When President Woodrow W... [barcode: P9-CKQ-676] Paul S. Reinsch minister to China in 1913, he gave the University of Wisconsin political scientist and expert in international relations a mandate to make the Open Door work. Reinsch eagerly accepted the task and quickly launched a hard-headed program to win for the United States a large share in the fabled markets of China and a position of real influence in East Asian affairs. Bold, pragmatic, and resourceful, he defended American rights and Chinese integrity against the foreign powers as well as against the corrupt and conniving Chinese politicians and warlords.

But at times, Reinsch demonstrated naiveté, lack of realism, ignorance of Chinese affairs, and irresponsibility. Reinsch, however, was placed in an impossible situation due to developments in China and elsewhere. World War I diverted European and American attention from China, giving Japan a golden opportunity to realize its ambitions on the Asian mainland. Although his program was undermined by the actions of Chinese leaders, American businessmen, and United States officials, Reinsch struggled to defend the Open Door even though that effort ruined his health and tested his ethical system. Consequently, Reinsch tended to blame Tokyo for his problems and the disintegration of China, and in the final, tragic years of his life he viewed militaristic, expansionist Japan as the embodiment of evil and the future source of strife in the world.

American cooperation, and the interpretation and redefinition of the Open Door policy.

NOEL H. PUGACH is presently Assistant Professor of History at the University of New Mexico, Albuquerque. He was previously an instructor at Kent State University. Professor Pugach received his B.S. degree from Brooklyn College and his M.A. degree and Ph.D. from the University of Wisconsin at Madison. His research interests have been centered on United States-East Asian relations in the twentieth century. He has published several articles in such leading historical journals as *The Journal of American History*, the *Pacific Historical Review*, *Business History Review*, and *The American Neptune*.

PAUL S. REINSCH
Open Door Diplomat
in Action

KTO STUDIES
IN
AMERICAN HISTORY

Consulting Editor: Harold M. Hyman
William P. Hobby Professor of History
Rice University

Paul Samuel Reinsch, no date, apparently his "academic picture," taken some-time during his teaching career at the University of Wisconsin. By permission of Iconographic Collection, State Historical Society of Wisconsin.

PAUL S. REINSCH
Open Door Diplomat
in Action

Noel H. Pugach

kto press

A U.S. Division of Kraus-Thomson Organization Limited
Millwood, New York

First printing

Printed in the United States of America

Library of Congress Cataloging in Publication Data

Pugach, Noel H
  Paul S. Reinsch, open door diplomat in action.

  (KTO studies in American history)
  Bibliography: p.
  Includes index.
  1. Reinsch, Paul Samuel, 1869–1923.   2. United States
—Relations (general) with China.   3. China—Relations
(general) with the United States.   4. Eastern question
(Far East)   5. Diplomats—United States—Biography.
I. Title. II. Series.
E748.R33P83   327.2′092′4   79-1503
ISBN 0-527-73050-5

In Memory of
Jules

CONTENTS

PREFACE

During the last third of the nineteenth century, American policy makers proclaimed that the United States had to go abroad in search of foreign markets, raw materials, investment opportunities, naval bases, and coaling stations. The great depression of the 1890s combined with the revival of Western imperialism created a consensus and a sense of urgency for overseas expansion. The Spanish-American War, the acquisition of the Philippines and other insular possessions, the assumption of a protectorate over Cuba and the Caribbean, the invigoration of the Monroe Doctrine and its reinterpretation in the Olney and Roosevelt Corollaries and, finally, the reassertion of the principles of the Open Door in the Hay Notes of 1899-1900 confirmed the fact that the United States was a world power with global interests. Statesmen, businessmen, and publicists looked primarily to the underdeveloped countries, above all China, as the proper field for American political, educational, religious and, of course, economic enterprise. They also believed that the Open Door policy—equal opportunity for American goods and ideas and respect for the integrity of semi-independent states—offered the best means of accomplishing America's objectives.

The events of the 1890s made a profound impression on the keen, sensitive, maturing mind of Paul S. Reinsch. He followed closely contemporary trends at home and abroad and took up the task of interpreting and publicizing them. He also accepted the validity of the assumptions and prescriptions of American policy makers. And even though he was excited about developments in Latin America, it was China that really captured his imagination. While Reinsch made the study of

modern imperialism and Oriental affairs the subjects of his scholarly and
literary endeavors in the busy years of his academic career at the University of Wisconsin, American overseas expansion became his personal
crusade before, during, and after his diplomatic service. Therefore, when
Woodrow Wilson appointed Paul Reinsch minister to China in 1913, he
selected the perfect instrument to implement America's Open Door
policy.

While several students of Wilsonian Far Eastern policy have discussed aspects of Reinsch's diplomatic career, this work focuses on the
view from the American legation in Peking. It is, in brief, an examination of Paul Reinsch's attempt to make the Open Door a reality and the
problems that he subsequently encountered. As much, if not more than
John Hay, W. W. Rockhill, and Woodrow Wilson, Reinsch sought to
translate the theory of American policy makers into fact and hoped,
thereby, to serve the interests of the United States, China, and the world.
It proved to be a long, bitter struggle which broke his health, tormented
his spirit, and tested his ethical and ideological framework. At the same
time, this study subjects to analysis Wilsonian Far Eastern policy, the
conduct of American business abroad in the first two decades of the twentieth century, the interpretation and redefinition of the Open Door, and
the issue of Japanese-American cooperation.

The spelling and use of Chinese names in this work requires an
explanation. Rather than adopt one of the standard forms of romanization of Chinese names and sounds, I chose to follow the general usage in
the State Department correspondence. However, where there were major
errors and inconsistencies (which are numerous), I selected the closest
standard form. Although this system is admittedly not very rigorous, I
thought that it might present fewer problems for those following the
State Department correspondence and the names mentioned in quotations. I have also adopted the recent, common practice of dropping the
umlaut (ü) in those cases where it does not affect the meaning (e.g.,
Yuan, Hsu). Except for those figures whose names were commonly Westernized (e.g., V. K. Wellington Koo, W. W. Yen), I have followed the
Oriental system of placing the surname first.

I take full responsibility for the analysis, conclusions, and errors
that follow. However, during the many years I have labored on this biography of Reinsch's public career, I have incurred many obligations which
I hereby acknowledge.

Professor William A. Williams first drew my attention to the career
of Paul Reinsch and then directed my dissertation on his diplomatic
career. From the very beginning he has been a constant source of wisdom,

encouragement, and helpfulness. My intellectual debt to William A. Williams will be evident to the reader of this book.

Several members of Reinsch's family have rendered invaluable assistance by answering my questions and providing me with information and documentary material. I therefore express my gratitude to the late Mr. and Mrs. Horatio Bates Hawkins (Reinsch's brother-in-law and sister-in-law) and to Reinsch's daughters, Mrs. Claire Cadura and Mrs. Pauline Thomas. The late Stanley K. Hornbeck and the Honorable V. K. Wellington Koo gave generously of their time in conversations and correspondence. Dr. Fred Harvey Harrington, formerly president of the University of Wisconsin, kindly shared his thoughtful ideas on Paul S. Reinsch in a lengthy interview. Ms. Betty L. Hale, Director of Public Relations of the Mobil Oil Corporation, supplied helpful information on the activities of the Standard Oil Company of New York in China. I also thank Professor Robert J. Gowen for lending me his microfilm copy of the Sir John Jordan Papers.

My research has taken me to numerous libraries and archives. I express my appreciation to the directors and personnel in the manuscript divisions of the following institutions: Library of the American National Red Cross; Library of Columbia University; Library of Congress; Library of Cornell University; Library of the Hoover Institution on War, Revolution and Peace; Library of The Johns Hopkins University; Library of the Institute of Current World Affairs; the National Archives; the Library of the State Historical Society of Wisconsin; the Library of the University of Wisconsin; Library of Yale University. I express my special thanks to the continuous assistance given to me by Dr. Josephine Harper at the State Historical Society of Wisconsin. Finally, I wish to thank the staff at the University of New Mexico Library, particularly in the interlibrary loan office.

The *Business History Review* and the *Pacific Historical Review* kindly gave me permission to use lengthy excerpts from articles I had published in them.

I wish to thank the Research Allocations Committee of the University of New Mexico for giving me travel grants which enabled me to research various parts of this study. I also express my appreciation to the many research assistants I have had in the past eight years, who have been supported under the work-study program at the University of New Mexico.

I am especially grateful to Dr. Margaret Szasz for critically reading and editing the manuscript. I am greatly indebted to her for her wise advice and expert assistance. Marion Honhart, Penny Katson, and Holly

Ward typed the final manuscript and cooperated to meet my tight schedule. Margaret Weinrod typed an earlier version, and Patricia Pabisch and Angela Juzang performed a host of secretarial services in connection with this work. I am pleased to express my appreciation to all of them.

Finally, I wish to thank Professor Harold Hyman, the consulting editor of KTO Studies in American History. Professor Hyman generously offered his wise, efficient, and professional editorial assistance and guidance in a most humane and sympathetic manner. I could not ask for better. Indeed, the staff at KTO Press, which collaborated in the publication of this work, proved most cooperative and helpful.

In closing, I reserve my heartfelt appreciation for my family—my wife, children, and parents—and friends for their moral support and encouragement over these many years. My wife and children bore the burden of an absent and tired husband and father. To Sheila, Michael, and Laura belong my infinite gratitude.

Noel Pugach

Albuquerque, New Mexico

PAUL S. REINSCH:
OPEN DOOR DIPLOMAT
IN ACTION

Chapter I

GETTING STARTED IN WISCONSIN

It was June 30, 1913, an early summer day in Madison, Wisconsin. Sometime that Monday, a Western Union messenger stopped at the residence of Professor Paul S. Reinsch and delivered a telegram. It was from the White House. "Would it be possible and convenient for you to come to Washington the middle of next week?" President Woodrow Wilson asked Reinsch. "I should like to have a brief conversation with you on a matter of important business."[1] Was it finally happening? Reinsch wondered. Did the president intend to offer him that long sought after diplomatic appointment? The Peking post, after all, had been vacant for months. Reinsch had been following such things for more than ten years. And yet, he hesitated to raise his hopes. He had already suffered too many disappointments.

But this time it was different. During his visit to Washington, Reinsch's conversation with President Wilson and Secretary of State William Jennings Bryan centered on the problems of the Far East. On July 16, 1913, the president announced his intention of naming Reinsch to head the United States diplomatic mission in China. "It was said today," the *New York Times* reported, that the president believed "that in Prof. Reinsch he had obtained a man who was capable of handling the delicate diplomatic situation in the Far East."[2] Excitement and a feeling of relief now reigned in the Reinsch household. After years of preparation, achievement, and hard political lobbying, Paul Reinsch was going to China.

*   *   *

During the Civil War, Paul's parents joined the stream of German immigrants flowing to the shores of the United States in the middle years of
the nineteenth century. George J. Reinsch came to the United States in
1861 and then sent for his betrothed, Clara Witte. Clara arrived in 1863,
and two years later they made their home in Milwaukee, which was fast
becoming "die deutsche stadt." There, Paul Samuel Reinsch was born on
June 10, 1869. For many years he was their only child; always, he was
their chief source of joy and their strongest family link. Even after the
Reinsches adopted a daughter, Martha, he remained their favorite and
she learned to live in her brother's shadow.[3]

Family life was far from placid. The Reinsch marriage was stormy,
punctuated by many separations. Sometimes George Reinsch's work
enabled him to leave home for several months; at other times, when Clara
made life particularly unbearable, he boarded with friends until tempers
cooled and differences were temporarily patched up. With the best of
intentions, they tried to keep the small Reinsch family together, but it
was an obvious case of incompatibility of personality and outlook.

O-Papa, as he was known in the Reinsch household, was an intelligent, educated, patient, and amiable man; he was well loved and highly
regarded by his friends and associates. But he lacked ambition and never
found his proper calling. Family pressure had forced him into the
Lutheran ministry, but it could not sustain him through the years of
unhappiness with his work. The Reverend George Reinsch served as
chaplain to German-speaking soldiers in the Union Army during the
Civil War. Afterwards, he was the pastor of several churches in Wisconsin. Although he was happier as an accountant, apparently he was not
very successful in this work. Finally, he settled for various jobs with the
federal government.[4]

O-Mama was made of very different stuff. Undoubtedly brighter
and shrewder than her husband, Clara Reinsch came from an educated
and somewhat illustrious Schleswig-Holstein family. The ambition for
distinction and achievement that she might have once had for her husband were transferred to Paul and she became entirely wrapped up in his
life. She often praised Paul in front of others while belittling his father.
O-Mama was also taciturn, pietistic, domineering, and demanding.
Except when she looked at Paul, she wore an "intolerant expression." To
the distress of family members and friends, she tyrannized Martha and
was generally difficult with other women.[5]

The family turmoil, occasional financial stringency, a sometimes
absent father and a doting, protective mother certainly affected Paul, but
apparently left no traumas. His father, to whom Paul was deeply at-

tached, taught him the pleasure of good company, the value of friendship, and the enjoyment of life; George Reinsch was a very healthy antidote to O-Mama's straitlaced, narrow, and stern outlook. Physically, Paul took after his mother and he acquired her inner toughness and ambition. He appreciated all she had done to make him a success, and he repaid her with respect, kindness, and devotion. There were also compensations. An only son with recognized abilities, Paul received love, attention, and encouragement. Everyone adored him, though his mother idolized him most of all. Nothing was ever too good for Clara Reinsch's son, who was destined for some greatness.[6]

Religion also played a significant role in his childhood. The Reinsch home was imbued with Lutheran teaching and observance, far more because of Clara's fierce devotionalism than George's position as a pastor. Paul was sent to Lutheran schools where memorization of the Scriptures and the catechism predominated along with continuous study of German and Latin. Well into his high school years, it seemed that Paul might fulfill his mother's fondest hopes and enter the ministry. Paul, however, discovered a different and broader outlook: he rejected the formal denominationalism and narrow theology of his parents and teachers and acquired liberal views and a sympathetic understanding of other religions. But he remained a Christian and an occasional churchgoer, though he refused to identify with any particular denomination. Moreover, he drew from the Scriptures and his religious training a deep humanitarianism and a strong ethical system that guided his conduct throughout his life.[7]

Meanwhile, Paul drank deeply from the German content that surrounded him. German was his first language; it was spoken in his home, in the private Lutheran schools he attended as a boy, and in the neighborhood streets of Milwaukee. In criticizing Paul's first major book, Charles K. Adams pointed to the "German complications" still present in his sentences; and years later John V.A. MacMurray, the first secretary of the United States legation in Peking, expressed pique with the American minister's correction of his writing, coming as they did from a man who seemed more fluent in German than English. Although Paul's home was characteristically American, Reinsch retained an everlasting attachment to the language and culture of his parents, while opposing the militarist cast and political aims of the ancestral land. To his admirers, therefore, Paul Reinsch represented "painstaking German ability" and "the developed German-American type" in the worthy Carl Schurz tradition.[8]

In anticipation of Paul's entrance into the University of Wisconsin in the fall of 1888, the Reinsches moved to Madison. They rented various

homes on Frances, Lake, and State Streets, within easy walking distance
of University Hill. George Reinsch's work soon forced him to return to
Milwaukee, but O-Mama and Martha remained in Madison. Clara
wanted to insure that Paul would suffer no unnecessary distractions or
lack of comfort as he pursued his studies, to keep her watchful eye on her
precious son, and to save on the cost of his room and board.[9]

Despite the financial sacrifice and the uprooting of the Reinsch
family, there was never any question that Paul would attend the university. In addition to his own ambitions and the aspirations of his parents,
Paul had demonstrated at an early age real academic ability and scholarly
self-discipline. He was also better qualified than most of his classmates
for the classical education which still dominated the university cur-
riculum at the end of the nineteenth century. At Concordia College, an
Evangelical Lutheran preparatory school modeled after the German *gym-
nasia*, Paul had received a rigorous education that emphasized Greek,
Latin, and mathematics as well as German and religious instruction for
prospective ministers.[10]

Paul's undergraduate years at Wisconsin were happy and eventful.
They broadened his mind, matured him socially and personally, and
marked a major turning point in his life. The university, from the outset,
exhilarated him intellectually; and Madison, his adopted city and "ideal
college town" captivated him. "The first Sunday morning of my
freshman year, as I walked along the path skirting the lake shore," he
recalled some thirty years later, "I praised my fortune looking forward to
four years in such surroundings."[11]

Paul chose the broad liberal education of the bachelor of arts program and for the first three years took heavy doses of the classical and
modern languages, mathematics, and the sciences. Then he discovered
history and the social sciences. He crammed into his senior year political
economy, Frederick Jackson Turner's offerings in American history, and
Charles Homer Haskins's courses on English and institutional history.
Three of the four professors who impressed him most taught him history:
William F. Allen, Wisconsin's pioneer historian and Turner's mentor,
"the first leader in the modern development of Wisconsin," Reinsch
noted; Turner himself, "whose eyes could say more than most men's
oratory"; and Haskins, "then a youthful prodigy of astounding knowledge and memory power." Finally, Reinsch singled out Charles Van
Hise, the university's outstanding geologist and later one of its greatest
presidents, whom he recalled "as a man of science" always ready to talk
with the debaters on any question "under the sun" and from whom "we
always went away full of new ideas." Paul was an excellent student and

compiled a brilliant scholastic record, graduating with a 95 average when he received his B.A. in 1892. He was also elected to Phi Beta Kappa and was known as the prize pupil of Alexander Kerr, Wisconsin's noted professor of Greek.[12]

Paul, however, was no bookworm. He was a joiner and an organizer who participated in almost every aspect of campus life. He was a champion debater and in his senior year he was co-editor of *The Aegis*, the literary magazine and newspaper, and *The Badger*, the school yearbook. As a spectator, he shared the growing interest in football and other intercollegiate sports, tolerated by President Thomas C. Chamberlin and boosted by President Charles K. Adams. He was a good swimmer, an avid boater on Madison's beautiful lakes, and a hardy hiker who loved to tramp through the Wisconsin countryside.

Reinsch kept up his German ties by joining the Bildungsverein, but after his initiation into Delta Upsilon became a loyal supporter of the Greeks. Delta Upsilon carried him into the mainstream of American society and established friendships that would be maintained throughout his lifetime. The DU fraternity house located on State Street, almost diagonally across from his mother's Lake Street house, became a refuge from O-Mama's watchful eye. Musical and graceful, Paul was also a hit at the college dances that were becoming a popular part of campus social life. Paul was unable and unwilling openly to defy or offend his mother, who frowned on dancing and even considered it sinful, but neither was he able to give up his love for the dance floor. He would therefore pretend that he was studying in his second floor room and then quietly lower himself out of the window by means of a rope to attend to the waltz. The stratagem apparently worked, for Clara never indicated that she knew what he had done.[13]

Shrewd, intelligent, ambitious, and determined to raise his social and financial status, Paul now wrestled with the choice of a profession. He considered journalism as a career—he enjoyed writing and searching out information—and never completely eliminated that possibility. He also dreamed of graduate study in Germany, but his family's limited financial means ruled out that objective for the immediate future. Finally, he settled on the law. He enrolled in the University of Wisconsin law school in the fall of 1892 and two years later was graduated and admitted to the Wisconsin bar.

With high expectations, Paul opened his law practice in Milwaukee. He was quickly disenchanted with the life of a young, inexperienced attorney struggling to earn a living and a reputation in that bustling city during the Gilded Age. From the outset, he confronted the dilemma of advancing in his chosen profession without compromising his ethical system. In one instance, Paul advised a shocked client, who was being sued for supplying inferior lumber, to settle out of court and to replace the defective material. The rest of the petty cases that came his way only bored him, deflated his ego, shattered dreams of greatness, and robbed him of the opportunity to read, write, think, and travel. His life stood in gray contrast to the exciting developments taking place at the University of Wisconsin, the spirit of commonwealth percolating in the state, and the powerful forces at work in the nation and the world, which he had already felt while a law student at Madison.[14]

These positive forces, above all, drew him back to the university and city that he loved—and never really left. In the 1890s, the University of Wisconsin was growing rapidly and, more important, was emerging as a great seat of learning, a major center for research and graduate work, a laboratory for new ideas and programs, and a training ground for a generation of public leaders. When Richard T. Ely founded the School of Economics, Political Science and History in 1892, he established Wisconsin as a pioneer in the social sciences. The Department of History became a national institution under the guidance of William F. Allen, who planted the seed, and Frederick Jackson Turner and Charles Haskins, who harvested the rich crop. Similar exciting developments were taking place in other departments. Consequently, President Adams's offer of an instructorship in the history department settled the matter. In the fall of 1895, Paul Reinsch returned to Madison and enrolled as a Ph.D. candidate in history and political science.[15]

Paul's return to Madison was by no means an admission that he had wasted three precious years of a short lifetime. The law, albeit from a scholarly and theoretical standpoint, always fascinated him and he continued to lecture and write extensively on constitutional, administrative, and international law. Paul's legal studies and brief legal practice also served him well in later years. They led to lifelong friendships and valuable associations with Joseph Davies, Henry Cochems, Theodore Kronshage, Francis McGovern (who with Reinsch were known as "The Five"), and many other classmates and colleagues who made their mark in public life. They proved highly useful when, as minister to China, he negotiated and drafted contracts for American business firms. And in the final years of his life, he returned to the practice of law and served as legal counselor to the Chinese government.[16]

Nor did the choice of an academic career signify a hasty retreat from the practical world to the safe seclusion of the ivory tower. Reinsch and his contemporaries never made such a distinction, and the Progressive

Era, especially in Wisconsin, refuted such an interpretation. From the presidency of John Bascomb through the terms of Chamberlin, Adams, and Charles Van Hise, the Madison campus was infused with the idea of close interaction between university and society. Throughout his academic career, Paul related his teachings to current events and contemporary concerns and he valued the views of America's political and economic leaders. He maintained close ties with the bankers and businessmen who invited him to Milwaukee and Chicago for consultations and lectures, and the politicians who sought his advice. As he operated in the world, however, Paul Reinsch functioned chiefly as a teacher, scholar, artist, and man of ideas.[17]

Paul's years in graduate school matured his thinking, laid the foundation for his future studies and ideas, and brought him into closer contact with Turner, Ely, and other members of the distinguished faculty. Although he increasingly identified himself with the emerging discipline of political science, Reinsch drew heavily from all of the social sciences and kept in touch with the major trends on the Wisconsin campus. Pointing to America's world-wide opportunities and responsibilities after the Spanish-American War and the complaints of inefficiency and ignorance in the consular service, John B. Johnson, the new dean of the College of Engineering, pleaded for the creation of a School of Commerce that would train young Americans in foreign languages and the technicalities of foreign trade. Richard T. Ely stimulated Paul's dedication to a better society and his School of Economics, Political Science and History fostered a broad integrated approach as well as a historical point of view. And Frederick Jackson Turner, Paul's chief mentor and dissertation adviser, not only trained him as a historian and turned his attention to international relations, but also led him to discover the social and economic forces that underlay all social development. Thanking Reinsch for his contribution to the festschrift dedicated to Wisconsin's pioneer historian, Turner observed: "I am particularly pleased by the emphasis which you lay on the 'deeper forces' of economic and social life, for this is exactly in line with my own interest in the study of history."[18]

Reinsch chose a dissertation topic that enabled him to combine his interest in the law with his field of American history. Published in 1899 as *English Common Law in the Early American Colonies*, Reinsch's thesis mirrored the Turnerian influence. Reinsch argued that the early American colonists fashioned an original legal system, which developed simplified, informal procedures geared to frontier needs. Not until the end of the seventeenth century, when pressure from the English authorities, the growing complexity of life, and the appearance of trained lawyers created new conditions, did the American colonies incorporate the English system. Even then, however, it continued to show the influence of the early, popular law. F. W. Maitland, the dean of English constitutional historians, found Reinsch's interpretation "very new at least on this side of the ocean," but highly praiseworthy, nevertheless. Indeed, Paul's first scholarly work received a cordial and generally favorable reception.[19]

Paul, however, had been writing for the popular audience for several years. His early efforts were largely travel accounts drawn from his trips to Washington, D. C., and Europe in the 1890s, which he wrote for the German press and, under the name of "Arno," for the *Milwaukee Sentinel*. Toward the end of the decade, Paul extended his range into analyses of world politics, some of which appeared as editorial articles in the *Milwaukee Sentinel*. It was an enjoyable and profitable experience. Paul's early newspaper work satisfied his lingering impulse for journalism, helped defray the cost of European travels and studies, gave him practice in reaching the mass public audience, and brought his name to the attention of newspaper and magazine editors who would request contributions in the future. Reinsch mixed easily with reporters, gained an appreciation for newspapermen and, as minister to China, turned to them as informants and confidential agents.[20]

After receiving the Ph.D. in June 1898, Paul decided that the time had arrived to realize his dream of studying at the great European centers of learning and research. He had already spent two summers touring Europe. But now, with the assistance of a John Johnston scholarship, supplemented by savings and earnings from his newspaper articles, he took off most of the following academic year to study, read, and travel.

Paul attended lectures in Bonn, Leipzig, Berlin, Rome, and Paris, and read extensively, especially in international politics and sociology, at libraries and archives in England and on the continent. And he did so with a special purpose. He believed that the world was entering a new constructive age in politics, art, and civilization, and felt a personal need to analyze and explain it. With the guidance of Turner, who was himself an able diplomatic historian, Reinsch's quick mind was drawn, in particular, to the revival of Western imperialism and the fierce scramble for empire in the Far East. As early as the summer of 1897, he had formulated the major themes; now, with the rapidly changing situation in China, he refined his ideas and collected the basic material that would fill the pages of *World Politics*.[21]

When Paul returned to Madison in the spring of 1899 to resume his teaching duties, he could show his colleagues an almost complete draft of a potential book. That was fortunate, for Wisconsin was considering the addition of an assistant professor in political science. Henry Parkinson represented an outmoded approach and the growing university needed a dynamic young man to update the offerings in political science. The head of the School of Economics, Political Science and History gave Paul (known as "one of Dr. Ely's young men,") his crucial support. Turner wanted to bring in new blood trained at other universities, but did not try to block the promotion for his esteemed student. Paul had impressed his professors and the university's president as a brilliant student and effective teacher, but it was his promise as a writer and scholar that persuaded Adams to recommend his promotion to the Board of Regents and offer him the appointment of assistant professor of political science.[22]

Ely knew a winner. He recognized the timeliness, importance, and merit of Reinsch's manuscript and offered to help get it published. In fact, Ely wanted *World Politics* for his Citizen's Library, which he edited for Macmillan. Citing the recommendations of Turner and Haskins, Ely urged that Macmillan publish it as the initial number in the series. "On account of the interest in the subject of expansion," Ely argued "this book should be pushed forward as rapidly as possible." After revisions and extensive rewriting, Paul Reinsch's first major work appeared in July 1900, under the title, *World Politics at the End of the Nineteenth Century as Influenced by the Oriental Situation.*[23]

World Politics was more an analysis of the forces undergirding contemporary international relations than a narrative of recent events; its recurring theme was the importance of the Oriental Question. Reinsch examined the nature of modern national imperialism, sketched the history of the opening of China and the scramble for concessions, made an original evaluation of the impact of the Western intrusion on China, and concluded with an analysis of German imperialism and American expansion. *World Politics* underscored and introduced to the public Reinsch's intellectual and personal concerns: his opposition to colonialism and his concurrent support for Open Door expansion; the dangers of national imperialism to world peace and its threat to domestic institutions and internal reform; the impact of modernization on traditional societies and economically backward nations; and the interest in China and its future importance to world civilization. *World Politics* expressed the hope that human wisdom, reason, and enlightened self-interest would prevail, that mankind, in the twentieth century, would create a peaceful, prosperous, and dynamic world order.[24]

Reinsch's ideas were somewhat fragmentary and the book was probably rushed into print to take advantage of the widespread interest in China and to beat the competition from numerous other writers. Nevertheless, for a young scholar, it was a provocative and seminal work. In fact, *World Politics,* which would go through several editions in the United States and England, was widely reviewed and generally acclaimed as a minor classic.[25]

The success of *World Politics* launched Reinsch's reputation as a scholar, brought his name into the public domain, and resulted in numerous requests for lecture appearances and contributions to popular magazines. Ely, meanwhile, discussed with Paul the need for a textbook on colonial politics and urged Macmillan to offer him a contract. "He is an unusually successful teacher and he is also an unusually successful popular lecturer," Ely reminded George Brett, Macmillan's vigorous president. "With these qualities he ought to give us a good work. I should naturally expect that his second work would in many ways show an improvement upon his first."[26]

With the publication of *World Politics* assured and the promise of a bright career, Paul could turn his eyes and heart to other important matters—love and marriage. He was already thirty years old, responsible and mature, but not unemotional or unromantic. In his student days he had been popular with the ladies, but had no burning romance—at least he left no record of any. But in the fall of 1899, he met and pursued Alma Marie Moser.

Alma was seven years his junior and still an undergraduate at Wisconsin, but shared a common background and similar interests. Her parents emigrated to Wisconsin from Switzerland and Saxony and, after their marriage, settled in Ashland, where John Moser operated a Farm Insurance agency until his untimely death in 1897. Her mother, Pauline, then went to Madison as housemother for Alma's sorority, Pi Beta Phi, and after her daughter's marriage moved in with the Reinsches. Alma's sister, Hildred ("Daisy"), also lived with them while she attended the University of Wisconsin.[27]

Alma was an intelligent, independent-minded, attractive, and vivacious woman. She had been active in the social life of the university and had been an excellent student, until Paul started to court her and took her mind off books and class assignments. She was gifted in languages and the social graces, fond of art, music, dancing, and parties, and like Paul an avid reader, traveler, and hiker. "Mrs. Reinsch is a corker," Mac-Murray reported to his mother; "she is simple and unaffected (though by no means artless) with a great deal of intelligence and of information and a habit of looking one straight in the eye."[28]

Paul and Alma announced their engagement shortly before her graduation in June 1900, and they were wed at the Pi Beta Phi house on Wednesday, August 1, 1900. Their marriage was filled with mutual love and respect, tenderness, and happiness. Paul was also a proud and doting father. Claire, who arrived in 1905, in Madison enjoyed his attention and she was very close to him. But Pauline (1915) and Paul John (1916) were born in China, when Reinsch suffered from physical exhaustion and mental strain. Consequently, he had less patience and spent less time with them. But Alma, Daisy, and Granny Moser were aware that Paul was not the domestic type, and they did their best to free him from household chores and family distractions in order that he could work undisturbed in the seclusion of his study.[29]

For the first two years of their marriage, Paul and Alma rented from the Turners and the Elys, when they were away on sabbaticals. But after Paul's promotion to full professor in 1902, they felt financially secure enough to buy 423 Wisconsin Avenue, a four-story house at the corner of East Gilman and just opposite the mansion of Senator William F. Vilas. Their large home always buzzed with activity. The Reinsches socialized with their prominent neighbors who lived between Capitol Square and Lake Mendota—Vilas, Spooner, La Follette—as well as Paul's university colleagues. Members of "The Five" and other friends often converged at Reinsch's Wisconsin Avenue home for football weekends, informal reunions, and parties. And Joe Davies, with whom Paul had a special friendship, was a frequent guest. They had met at college and Delta Upsilon. But their friendship was forged when they shared a room together and Paul read law books to Joe, whose eyesight had temporarily failed after a tennis court accident.[30]

Meanwhile, Reinsch emerged as one of America's foremost political scientists. As Frank J. Goodnow was regarded as the leader in public administration and municipal government and Woodrow Wilson was recognized for his preeminence in American government, so Reinsch was hailed as the nation's expert in colonial studies and international relations. With these and other luminaries, Reinsch launched the American Political Science Association and helped to develop it into a major professional society. For many years, political scientists held their meetings in conjunction with the American Historical Association and the American Economic Association. But in 1902 Reinsch was named to a committee, chaired by Jeremiah Jenks of Cornell, which considered the formation of a separate professional organization. Concluding that political science had come of age as an independent discipline, and that it possessed different interests and methods from history and economics, the committee recommended the formation of the American Political Science Association.

At the annual meeting in New Orleans in December 1903, the founding members formally established the American Political Science Association and elected Goodnow president and Wilson first vice-president. Although he was a younger scholar and not part of the East Coast establishment, Reinsch was chosen second vice-president. In the following years, Reinsch chaired several committees and served on the editorial board of the *American Political Science Review,* which made its appearance in 1906. However, it was not until 1920, after he gained fame as minister to China, that Reinsch was elected president of the association.[31]

As Reinsch's star rose, Stanford University made a serious effort to lure Reinsch away from Madison. In April 1901, President David Starr Jordan offered Reinsch a salary of $2,500 (a thousand dollars more than he was receiving at Wisconsin), an associate professorship, and a pledge of California's political support for a diplomatic position. To the delight of his colleagues and President Adams, Reinsch decided to remain at Wisconsin when he was given a promotion to full professor and a raise to $2,000. But Jordan, anxious to build a great university, persisted. Later that year, he invited Reinsch to deliver a series of lectures at Stanford so that he could see things for himself. Jordan painted a bright future for Stanford and agreed that all of Reinsch's requirements were reasonable —a great library in Oriental Studies, more emphasis on graduate training, frequent leaves of absence, and an assistant to handle the details of administration. But he also admitted that Stanford was still in the "Stone Age" and that he could not make concrete promises.[32]

Reinsch was impressed with Stanford and now faced a difficult decision. Afraid Reinsch might indeed leave, Wisconsin countered again with another large salary increase, a flexible teaching schedule, frequent leaves of absence, and assurances of the university's support for a diplomatic appointment. Moreover, Wisconsin was already building a fine library and was developing an excellent graduate program. In addition, Reinsch was deeply troubled by the recent threats to academic freedom at Stanford. "Unless I can feel that I could work there without in any way putting myself in a false or strained position, I shall not go," he explained to Ely. Those considerations, and his deep attachment to Madison, decided the issue. Reinsch firmly rejected Stanford's offer and shortly afterward also refused an invitation to move to the University of Chicago.[33]

Wisconsin had been kind to Paul Reinsch thus far. He had moved from the self-contained German community in Milwaukee and the tense, unhappy home of his parents to a respected position in his profession, a rising reputation at the state university, and a happy marriage to a woman who shared his dreams. He was still in a hurry to make good. In that effort, Madison would serve as his base of operations for the next ten years of active and productive work.

NOTES TO
CHAPTER I

1. Wilson to Reinsch, 30 June 1913, Paul S. Reinsch Papers, The State Historical Society of Wisconsin, Madison, Wisconsin (hereafter cited Reinsch Papers).

2. *New York Times*, 17 July 1913.

3. Tape recordings by Horatio B. Hawkins and Hildred "Daisy" Hawkins (Paul Reinsch's brother-in-law and sister-in-law), 1963, Reinsch Papers (hereafter cited Hawkins Tapes, and number); Horatio B. Hawkins to author, 23 May 1965; Claire Reinsch Cadura to author, 24 January 1970; *Milwaukee Sentinel*, 21 October 1932.

4. Author's interview with Horatio Hawkins, 10 August 1971, Albany, California; Claire Reinsch Cadura to author, 24 January 1970; Alma Reinsch to Paul Reinsch, [1909?], Reinsch Papers; *Milwaukee Journal*, 26 January 1923.

5. Hawkins Tapes, 2; Hawkins to author, 23 May 1965.

6. Paul Reinsch to Alma Reinsch, 23 August 1901, Reinsch Papers; Hawkins, annotations, *ibid.;* Hawkins Tapes, 2; Hawkins to author, 23 May 1965, 30 January 1970; Reinsch to Richard Ely, 1 April 1912, Richard T. Ely Papers, The State Historical Society of Wisconsin (hereafter cited Ely Papers).

7. Lauros G. McConachie, "Paul S. Reinsch," *World Today,* reprinted in the *Milwaukee Free Press,* 31 July 1906; Hawkins Tapes, 5; author's interview with Hawkins, 10 August 1971, Albany, California.

8. McConachie, "Paul Reinsch"; Charles K. Adams to Reinsch, 17 August 1900, Reinsch Papers; John V. A. MacMurray to his mother, 19 February 1914, John V. A. MacMurray Papers, Princeton University (hereafter cited MacMurray Papers); Yamei Kin to Roger H. Williams, 2 June 1917, Charles R. Crane Papers, Institute of Current World Affairs, New York (hereafter cited Crane Papers); Paul S. Reinsch, *World Politics at the End of the Nineteenth Century as Influenced by the Oriental Situation* (New York, 1900), 50; Claire R. Cadura to author, 12 March 1974.

9. Hawkins to author, 23 May 1965; Hawkins Tapes, 2, Reinsch Papers; McConachie, "Paul Reinsch"; Louis P. Lochner, "The Roosevelt Exchange Professor," *Wisconsin Alumni Magazine*, XIII (February 1912), 231–34; Merle Curti and Vernon Carstensen, *The University of Wisconsin: A History 1848–1925,* 2 vols. (Madison, 1949), 1, 661–62.

10. Hawkins Tapes, 6; McConachie, "Paul Reinsch"; Ray Allen Billington, *Frederick Jackson Turner: Historian, Scholar, Teacher* (New York, 1973), 17–18.

11. Reinsch, "What Has Wisconsin Meant to Me," *Wisconsin Badger,* 1923, written in December 1921, Reinsch Papers; Reinsch, "The Ideal College Town," *The Aegis,* 5 June 1891.

12. Reinsch, "What Has Wisconsin Meant to Me"; Paul S. Reinsch's undergraduate transcript, University of Wisconsin Archives, Memorial Library, University of Wisconsin (hereafter cited UW Archives); Hawkins Tapes, 2, 6; McConachie, "Paul Reinsch."

13. Reinsch, "What Has Wisconsin Meant to Me"; Hawkins Tapes, 2, 6; Hawkins to author, 23 May 1965; McConachie, "Paul Reinsch."

14. Hawkins Tapes, 15; Hawkins to author, 23 May 1965; McConachie, "Paul Reinsch."

15. Charles K. Adams to Reinsch, 10 May 1895, Reinsch Papers; McConachie, "Paul Reinsch"; Curti and Carstensen, *The University of Wisconsin,* I, 501–739; J. F. A. Pyre, *Wisconsin* (New York, 1920), 250–51.

16. Hawkins to author, 21 January 1965.

17. Reinsch, "The Ideal College Town"; Curti and Carstensen, *The University of Wisconsin*, I, 288, 541, 569–70, 631–32.

18. Turner to Reinsch, 3 February 1911, Reinsch Papers; Curti and Carstensen, *The University of Wisconsin*, I, 638–39; Billington, *Frederick Jackson Turner*, 166–71, 486; Patrick John Scanlan, "Commerce and Diplomacy: The Policies of Paul S. Reinsch American Minister to China, 1913–1919" (M.A. thesis, University of Wisconsin, 1967), 3.

19. Reinsch, *English Common Law in the Early American Colonies* (Madison, 1899); F. W. Maitland to Reinsch, 26 April 1900, Reinsch Papers; *American Historical Review*, VI (April 1901), 584–85.

20. "The Philippine Question in its International Aspects," *Milwaukee Sentinel*, n.d.; various clippings of other Reinsch articles, Reinsch Papers; Hawkins annotations, no. 45, 4 October 1963, *ibid.*; Hawkins Tapes, 6, 8; Turner to Theodore Roosevelt, 10 December 1902, Appointments and Recommendations File, "Paul S. Reinsch," Department of State, National Archives (hereafter cited DSNA).

21. Hawkins-Knaplund conversation, Hawkins Tapes, 3; Hawkins Tapes, 6; Reinsch, "A Changing World," *The Kingdom*, 8 December 1898, Reinsch Papers; Reinsch's Wisconsin Teaching File, UW Archives; Louis P. Lochner, "The Roosevelt Exchange Professor"; McConachie, "Paul Reinsch."

22. Ely to Harper & Bros., 2 September 1899, Ely Papers; clipping, *Wisconsin State Journal*, 27 July 1900, Reinsch Papers; Curti and Carstensen, *The University of Wisconsin*, 1, 636–37, 642.

23. Ely to Reinsch, 10 September 1899, Reinsch Papers; Reinsch to Ely, 12 September 1899, Ely Papers; Ely to Harper & Bros., 2 September 1899, 25 September 1899, *ibid.*; Ely to A. G. Goodrich, 21 January 1900, *ibid.*; Ely to George P. Brett, 8 June 1900, *ibid.*

24. Reinsch, *World Politics, passim*.

25. *Political Science Quarterly*, XV (December 1900), 719–22; *The Dial*, XXIX (16 October 1900), 270.

26. Walter H. Page to Reinsch, 29 August and 8 September 1900, Reinsch Papers; Ely to George P. Brett, 17 July and 29 September 1900, Ely Papers.

27. Hawkins to author, 15 November 1969, 30 January 1970; Hawkins Tapes, 10.

28. Various undated letters of Alma to Paul, Reinsch Papers; Hawkins to author, 8 December 1964, 15 November 1969, 30 January 1970; Horatio Bates Hawkins, "A General Explanatory Note, Reflecting the Circumstances and Background of These Reports in the Reinsch Papers" (hereafter cited Hawkins, "A General Explanatory Note," Reinsch Papers); Hawkins Tapes, 10; MacMurray to mother, 8 February 1917, MacMurray Papers.

29. Paul to Alma, 23 August 1901, 29 August 1901, and various undated letters Alma to Paul, Reinsch Papers; Hawkins Tapes, 2, 10; Hawkins, "A General Explanatory Note," Reinsch Papers; Hawkins to author, 8 December 1964, 30 January 1970.

30. Hawkins Tapes, 1, 2, 5–8, 10, 11; Davies to Reinsch, 12 January 1909, Reinsch Papers; Hawkins to author, 8 December 1964, 13 December 1965, 30 January 1970.

31. Reinsch, "The American Political Science Association," *The Iowa Journal of History and Politics*, II (April 1904), 155–61; Jenks to Reinsch, January 1903, Reinsch Papers; Goodnow to Reinsch, 19 March 1904, 20 January 1905; Reinsch to Goodnow, 22 March 1904, 11 February 1907, Frank J. Goodnow Papers, Johns Hopkins University, Baltimore, Maryland (hereafter cited Goodnow Papers); Albert Somit and Joseph Tanenhaus, *The Development of Political Science: From Burgess to Behavioralism* (Boston, 1967), 49–51.

32. Jordan to Reinsch, 13 April 1901, 6 January 1902, Reinsch Papers; C. K. Adams to Birge, 16 April 1901, Edward A. Birge Papers, The State Historical Society of Wisconsin.

33. Ely to Reinsch, 14 November 1901, Ely Papers; Reinsch to Ely, 19 November 1901, *ibid*.; Jordan to Reinsch, 6 January 1902, Reinsch Papers; Turner to Theodore Roosevelt, 10 December 1902, Appointments and Recommendations File, "Paul S. Reinsch," DSNA.

Chapter II

WISCONSIN TEACHER, SCHOLAR, AND PROGRESSIVE-EXPANSIONIST

In his teaching days at Wisconsin, Reinsch cut an imposing figure. Always careful about his appearance, he dressed well by buying good clothes of moderate cost during his trips to Europe. He wore a frock coat to his lecture classes, but appeared at his best in tailored brown business suits. Lean, sinewy, and tall, his long arms and long fingers stood out from an otherwise well-proportioned body. Paul had a round, broad forehead, which in later years was accented by a receding hairline. He parted his brown hair in the middle and wore a full, well-trimmed mustache that curled slightly as it passed the ends of the upper lips. His eyeglasses rested on a prominent nose and large ears, while heavy eyebrows arched his beautiful and expressive brown eyes.[1]

Outwardly, Reinsch looked scholarly, dignified, and polished. But underneath lay a very "human sort of person." Most people found him charming, witty, gregarious—a pleasant companion and a good conversationalist. Although he was always busy, Paul was generous with his time, kind, thoughtful, and good-natured—at least until the last years of his life when the strain of his work and a developing brain tumor began to take their toll. The writer of one obituary testified: "It may be truthfully said—and it is said here on the ground of thirty years of personal knowledge of the man and his work—that there was not one mean or ignoble trait in the character of Paul S. Reinsch."[2]

Reinsch's academic career spanned an exciting era in Wisconsin, in particular, and in America as a whole. During the two decades preceding World War I, the American university educated a larger and more diverse student body, became a center for research and scholarship, and

devoted itself to the service of state and citizenry. New fields of knowledge were explored and, correspondingly, new departments had to be
created and staffed at the larger schools. With President Van Hise at the
helm, the University of Wisconsin advanced to the forefront of American
higher education and acquired an international reputation for its service
to the state. Concurrently, Robert M. La Follette, Francis McGovern,
and their followers made the state the very model of progressive reform,
drawing heavily on the talent and resources of the University of Wisconsin.[3] Meanwhile, the United States acquired a colonial empire, com-
peted energetically for foreign markets and investment opportunities,
and assumed a more vigorous role in world affairs.

During those years, Reinsch represented Wisconsin at its best.
Often mentioned in the same breath with Van Hise, Turner, Ely, and
John R. Commons, the school's leading economist, Reinsch was regarded as one of the university's academic stars. He developed an agenda
for progressivism and made important contributions to reform in Wisconsin. Still, his focus of scholarship and his overriding personal concern
remained modern diplomacy and imperialism. These activities established Reinsch as an authority on international relations, a pioneer in
colonial studies, one of America's leading experts on the Far East and
herald of the Pacific Era, an ardent economic expansionist, and an advocate and architect of international peace and cooperation.

*   *   *

Reinsch was one of Wisconsin's most effective, innovative, and popular
teachers. He offered a wide variety of courses, ranging from the history of
English and American law to American Diplomacy and Oriental Politics, which reflected his catholic interests and many talents. In 1906,
Reinsch introduced Contemporary International Politics, described in
the university catalogue as a "course of weekly lectures on questions of
international politics, which are of special importance at the present
time." These lectures were opened to the public and were frequently
covered by the local press and the *Daily Cardinal*, the student newspaper.
In the days before syndicated columnists and radio and television com-
mentators, Reinsch treated Madison's students and townspeople to a
personal analysis of international affairs.[4]

Charles McCarthy, who took Reinsch's course on political thought
while working on his Ph.D. under Turner, described him as "a very
brilliant man" and reported that "the course is one of the best I have
taken." Reinsch was an accomplished speaker, intense, reflective, and

enthusiastic. He conscientiously updated his material and filled his lectures with references to contemporary developments, embellished with anecdotes from his diplomatic missions and meetings with leading men of the day.[5]

Moreover, Reinsch experimented with his classes to make them more exciting and to break away from the formality and sterility of the lecture-textbook system. Hoping to encourage the use of primary sources and classroom discussion, Reinsch edited collections of documents on federal and state government. Charles Beard, Columbia University's controversial, progressive historian and political scientist, declared the experiment would help "to make a revolution for the better in our university instruction in American Government and Politics."[6] At the suggestion of Charles McCarthy, then head of the Legislative Reference Library, Reinsch offered a practical course in comparative legislation in the spring of 1904. After researching a particular social or economic problem, the students drafted a bill and, with McCarthy's tactful assistance, tried to secure its passage in the state legislature. Reinsch was so impressed with the success of the course, which he felt gave students an insight into the practical, economic, and legal aspects of legislation, that he made it a regular offering, later taught by McCarthy himself, whenever the legislature was in session.[7]

Reinsch attracted students from all parts of the country: Horatio Bates Hawkins from California, Stanley Hornbeck from Colorado, and S. Gale Lowrie from Illinois. And as Reinsch earned a reputation as one of America's foremost experts on colonialism and the Far East, many Asian students (Chinese, Japanese, and Indian) came to Wisconsin to study under him. The Chinese students paid Reinsch the highest compliment when the called him a Second Confucius.[8]

Reinsch had special relationships with two of his students. Horatio Bates Hawkins was a freshman at Stanford University in 1901 when he heard Reinsch deliver a series of lectures and read *World Politics*. They made such a profound impression on him that Hawkins transferred to Madison in 1904. During the next two years, while he completed his senior course work and finished most of the requirements for the Master's degree, Ray Hawkins was at Reinsch's beck and call. He served Reinsch as an amanuensis, editor, research assistant, and typist. The Reinsches made him feel like a member of the family and gave him the large front room of the attic. Meanwhile, Ray had fallen madly in love with Alma's younger sister, Hildred. Ray pursued her for several years until she consented to marry him, thereby further cementing Hawkins's ties to the Reinsch family.[9]

Stanley K. Hornbeck, whom Reinsch probably regarded as his most able student, occupied a different place. Paul came to consider Stanley as his equal, as a worthy successor in his life's work, and as his confidant during his last years. Hornbeck had been studying at Oxford on a Rhodes fellowship when he was steered to Wisconsin by Richard Scholz, another Rhodesman and Paul's former student. Hornbeck shared Reinsch's interest in the Orient, the Open Door policy, and American economic expansion, and was determined to follow in his footsteps. After receiving the Ph.D. at Wisconsin, Hornbeck went to the Far East to teach at Chinese colleges and to gather material for a book on the Open Door. Later, when Reinsch was serving as minister to China, Stanley took over his courses in Madison (1914–1917). Hornbeck soon became known as a Far Eastern specialist in his own right and eventually realized his ambition to shape American Far Eastern policy by securing the appointment as chief of the Far Eastern Division in the Department of State and later as adviser to Secretary of State Cordell Hull.[10]

*   *   *

Development of the political science department was one of Reinsch's major achievements. The University of Wisconsin recognized the emergence of political science as an independent discipline and, in 1901, it divorced political science from history and established it as a separate department. Reinsch was named chairman and served in that capacity until his departure in 1913. Political science never quite attained the excellence and reputation that history had at Wisconsin. But, by the time he left for China, Reinsch made Wisconsin a center of study in international affairs, Latin American and Far Eastern politics and Oriental studies, a tradition carried on by Chester Lloyd Jones and Hornbeck.

However, Van Hise, Dean Edward Birge, and some members of the political science department felt that Reinsch had failed to provide a balanced and well-integrated program. McCarthy, who secured a part-time appointment through Reinsch's efforts, complained that his friend was too busy running around to give full attention to upgrading the department. Reinsch attributed part of the problem to his inability to draw certain scholars to Wisconsin. In fact, the strength of Wisconsin's political science department rested to a considerable degree on Reinsch's enthusiasm, the force of his personality, and his own contributions as a teacher and scholar. It was almost, but not quite, a one-man show. Unfortunately, Reinsch often operated in that fashion.[11]

Reinsch's service to the University of Wisconsin extended beyond concern for his own department. To provide intellectual stimulation and cultural enrichment, he brought the first major art collection to Wisconsin. During his tenure as Roosevelt Professor, Reinsch purchased more than one hundred Dutch, Italian, French, Spanish, and German paintings; some he acquired for himself, but most, especially the more valuable works, he planned to sell to wealthy friends and acquaintances. Upon his return to Madison, Reinsch loaned his collection to the university. In addition, he persuaded Charles R. Crane, the Chicago plumbing industrialist, philanthropist, and progressive, and Colonel William Brumder, scion of an influential German-American family in Wisconsin, to donate most of their paintings. [12]

Reinsch also contributed directly to the excellence of Wisconsin's library. On his trips to Europe and Latin America, Reinsch scoured the book stores and publishing houses for basic works, collections of documents, and little-known gems. Occasionally, he exceeded the amount budgeted by the university, which led to rumors that he was irresponsible with other people's money. On one trip to South America, Reinsch supposedly sent back to Madison books costing between 1,500 and 2,000 dollars, when he was authorized to spend only 500 dollars. Reinsch, to be sure, was unorthodox in his methods, especially when judged by the proper standards of his Eastern critics. But he felt that he could not pass up rare opportunities to enhance Wisconsin's library holdings. Furthermore, his seemingly impetuous spending was, in fact, based on the knowledge that wealthy friends, such as William Vilas, would support his purchases, if that became necessary. These experiences, however, may have reinforced Reinsch's faith when he was minister to China that his superiors would back him up when he had to make a difficult decision or found himself in a delicate situation. [13]

Finally, Reinsch emerged as a leading defender of the university during the heated conflict with the regents in 1909–1910. The issue came to a head during the summer of 1909 when the associate editor of *Collier's*, Richard Lloyd Jones, charged, in an article which appeared in that magazine, that some of the more conservative and powerful regents were interfering in purely academic affairs and were even planning to depose President Van Hise. To calm the alarmed faculty and air their complaints, Van Hise suggested a meeting between the regents and a faculty committee. Reinsch's strong support for responsible academic freedom made him a natural choice for a place on the committee.

Reinsch took a leading part in the discussions, held on December 10, 1909, which resulted in a victory for the faculty. When the regents referred to the complaints voiced throughout the state about the teaching of socialism, Reinsch retorted that a university could not teach "socialism" or thrust any dogma upon students. Nevertheless, he insisted, "you cannot close any field of inquiry without impairing the student's faith in the honesty of teaching." Reinsch stated the faculty case: if the regents would adhere to the spirit as well as the letter of the university bylaws, if they would leave matters concerning teaching, time for research, promotions, and appointments to the administrators they selected, and if they would respect the faculty's judgment of the ability of the university personnel, a considerable degree of harmony would be restored. At the end of the meeting, the regents agreed not to interfere with the customary methods of administration and to give the faculty the initiative in formulating educational policy.[14]

* * *

Reinsch's reputation, however, rested primarily on his scholarship and prodigious writings. The thirteen years between the appearance of *World Politics* and his appointment as minister to China yielded five major books, two collections of documents, a successful high school civics textbook, *Civil Government*, several extended essays and dozens of articles for scholarly journals and popular magazines.[15] Like scholars then and now, Reinsch enhanced his bibliography by borrowing articles from forthcoming books. But he was also a tireless worker who often put in a fourteen-hour day. Blessed with a keen mind and great powers of concentration, Paul could read rapidly and critically. Thanks to his linguistic talents and broad background, Reinsch was able to draw on a wealth of material. In addition, he had the journalist's eye for detecting a good story and the good sense to take advantage of every opportunity; a trip to South America or Europe, a dramatic event in domestic or world affairs, might result in an article or a chapter in a book.[16]

Reinsch stood above many of his contemporaries in his extensive and ingenious use of primary source material. He carefully watched the American press for developments in American political life and foreign journals for information on international affairs. He opened the "untapped mine" of court opinions and the minutes of bar association meetings to political scientists and historians. He pored through state, federal, and foreign government publications (especially census reports, consular and trade reports, the *Congressional Record*, and House and Senate committee hearings), and with the help of friends in Washington and in other countries, he solicited information from government departments and agencies.[17]

Finally, Reinsch resourcefully compensated for his inability to visit the Orient and to learn Chinese or Japanese. When Ray Hawkins planned to apply for the United States Philippine Service in 1905, Paul suggested that instead he enter the Chinese Imperial Maritime Service and then rejoin him in Madison to collaborate on a study of Far Eastern politics. For the next five years, Hawkins served as Paul's eyes and ears. Hawkins learned Chinese and through his Chinese friends acquired information and a feel for China which could not be obtained from the books, periodicals, and newspapers he scoured for his mentor. Hawkins sent back to Madison lengthy analyses of political, intellectual, and social trends in China and interesting anecdotes to enliven Reinsch's lectures and writings.

Realizing that this arrangement was inefficient and time-consuming, Hawkins trained adult Chinese students, familiar with Chinese classical learning and modern trends, and sent them to work with Reinsch in Madison. In similar fashion, Reinsch turned for translations and information to the Chinese, Japanese, and Indian students whom he drew to Wisconsin. Without the help of Hawkins and those foreign students, Reinsch could not have written *Intellectual and Political Currents in the Far East*, and he gratefully acknowledged his debt to them. By 1911, when he married Daisy Moser, Hawkins had trained enough Chinese students so that Reinsch no longer needed him in China. Paul invited Ray to become an assistant in the political science department while he pursued his Ph.D. But Hawkins decided to return to China, where he served in the Maritime Service until his retirement in 1940.[18]

Suspicious of dogma, Reinsch never tried to fit his writings into an all-encompassing framework. Similarly, Reinsch had no precise methodology and owed allegiance to no particular school of thought. He was influenced by John Marshall in constitutional law, Hugo Grotius in international law, Wang Yang-ming in energism (an ethical doctrine of self-realization), Ludwig Gumplowicz and Gustave Ratzenhofer in sociology, as well as by Gustave Le Bon, Paul and Pierre Leroy-Beaulieu, Woodrow Wilson, Frederick J. Turner, and Richard T. Ely. He respected them, but worshipped no one.

Reinsch dismissed the deductive method as sterile and subjective. Although he frequently talked of making the study of politics scientific, Reinsch did not really think political and social problems could be solved in the same manner as the natural sciences and often warned against making broad generalizations. Being scientific meant to Reinsch the accumulation of large amounts of data and statistical investigations and, especially, the comparative historical study of political institutions. In practice, it amounted to empirical common sense. Nor did Reinsch imply or advocate cold objectivity. *A priori* ethical considerations were necessary to preserve human decency, democracy, and idealism and to prevent the triumph of amoral Machiavellianism. Drawing upon his classical education, Reinsch pointed out that the ancient Greeks never separated politics from ethics; indeed, they believed that politics gave form to ethical ideals. The Greek sense of concrete vision, however, prevented them from confusing the existing reality with the ideal schemes of the philosophers.

Reinsch therefore opposed the philosophical construction of the state by the Hegels and Bosanquets. He rejected the juristic view, and the supporting theory of natural law, because government policy was deduced from constitutions and enshrined precedents. Reinsch found much merit in the influential historical-evolutionary school, but was also highly critical of its methods and assumptions. It tended to be aristocratic, and could become reactionary; it led to understanding rather than to action; and it considered man helpless against the forces that shaped nations. Reinsch also felt that history was not sufficiently present-minded and that sociology and economics offered as much insight to the political scientist. "Not only is political science largely determined by economic power," he wrote in the entry "Political Science" for the *New International Encyclopedia*, "but the constant interference of political agencies with economic interests and processes makes it necessary for political science to give special attention to economics." Here he owed much to Turner, Ely, and the Austrian sociological school. Reinsch anticipated later American scholars by borrowing from Gumplowicz and Ratzenhofer the idea that political life was a struggle among interest groups. Finally, Reinsch accepted the position of the realists that political science should focus on real people and deal with the actualities of political life.

In brief, Reinsch was eclectic. His studies lacked systematic formulation and his thinking sometimes suffered from inconsistencies and internal contradictions. But by creating his own synthesis out of the best he could find, Reinsch retained the open-mindedness, sensitivity, and flexibility that might escape the more rigorous thinker or theorist.[19]

Reinsch wrote for many audiences—the intelligent reader and the concerned citizen as well as for the specialist and the college student. He considered himself not only a scholar but also a publicist and social critic, charged with the duty to speak out on the issues of the day and to influence public policy. Reinsch was therefore overwhelmed with requests to lecture to business and civic groups and to contribute to leading popular publications. "Your specialty of World Politics makes you a victim of our magazine," La Follette explained to Reinsch. Richard Lloyd Jones repeatedly asked Reinsch to submit his thoughts to *Collier's*. "Turn yourself loose, so to speak, and through us address the public," Jones wrote his friend.[20] Reinsch, indeed, welcomed these opportunities as he searched for ways of translating his theories into concrete action.

*   *   *

Reinsch's study of the American political system, begun in the 1890s with newspaper reports from Washington, culminated in the publication of *American Legislatures and Legislative Methods*. It was both a careful analysis of how American legislatures actually operated at the federal and state levels and a progressive indictment of the perversion of the legislative process by economic interests and political machines. While Reinsch was concerned with the elimination of political corruption, he felt that the greater problem facing progressive reform was to meet the challenge of a highly industrialized, technological, and urbanized society. In essence, America had to learn how to control the new concentrations of power while fostering cooperation between the various elements of American society, ensuring efficiency to meet foreign competition and to raise the standard of living, and preserving and strengthening political democracy and human values. Or, as Reinsch often explained, it meant the restoration of commonwealth—government acting in the common interest to produce a better society. The Founding Fathers had inherited that concept from ancient Greece and seventeenth-century England, but it had been shattered by the Civil War and had disappeared during the era of "unrestrained individualism" and gross materialism that followed. Reinsch believed that his generation wished to return to the concept of government that had reigned in Athens and during the early national period in the United States. Interpreting for the *Wisconsin State Journal* the strong popular vote for progressive candidates in the election of 1910, Reinsch observed: "They want the spirit of our legislation to be progressive, in the sense that the test of any measure shall not be a special interest but the idea of commonwealth in its old and true meaning."[21]

While most progressives, especially in Wisconsin, defined the problem of reform in similar terms, they differed on the means of attaining their objectives. Reinsch clearly rejected a return to a simpler past and a restoration of mythical free competition. He deplored the political power of big business, but taught that America must accommodate itself to the large corporation and to "the age of solidarity and cooperation." Unlike some Midwestern progressives, he opposed the rigid enforcement of the antitrust laws and maintained that large-scale enterprise was necessary for efficiency. In fact, Reinsch admired the American corporation as a creative institution for organizing vast amounts of capital and skill for constructive work, and he considered it a model for backward nations. As minister to China, Reinsch enlisted the corporation in his program to extend American influence and to develop a modern progressive nation. Reinsch, however, shared the Midwestern distrust of the large Eastern investment banks which tried to extend their power nationally and which over-capitalized the corporate giants. He therefore supported the Federal Reserve Act as the first step in decentralizing banking in America. Furthermore, he carried to China a grudge against Wall Street for its refusal to float loans for Wisconsin in retaliation for La Follette's progressive reforms.[22]

Reinsch was also harshly critical of the continued attachment to the liberal state and laissez-faire economics. He was convinced that it permitted powerful groups to control American society and did not conform to reality. He argued that society was composed of interests as well as individuals, that property rights were not unlimited, and that liberty was the opportunity to develop one's personality rather than the absence of restraint. The state, he insisted, had to be an active force in the lives of its citizens.

Reinsch therefore toyed with the idea of replacing representation based on numbers with the representation of interests as they existed in society—leading industries, chambers of commerce, farmer organizations, labor unions, educational institutions, and professional associations. Such a system, he maintained, "affords a recognized position to all the leading interests of a given society and can thus be expected to free political life very largely from that striving for secret control which has corrupted contemporary politics. Moreover, each interest naturally desires to be represented by some man who stands preeminent as a leader in his business or profession, and the trade of the legislative politician would disappear."

But while this form of syndicalism might be instituted by countries lacking experience in representative government and frontier individualism, Reinsch hesitated to apply it in the United States. In part, Reinsch shared with other progressives an innate political conservatism and a deep attachment to American institutions; in part, he feared for the survival of democracy and social stability if the change were made. In addition, he was always reluctant to advocate the complete adoption of another country's system for the United States or for any other society. Instead, selective borrowing and ongoing experimentation might enable the United States to perfect its political institutions within its own historical context.[23]

Working within the existing democratic-capitalist system, Reinsch thought that by means of "executive leadership, expert administration and direct legislation," it would be possible to create "a new governmental machinery which will be thoroughly and flexibly representative of the underlying needs of a more social democracy." The central government must first be strengthened to enable it to control the new social and economic forces and to institute necessary reforms. It required a powerful executive, particularly in foreign affairs where the Senate used its prerogatives to hobble action in the national interest. It also entailed greater cooperation between the executive and legislative branches and changes in congressional procedures to speed the enactment of vital legislation. Second, Reinsch called for improved methods to recruit, train, and retain able statesmen and legislators. At one point he urged that capable congressmen be elevated to the Senate and that cabinet officers be selected from Congress. Finally, Reinsch maintained that the increasing complexity of modern life necessitated greater dependence on impartial, scientifically oriented administrative bodies, staffed by experts and motivated solely by the general welfare. "The ideal of commonwealth demands that the ordinary administration of the state be placed as much as possible outside of the sphere of personal struggles for political power," Reinsch declared. This really meant *the elevation of administration above politics.*[24]

Reinsch's emphasis on expertise and administration reflected the development of his age and the concern of his profession. Since the 1890s regulatory and administrative commissions had mushroomed on all levels of government. Meanwhile, political scientists, economists, historians, and sociologists were recruited to staff the growing bureaucracies. Hailing this development, Reinsch wrote: "The development of a highly efficient, conscientious, and public spirited expertship is therefore one of the prime needs of free government."[25]

But above all, Reinsch was influenced by the Wisconsin experience. "Education," "efficiency," and "applied human effort directed to progress" were the themes that rang out from Madison. Ely brought back from Germany the idea that the problem of the age was "fundamentally one of administration." Heralded by Charles McCarthy and Frederic Howe, a former instructor at the University of Wisconsin and a leading exponent of progressive reform, the Wisconsin Idea emphasized the involvement of experts in framing and administering legislation that would insure political honesty, regulate corporate wealth in the public interest, provide greater social justice, and create a more efficient society. McCarthy, in fact, equated efficiency and expertise with honesty and justice.

During the administrations of Robert La Follette and Francis McGovern, the application of the Wisconsin Idea thrust the state into the national limelight and provided the dynamism for much progressive reform in Wisconsin. La Follette worked closely with his friend Charles Van Hise and together they chanted the themes of progress through administration and expertise and service to the commonwealth. Counting forty-six faculty members in various state positions in 1910–1911, McCarthy declared: "It is hardly too much to say that the best hope of intelligent and principled progress in economic and social legislation lies in the increasing influence of American universities.[26]

Reinsch echoed these sentiments by maintaining that the university could no longer be apart from the people. "It interests itself in the general welfare of the state," he explained. "It works to improve the agriculture, the manufacturing activities, the engineering work, the health, the power of the Commonwealth. It exists for every citizen." He became enamoured of Charles McCarthy's Legislative Reference Library, which he viewed as a "scientific" device to demonstrate how legislation could be made and administered. Reinsch worked closely with McCarthy, encouraged him to go to Europe to examine different legislative bodies, and publicized the work of the library.[27]

Moreover, as an adviser to La Follette and McGovern, Reinsch exerted direct influence on the reform movement in Wisconsin. Along with Van Hise, Ely, Commons, Turner, and McCarthy, Reinsch was a regular member of the Saturday Lunch Club, where state officials and professors met to discuss forthcoming legislation and state problems. During the election campaign of 1920, McCarthy testified that Reinsch had been "called in on nearly every constructive piece of legislation that was up before the state legislators." But while he doggedly pursued a diplomatic position, Reinsch refused to serve in any official or paid capacity in Wisconsin. In fact, taking Wisconsin academic progressivism to the extreme, Reinsch scrupulously avoided partisan politics and was not an active La Follette adherent. A Gold Democrat in the 1890s, opposing both the unlimited coinage of silver and radical Populism, Reinsch voted for McKinley and Roosevelt for president and La Follette and McGovern for governor; then, in 1912, he supported

Woodrow Wilson. Reinsch saw himself as an impartial critic and expert. He was on good terms with the leaders of different movements, parties, and ideological positions. Only in 1920, did Reinsch engage in partisan politics—and then as a reluctant candidate for the United States Senate. He ran on the Democratic ticket, but campaigned under the banner of extended progressive reform.[28]

Reinsch marched in the ranks of Progressive America. But he remained open-minded, avoided the clichés of many reformers, and created his own synthesis from the currents that swept through America during the great era of Populist-Progressive reform. His faith in private enterprise, the sanctity of property, and individual rights as the basis of the American system, was tempered by his suspicion of Wall Street, dislike of speculation, and concern for social justice. He was clearly one of those progressives who questioned the value of liberal political reform, who called for experts to save democracy, and who talked of social control, national guidance, and the end of laissez-faire. Plainly, Reinsch looked more to the future than to the past. Still, Reinsch's goal remained constant. Impelled by his Christian upbringing, his deep humanitarianism, his image of classical Athens and his Wisconsin experience, Reinsch worked for a true commonwealth of men on earth.

*   *   *

Nations ought to concentrate their energies on domestic problems, Reinsch taught, and "national worth, welfare and strength are developed from within, not conquered or acquired from without." Reinsch shared the Puritan fear of "a wealth too easily gained" and the anti-imperialist concern of becoming "untrue to our real social and political mission." He understood that all forms of imperialism tended to undermine domestic reform, to centralize economic and political power, to weaken individual liberty, and to encourage blind nationalism. Reinsch also worried because the contemporary race for empire appeared to be controlled by "grim, silent, passionate forces"; the American public and most of its leaders seemed to look abroad without developing a national policy on expansion.

Nevertheless, Reinsch accepted the fact that the United States would have to develop a dynamic foreign policy and establish its own world empire. "We are no longer an agricultural nation," he lectured his students at Wisconsin. "We are a manufacturing nation, & we can be successful and rich only by tending to foreign markets. We can no longer afford to live isolated." Reinsch indeed became an avowed expansionist.

His problem, during the years that spanned his academic career at Wisconsin, was to find the means to ensure that expansion brought prosperity, progress, peace, and justice to the United States and the rest of the world. In numerous essays and in his major books, *World Politics, Colonial Government: An Introduction to the Study of Colonial Institutions, Colonial Administration,* and *Public International Unions,* Reinsch attempted to examine modern imperialism, educate the American public, and guide policy makers and diplomats. Greatly influenced by the policies of Secretaries of State John Hay and Elihu Root, Reinsch thought he found the solution in the updating and elaboration of traditional American policies—the Open Door, the Monroe Doctrine and Pan Americanism, anti-colonialism, and international law and cooperation.[29]

While Reinsch recognized the significance of missionary work, racism, the role of the navy, and the emulation of Britain as causal factors, he maintained that the primary force behind modern national imperialism was economic. Industrialism and technological progress had produced surpluses which home markets could not absorb; in order to prevent economic depression and social dislocations, the advanced nations had to find foreign outlets, particularly in the underdeveloped areas of the world. "To-day the primary object is the search for markets, and the chief purpose of commercial expansion has come to be the desire to dispose of the surplus product of European industry," Reinsch wrote in *Colonial Goverment.* Similarly, capital in the industrialized countries had accumulated beyond the possibility of profitable investment at home. In addition, Reinsch taught that commerce depended on foreign investment to create markets for sophisticated industrial goods, to gain access to needed raw materials, and eventually to raise the purchasing power of the underdeveloped countries. "You see, it is difficult to foster trade by itself alone," he instructed businessmen upon his return from Rio de Janeiro in 1906, "there must be other interests in the country back of it—banking and shipping interests, investments in railroads and other public service enterprises and the like."[30]

For the United States to succeed abroad, however, it had to rationalize and coordinate its overseas activity. Reinsch labored to disabuse American businessmen of the popular notion that an Eldorado existed in China and Latin America, with millions of people anxiously waiting to buy American goods. Rather, Americans had to cultivate these markets through hard work and in stiff competition with more experienced British and German businessmen, from whom they had much to learn. Reinsch therefore emphasized that overseas enterprise was a long-term matter that would eventually yield "to the consistent processes of scientific exploitation backed by courage, character [and] wealth."[31]

This commercial and industrial expansion, Reinsch believed, was not only inevitable, it was also justified. The advanced nations therefore had the right to insist on the security of trade and investment. Occasionally resorting to the rhetoric of the White Man's Burden, Reinsch argued that expansion was based on the needs of the human race for raw materials, manufactured goods, and economic growth; it would also result in progress, the "industrial conquest of the world" and an improved standard of living for all. Economic competition would encourage the invention of new techniques and greater efficiency. And, finally, economic interdependence would unite mankind in peace and mutual assistance.

Nevertheless, Reinsch recognized that imperialism posed the danger that one or more nations, impelled by excessive nationalism, missionary zeal, an insatiable lust for power, or a Nietzschean exercise of will, might attempt to seize large amounts of territory, to subjugate other peoples, and to destroy the delicate equilibrium developed over the years. This frightening prospect was present in the imminent partition of China and especially in Russian expansion in East Asia.[32]

Reinsch therefore urged the powers to limit their ambitions and to recognize that there was sufficient opportunity for all in developing and civilizing the backward regions of the world. In the great debate over imperialism in 1898–1900, Reinsch supported the annexation of the Philippines to obtain a trading and naval base with which to protect and expand America's markets in China. But since modern expansion was primarily economic, Reinsch condemned any general policy of territorial acquisition or formal imperialism. Industrial nations needed ample facilities for trade, industry, banking, communications, naval depots, and coaling stations. Consequently their best interests would be served "were law and order established throughout the world, but were it considered indifferent which particular power holds sovereignty over any given region." Lively economic competition under the aegis of the Open Door, Reinsch concluded, was the best guarantee for a progressive, prosperous, dynamic, and stable world.[33]

*   *   *

Reinsch was very much worried about solving the economic problems of the United States and the other industrialized nations and preventing conflict between them. But he was also deeply concerned with the impact of Western expansion on traditional societies and underdeveloped nations. Consequently, Reinsch emerged as a leading critic of colonialism and "rough-shod assimilationism." Reinsch maintained that every society had a life purpose and unity; every people had a right to survive and to determine its destiny. Viewed in this light, assimilation made the unjustifiable and harmful demand that societies abandon "the entire complex of customs and beliefs which has thus far guided them through life, and by an act of selective reason" adopt institutions alien to their experience. Reinsch argued that not even those things that Western man cherished most highly—private property, literary education, individualism, or representative government—should be imposed on other peoples. He also showed how the massive introduction of Western civilization threatened the livelihood and skills of thousands of workers and destroyed the stability of Oriental thought and character, thereby creating revolutionaries such as the Boxers. "It is impossible to avoid the conclusion," Reinsch insisted, "that what to some societies is the breath of life becomes to others a deadly poison."[34]

While he did not ask the colonial powers to grant immediate independence to their colonies, Reinsch did expect them to foster political and economic development. That meant giving colonial societies the greatest possible amount of autonomy—best found in the protectorate—and acceptance by the powers of the greatest diversity in their empires. It required that the powers eradicate disease and the threat of famine, build the roads, railways, and utilities needed by a modern economy, protect native agriculture and handicrafts from capitalist plantations and foreign imports, and institute an educational system which offered practical training and preserved traditional culture. Finally, it demanded a commitment to low taxes and tariffs, a simple and inexpensive administrative machinery, an open door for foreign trade and investment, and meaningful industrialization. It would be criminal, Reinsch wrote, for the West to deny the backward nations the "same freedom of economic development" that made it "powerful and prosperous."

Realizing that modernization was a long and painful process, Reinsch asked the West to show patience and forbearance. He also called for a new kind of colonial administrator—not the adventurers, missionaries, and merchants of the past, but wise, efficient broadminded experts. For "the blessings of civilization" could not be bestowed by force, legislation, or exhortation; change could come only through "*example freely followed.*" Gradually, Reinsch thought, the colonials would recognize Western superiority in technology, industry, and practical affairs, and they would adapt them to their own values and institutions. "We shall never succeed in making Americans of the Filipinos," he declared. "But we may hope by a careful, considerate policy, to assist in raising their life to a higher plane, though it must remain their life, and will never be ours."[35]

Reinsch saved some of his harshest criticism for American colonial policy in the Philippines. He complained that the United States was extending its institutions—suited for a rich, highly developed nation —to the poor and backward Philippines with no intention of granting American citizenship or statehood. "We have been telling the Filipinos that if they learn English and vote they will be happy," he declared in his stirring keynote address at the first annual meeting of the American Political Science Association. "But what we must do is give them an opportunity to live." Reinsch's remarks attracted national attention. "Professor Paul Reinsch of the University of Wisconsin," the *New York Times* editorialized, "is a man who should be listened to when he speaks of our colonial dependencies. He is among the most careful, acute, candid, and patient students of the questions they involve, not a theorist, still less a partisan, but a practical, clear-headed man of unusual ability who has given a great deal of time and labor to the study of the subject."[36]

Important as the Philippines were, Reinsch stressed that China presented a far more formidable challenge. The Boxer Rebellion, he observed, was a mere hint of the convulsions and anti-foreign sentiment that would eventually spread through China and possibly the entire Orient. And yet the West was sadly lacking in information and understanding of this area of growing importance. In an effort to educate policy makers and the general public about developments in Asia and to interpret Oriental thinking to the West, Reinsch wrote *Intellectual and Political Currents in the Far East*. Reinsch pointed out that the Orient had a unity of its own and could be expected to react sharply against imperialism and forced modernization. But he denied that an irrepressible antagonism existed between Asia and the West. He thereby attempted to demolish the popular myth of the "Yellow Peril." He also warned against the growth of irrational and unscientific pessimism and the longing for a vague mystical spirit that was to be found in the Orient. Finally, he stressed the shared ideals of both civilizations and the positive side of the Orient: its preeminently peaceful temper, its appreciation for the beauty of nature, its concern for the human spirit and brotherhood of man, and its understanding that "machinery kills souls, that mechanism destroys human feeling."[37]

Reinsch's analysis of the impact of Western imperialism was

noteworthy for its sensitivity and breadth of vision. His deeply rooted humanitarianism echoed throughout his writings as his demand for fair play later rang out in his diplomatic dispatches. He always tried to express his religion in deeds; he hated propaganda, cant, and tyranny wherever they existed. He felt the age-old suffering and persecution of the Jews, the fatigue and cruel exploitation of the overworked coolie and the enslaved Congo native, even the eyestrain of the carver of wood or ivory.[38]

But Reinsch offered more than the "broad human sympathy," which several writers have attributed to him. He was a constant and biting critic of Western colonialism and "the profound discrepancy between Christian profession and practice." He not only believed in the right of self-determination, but actively supported the Finns against the Russians, sided with the Boers against the British, and later endorsed the Zionist demand for a national Jewish homeland. He designed policies to prepare dependencies for eventual independence and grappled with the nature of revolution. Reinsch believed that no nation, however benevolent, could bestow independence upon another. "Autonomy means the self-determination of a people," he insisted. "History has shown that the autonomy of one nation has never been created by the efforts of another." Finally, Reinsch recognized that true independence required both political and economic freedom.[39]

*   *   *

Confronted by the mighty forces of industrialization, imperialism, and impending revolution, Reinsch joined other men of his day in the search for world peace. He thought that war was an irrational perversion of humanity, but he also believed that pacifism cut against the bursting energies of his era and that the idea of a world state was a naive abstraction. Peaceful Open Door competition and the drive for national excellence offered a partial solution. Anticipating by some fifteen years the House-Wilson démarche of 1914, Reinsch wished to divert the industrialized nations from the arms race to the development of the backward nations. "We must constantly emphasize the thought that there is sufficient work for all nations in developing and civilizing primitive regions," Reinsch declared. "Each one of the leading nationalities can fully develop its own character and impress its best elements on the civilization of the world, without desiring the downfall and ruin of other powers."[40] However, Reinsch's more complete prescription included a combination of practical international cooperation, an expansion of international law, a new diplomacy, and disarmament.

Ironically, science, technology, and industrialism provided the starting point for international cooperation. In the modern age, economic activity had become international in scope and science knew no national boundary. "The great fact that the world is a unit," Reinsch explained, "rests upon the underlying conditions of modern invention and science which the dictum of no government can destroy." More than a hundred public international unions had developed to provide information, facilitate joint action, maintain standards, and regulate certain activities. A random listing of these international organizations—the European Freight Union, the Universal Postal Union, the Pan American Sanitary Union, and the International Opium Commission—provided a sense of their range and indicated the need to take other kinds of international action "out of the field of resolutions" and make them part of the realities of human life. These unions recognized the existence of national states, based on history and ethnic identity, as constructive units in a cooperative world. But they were also permanent political organizations possessing executive bureaus, legislative commissions, and arbitration tribunals and developing a positive, practical international administrative law.[41]

These objectives, in turn, called for a new concept of diplomacy which aimed at establishing mutual cooperation among all nations instead of seeking special advantages by means of shrewd negotiations, threats of force, and the "nice balancing" of political interests. Eventually, administrative conferences would take the place of bilateral diplomatic conversations and underhanded pressures; legations and embassies would become the center for diverse helpful activity, with attachés for commerce, education, and science playing as important a role as political and military specialists. Thus, the successful diplomat would be, in the words of John Quincy Adams, a man of "great energy of mind, activity of research, and fertility of expedients," who would master the intricate interaction of those world-wide "industrial, commercial and scientific forces which give to national life new and broader significance." In this way, caste diplomacy and secret diplomacy would be purged from international relations.[42]

Finally, there remained the problem of disarmament. Reinsch recognized that strong military preparedness was often a deterrent to violence: he was concerned with the disorganization of the American army and supported the building of a strong navy, "the most important branch of national defense," but he believed that the burgeoning arms race before World War I bordered on insanity, was driving nations into bankruptcy, and was dangerous to world peace. Rather than wait for an agreement among all the powers, Reinsch suggested that the United States and

Britain enter into a compact with several other nations to limit naval strength in proportion to their population and sea-borne commerce. Non-signators would then be forced to limit their navies proportionately or face the combined strength of the members of the compact.[43]

Reinsch was directly involved in the multifaceted peace movement during the first two decades of the twentieth century. He joined Elihu Root, Oscar Straus, Nicholas Murray Butler, and other supporters of international arbitration at the Lake Mohonk conferences. He collaborated with Root, Robert Lansing, John Bassett Moore, and other members of the Eastern establishment in forming the American Society of International Law.[44] But it was in the Carnegie Endowment for International Peace (CEIP) that he found an organization perfectly suited to his views. The Endowment, created in 1910, was based on the premise that universal peace and law were the ends of human existence, but admitted that time, skilled effort, and sacrifice were needed to gain universal acceptance. Through a program of study, propaganda, and action, the Endowment sought to educate mankind to the folly of war and the need for international cooperation. Reinsch labored primarily for the Endowment's Division of Economics and History, whose purpose was to make a "thorough, systematic and scientific inquiry into the economic and historical aspects of war." His major contribution was to recommend, solicit, and coordinate studies subsidized by the Carnegie Endowment. While some of his recommendations were considered impractical or beyond the scope of the Endowment, the directors generally valued his contributions. Reinsch attended the Berne Conference (August 1911), which "inaugurated the scientific work in the study of warfare and international relations." Subsequently, he was asked to participate in the Lucerne Conference, called for August 5, 1914, to evaluate the work launched at Berne and to formulate plans for future research.[45]

The peace movement which blossomed before World War I had produced a diverse group of advocates that ranged from cautious legalists and arbitrationists to more ambitious world staters and sanctionists. Like most American leaders, Reinsch hewed to a moderate, gradual, and practical approach, but he also broke new ground. He was one of the early proponents of functionalism and the doctrine of "transferability" —the belief that cooperation in technical and economic matters could be transferred to cooperation in the political sphere. Comfortable with the Anglo-American legal system, he felt that a viable system of international law and arbitration could be built on meaningful precedents. He also sought to marry the idealism of the philosophers of peace (Kant and Saint Pierre) and the world community concept of the founders of international law (Grotius and Suarez) to the reality of strong, self-conscious national states. Reinsch saw internationalism operating, in the words of Inis Claude, "like a pebble dropped in the international pond, giving rise to a series of circles of cooperation which will expand from the limited area of technical agencies to the vast circumference of a global political and security organization." The outbreak of World War I deeply troubled Reinsch and advanced his internationalist thinking. It caused him to sketch a plan for a League of Nations, which he sent to President Woodrow Wilson in January 1915, and he supported the idea for the rest of his life. He hoped that eventually an international consciousness would replace the national state as the focal point of loyalty; then a comprehensive international law would govern a truly universal community of man.[46]

*   *   *

Reinsch's analysis of international affairs contained numerous inconsistencies, some of which he recognized. He believed that the resentment of the Boxers was justifiable, but he still maintained that the Western powers had "the right and duty" to protect their citizens in China and he also held Peking responsible for the destruction and losses caused by the rioters. Even with the encouragement of Dollar Diplomacy, Reinsch witnessed the difficulties in getting private capital to serve the national interest in China and Latin America. Gradual expansion on the basis of real need and actual power might serve the United States, but it might not be acceptable to other nations. Nor was there any assurance that native leaders, during the process of decolonization, would institute the social and economic reforms expected of them. Moreover, the maintenance of a system of international peace also seemed to require that some nations would play a special role, perhaps even policing the system.[47]

Because of Reinsch's intellectual framework and assumptions, these problems could not be easily resolved and they would continue to plague him as minister to China. After all, he was very much a product of his age. In an eclectic fashion, he combined the best thinking of his day, the heritage of the past, and some of his own original ideas, to produce a synthesis that would guide him and his contemporaries in coping with the intricate problems facing Americans at home and abroad. He was a progressive who, influenced by the Wisconsin Idea, called for political honesty, public morality, efficiency, material improvement, social justice, and a renewed commitment to the spirit and practice of commonwealth. He also personified Open Door expansion, in the sense so ably defined by William Appleman Williams,[48] and he called for its globalization and the rationalization of its techniques. While he vigorously opposed excessive nationalism and formal imperialism or colonialism, Reinsch insisted that the world be open to American goods, capital, and ideas.

Reinsch, therefore, was both a progressive and an expansionist. Some historians have challenged the viability of the concept of progressive-imperialism and the existence of any real linkage between the two movements. Nevertheless, Reinsch fits nicely the composite of the progressive-imperalist drawn by Gerald Markowitz, and his own synthesis suggests that the concept has a certain validity.[49] Aware of many of the underlying conflicts, how did he resolve the dilemmas of liberal internationalism in the early twentieth century? And what common basis did he find for continued reform at home and "benevolent" imperialism abroad?

To begin with, Reinsch and his contemporaries were overwhelmed with the need to solve simultaneously two very difficult and pressing problems: on the one hand, the United States had to adjust democratic capitalism to a highly industrialized and urbanized society; on the other hand, the United States had to take its place in world affairs. Abetted by the fact that they were not doctrinaire nor very rigorous in their thinking, they muddled through the contradictions in desperate, sloppy fashion. In addition, Reinsch, along with Wilson and other American leaders, glorified definitive action and often adopted a casual attitude toward their means as long as they were convinced that their cause was just. But one must be careful in applying William Leuchtenburg's thesis to Reinsch.[50] For while, as minister to China, he would withhold information, practice a little deception, and engage in questionable deals, Reinsch distinguished between acceptable and improper kinds of behavior.

More important, Reinsch saw direct and positive interrelationships between progressivism and expansion, particularly as he called for the globalization of the American system. Both aimed at moral regeneration and material improvement; both required flexible, organic law to realize reform, progress, peace, and stability. The progressive experience taught Reinsch the need for efficiency in foreign relations and for a new breed of colonial administrators and experts—scientists like himself who would study and control complex forces for human betterment. America's success in achieving a democratic, federal commonwealth might indeed serve as a model for others to follow. But, like his fellow progressives, Reinsch believed that foreign markets and investment were essential for prosperity and tranquility at home that would in turn support the democratic commonwealth. Practical economic and political considerations combined with humanitarianism (partially garbed in self-righteousness and self-fulfilling superiority) therefore required that the United States go abroad and assume the role of world power. However, the insistence upon peaceful Open Door expansion, cultural diversity, and national self-determination offered safeguards against the evils inherent in any form of imperialism; international cooperation and the rule of international law promised still more.

Weaving these themes together, Reinsch offered a vision of a better world:

> No one can behold the new fields and possibilities opened to the human race by the developments which we have just traced without the thought, that for centuries to come there is here provided work in abundance for willing hands. Could the crying injustice to natives, the utter disregard of human rights, that so often marked the work of the greatest pioneers of industrial advance be shut out from our vision, the picture of teeming resources only awaiting a master hand to be turned into wealth and bountiful sustenance for whole nations would fill us with pure gratification. What a school for hardy training in bold purpose and iron will power, what risks to face, what dangers to overcome, what prizes to win! . . . May the ideal side, the obligations to humanity, of this great movement be realized more fully, to the end that it may become humanized and refined, . . . May industrialism also forbear to reduce the life of the world to the sordid uniformity of a dead mechanism, but taking account of the rich variety of human existence, aid the peculiar genius of race and locality to find the best means of expression. Thus would the world be truly enriched by the industrial conquest.[51]

And being basically optimistic by nature, Reinsch was confident that in the end reason, enlightened self-interest, and humanitarian impulses would triumph, showering mankind with the blessings of peace, prosperity, and progress.

*   *   *

Reinsch contributed much to Wisconsin: fine scholarship and leadership in his discipline that brought stature and recognition to his school and state; dynamic classes and well-trained students who carried his teachings to the far corners of the globe; a separate political science department that he helped to create and develop; a collection of art works and research works for all to enjoy; a ringing defense of academic freedom and unhampered inquiry not only in Madison but everywhere; and service in the cause of progressive reform. His legacy also included his devotion to the University of Wisconsin and his state, the ideas and inspiration that he gave to students, colleagues, political associates, and business friends.

Wisconsin reciprocated. It gave him a springboard for success and status; a great university and a friendly environment in which to pursue his work; and political and moral support for both his personal and professional ambitions. Later the University of Wisconsin recognized his achievements by awarding him an honorary degree, while many of his fellow citizens showed their respect and admiration by supporting his candidacy for one of Wisconsin's seats in the United States Senate. But, as he noted with gratitude in the *Wisconsin Badger* of 1923, Wisconsin also gave him a faith and an outlook:

> Wherever I have gone later in life, whatever situations I have had to face, whatever work fell to my lot, I was helped by the inspiration of the new life of a great commonwealth which was becoming conscious of itself in those last years of the nineties. The broadening view of human relationships, the idea of the State as a big family, the devotion of the best talent therein to work for the good, the testing of all human rights by their just subservience to human welfare, the aims so clearly expressed in the Wisconsin Idea, helped me beyond words, in facing the difficulties and responsibilities of an arduous time.[52]

The Wisconsin years would be the happiest of his life. But for more than a decade he had looked beyond his university, city, and state to the momentous developments occurring in world politics. And he was determined to play a role on the larger stage of international diplomacy. He received his chance in 1913, and thereby closed a major chapter in his career. Reinsch would always carry the mark of his Wisconsin experience, though he would never again return permanently to his university and state.

NOTES TO
CHAPTER II

1. Hawkins Tapes, 5, 6.

2. Author's interview with Walter S. Rogers, 21 April 1965; Reinsch's obituary, *Milwaukee Wisconsin News,* 27 January 1923.

3. Curti and Carstensen, *University of Wisconsin,* II, 3–26.

4. Lochner, "The Roosevelt Exchange Professor"; Hawkins Tapes, 5; University of Wisconsin Catalogues, 1895–1913, UW Archives; *Daily Cardinal,* 1907–1910.

5. McCarthy to Jameson, 10 March 1900, "Letters: Charles McCarthy to J. Franklin Jameson," ed. Elizabeth Doonan and L. F. Stock, *Wisconsin Magazine of History,* XXXIII (September 1949), 71–72; Hawkins Tapes, 5; author's interview with Stanley K. Hornbeck, 20 January 1965.

6. Hawkins Tapes, 2; Reinsch, ed., *Readings on American Federal Government* (Boston, 1909); Reinsch, ed., *Readings on American State Government* (Boston, 1911); Charles A. Beard to Reinsch, 12 April and 12 August 1911, Reinsch Papers.

7. McCarthy to Jameson, 24 February 1904, "Letters: Charles McCarthy to J. Franklin Jameson," 78–79; Reinsch, "News and Notes," *American Political Science Review,* I (February 1907), 322.

8. Hawkins Tapes, 5.

9. Hawkins to author, 8 January 1972; Hawkins, "A General Explanatory Note," Reinsch Papers.

10. Hornbeck to Reinsch, 20 March 1907, Reinsch Papers; Hornbeck to Reinsch, 16 April 1912, Stanley K. Hornbeck Papers, Hoover Institution on War, Revolution and Peace, Stanford, California (hereafter cited Hornbeck Papers); Claire R. Cadura to author, 12 March 1974.

11. Reinsch to Van Hise, 13 December 1911, Papers of the Presidents (Van Hise), UW Archives; Birge to Reinsch, 27 March and 6 June 1912, College of Letters and Science, Edward A. Birge Papers, UW Archives (hereafter cited Birge Papers, UW); Birge to McBain, 12 July 1912, *ibid.*; McCarthy to Van Hise, 5 October 1911, Charles McCarthy Papers, The State Historical Society of Wisconsin (hereafter cited McCarthy Papers); McCarthy to Ely, 24 May 1912, *ibid.*; Hawkins to author, 8 January 1972; Pyre, *Wisconsin,* 295; Curti and Carstensen, *University of Wisconsin,* II, 338–39.

12. Hawkins Tapes, 8; List of Paintings, Reinsch Papers; clipping, *Milwaukee Free Press,* 19 January 1913, *ibid.*; Reinsch to Ely, 1 April 1912, Ely Papers; Reinsch to Charles Crane, 14 February 1913, Crane Papers; Van Hise to Crane, 22 September 1913, *ibid.*; *Biennial Report of the Board of Regents 1912–1913 and 1913–1914* (Madison, 1914), 10–11.

13. Author's interview with Hawkins, 10 August 1971; Hawkins to author, 2 October 1971; Vilas to Reinsch, 19 February 1908, Reinsch Papers; Charles Eliot to Nicholas M. Butler, 11 February 1913 and Butler to Eliot, 12 February 1913, Papers of the Carnegie Endowment for International Peace, Special Collections, Columbia University (hereafter cited CEIP Papers).

14. Ely to Richard Lloyd Jones, 9 November 1909, Ely Papers; Jones to Ely, 12 November 1909, *ibid.*; Billington, *Frederick Jackson Turner,* 290–305; Curti and Carstensen, *University of Wisconsin,* II, 49–50, 57–66, 99–100.

15. William F. Young to Reinsch, 29 July 1915, Reinsch Papers; Hawkins, "A General Explanatory Note," *ibid.*

16. Hawkins Tapes, 1, 5.

17. Hawkins, "A General Explanatory Note," Reinsch Papers; Hawkins Tapes, 5;

Hawkins to author, 21 January 1965, 8 January 1972; Reinsch, *Readings on American Federal Government,* ii–iv; Reinsch, *Readings on American State Government,* iii; Spooner to Reinsch, 24 December 1901, 11 October 1905, John C. Spooner Papers, Library of Congress (hereafter cited Spooner Papers); Reinsch to Spooner, 24 March 1904, *ibid.*; Spooner to Taft, 5 July 1905, *ibid.*; La Follette to Reinsch, 8 May 1911, La Follette Family Papers, Library of Congress (hereafter cited La Follette Papers, L.C.).

18. Hawkins Tapes, 1, 2, 5; Hawkins, "A General Explanatory Note," Reinsch Papers; Reinsch, *Intellectual and Political Currents in the Far East* (Boston, 1911), vii; Hawkins to author, 8 January 1972.

19. Reinsch, "Political Science," *The New International Encyclopedia* (New York, 1903), XIV, 315–320; Hawkins's Lecture Notes on Reinsch's Course on the History of Political Thought, Reinsch Papers; Reinsch, MS, "Foundation Principles of Government," *ibid.*; Hawkins to Reinsch, 5 March 1910, *ibid.*; Turner to Reinsch, 3 February 1911, *ibid.*; Reinsch, "Some Notes on the Study of South American History," *Essays in American History Dedicated to Frederick Jackson Turner,* ed. Guy S. Ford (New York, 1910), 269; Hawkins to author, 21 January 1965; Bernard Crick, *The American Science of Politics: Its Origins and Conditions* (Berkeley & Los Angeles, 1959); Albert Somit and Joseph Tanenhaus, *The Development of Political Science,* especially, 21–85.

20. Reinsch, *World Politics,* 80; Richard Lloyd Jones to Reinsch, 24 December 1903, 1 December 1904, *ibid.*; La Follette to Reinsch, 28 April 1909. Robert M. La Follette Papers, The State Historical Society of Wisconsin, (hereafter cited La Follette Papers, Wisconsin).

21. Reinsch, MS, "Foundation Principles of Government," Reinsch Papers; interview with Reinsch, *Wisconsin State Journal,* 16 November 1910, *ibid.*; Reinsch, *American Legislatures and Legislative Methods* (New York, 1907), *passim*; Reinsch, *Civil Government* (Boston, 1909), especially, iv, 11, 157; Reinsch, "Political Science," 316.

22. Clipping, Reinsch address before the Milwaukee Chapter of the American Institute of Bank Clerks, *Milwaukee Sentinel,* 10 October 1902, Reinsch Papers; *Milwaukee Journal,* 25 September 1913, 26 September 1920; Reinsch, *American Legislatures,* 233; author's interview with Hawkins, 10 August 1971.

23. Hawkins notes on Reinsch lectures, Reinsch Papers; Reinsch, MS. "Foundation Principles of Government," *ibid.*; MS, n.d., no title, Box 14, *ibid.*; Reinsch, *American Legislatures, passim*; Reinsch, *World Politics,* 340–44. William A. Williams has pointed out that an American syndicalism based on "organizing, balancing and co-ordinating different functional groups" was a significant element in progressive thought. William A. Williams, *The Contours of American History* (Cleveland, 1961), 356–60.

24. Reinsch, MS, "Foundation Principles of Government," Reinsch Papers; Reinsch, "The Speaker's Great Powers," *Milwaukee Sentinel,* 25 April 1897, *ibid.*; Reinsch, "The Education and Selection of Statesmen," *ibid.*; Reinsch, *World Politics,* 340–41; Reinsch, *American Legislatures,* iv, 34–48, 67–70, 79–86, 105–07; Reinsch, "Political Science" (author's emphasis).

25. Reinsch, MS, "Foundation Principles of Government," Reinsch Papers; Samuel Haber, *Efficiency and Uplift: Scientific Management in the Progressive Era 1890–1920* (Chicago, 1964); Robert H. Wiebe, *The Search for Order 1897–1920* (New York, 1967).

26. Author's interview with Hornbeck, 20 January 1965; Richard T. Ely, *Ground Under My Feet: An Autobiography* (New York, 1938), 114, 198; Frederic C. Howe, *Wisconsin: An Experiment in Democracy* (New York, 1912); Charles McCarthy, *The Wisconsin Idea* (New York, 1912), especially 16–17, 21–31, 137–40, 252–53; Merle Curti and Vernon Carstensen, "The University of Wisconsin: To 1925," *The University of Wisconsin: One Hundred & Twenty-Five Years,* ed. Allan Bogue and Robert Taylor (Madison, 1975),

29–31: Robert S. Maxwell, *La Follette and the Rise of the Progressives in Wisconsin* (Madison, 1956), 10–11, 59, 132.

27. Reinsch, *American Legislatures*, 295–98; Hawkins Tapes, 11; McCarthy to Crane, 2 June 1909, McCarthy Papers.

28. Hawkins Tapes, 5, 15; Hawkins to author, 5 December 1964, 13 December 1965; Robert M. La Follette, *La Follette's Autobiography: A Personal Narrative of Political Experiences* (Madison, 1921), 30–32; *Milwaukee Journal*, 17 October 1920.

29. Reinsch, *World Politics*; Reinsch, *Colonial Government: An Introduction to the Study of Colonial Institutions* (New York, 1902), 2; Reinsch, *Colonial Administration* (New York, 1905), 10–11; Reinsch, *Public International Unions* (Boston, 1911); Alfred T. Flint lecture notes for Reinsch's Course on Contemporary International Politics, 1910–1911, Alfred T. Flint Papers, The State Historical Society of Wisconsin; Robert D. Schulzinger, *The Making of the Diplomatic Mind: The Training, Outlook and Style of United States Foreign Service Officers 1908–1931* (Middletown, Conn., 1975), 22–24, 34–35.

30. The above discussion is based on the following writings and speeches of Reinsch: *World Politics; Colonial Government; Colonial Administration;* "Latest Developments of German Imperial Politics," n.d., Reinsch Papers; clipping, *Milwaukee Free Press,* 24 October 1906, *ibid.*; "The Political Spirit of the Last Half Century," *The Conservative Review,* IV (December 1900), 340–51; "The New Conquests of the World," *World's Work,* 1 (February 1901), 425–31; "The New South America, IV: Developing Railways in a Unique Continent," *World To-Day,* XVII (September 1909), 951–61.

31. Reinsch, *World Politics,* 35–36, 314–16; Reinsch, *Colonial Administration,* 204–05; Reinsch, "A New Era in Mexico," *Forum,* XXXII (January 1902), 528–38; Reinsch, "The New South America, II: Argentina," *World To-Day,* XVI (June 1909), 591–601; Reinsch, "The New South America, IV: Developing Railways in a Unique Continent"; lecture, "Conditions in South America," 29 November [1907], Reinsch Papers; clipping, 13 March 1909, *ibid.*

32. See the following writings by Reinsch: *World Politics,* especially 40–43; *Colonial Government,* 84–86; *Colonial Administration,* 5–11; "The New Conquests of the World"; "Cultural Factors in the Chinese Crisis," *Annals of the American Academy of Political and Social Science,* XVII (November 1900), 444; "Governing the Orient on Western Principles," *Forum* XXXI (June 1901), 398.

33. Reinsch, *World Politics,* 26–37, 70, 253, 257, 284–87, 311–12, 323–26, 361–62; Reinsch, *Colonial Government,* 70; Reinsch, "The Philippines in Its International Aspects," clipping, *Milwaukee Sentinel,* 17 December 1899, Reinsch Papers; Reinsch, "American Love of Peace and European Skepticism," *International Conciliation,* No. 68 (July 1913), 1–14.

34. See the following writings by Reinsch: *World Politics,* 88–89; *Colonial Government,* 224–35; *Colonial Administration,* especially, 15–26, 59; "Colonial Autonomy, with Special Reference to the Government of the Philippines," *Proceedings of the American Political Science Association,* Chicago, Illinois, 28–30 December 1904; "Governing the Orient on Western Principles," 387–400; *Intellectual and Political Currents,* 73–74, 114–15.

35. Reinsch, *Colonial Government,* 88–89, 226–33, 300, 308; Reinsch, *Colonial Administration,* especially, 82, 92–93, 177–78, 233; Reinsch, "Colonial Autonomy"; Reinsch, "Governing the Orient on Western Principles"; Reinsch, "Can the United States Americanize Her Colonies?" *World To-Day,* XV (September 1908), 950–54; clipping, *Chicago Post,* 29 December 1904, Reinsch Papers. (Reinsch's emphasis).

36. Reinsch, "Colonial Autonomy"; clipping, *Chicago Post,* 29 December 1904, vol. 2, Reinsch Papers; editorial, *New York Times,* 31 December 1904.

37. Reinsch, *World Politics,* 61, 87–89, 98, 185–87, 231; Reinsch, *Intellectual and*

Political Currents, passim; Reinsch, "China Against the World: The National Uprising Against Foreigners," *Forum,* XXX (October 1900), 67–75; Reinsch, "Cultural Factors in the Chinese Crisis"; Reinsch, "Governing the Orient on Western Principles"; Reinsch, "Japan and Asiatic Leadership," *North American Review,* CLII (January 1905), 48–57; Reinsch, "The Ideal of Oriental Unity," *Atlantic Monthly,* CII (July 1908), 23–33; Reinsch, "Energism in the Orient," *International Journal of Ethics,* XXI (July 1911), 407–22.

38. Reinsch, *World Politics,* 70; Reinsch, "Real Conditions in the Congo Free State," *North American Review,* CLXXVIII (February 1904), 216–21; Hawkins Tapes, 5, 6; Reinsch obituary, *Milwaukee Wisconsin News,* 27 January 1923.

39. Reinsch, *Colonial Administration,* 311–12; Reinsch, "Colonial Autonomy"; Reinsch, "The Ideal of Oriental Unity"; Reinsch, "Justice of War in Transvaal," clipping, *Milwaukee Sentinel,* 15 October 1899, Reinsch Papers; E. S. Kadoorie and N. E. B. Ezra to Reinsch, 20 December 1918, *ibid.*; Reinsch to Kadoorie and Ezra, 24 December 1918, *ibid.*

40. Reinsch, *World Politics,* 5–6, 24–26, 69–70; Reinsch, *Colonial Administration,* 11–12; Reinsch, *Public International Unions,* 1–2, 8; Reinsch, "Precedent and Codification in International Law," *Judicial Settlement of International Disputes,* no. 12 (May 1913), 23–24; "Interdependence vs. Independence of States," address by Reinsch at the Second National Peace Congress, 3 May 1909, Reinsch Papers.

41. Reinsch, *Public International Unions, passim*; "International Administrative Law and National Sovereignty," *American Journal of International Law,* III (January 1909), 1–45; Reinsch, "Precedent and Codification in International Law," 1–27; Reinsch, "The Codification of International Law," address before the American Society of International Law, n.d., Reinsch Papers; Reinsch, "American Love of Peace and European Skepticism."

42. Reinsch, *Public International Unions,* 145; Reinsch, "International Administrative Law and National Sovereignty," 15; Reinsch, *Secret Diplomacy: How Far Can It Be Eliminated?* (New York, 1922), especially, 218.

43. Reinsch, *Civil Government,* 122, 124; Reinsch, *Public International Unions,* 81; Reinsch, "The Declaration of London," *North American Review,* CXC (October 1909), 479–87; Reinsch, "The Carnegie Peace Fund," *North American Review,* CXCIII (February 1911), 180–92; Reinsch lecture, "The Army of the United States," Reinsch Papers; Reinsch, "A Possible Approach to the Limitation of Armaments," n.d., *ibid.*

44. Invitations to Reinsch to attend Lake Mohonk Conferences, Reinsch Papers; "The Seventeenth Annual Lake Mohonk Conference on International Arbitration," *American Journal of International Law,* VI (October 1911), 748–52; Warren F. Kuehl, *Seeking World Order: The United States and World Organization to 1920* (Nashville, 1969), 40–41, 78.

45. Reinsch, "The Carnegie Peace Fund"; Reinsch, "The Carnegie Endowment Conference on War at Berne," *Independent,* LXXI (14 September 1911), 589–90; Root to Reinsch, 20 May 1911, 9 June 1914, Reinsch Papers; Clark to Reinsch, 2 February 1912, 3 May 1912, *ibid.*; Reinsch to Clark, 30 November 1911, *ibid.*; Reinsch memo on work to be done by the Carnegie Endowment, *ibid.*; Clark to James B. Scott, 21 November 1911, Division of Economics and History, 1–A, CEIP Papers; Reinsch to Clark, 23 October 1911, *ibid.*; Reinsch to Scott, 13 December 1911, *ibid.*

46. Kuehl, *Seeking World Order;* Inis Claude, Jr., *Swords into Plowshares: The Problems and Progress of International Organization,* 2nd ed. (New York, 1959), 380–81; Reinsch to Wilson, 4 January 1915, Woodrow Wilson Papers, Library of Congress (hereafter cited Wilson Papers); Reinsch, *Public International Unions,* 3–4, 9–10; Reinsch, "International Administrative Law and National Sovereignty."

47. Reinsch, "The Far East as a Factor in International Development," in *The History and Nature of International Relations,* ed. Edmund A. Walsh (New York, 1922), 220. Reinsch, "China Against the World"; Reinsch, "Cultural Factors in the Chinese Crisis."

48. William Appleman Williams, *The Tragedy of American Diplomacy,* rev. ed. (New York, 1962).

49. Gerald Markowitz, "Progressive Imperialism: Consensus and Conflict in the Progressive Movement on Foreign Policy, 1898–1917," (Ph.D. dissertation, University of Wisconsin, 1971). Unlike a number of historians who have counted congressional votes on specific foreign policy issues, Markowitz studies the ideas of a broad group of progressives and finds that they formulated foreign policy around the three basic issues of peace, commercial expansion, and the development of backward areas. The relation between progressivism and imperialism has been explored by many historians since the appearance of William Leuchtenburg's seminal essay in 1952. For example, see the following for different positions and analyses of the debate: Barton J. Bernstein and Franklin A. Leib, "Progressive Republican Senators and American Imperialism, 1898–1916: A Reappraisal," *Mid-America*, L (July 1968), 163–205; Jerry Israel, *Progressivism and the Open Door: America and China, 1905–1921* (Pittsburgh, 1971); Padraic Colum Kennedy, "La Follette's Foreign Policy: From Imperialism to Anti-Imperialism," *Wisconsin Magazine of History,* XL (Summer 1963), 287–93; William L. Leuchtenburg, "Progressivism and Imperialism: The Progessive Movement and American Foreign Policy, 1898–1916," *Mississippi Valley Historical Review,* XXXIX (December 1952), 483–504; Joseph M. Siracusa, "Progressivism, Imperialism, and the Leuchtenburg Thesis, 1952–1974: An Historiographical Appraisal," *Australian Journal of Politics and History,* XX (December 1974), 312–25; Walter I. Trattner, "Progressivism and World War I: A Reappraisal," *Mid-America,* XLIV (July 1962), 131–45; Williams, *The Tragedy of American Diplomacy.*

50. Leuchtenburg, "Progressivism and Imperialism."

51. Reinsch, "The New Conquests of the World," 431.

52. Reinsch, "What Has Wisconsin Meant to Me."

Chapter III

SEARCHING
FOR A DIPLOMATIC
POSITION

Had he been so inclined, Paul Reinsch could have looked back with satisfaction in 1913 on a crowded and successful career. At the age of forty-four, he had acquired an international reputation as a teacher, scholar, and expert on colonial and Far Eastern questions. Several of his books had been translated into German, Spanish, Japanese, and Chinese and were read at home and abroad by statesmen as well as by scholars and the educated middle class. Reinsch was respected by his colleagues at the University of Wisconsin, by political scientists throughout the nation, and by political and business leaders who turned to him for honest, sound, and nonpartisan advice. His abilities and achievements had been widely recognized and he had been hailed as "a leader in the movement to effect a direct coupling between higher education and the world's work."[1] Moreover, Reinsch's professional work and public service had enabled him to mix with America's intellectual, political, and business elite. He moved along the rim of the establishment, but never really entered into it.

Reinsch also had a happy marriage and family life, though severe and unexpected illnesses befell him and Alma. Following her very difficult pregnancy with Claire, Alma remained weak and in pain for several months. Finally, a Chicago physician discovered abdominal ulcers and saved her life with a timely operation. It was a terrible ordeal for Paul and the entire family.[2]

Alma, in turn, was endlessly worried by the energy and long hours Paul expended on his work, which not only made him susceptible to colds but also brought him to the brink of nervous breakdowns. Medical attention, rest, and a temporary let-up in his activity enabled him to recover fairly rapidly, but it became a recurrent pattern which intensified in his later years.

However, a near tragedy struck the Reinsch family on May 10, 1910. Paul, Alma, and his parents were about to leave for a weekend ride and picnic when a runaway horse crashed into his buggy. Paul was thrown to the ground and suffered a severe concussion. Although he was incapacitated for several weeks, Reinsch insisted on leaving in June with the American delegation to the Fourth Pan American Conference. But he was never again his old self. Thereafter Reinsch suffered from occasional headaches and became increasingly irritable, so that he could never stand the crying of his younger children.[3]

Reinsch had a reasonably good life. And yet he drove himself mercilessly and disregarded the pleas of Alma and his friends to slow down. He was always restless and tried to do more than he could possibly accomplish. Working to the last minute, Reinsch always ran to catch a train and he often forgot to pack something. But he could not stop. He was a bundle of nerves and was frequently unable to sleep. Fortunately, he found release by working out improvisations on the piano or by taking refreshing walks along Lake Mendota.[4]

What impelled this behavior? Reinsch accepted the theory, originally advanced by Dr. William Osler, a noted professor of medicine at Johns Hopkins University, that creative men throughout history did their work before forty years of age. Besides, he intuitively felt that he would die young; and the carriage accident further convinced him that death was only a few years away. He therefore believed that he was working against time and that his most important projects had to be completed as soon as possible. Undoubtedly, Reinsch was pushed, both consciously and unconsciously, by his mother's image of him as a brilliant, successful son. For this reason he was ambitious to excel in his profession, and being a perfectionist further increased his burden. Moreover, Reinsch very likely saw himself as a classical or renaissance man, broadly talented and active in all phases of human affairs.[5]

In addition, Reinsch constantly struggled to give his family financial security and himself the financial freedom to carry on his work. The maintenance of their large house, their high medical bills, Alma's precarious health, and the premonitions of his own early death caused Reinsch continuous worry about providing for his wife and family. The Reinsches were fond of traveling, enjoyed entertaining and serving fine wines. Although Alma was careful with the household budget, they found it difficult to meet the rising cost of living, especially since they were tempted to keep up with the Turners and the Elys.

Since Reinsch's university salary just enabled them to get by, Paul looked to his publications and outside lectures to support the extras and to ensure a future income for Alma. With the advice and help of Davies and business friends, Reinsch sought out profitable investments. He joined Davies in several ventures, invested in a land company organized by Ely, and occasionally dabbled in the stock market. He also bought and sold art works—paintings in Europe, silver objects in South America, embroideries, rugs, and porcelain in China—partly for profit and partly to finance his own collections. Reinsch tended to be an optimistic investor and was sometimes taken in by a deal or prospectus. He made money in Madison real estate, but lost substantial amounts in Washington timber land.[6]

But beyond those considerations, Reinsch desired to influence policy making, to be more than just a voice "crying in the wilderness," as a reviewer of *World Politics* noted. Like so many of his university colleagues during the Progressive Era—John Bassett Moore, Nicholas Murray Butler, Jeremiah Jenks, Leo S. Rowe, Jacob Gould Schurman—he wanted to participate in the exciting developments of his day. He was proud and self-confident; he could contribute as much as they did. At the same time, he would give glory to his own school and state.

Reinsch had a fear—almost an obsession—of being restricted to the theoretical. He believed in the power of ideas and he wanted to test them in the real world. Having helped to form the political science department at Wisconsin, the American Political Science Association, the American Society of International Law, and the Milwaukee Chapter of the American Institute of Banking, Reinsch repeatedly demonstrated that he was an organizer, an experimenter, a doer, and a fighter. Paul Reinsch saw himself as a master hand and chose diplomacy as his field of operation.[7]

To realize all of these objectives, Reinsch actively sought a regular diplomatic appointment. He preferred a post in the Far East, where he could continue his pioneering studies on the spot, or in Latin America, in which he had serious interest. Beginning around the turn of the century, Reinsch shrewdly and persistently presented his case to those with influence. He established his first base of support in the University of Wisconsin and the Wisconsin delegation to Congress, especially Senators Spooner and La Follette. He also cultivated leading men in Washington, such as Roosevelt, Root, Taft, and Knox, and befriended such influential figures as Charles Crane. Finally, Reinsch used his writings and speaking engagements to keep his name before the public.[8]

*   *   *

Reinsch made his first serious bid in December 1902, when Alfred E. Buck, the United States minister to Japan, died suddenly in Tokyo. "Has successor of Japanese Minister been selected?" he immediately wired. "Would apply for two-year appointment supported by the University and State." Acting President Edward A. Birge and the university regents lost no time in dispatching their endorsements, while Turner wrote a personal letter to Roosevelt. In Washington, Spooner badgered the State Department, and when it seemed that John Barrett was the president's first choice, suggested that Reinsch go to Tokyo as first secretary of the legation. Spooner was informed that the administration had no plans to change the staff in Tokyo and had no other openings in the Far East. But since the president and State Department were impressed by his credentials, Reinsch's name would be kept on file for future vacancies. "Reinsch of Wisconsin is a first-class man—a writer of some note—standing very high in the University of Wisconsin," Roosevelt noted to Secretary of State John Hay. "He wants to go to the east. I should like to give him a secretaryship or consulship in China or Japan if the chance opens."[9]

Determined not to lose the momentum, Spooner secured an interview for Reinsch with Secretary of State Hay. In Washington, Reinsch indicated that he would also accept a temporary position in South America. Roosevelt thereupon offered Reinsch the secretaryship of the legation in Guatemala and the consulship at Callao, Peru. But Reinsch declined both positions because they would not serve his purpose of combining research with diplomatic experience of some importance. Reinsch then asked Spooner if he should apply for the attorney-generalship of Puerto Rico. For, he explained, "some appointment which would bring me into direct contact with either our great diplomatic affairs, or our colonial administration, would *just now* be very helpful to me. Later it would be less so. Also, having had the University make an effort for me in this matter, I am naturally anxious for it not to fail." Spooner appreciated Reinsch's feelings, but advised Reinsch not to apply for the position and counseled patience.[10]

In May 1903, Reinsch decided to withdraw from active pursuit of a government appointment. He was clearly embarrassed by Senator Joseph Quarles's insinuation that he had been seeking just any post. Nor did he want to undercut Richard Ely, who was then seeking an official position. "Now I consider it of the greatest importance that the University of Wisconsin should be given some representation in the National Capital, as all prominent universities have," he wrote asking Spooner to assist his colleague. He also felt that he had been imposing on Spooner, who owed him nothing.[11]

But the desire for involvement in current affairs remained powerful. In December 1905, Reinsch formally applied to the State Department for a diplomatic position in the Orient or Latin America. Shortly afterward, when a bitter patronage struggle erupted between Spooner and La Follette, Reinsch's name was proposed as a compromise for the post of consul-general at Hong Kong. Spooner had nominated Dr. Amos P. Wilder, editor and publisher of the *Wisconsin State Journal*, whose cause he had championed for over a year. But the newly elected progressive senator was determined to defeat Wilder, whom he regarded as one of the more effective leaders of the Wisconsin "Stalwarts." Reinsch's friends, led by Francis McGovern, Henry Cochems, Theodore Kronshage, and Joe Davies, used the opportunity to suggest that the appointment go to the University of Wisconsin. In the end, however, Wilder went to the Far East and served with distinction at Hong Kong and later at Shanghai.[12]

Reinsch, meanwhile, had his eyes fixed on the approaching Third Pan American Conference (1906). Like other American leaders who had turned their eyes southward after 1900, Reinsch had devoted considerable attention to the redefinition and modernization of the Monroe Doctrine and to the expansion of United States markets and influence in Latin America. Just as he depended on the Open Door to secure America's markets in Asia, Reinsch hailed the Monroe Doctrine as "sort of an unconscious stroke of genius in statesmanship in that it has preserved South America for us now that we are ready to enter into our possession." Arguing that the United States would have to "supply the ultimate responsibility for the states of the region that come within the purview of the Doctrine," Reinsch endorsed the principle of the Roosevelt Corollary as part of the "positive side of the Monroe Doctrine." But while wielding the Big Stick was necessary in some instances, Reinsch believed that the Pan American movement was a far better instrument for extending American influence in Latin America, capturing its trade, and ensuring peace and stability in the area.[13]

Realizing that the United States delegation would be selected on a geographical and professional basis, Reinsch was plainly worried when he learned that Edwin James, president of the University of Illinois, would attend the conference. "Will this stand in the way of my appointment?" he nervously asked Spooner. "I am ready to send you a bushel of endorsements as soon as you want to use them in my behalf." And, indeed, Reinsch and Governor A. J. Montague of Virginia were late substitutes for President James and James S. Harlan who were forced to withdraw for personal reasons. Nevertheless, Reinsch was delighted

with Root's invitation and served diligently at the Rio de Janeiro Conference. Appropriately assigned to the Commerce Committee, Reinsch was
largely responsible for the resolutions adopted at the Rio Conference to
make a scientific study of the mining, forestry, and land laws of the
American states and the means to stimulate improvements in rail,
steamer, telegraphic, and postal communications.

Afterwards, Reinsch served on several State Department committees designated to follow up the work of the Rio Conference and helped
to draft memoranda for the use of the American delegation to the Fourth
Pan American Conference. Concurrently, Reinsch lobbied hard for a
place on the American delegation to the First Pan American Scientific
Congress, which would convene in Santiago, Chile, in 1909. Like so
many of his progressive contemporaries, Reinsch believed that the
United States could also exert influence by exporting its ideas and technical skills as well as its surplus goods and capital. Reinsch won his
appointment and was subsequently named vice chairman of the United
States delegation.[14]

Reinsch found the two Pan American conferences enjoyable and
rewarding; he accumulated material for several articles and lectures and
made important contacts with leading men in the United States and
Latin America. But he still longed for a regular diplomatic appointment,
especially in the Orient. William Howard Taft's election to the presidency led to new initiatives by Reinsch and La Follette, upon whom he
now depended. The sudden firing of Charles Crane as minister to China
again enabled La Follette to propose Reinsch for the Peking post.
Reinsch was therefore crushed with disappointment when William J.
Calhoun, a Chicago lawyer and former United States Steel executive with
minor diplomatic experience in Latin America, was chosen by Taft.[15]

Reinsch's appointment to the Fourth Pan American Conference
(Buenos Aires, 1910) a few months later gave him only partial consola-
tion. But Reinsch, who had not fully recovered from the severe injuries
he sustained in the carriage accident of May 1910, was not at his best.
Indeed, Henry White, the chairman of the United States delegation,
questioned Reinsch's performance in a note to Secretary of State Knox:
"Of all the delegates the only one who did not 'pan out' well was Reinsch.
. . . The rest of us thought him rather a light weight, which I mention
chiefly because I rather suspect that he aspires to succeed John Barrett
[Director-General of the Pan American Union], and I really don't think
him at all adapted to that post."[16]

Reinsch returned from the South American tour with little hope of
further recognition from the Taft administration. Besides, he had already

agreed to represent American academia as Roosevelt Exchange Professor in Germany during the 1911–1912 school year. During the fall semester at the University of Berlin, Reinsch taught a course on American government and politics, conducted a seminar on American foreign affairs, and gave a weekly lecture on contemporary American developments. In the spring of 1912, Reinsch lectured at the University of Leipzig, the University of Kiel, and the Merchants' Union in Bremen. The demands for public talks and articles put a heavy strain on Reinsch, who was also burdened by Alma's illness, his father's death, and his commitments to the Carnegie Endowment for International Peace. Nevertheless, Reinsch enjoyed the renewed contact with European scholarship, the honors bestowed upon him, and the opportunity to mix with European society.[17]

*   *   *

In the fall of 1912, Reinsch returned to Madison to resume his teaching and administrative duties and to develop a major project on international law. Probably unbeknown to Reinsch, the trustees of the Carnegie Endowment, in February 1913, briefly considered nominating him constitutional adviser to the Chinese government. But Charles Eliot, president emeritus of Harvard, had heard that Reinsch was too quick in his judgments and, based on reports that Reinsch had overspent an allocation to buy books for the University of Wisconsin in South America, too loose with other people's money. "Any obscurity about financial obligations would be highly objectionable in China on the part of any person selected by the Carnegie Endowment," he argued. "Peking is a place of great temptation for commission seekers and curio buyers." The Eastern establishment, in fact, had a certain animus against Wisconsin, which was directed mainly against Ely, but affected Reinsch as well. The trustees subsequently selected Frank J. Goodnow, a Columbia University expert on public administration and constitutional law, who would later commit his own indiscretions in China.[18]

Meanwhile, the Democratic victory in 1912 encouraged Reinsch to try again for a diplomatic appointment. Reinsch had known Wilson personally and professionally. Moreover, Reinsch could depend on Joe Davies, who had managed Wilson's campaign in Wisconsin and who was now dispensing the patronage for his state. But realizing that this was probably his last opportunity, Reinsch left nothing to chance. He dashed off to see Wilson in New Jersey, ostensibly to argue Davies's case for an ambassadorship but also to make known his own availability.

Reinsch further cultivated Charles Crane who had been impressed by Reinsch's work and was then helping him to assemble Wisconsin's art collection. This "inscrutable" Chicago millionaire, world traveler, and philanthropic "angel" to numerous causes had taken a keen interest in the University of Wisconsin and Wisconsin politics. A well-known and active progressive, Crane had originally supported La Follette's bid for the presidency. But in the beginning of 1912, he joined the Wilson movement and became its biggest financial contributor. Now he was informally advising Wilson on State Department appointments. "There are a great many things in our foreign situation which I should like to talk over with you," Reinsch wrote to Crane in February 1913. "I believe that there is great work waiting for Mr. Wilson's administration, in reestablishing the prestige of our diplomacy in Asia, and in reassuring our Latin American neighbors." Responding to his overtures, Crane recommended Reinsch as assistant secretary for Latin American Affairs.[19]

But there was no quick success, and the passing weeks seemed to dramatize the futility of his quest. Complicating things for Reinsch was the interest of his Wisconsin colleagues in entering the diplomatic service. While urging Reinsch for the Latin American area, Crane thought that Edward A. Ross should go to Peking.[20] More embarrassing to Reinsch, however, was the support Richard T. Ely was receiving for the appointment to the Hague from Van Hise and others. T. K. Urdahl, acting chairman of the Department of Economics, and a leader of the Ely campaign, reported that Bryan was favorably disposed, but that everything depended on Davies. "He does not seem inclined to do anything at the present, since he claims that he is pledged to someone else," he told Ely, who was then doing research in Europe. "Who this someone else is you will probably be able to guess."[21]

Ten years earlier, Reinsch was willing to throw the undivided support of the university and the state's congressional delegation behind Ely. But in 1913, older and more anxious to realize his life goals, Reinsch would only aid his mentor if it did not interfere with his own objectives. "I am told that I did not receive sufficient support in a certain Wisconsin quarter which I take to be a friendly one," he wrote Reinsch after Henry Van Dyke, Princeton's English scholar, was named minister to Holland. "I suppose there were strong claims which pulled in another direction."[22]

Meanwhile, the United States was without a minister to China as Wilson was determined to selct the right man for one of his most important diplomatic appointments. Wilson believed in the frontier thesis and the Open Door and hoped to export to China America's goods, democratic institutions, and Christian values. He had just broken with the policies of the Taft administration by withdrawing from the Six Power Financial Consortium and by unilaterally recognizing the Chinese Republic. For his minister to China, therefore, Wilson sought a man of "profound Christian character" and an Open Door expansionist, who could implement his independent Far Eastern policy.

Before he rewarded Bryan with the secretaryship of state, Wilson thought of sending him to Peking. Wilson first formally offered the Chinese mission to Charles Eliot whose Unitarianism distressed Bryan. When family opposition forced Eliot to decline, Wilson decided that he must have John R. Mott, the dynamic foreign secretary of the International Committee of the Y.M.C.A. But Mott's firm decision to devote himself to the work of international Christian service now forced Wilson to consider the host of names presented to him. Henry Morgenthau, later appointed ambassador to Turkey, did not qualify as an evangelical Christian. To his credit, E. A. Ross had a year of study and travel in China, a book entitled *The Changing Chinese*, and the support of Charles Crane. But with Wisconsin brought to mind by Ross and Crane, Reinsch seemed more and more the natural choice. For years Reinsch had trumpeted the future importance of China and had strongly pushed for the expansion of America's foreign markets; he was, moreover, a genuine progressive and exponent of the Wisconsin Idea.[23]

To help him decide the matter, Wilson called in Davies, his new commissioner of corporations, for a discussion of the respective merits of Reinsch and Ross. Davies suggested that Wilson read Reinsch's *Intellectual and Political Currents in the Far East* and reminded him that Reinsch was a recognized authority on colonial government and Far Eastern questions. He was also "safe, careful, and judicious in making judgments of men or conditions, and that by reason of his mental poise, there is absolute safety in his treatment of any delicate situation that might arise." Ross, on the other hand, was imprudent, undiplomatic, and unaffiliated with any church; nor did he possess Reinsch's expertise on international law and the Far East. Knowing full well the mind of the president, Davies added the following tribute:

> In the sympathetic appreciation and aid to the aspirations of young men, Reinsch stands out most prominently in our university life. He is universally beloved. His sympathy and the inspiration he arouses have meant much to many students, not only from our country, but from the Far East as well. Qualities of heart and mind such as these must react similarly when dealing with a people such as the Chinese, struggling as they are with

these new problems of self-government under world-old conditions.[24]

Davies's arguments must have been effective. On June 30, 1913, Wilson asked Reinsch to come to Washington and two weeks later offered him the Peking mission. After checking with La Follette, who replied that "a better man for the Chinese post" could not have been selected, Wilson sent Reinsch's nomination to the Senate on August 5, 1913.[25]

Reinsch's friends were elated. "I want to congratulate you and congratulate the whole administration upon the appointment of Paul Reinsch," McCarthy wrote to Davies. "No better appointment could have been made from every standpoint." Richard Lloyd Jones, who had become the editor of the *Wisconsin State Journal* through Reinsch's intervention, asked Davies to be sure "that he was impressed with the importance of accepting it." Ely sent his best wishes, but could not mask his jealousy. "You have had and are having such opportunities as come to few," he wrote, "and are profiting from them in a manner which is gratifying to all your friends."[26]

Congratulatory messages and advice poured in from leading figures and acquaintances. Robert Lansing, who would sit at the secretary of state's desk in less than two years, commented on "this deserved recognition of your eminent qualifications for a post, which at the present time is one of the most interesting and important, as well as the most difficult in the diplomatic service of the United States." Henry White, who had earlier questioned Reinsch's abilities, pointed to the opportunity for "distinction and valuable work," as well as the enormous problems he would face. "What with Russia on the one hand and Japan on the other, it will take you all of your time to prevent the 'Open Door' from being more or less closed, if indeed it can be said not to be much more than ajar; and when in addition to this one thinks of the guidance and counsel the Chinese will expect of you in their uphill journey toward the establishment of a bona fide Republic your hands will be filled to overflowing."[27]

While his name was before the Senate, Reinsch set off on a walking tour of central Wisconsin in order to get some much needed rest and relaxation. It was a short vacation, and at the end of August he moved his headquarters to Chicago, so that he could be more centrally located as he prepared to leave for China. In Chicago, Charles Crane took him under his wing and introduced him to men "who knew China," a group that included John W. Foster, John R. Mott, and Fletcher A. Brockmann, Mott's representative in China. Crane's China experts were delighted with Reinsch. "I believe he will do good work for you there," Crane reported to Wilson.[28]

After receiving Senate confirmation on August 15, 1913, Reinsch returned to Washington at the beginning of September for final consultations with the State Department and the president. While he was in Washington, Reinsch also met and conferred frequently with John V. A. MacMurray, who had just been designated as the first secretary of the legation in Peking. At this point, MacMurray spoke approvingly of his new "Chief" to his mother:

> He is an unpretentious man with a broad Wisconsin accent and a professional manner; just a trifle unworldly, but evidently a gentleman; a good deal of a theorist, but possessed of a level head and a willingness to face facts; a plodder in his own field of political science, but with a considerable outlook upon other interests and a great deal of information and of intellectual alertness: self-assured (though without conceit) and confident and independent, but ready to hear and consider other judgments; and withal very kindly and attractive and sympathetic, and apparently disposed to be both a good Chief and a good companion. I had been afraid that his views on China would be visionary and idealistic and unreal; but in talking with him I have not found them so.

MacMurray was especially pleased that Reinsch understood the need for a first hand "acquaintance with China" and planned to do a lot of traveling in the country. "Altogether," the critical MacMurray concluded, "I think him a very promising chief to serve under."[29]

Afterwards, Reinsch dashed up to New York for crucial talks with Wall Street leaders and other businessmen, who were anxious to meet him. Wall Street was still dismayed and stung by Wilson's withdrawal of support from the Chinese Consortium and, despite the administration's concerted effort to convince the business community of its desire to foster legitimate foreign enterprise, it remained suspicious and skeptical of the New Freedom at home and abroad. Wall Street was unfamiliar territory for Reinsch, but he was partially successful in making contacts and opening a dialogue, especially with Willard Straight. Straight had been United States consul in Mukden, Far Eastern adviser in the State Department, and a major architect of Dollar Diplomacy in China; now he was overseeing J. P. Morgan & Co.'s interests in the Orient.

Straight was favorably impressed with Reinsch and pleased with his declared intention "to do everything possible for American trade." "I am sure you will like him," Straight wrote to James A. Thomas, British-American Tobacco's manager in China, "and that he will prove a most distinguished public servant. My only doubt is as to whether he will find any Government at Peking with which to deal." Straight urged Reinsch to return to New York for further conversations with business leaders. "If you will but say to them what you said to me," Straight opined, "I am sure that they will look towards the future with less apprehension, and that they may be encouraged to feel all is not yet lost." Reinsch's busy schedule prevented his return, but a unique relationship between Reinsch and Straight had already been formed. Although they would disagree, sometimes sharply, on the policies and actions of Washington and New York, Reinsch and Straight began an interesting and candid exchange of views that was to last for several years.[30]

When he returned to his native city in September, Reinsch was feted at luncheons and dinners by the Milwaukee Chapter of the American Institute of Banking, the Wisconsin Alumni, and a host of other groups. At a grand banquet held in his honor at the Hotel Pfister, Reinsch delivered a farewell address in which he sounded the theme that would characterize his diplomatic mission:

> I believe that the great drama of the future is to be enacted in the Orient. There are many points of contact between this nation and the new Chinese Republic. I feel that this period is one of tremendous importance to this nation; it is now that American industry must get a hold on the vast, undeveloped resources of the Orient.

When he was finished, the hall resounded with applause. "This native Milwaukeean's ripe scholarship, his mastery of international law, his broad powers of comprehension, his finely tempered judgment, and his simple, charming personality all tend to fit him ideally for the service in the diplomatic field," the *Milwaukee Journal* noted in its editorial.[31]

*　　*　　*

On October 1, 1913, Reinsch moved his family to San Francisco, where he held numerous meetings with businessmen and the Chinese Chamber of Commerce. A week later, he settled Alma, Claire, and Granny Moser aboard the *Tenyo Maru* (symbolic of Japan's rising predominance in Pacific shipping) for the long voyage to Shanghai.

Paul Reinsch was finally going to China. Plainly, he had not been Wilson's first choice. Nevertheless, he had won the diplomatic assignment which he had long sought and which seemed meant for him. Reinsch had a grand vision of his mission and, as usual, set for himself enormous objectives. But this time he faced a different and much greater challenge—one that would fully test his abilities, wisdom, strength, and perseverance.

NOTES TO
CHAPTER III

1. Clipping, vol. 2, Reinsch Papers.
2. Hawkins, "A General Explanatory Note," Reinsch Papers; Hawkins to author, 8 December 1964, 30 January 1970.
3. Undated Paul–Alma Reinsch letters, Reinsch Papers; clipping, *Milwaukee Free Press*, 11 May 1910, *ibid.*; Hawkins Tapes, 10; *Daily Cardinal*, 11 May 1910; Bernadotte Schmitt's Account of Reinsch's Accident, Hornbeck Papers; author's interview with Hawkins, 10 August 1971.
4. Alma to Paul, n.d. (1904?), Reinsch Papers; Reinsch to Birge, 6 August 1910, Birge Papers, UW; Reinsch to Ely, 23 January and 1 April 1912, Ely Papers; Hawkins Tapes, 2, 6; author's interview with Hawkins, 10 August 1971.
5. Author's interview with Hawkins, 10 August 1971.
6. Alma to Paul, November 1901, and various other Alma–Paul Reinsch letters, Reinsch Papers; Davies to Reinsch, n.d., *ibid.*; Ely to Reinsch, 2 December 1909, 17 February 1912, Ely Papers; Reinsch to Ely, 1 April and 22 August 1912, *ibid.*; Reinsch to Crane, 14 February 1914, Crane Papers; Hawkins Tapes, 8, 10; Hawkins to author, 8 December 1964; author's interviews with Hornbeck, 5 and 20 January 1965.
7. Clipping, review of *World Politics,* in the *Philadelphia Public Ledger,* Reinsch Papers; Hawkins, "A General Explanatory Note," *ibid.*; author's interview with Stanley K. Hornbeck, 20 January 1965.
8. Hawkins to author, 15 November 1969.
9. Reinsch to David J. Hill, 5 December 1902, "Paul S. Reinsch" file, Bureau of Appointments, DSNA; Turner to Roosevelt, 10 December 1902, *ibid.*; University of Wisconsin regents to Spooner, 13 December 1902, *ibid.*; Roosevelt to Hay, 13 December 1902, *ibid.*; Hill to Reinsch, 8 December 1902, Reinsch Papers; Hay to Spooner, 9 December 1902, Spooner Papers; Birge to Spooner, 18 December 1902, *ibid.*
10. Spooner to Reinsch, 16 December 1902, 14 January, 22 January, 25 March, 21 April 1903; Reinsch to Spooner, 3 January, 11 April, 19 April, 19 May 1903; Hay to Spooner, 18 December 1902; Spooner to Van Hise, 20 December 1902, Spooner Papers (Reinsch's emphasis).
11. Reinsch to Spooner, 19 May 1903, *ibid.*
12. Reinsch's application, 6 December 1905, "Paul S. Reinsch" file, Bureau of Appointments, DSNA; Hawkins, "A General Explanatory Note," Reinsch Papers; Hawkins Tapes, 1; Roosevelt to Spooner, 14 March 1905, Spooner Papers; Wilder to Spooner, 23 February 1906, *ibid.*; Richard L. Jones to Joe Davies, 17 July 1913, Record Group (RG) 59, General Records of The Department of State, Decimal File 123.W641/90, National Archives. (Hereafter, documents from this file will be cited by file number, DSNA.)
13. Clipping, *Milwaukee Free Press*, 24 October 1906, Reinsch Papers; clipping, Reinsch talk before the Milwaukee Bankers' Club, 4 November 1906, *ibid.*; clipping, "Rio Conference Work Praised by Speakers," *ibid.*; Reinsch, "The Positive Side of the Monroe Doctrine," *The Independent,* LV (1 January 1903), 9–11.
14. Reinsch to Spooner, 28 February 1906, Spooner Papers; Spooner to Van Hise, 11 June 1906, *ibid.*; clipping, *New York Tribune*, 9 June 1906, Reinsch Papers; Root to Reinsch, 10 May 1906, 19 February 1908, *ibid.*; "Resolutions and Introductory Note on the Development of Natural Resources in the American Republics submitted by Paul S. Reinsch, a delegate of the United States of America," *ibid.*; "Preliminary Report Submit-

ted to the American Committee on the Development of Natural Resources," *ibid*.; Van Hise to Root, 27 May 1908, Papers of the Presidents (Van Hise), UW Archives; Reinsch to Root, 14 May 1906, "Paul S. Reinsch" file, Bureau of Appointments, DSNA; "Special Report of Paul S. Reinsch, on the Third Pan American Conference," RG 43, Records of International Conferences, Commissions, Expositions, and Committees (The Third International Conference of American States), Box 24, NA; James Brown Scott, ed., *The International Conferences of American States, 1889–1928* (New York, 1931), 113–50.

15. Hawkins to author, 2 October 1971; La Follette to Reinsch, 7 May 1908, 28 April and 3 May 1909, Reinsch Papers; Hawkins to Reinsch, 5 March 1910, *ibid*.; Hawkins annotation, 4 October 1963, *ibid*.; La Follette to Knox, 8 December 1909, "Paul S. Reinsch" file, Bureau of Appointments, DSNA.

16. Knox to Reinsch, 14 March 1910, Reinsch Papers; clipping of article by William Curtis, 4 March 1910, *ibid*.; White to Knox, 24 October 1910, referred to in an undated handwritten note, "Paul S. Reinsch" file, Bureau of Appointments, DSNA; Hawkins to author, 2 October 1971.

17. Reinsch to Van Hise, 10 April 1910, 13 December 1911, Papers of the Presidents (Van Hise), UW Archives; Reinsch to Butler, 30 September 1912, John W. Burgess Papers, Special Collections, Columbia University; Reinsch to Ely, 18 November 1911, 23 January and 1 April 1912, Ely Papers; Hawkins to author, 30 January 1970; Lochner, "The Roosevelt Exchange Professor."

18. Eliot to Butler, 30 January and 11 February 1913; Butler to Eliot, 12 February 1913, Division of Intercourse and Education, CEIP Papers. For a discussion of Goodnow's appointment and work in China, see Noel H. Pugach, "Embarrassed Monarchist: Frank J. Goodnow and Constitutional Development in China, 1913–1915," *Pacific Historical Review*, XLIV (November 1973), 499–517.

19. T. K. Urdahl to Ely, 18 April 1913, Ely Papers; Reinsch to Crane, 14 February 1913, Crane Papers; Crane to Wilson, 21 and 24 March 1913, Wilson Papers; Wilson to Crane, 21 March 1913, Ray Stannard Baker Papers, Library of Congress (hereafter cited Baker Papers); *New York Times*, 20 July 1913; Israel, *Progressivism and the Open Door*, 109–10; Arthur Link, *Wilson: The Road to the White House* (Princeton, 1947), 403–4, 481–82, 485; Arthur Link, *Wilson: The New Freedom* (Princeton, 1956), 106.

20. Crane to Wilson, 21 March 1913, Wilson Papers; Crane to Wilson, 8 April 1913, Crane Papers.

21. Van Hise to La Follette, 29 March 1913, La Follette Papers, LC; Van Hise to Davies, 29 March 1913, *ibid*.; La Follette's secretary to Urdahl, 30 March 1913, *ibid.;* Urdahl to Ely, 18 April 1913, Ely Papers.

22. Ely to Reinsch, 27 June 1913, Ely Papers.

23. Wilson to Bryan, 16 January and 21 February 1913, William J. Bryan Papers, Library of Congress (hereafter cited Bryan Papers); Wilson to Mott, 21 March 1913, Wilson Papers; Wilson to Cleveland Dodge, 10 March 1913, *ibid*.; Wilson to Norman Hapgood, 27 February 1913, *ibid*.; Edward House Diary, vol. 1, entries for 17 and 24 January and 13 February 1913, Edward M. House Papers, Yale University Library (hereafter cited House Papers); Israel, *Progressivism and the Open Door*, 112–19; Tien-yi Li, *Woodrow Wilson's China Policy, 1913–1917* (New York, 1952), 16–18; Williams, *The Tragedy of American Diplomacy*, 61–83.

24. Davies to Wilson, 10 June 1913, "Paul S. Reinsch" file, Bureau of Appointments, DSNA.

25. Wilson to Reinsch, 30 June 1913, Reinsch Papers; *New York Times*, 17 July 1913; *Wisconsin State Journal*, 16 July 1913; La Follette to Wilson, 2 August 1913, La Follette Papers, LC.

26. McCarthy to Davies, 30 July 1913, McCarthy Papers; Jones to Davies, 17 July 1913, 123.W641/90, DSNA; Ely to Reinsch, 18 August 1913, Ely Papers.

27. Lansing to Reinsch, 6 August 1913; Henry White to Reinsch, 28 July 1913, Reinsch Papers.

28. *Wisconsin State Journal,* 6 August 1913; clipping, *Chicago Inter-Ocean,* 22 August 1913, Reinsch Papers; Crane to Wilson, 1 October 1913, Crane Papers.

29. Bryan to Reinsch, 9 September 1913, Reinsch Papers; MacMurray to mother, 2 and 10 September 1913, MacMurray Papers.

30. Frank Vanderlip to James Stillman, 21 March 1913, Frank A. Vanderlip Papers, Special Collections, Columbia University (hereafter cited Vanderlip Papers); Straight to Thomas, 22 September 1913, Willard Straight Papers, Cornell University Library (hereafter cited Straight Papers); Straight to Reinsch, 17 and 30 September 1913, Reinsch Papers. For an excellent study of Straight's career to 1913, see Helen D. Kahn, "The Great Game of Empire: Willard D. Straight and American Far Eastern Policy" (Ph.D. dissertation, Cornell University, 1968).

31. Clipping, *Milwaukee Free Press,* 1913, Reinsch Papers; editorial, *Milwaukee Journal,* 25 September 1913.

Chapter IV

GETTING SETTLED
IN PEKING

When the Reinsches disembarked at Shanghai on the afternoon of November 1, 1913, the Japanese wharf was lined with a large welcoming party headed by Consul-General Amos P. Wilder. The presence of Daisy Hawkins and Stanley Hornbeck helped to bridge the vast distance that separated Asia from America. Following brief introductions, Reinsch was whisked off to the weekly tiffin (the Anglo-Indian lunch or high tea) of the Saturday Club, the discussion center for Shanghai's Westerners and Chinese. Afterwards, he was the guest of honor at a Wisconsin reunion that included Chinese students who had studied under him. During the next two days, Reinsch observed a session of the United States Court for China, a symbol of the extraterritorial privileges enjoyed by the foreign powers, inspected the Episcopalian-sponsored St. John's University and addressed a convocation of its student body, and conferred with Wilder and the consulate staff on the situation in Shanghai and the rest of China.[1]

Reinsch's speeches and press interviews in Shanghai were carefully scrutinized for any hint of the policies that he would pursue. But Reinsch stuck to generalities. He would follow America's traditional policy toward China, he would carry forward President Wilson's great interest in China's constitutional and economic development, and he would extend the activity of the legation to economic, agricultural, and educational concerns, thereby providing "all kinds of mutual helpfulness in vital phases of national reorganization."[2]

On the evening of November 3, Reinsch, his family, Daisy, and Hornbeck boarded the special railway car provided by the Chinese gov-

ernment for the trip to Peking. The long northward journey offered
Reinsch some glimpses of a many-sided China. Helpful interpretations
were supplied by Hornbeck and especially by Roy S. Anderson, whom
Reinsch described as "an American uniquely informed about the
Chinese." Anderson joined the Reinsch party at Nanking and would
serve the minister as an adviser and confidant for the next six years.
Nanking, which had been recently sacked by the semi-barbarous troops
of General Chang Hsun, was a disheartening sight. The train then passed
through the fertile but flood-ravaged Huai River Valley, which would
become Reinsch's keystone for American investment and assistance to
China, and the rich province of Shantung, which would embroil him in
controversy with Japan. Reinsch was lavishly entertained in Tientsin,
which had been policed by foreign troops and forbidden to the Chinese
army since the suppression of the Boxer Rebellion.[3]

Arriving in Peking on November 6, Reinsch was met by a large
crowd of officials and spectators, which included Edward T. Williams,
the chargé d'affaires, and the Chinese foreign minister who represented
the Chinese government. After greetings were exchanged and the national anthems were played, Reinsch was escorted to the Legation Quarter, the self-contained community of foreign offices, residences, and
hotels that occupied the southeastern corner of the Inner City (or Tatar
City). Nestled in the shadow of the impressive Gate of Heavenly Peace
(the T'ien-an Men), the American properties comprised four sections.
The marine barracks, housing about three hundred men, were situated at
the southwestern corner of the Legation Quarter. Adjacent to it was the
legation compound, which contained the chancery, the legation offices,
and the houses assigned to the ministers and the secretaries. Farther east,
separated by the Dutch legation, were the military storehouses and cor-
rals, and former Chinese temples which had been taken over as residences
for the military attachés, clerks, and student interpreters. Most of the
buildings were designed by a Treasury Department architect, who had
spent his career planning post offices in the United States. But thanks to
William W. Rockhill, the minister's home was built in "stately colonial
renaissance style." Reinsch found the residence "simple but handsome,"
its interior combining "the spaciousness needed for official entertaining
with the repose of a real home."[4]

While the ladies settled into their new home, the minister ac-
quainted himself with the chancery operations and met with his staff.
The first secretary, Edward T. Williams, was an able and highly regarded
diplomat, thoroughly versed in the Far Eastern situation. Sent to China
in 1887 as a missionary for the Disciples of Christ, Williams chose to

enter the diplomatic service in 1896. He served as Chinese secretary in Peking, consul-general at Tientsin, assistant chief of the Far Eastern Division in the Department of State, and finally as first secretary and chargé d'affaires in Peking. He would soon return to Washington as chief of the Far Eastern Division, where he proved to be a sympathetic ally. Although he differed with Reinsch on details and methods, Williams was devoted to the Open Door and to Reinsch's program to expand America's economic interests in China.[5]

Williams's young replacement was John V. A. MacMurray, who had served in Bangkok (1907), St. Petersburg (1908–11), and in Washington, where he rose quickly to the post of assistant chief of the Division of Near Eastern Affairs. Wherever he went, MacMurray impressed his superiors, including Reinsch, with his knowledge, keen analytical mind, organizational ability, and fine bearing. He had, Reinsch observed, "an almost religious devotion to the idea of public service," and he emerged as one of the State Department's super-professional officers. But MacMurray was also snobbish, prejudiced, and somewhat austere; although he possessed a genuine interest in things Chinese, he never acquired Reinsch's warm attachment to China. While MacMurray held Reinsch in high regard as a person and respected his insights into the Chinese situation, they frequently clashed in the chancery—mainly over the delegation of duties and methods of operation rather than over American policy toward China.[6]

Willys R. Peck, who had accompanied Reinsch from Tientsin to Peking, held the important post of Chinese secretary, an interpreter of Chinese affairs as well as a translator. Peck spoke colloquial Chinese with ease. He was tactful, subtle, and sophisticated in dealing with people, but at times he could be bluntly outspoken. In the spring of 1914, however, Peck was named consul at Tsingtao.[7] His successor was Dr. Charles D. Tenney, a former missionary educator with a broad knowledge of Chinese life. Tenney served Reinsch faithfully for the remainder of Reinsch's tenure and was often assisted by his conscientious son, Raymond, who held the title of assistant Chinese secretary.[8]

During the next six years, dozens of men passed through the legation as military and naval attachés, assistant secretaries, student interpreters, clerks, and consuls. The outbreak of World War I and the reinvigorated effort to extend American interests brought a host of other officials to China: commercial attachés, agricultural experts, trade commissioners, and communications and railway advisers. A handful of these men became trusted advisers and confidants to Reinsch. But the most important was Julean Arnold, a former consular officer who became the first American commercial attaché in Peking. Strongly committed to the Open Door policy, Arnold helped Reinsch in designing a blueprint for capturing the China market.

But Reinsch often went outside of his official family—especially to newspapermen—and relied heavily on a Kitchen Cabinet. He had always been unorthodox in his methods when the situation required. The need for information, contacts, and influence in this very strange and different country, where the traditional rules of diplomacy were generally broken or subverted and where internal chaos often reigned, led Reinsch to assemble an unofficial group of advisers, informants, and agents—Americans, Britishers, and Chinese. These men had access to Reinsch twenty-four hours a day, by means of correspondence, chits, the telephone, and under cover of night, the backdoor of the chancery.

Reinsch's most valuable and faithful agents were Roy S. Anderson and William H. Donald, two colorful adventurers who knew China intimately and had the confidence of different Chinese political figures and factions. They were frequently indispensable in providing Reinsch with useful information and serving as intermediaries during sensitive negotiations involving the United States legation, American business firms, and Chinese officials. The son of an American missionary, Anderson had mastered the Chinese language, the workings of Chinese politics, and the nuances of Chinese ways. He was a journalist who wrote under the name of "Bruce Baxter," a sometime adviser to the Chinese government as well as to key politicians and military leaders, and an agent for Standard Oil, the American International Corporation, and other companies. Reinsch implicitly trusted this lover of China and straightforward American who shared the American minister's objectives and dreams.

Donald, an Australian newspaperman, who wrote at various times for the *China Mail*, George Bronson Rea's *Far Eastern Review*, and the *New York Herald* never really learned Chinese. But he gained the confidence of many Chinese officials and was well known as a troubleshooter, who was not above dabbling in intrigue and even a little blackmail. An ardent supporter of Chinese nationalism, Donald was one of the few Westerners to become attached to Sun Yat-sen and reportedly wrote all of his early pronouncements; later, he became an admirer of Chiang Kai-shek and served the generalissimo as a faithful adviser. "He had a heart for the Chinese, as if they had been his own people," Reinsch recorded in his memoirs. "He worried about their troubles and fought their fights."[9]

But there were also others. James A. Thomas, for many years manager of the British-American Tobacco Company, occasionally provided assistance to Reinsch. Dr. George E. Morrison, the Australian adviser to

President Yuan Shih-k'ai, had an encyclopedic knowledge of Chinese public men and politics. Finally, Reinsch's intimate circle included a number of Chinese: V. K. Wellington Koo, the young but rising diplomat; Hollington Tong; Admiral Tsai T'ing-kan; C. C. Wang; C. T. Wang; and Chou Tzu-ch'i. These men were drawn both from the Young China Movement, which Reinsch encouraged from the day he arrived in China, and the progressive traditionalists.[10]

The afternoon of November 15, 1913, was set aside for Reinsch to present his credentials to President Yuan Shih-k'ai. Escorted by mounted detachments of United States Marines, Chinese police, and the presidential bodyguard, Reinsch and his aides were conveyed with great pomp to the presidential palace. He rode into the Imperial City in an ornate state carriage that had belonged to the Manchu Court; then he was rowed across the beautiful South Lake in an old barge. Old Imperial China, Reinsch observed in his memoirs, was very close indeed. The ceremonies, however, were simple and modeled after Western procedures. Sun Pao-ch'i, the minister for foreign affairs, formally presented Reinsch to the president; the new American minister read a short address and Yuan responded with appropritate remarks, translated by Columbia-educated V. K. Wellington Koo.[11]

*   *   *

Officially installed as representative of the United States government in Peking, Reinsch was ready to execute American policy. But what was the United States policy toward China? What were American attitudes toward that nation and its people? What was Reinsch's particular view of his mission?

Reinsch carried with him the baggage of more than one hundred and twenty-five years of Sino-American relations. The first principle of American diplomacy—in China and throughout the world, for that matter—was to secure equal opportunity for American merchants and manufacturers; in other words, the Open Door. That policy was rooted in the Model Treaty of 1776 and was formerly recognized in the Treaty of Wanghsia (1844), concluded by Ch'i-ying, who represented the Manchu Court, and Caleb Cushing, the enterprising son of a Newburyport merchant and the instrument of Websterian commercial diplomacy. In the following decade, Humphrey Marshall, the United States commissioner at Canton (1852–54), formulated its corollary. Fearing that the Taiping Rebellion and the pressures by the foreign powers would result in the partition of China, Marshall asserted the need to uphold the territorial and administrative integrity of China in order to maintain the viability of the Open Door. Although it generally abstained from military intervention against the decadent Manchu Empire, the United States demanded, under the most favored nation clause, the same treaty rights and extraterritorial privileges obtained by European powers: "Jackal Diplomacy," some have labeled it. On the other hand, the United States attempted to assist China to modernize its institutions and develop its resources by encouraging Chinese leaders and by providing technical assistance. An expression of American humanitarianism and patronizing sympathy for the suffering Chinese people, that goal also reflected the American realization that the Open Door could not function as intended without strengthening and developing China. In the course of the nineteenth century, therefore, the United States enjoyed a share of the much valued China trade and the fruits of European imperialism, while also establishing the popular myth at home that it was China's only true friend. And it did so with relatively little expenditure of its own resources.

However, at the end of the nineteenth century, the Open Door seemed to be endangered just as American economic interest in China revived. The balance of power had shifted decidedly to the industrialized nations and China's glaring weakness was underscored by its disastrous defeat in the Sino-Japanese War (1894–95). The powers thereupon staked out and obtained spheres of influence preparatory to their partition of China. Moreover, the struggling reform movement was quashed by the conservative reaction in 1898, and the Boxer Rebellion seemed to signal the demise of China.

To save the situation, Secretary of State John Hay returned to the cooperative strategy and reasserted the Open Door policy in his famous circulars of 1899 and 1900. Counting on British support and the rivalries among the powers, the United States asked for recognition of the principles of equal commercial opportunity within the "so-called" spheres of influence and respect for the territorial and adminstrative integrity of China. The Roosevelt administration was fully aware of the limited value of the vague acquiescence of the powers in the Hay notes. It therefore encouraged American enterprise in China in order to give Washington greater leverage in exercising American influence and in managing the balance of power in the Far East. However, American business failed to come through the Open Door and Japan's victory over Russia (1904–05) further upset the balance of power. As a result, Roosevelt virtually abandoned the rich province of Manchuria to Russia and Japan, and, in the Root-Takahira Agreement (1908), sought a temporary compromise in the western Pacific and a strengthened Japanese commitment to the Open Door in the rest of China. In adopting this approach, Roosevelt ignored Chinese initiatives to enlist American cooperation in the defense of their Manchurian frontier. Simultaneously, the administration was slow to respond to growing Chinese resentment against the more restrictive and insulting exclusion policy. In brief, America's support for the Open Door and its professions of sympathy for China sounded increasingly hollow.

The Taft administration, however, launched a vigorous offensive to make the Open Door a reality. John Hay had seen no sense in antagonizing the other powers by demanding equality of investment, since American businessmen were not seriously interested in making long-range financial commitments to China. But Secretary of State Philander Knox accepted the implications of modern state capitalism and, worrying about the situation in China, adopted the grandiose schemes of Willard Straight to establish developmental corporations for China. In imitation of what the other powers were already doing, Taft and Knox encouraged the formation of American financial syndicates. These were based around four Wall Street banks, which would pool resources and share the risks while enjoying official government support. In the name of the Open Door, they would serve as the instrument of American economic and political influence.

The Taft administration thereupon forced the Chinese government to admit the American Group of bankers into the Hukuang Railway concession, a series of railways in central and south China; it resurrected the Willard Straight–E. H. Harriman transportation project in the clumsy scheme to internationalize all Manchurian railroads; similarly, it bid for British support for the construction of the Chinchou-Aigun line, which would have also offset Russo-Japanese influence in Manchuria. Finally, convinced that cooperation with the other imperialist powers offered the only means of securing a share of business in China for the weaker, less experienced American interests, the State Department obtained for the American Group full participation in the Four Power International Banking Consortium (the Six Power Chinese Consortium after Russia and Japan thrust their banking groups into the British-French-German-American combination). The Consortium initiated negotiations with the Imperial government for a major loan to finance currency reform and economic development in Manchuria and China proper. But after the Chinese Revolution of 1911, Yuan Shih-k'ai wanted the Reorganization Loan, as it became known, to finance administrative expenses, and actually to cover budget deficits and to pay his armies.

Meanwhile, as long as the negotiations dragged on, the powers blocked other foreign loans to China and delayed recognition of the republic in order to extract additional concessions from the struggling Peking government.

By the end of 1912, the Taft-Knox cooperative policy was in shambles. The administration's well-intentioned efforts were designed to advance American interests and protect the Open Door. Instead, they antagonized the British, who thought that the American demands for security were excessive, inflamed the Russians and Japanese, who found their spheres of influence under attack, and frustrated the Chinese, who had relied on the Americans to protect their interests in Manchuria. In addition, American bankers became disenchanted with Chinese finance, and some of them looked to the incoming administration to bail them out.[12]

Without abandoning the commitment to the Open Door policy, the Wilson administration returned to the tactic of independent American action. Consequently, on March 18, 1913, Wilson condemned the Reorganization Loan and announced the withdrawal of official government support from the Consortium. In order to enhance America's position in China, Wilson also wanted the United States to be the first major nation to recognize the Chinese republic. Taking the reorganization of the National Assembly as a sign of progress in establishing parliamentary government, the United States, on May 2, 1913, formally recognized the Republic of China.

Wilson and Bryan were influenced by reports from missionary correspondents and the desire to be helpful to China. In castigating the monopoly features of the Consortium and the Wall Street bankers, they saw political advantage in appealing to progressives and in launching the New Freedom at home. But they also concluded that the United States had little leverage in the Consortium and that the cooperative policy had not worked out as it had been envisioned. The reshaping of the Reorganization Loan, moreover, undermined the American goals of developing China, reforming its burdensome and antiquated tax system, and generating exports for American industry, rather than merely assisting the bankers to float securities.

If Wilson's decision was made quickly—the bankers requested an immediate statement on the administration's China policy—it was not rendered on purely moralistic grounds or without some justification. If Wilson's public announcement was politically motivated, the decision itself won wide public support at home and in China. Furthermore, if the president misunderstood the Chinese situation and mistakenly thought that Americans could go it alone, he was still prepared to offer strong support for American enterprise and later he returned to the cooperative approach. "I feel so keenly the desire to help China that I prefer to err in the line of helping that country than otherwise," he reportedly remarked.[13]

Wilson also sought better ways of realizing America's traditional objectives in China and throughout the world. Wilson surpassed his predecessors in the vigor and zeal with which he sought to find markets for American industry and to encourage liberal parliamentary government. "Our interests are those of the open door—a door of friendship and mutual advantage," he declared in rejecting the Consortium. "This is the only door we care to enter."[14]

Wilsonian progressivism, at home and abroad, meant the rationalization of techniques and the institutionalization of ideas that had been experimented with on an ad hoc basis during the previous fifteen years. Responding to the needs of American commerce and finance, the Wilson administration would encourage the establishment of foreign branch banks under the Federal Reserve Act, would secure the Webb-Pomerene and Edge Acts to free business abroad from the restraints of the antitrust laws, and would greatly expand the activities of the Department of Commerce. Urging subsidies to revive the flagging merchant marine, Wilson declared in his annual message to Congress in 1914: "The Government must open the gates of trade, and open them wide; open them before it is altogether reasonable to ask private capital to open them at a venture."[15]

Following the withdrawal of support from the American Group, the Wilson administration took every opportunity to emphasize that it would uphold all legitimate foreign enterprise, without guaranteeing any particular venture and without favoring any one firm or group. In the summer of 1913, Secretary of State Bryan spelled out the administration's stand in a reply to E. T. Williams's request for clarifying instructions:

> This Government is not the endorser of the American competitor, and it is not an accountable party to the undertaking. It, however, stands ready, if wrong be done toward an American citizen in his business relations with a foreign government, to use all proper effort toward securing just treatment for its citizens. This rule applies as well to financial contracts as to industrial engagements.

Bryan added that within those broad guidelines, much must necessarily be left to the discretion and experience of the legation. And by citing

previous State Department instructions, Byran underscored the basic
continuity of American policy.[16]

Finally, in sending Reinsch to China, Wilson thought that he had
found a man who shared his vision of the Open Door and who could
implement his independent, competitive approach. Historians who have
contended that Wilson's China policy was misguided and moralistic have
seized upon the last sentence of Reinsch's account of the president's instructions while ignoring or deemphasizing the rest of it:

> From my conversations with President Wilson before departing
> for my post I had formed the conclusion that the President
> realized that as America had withdrawn from a cooperative ef-
> fort to assist in the development of China, it was incumbent
> upon her to do her share independently and to give specific
> moral and financial assistance; in fact, I received the President's
> assurance of active support for constructive work in China. In
> conversation he dwelt, however, more on the educational and
> political example and moral encouragement, than on the matter
> of finance and commerce.[17]

But Reinsch often used the same rhetoric and understood the president's intentions. During his first business conversation with Yuan
Shih-k'ai, the Chinese president had emphasized the educational bonds
between the United States and China, but also expressed the hope for
more American material aid. Taking up his cue, Reinsch replied that
economic assistance to China

> was a part, also, of the aim and desired policy of the President of
> the United States. The United States had withdrawn from the
> Sextuple Group not through indifference to China's needs, but
> because it was actuated by a desire to attain a position where
> such needs could be satisfied in a more independent manner on
> the part of the United States, and with greater benefit to China
> herself. He looked forward to the extension of American busi-
> ness enterprise in China and considered and hoped that such a
> result would conduce to *the breaking up of the localization of busi-
> ness interests in China in national spheres of influence*.[18]

In any event, Reinsch was largely on his own in interpreting and
implementing America's China policy. The legacy he inherited from
American policy makers was not as clearly defined, simple, and consis-

tent as the above summary may indicate. President Wilson and his advisers were often too concerned with domestic affairs, with Mexico, and with the European War to devote much attention to China. Besides, Reinsch brought to China his own preconceived ideas and plans.

First, Reinsch was obsessed with the need to find foreign outlets for America's surplus goods and capital. The severe depression of the 1890s, the economic upturn beginning in 1897, that was widely attributed to the revival of American exports, and the accounts of neglected commercial opportunities in the *Daily Consular and Trade Reports* (which he read, underlined, and used in his lectures and writings) molded his thinking and his diplomatic activity. Without ignoring Latin America, Reinsch concluded that China held the key to America's salvation. For Reinsch accepted somewhat uncritically the findings of Baron Ferdinand von Richthofen and other China enthusiasts and believed wholeheartedly in the myth of the China market. "We may consider it natural—even necessary—that, if free trade opportunities are maintained in China, we shall soon absorb our full share of the commerce of that magnificent market," he observed in 1900. When the Panic of 1907 seemed to presage a widespread economic collapse, he prescribed an increase in commerce "with South America, Japan, and China to act as a safeguard against such a crisis." Furthermore, the completion of the Panama Canal and the impending industrialization of China heralded the dawning of the Pacific Era and new opportunities for the United States. Shortly after receiving Senate confirmation, Reinsch declared:

> While we furnish a market for many of the Chinese products and soon will carry on a much greater trade here, that country also opens a big field for American industry. Too much cannot be said in this regard. China has been shut away from the rest of the world for ages. Today her vast country is in the process of rebuilding and advancement. She needs our modern inventions— you might also say, our facilities for civilization. She needs railroads, telephones, the telegraph, our iron manufactures and cotton products. And with the opening of the new highway across Panama this tremendous field of commerce will be automatically opened to us if we go after it.

Two years later, Reinsch told Secretary of State Robert Lansing that China contained "all the elements favorable to the establishment of American business interests . . . for a long time to come when European markets shall fail us."[19]

Second, Reinsch had great admiration for China and a strong desire to help it advance into the modern age. He often referred to the fact that China possessed the oldest civilization in the world and a great heritage of cultural and technological achievement. Although public corruption was a way of life, he stressed that the Chinese people were talented, hard-working, and personally honest. Measured against the industrialized nations, China was indeed backward. But once China mobilized its enormous population and resources and built the infrastructure of a modern economy, Reinsch predicted that China would become "the centre of the industrialized world."

At the turn of the century, Reinsch warned against any attempt to transform China too rapidly, for that would only exacerbate the existing antagonism toward the West and the inevitable suffering that accompanied industrialization. The Chinese, he observed, on the eve of the Boxer Rebellion, would tend to blame the "foreign devils" for the social and economic dislocations resulting from modernization. But impressed by the elimination of the traditional examination system, the introduction of scientific and practical studies, and the great increase in the number of Chinese studying abroad, Reinsch began to think that the Chinese would adopt Western style modernization more rapidly and extensively than the facts warranted. By 1910, Reinsch believed that these educational reforms were needed to make China "strong in a hurry," and he argued that they would unify and transform Chinese society.[20]

Even more striking were the political changes. Reinsch (somewhat simplistically) had viewed traditional China as a nonpolitical society unified by Confucian teachings and ethics; he also had stressed that the Chinese resisted any authority outside of the family, clan, and village. But now Chinese society was being politicized and was beginning to demand a responsible, representative parliament to enact a program of national reform. "The Chinese people are stirring," Reinsch told his Wisconsin friends before departing for Peking. "The idea of nationalism has dawned upon them. It means that they must cooperate more widely and with the idea of nationalism they must organize." Hawkins, himself fearing a wave of Jacobinism, was surprised that Reinsch, who had always emphasized the slow evolution of political institutions, embraced "Chinese Nationalism expressed in a Parliamentary way." But at the same time, Reinsch criticized those revolutionaries who would attempt to establish a democracy. Considering China's size and history, as well as the traditional popular aversion to the authority of the central government, he also advised the creation of a federal system of government. Finally, Reinsch warned that the road to political reform would be paved with mistakes, violent controversies, and intrigue. The "real work of reform must be done in administration," he therefore lectured. "There the confidence of the people must be won. The corrupt methods which have obtained in the past must give way to strict accountability, and to the maintenance of just and legal changes."[21]

Reinsch felt that the developed nations could assist China by investing in railroads, mines, and manufactures, by encouraging the adoption of commercial codes and legal reforms, and by supplying the technical assistance to develop a system of administration. Earlier, Reinsch thought that Japan, which was anxious to serve as a "mediator" in the Orient, might take a conspicuous part in the modernization of China.[22] But by 1913, Reinsch had concluded that the United States, alone, could assume a special role in China's development. The United States, after all, was the leading proponent of the Open Door and, unlike the other powers which sought political advantage, was solely interested in guaranteeing equal opportunity for all nations. Furthermore, he believed America's traditional concern for education and relief work implied a similar responsibility to extend concrete aid to China. Without critically examining the differences in their historical development, Reinsch felt that the United States could serve as a model for China. "Our system of commerce, railroading and business, because both nations are great in area, are best adapted to China," he explained to an American audience in September 1913. "From every point of view, political, industrial, there are points of contact." Finally, Reinsch envisioned the day when there would be a great, though by no means exclusive, partnership between the two industrial giants of the world.[23]

Reinsch believed that the Chinese earnestly desired American assistance in the development of their nation. They saw a reservoir of American good will, which the Chinese took to imply a readiness to give them "a certain amount of support in time of need." But, Reinsch hastened to stress, the Chinese looked for economic assistance and not political or military intervention. "I was therefore resolved," Reinsch wrote in the original draft of his memoirs, "to give every legitimate encouragement to constructive enterprise, whether it be in education, finance, commerce or industry, because I saw in every specific effort of this kind a definite advance towards helping the Chinese adequately to organize their own national life themselves, and thus preserving American rights and opportunities, and maintaining Chinese confidence in our country, which is one of our most valuable heritages. . . . " This meant, on the one hand, that the task of American diplomacy was to prevent any interference with the upbuilding of Chinese national life, and to resist attempts to secure privileged positions. On the other hand, it meant that the United States had to render sizeable assistance for the work of reconstruction and development.[24]

Third, Reinsch brought to China a reinterpreted and strengthened version of the Open Door policy as well as a fierce determination to make it work. America's late start, the commercial basis of its overseas expansion, and the immediate concern for the situation in China required that the United States assert the doctrine of equal opportunity. Moreover, America's enviable geographic location (straddling two oceans soon to be linked by the isthmian canal), its enormous industrial power and capital, its administrative and technological skills, and the model of its political system convinced Reinsch that the Open Door would best serve its long-range interests. "For what better economic situation could we wish for in the world," he asked, "than that its markets should be open without artificial political impediments to the enterprise of our commerce and industry."[25]

An admirer of John Hay, Reinsch considered the Open Door notes a "valuable achievement on the part of the American Department of State." Although the correspondence was informal in character and the replies of the powers were vague, if not evasive, the American initiative produced the first clear declaration for equal opportunity in China, it encouraged the British to stand by the Open Door, and it cleared the air by recognizing the spheres of influence as an established fact. In the debate that took place at the turn of the century, Reinsch sided with those who held that the spheres of influence were compatible with the Open Door. "As long as freedom of opportunity is preserved within these spheres," he wrote in *World Politics,* "as long as the treaty ports are kept open and their number is gradually increased, the policy designated by the term 'open door' is practically in force, even although the policing of the empire may have been divided up among the powers." Two years later, Reinsch insisted that the "open door policy may still confidently be said to be in the ascendant, both actually and potentially."[26]

Reinsch fully understood that China's weakness and financial problems combined with the grant of railway concessions and spheres of influence could lead to its partition and to the exclusion of the United States. But Reinsch counted on international rivalries and increased American economic influence to maintain the balance of power and to provide China with alternative sources of capital and aid. Moreover, he welcomed the growing rapprochement between the United States and Great Britain as a means of blocking France and Russia, which he singled out as the greatest enemies of the Open Door. Germany seemed to support the Open Door concept, but its different political system caused Reinsch to doubt the possibility of a close understanding with Berlin. On the other hand, Reinsch belonged to the sizeable group of American leaders and publicists who believed that "Japan was fighting our battle for us" and who encouraged Japan to influence Chinese development.[27]

By 1910, however, Reinsch had modified his views. The failure of American business to come through in China coupled with the changed siutation in East Asia, particularly in Manchuria, made Reinsch an advocate of Dollar Diplomacy. Reinsch saw Dollar Diplomacy as merely an extension of the traditional Open Door policy. It meant that the government was drawing upon private capital—giving it direction, assistance, and protection—in order to advance the national interest. Moreover, Reinsch had never distinguished between equal opportunity for commerce and investment, for he had always argued that under modern conditions they were inseparable. Thus, as Charles Beard later observed, "although he did not belong officially to the school of dollar diplomacy, Reinsch believed in its tenets."

Reinsch felt free to criticize some of the tactics and mistakes of the Taft administration in Latin America and China, notably the Knox Neutralization scheme, but he still supported its general objectives. He told his class in Contemporary International Politics that "if we can maintain the policy of President Taft in his attitude toward Chinese development . . . , and not grasp more than is due us, we shall take the position that was held by England up to 1908." In the process, Reinsch began to question the wisdom and justice of retaining the spheres of influence. "If China is to be saved the complete loss of her Manchurian dominion," he wrote in early 1911, "it will come about through the maintenance of international interest in that dependency, which compatible with the special interests acquired by Russia and Japan, will, nevertheless, keep alive the exercise of Chinese sovereignty until eventually China may be strong enough to exercise her power more effectively so as to prevent further encroachments and perhaps even to secure a retrocession of some of the things she has at present lost."[28]

By 1911, however, Hawkins had succeeded in disabusing Reinsch of his notions that the spheres of influence had permitted the Open Door to function and, especially, that Japan was sympathetic toward China and equal opportunity. Shortly after he arrived in China, Reinsch launched a campaign, which would engage his attention for the next ten years, to eliminate the spheres of influence completely. Moreover, although there is evidence that he questioned the wisdom of withdrawing from the Consortium, Reinsch was prepared to abandon, at least temporarily, the

cooperative policy in favor of aggressive independent American investment in China.[29]

Reinsch subsequently maintained that an independent American
effort was by no means inconsistent with the Open Door; nor was it
designed to play a lone hand to the disadvantage of the other powers.
American policy, he frequently asserted, was straightforward and simple. The United States was not engaged in the delicate and complicated
balancing of conflicting interests; it eschewed political interference in
the affairs of China and the reprehensible demands for special privileges.
"A united China, master of its own land, developing its resources, open
to all nations of the world equally for commercial and industrial
activity—should be the chief desideratum of American policy," he declared in his memoirs. "The United States does not represent a special
interest, but it trusts that a wise and suitable policy may be found in
supporting interests which are common to all, or nearly all the remaining nations."[30]

This was, after all, the essence of the Open Door as Reinsch conceived it: vigorous but fair economic competition, but without the special privileges and political influence conferred by the spheres of influence. Considering America's advantages, he was confident that the
United States would emerge victorious as long as American interests
entered China in strength. Finally, the success of the Open Door in China
might mean the establishment of a new world order—one in which
peaceful competition, international cooperation, progress, and prosperity would replace force, subterfuge, waste, and poverty.

*   *   *

Here were the roots of America's China policy. Here were the Wilsonian
modifications. Here, too, were Reinsch's ideas and his grand vision. But
what were the realities of the situation in the Far East? And did they offer
Reinsch any chance or hope of success?

The American business community in China lacked solidarity and
strong leadership. Moreover, it was greatly demoralized by the
withdrawal from the Consortium; it felt that this had left the United
States without any influence in China. Consequently, American businessmen in China were skeptical of the new American minister whose
ties to Wilson and to an academic background did not inspire much
confidence. The Shanghai community, in fact, had been restrained in
greeting Reinsch and was angry because he could not find the time to
hear its views. Speaking for the businessmen, the *China Press*—the lead-

ing American newspaper in China, published in Shanghai—chided Reinsch, saying that he could be a successful minister if he came to China merely as an observer. Coming to his rescue, Wilder expressed personal confidence in Reinsch's ability to do good work, but counseled him to stress the commercial aspects of his mission since "business men, as a rule, are still a little jealous of scholastics."[31]

The situation was little better at home. Even though some Wall Street interests had become disenchanted with the Consortium loan, most business organs continued to express disinterest in China and bitterness with the administration's handling of Chinese affairs. Henceforth, Wall Street spokesmen warned, American business would not go into places like China on a large scale unless "our Government is ready to stand as close to the financial and commercial enterprise of its citizens in foreign countries as the governments of Europe have long been accustomed to." Defending the Consortium policies of the Taft administration and the American Group, Straight predicted that any independent American effort would fail unless the United States was prepared to extend active military support to China. "This, you will agree, is impossible," Straight told his audience. Perhaps, Straight concluded, it was best that the United States had withdrawn from the Consortium, for the American public was not yet ready for overseas expansion: it still was unaccustomed to buying foreign securities, it still considered government support for monopoly un-American, it still did not know how to inaugurate a constructive and intelligent foreign trade policy, and it still did not know how to respect the interests and rights of other foreign powers.

Straight did not represent the entire American financial community. But his cooperation could be crucial if Reinsch was to make use of America's economic power in China. For while Straight had already given up on the Open Door in Manchuria, and Mongolia and was starting to lean toward an accommodation with Japan, he was still lured by the China market. And even though he remained critical of the Wilson administration, he came to appreciate both its desire to expand American enterprise abroad and Reinsch's individual efforts to use America's economic power to make the Open Door work.[32]

A greater threat to the American position in China came from the other foreign powers. Despite the completion of the Reorganization Loan in the summer of 1913, the cooperative policy was crumbling and the powers were scrambling for concessions. "At this rate it will not take many years for China to dispose of all her main trunk lines," D. A. Menocal reported to Straight, "and as they fall into the hands of the various foreign nations, they supply a pretext for zones of special interest which will probably be increasingly difficult to break into." Unless the United States government took immediate, effective action, he continued, it would soon find itself excluded from all business in China, thereby repeating its mistakes in Turkey and Persia where the Europeans obtained exclusive control of natural resources. Even the British were becoming alarmed at the French and Japanese incursions into their sphere of interest in the Yangtze. The French had tightened their grip on Yunnan and the Japanese were increasingly active in Fukien and south China. Henry White was right: the Open Door was scarcely ajar. [33]

Moreover, the foreign powers looked upon the United States with intense suspicion and hostility. Having divided up China, at least in their own minds, they viewed Americans as latecomers and interlopers. They also resented the attempt by the United States to use its moral influence to obtain special consideration from China while they expended their money, manpower, and energy and built up real territorial and commercial interests. The United States had forcibly interjected itself in the Hukuang Railway Loan, it had tried to neutralize the Manchurian railways, it had tried to use the Chinchou-Aigun concession to accomplish the same end, and it had obtained the right to float a currency loan, and yet the actual American investment remained negligible. Their ill-feeling was magnified by America's withdrawal from the Consortium and its recognition of the Chinese republic, which seemed to confirm the impression that the United States was trying to create for itself the image of China's only friend. And in the fall of 1913, this scholarly American minister was poised to carry out an independent policy while preaching the Open Door and America's friendship for China. [34]

Consequently, with the exception of the British organs, which always treated him fairly, the foreign press greeted Reinsch with scorn and abuse. On the day of his arrival in Peking, *Le Journal de Pekin,* the spokesman for French and Russian business interests, flayed Reinsch for his criticism of French imperialism and French subservience to Russian political interests in the Far East. Inveighing against the United States, in general, it asserted that "Bluff and Blunder" were the two chief characteristics of American diplomacy, of which the new minister was a worthy representative. German editorials in north China called Reinsch "chicken-hearted," and the Japanese controlled press soon accused Reinsch of stirring up revolutionaries during his excursions outside Peking. He was also charged with nepotism because he tried to have the American-owned International Banking Corporation recommend Hawkins for a district post with the Salt Administration. This was only the beginning. Throughout his six years in China Reinsch encountered constant intrigue, hostility, and the propaganda which came in part from France, but especially from Japan.[35]

Reinsch also discovered that China verged on the brink of disintegration while the fledgling reform movement was stymied and wandered in aimless confusion. What occurred in China in 1911–1912 was more than a palace coup but less than a revolution. Chinese hostility to the Manchus, disgust with their corruption and misrule, opposition to the centralizing tendencies of the Peking regime, and the desire of some intellectuals to reproduce Western parliamentary democracy in China brought down the imperial government and led to the creation of the Chinese republic. Although it was hardly a mass movement, the Revolution of 1911 crystallized the reformist tendencies that had been fermenting within Chinese society as well as the nationalist impulse to overthrow foreign domination.[36]

Sun Yat-sen, the spiritual father of the Chinese Revolution and the titular leader of the Kuomintang (KMT), or Nationalist party, was called from exile to serve as provisional president. But Sun recognized the weakness of his republican followers and the widespread support for Yuan Shih-k'ai; he therefore offered to resign, subject to certain conditions, in favor of Yuan.[37] Almost all factions regarded the former imperial viceroy with suspicion. Nevertheless, Yuan was considered the only figure who could avert civil war and foreign intervention. On February 15, 1912, therefore, the Provisional National Assembly in Nanking elected Yuan provisional president and a few days later chose Li Yuan-hung, the reluctant rebel hero at Wuchang, provisional vice president of China.

In order to placate the republicans and secure foreign recognition and financial assistance, Yuan allowed the election of a permanent National Assembly. The Kuomintang failed to make much headway in the more conservative northern provinces. But under the brilliant guidance of Sung Chiao-jen, who inherited the mantle of leadership from the erratic Sun and transformed a traditional Chinese secret society into a Western-style political party, the KMT won a majority in both houses of Parliament. The Kuomintang adopted Sun Yat-sen's three general principles of nationalism, democracy, and the people's livelihood. Distrustful of a strong centralized government and a powerful executive, it also favored provincial autonomy, cabinet government with a premier responsible to the National Assembly, and a weak president. Moreover, it opposed the Reorganization Loan because it feared increased foreign control and suspected that Yuan would use the funds to strengthen his position.

Yuan, naturally, had no intention of becoming a figurehead and plotted the destruction of his political opposition and his elevation as dictator of China. In the end, Yuan broke the stalemate by arranging for Sung's assassination and by signing the Reorganization Loan without the approval of the National Assembly. In response, some of the KMT leaders backed a rebellion that erupted during the summer of 1913 in the Yangtze Valley. Yuan, however, had a well-trained northern army, an alliance of northern and southern warlords, money from the Consortium loan, and the support of the foreign powers and the Chinese businessmen who feared instability and the disruption of commerce. Yuan quickly crushed the rebellion and scattered his foes into exile in Japan and Hong Kong or into hiding in the international settlements and distant provinces within China. Flushed with this victory, Yuan first had the National Assembly elect him to a five-year term as permanent president on October 6, 1913. Then, two days before Reinsch's arrival in Peking, Yuan expelled the Kuomintang from the National Assembly, and declared it illegal. Since the rump Parliament could not gather a quorum, Yuan's dissolution of Parliament on January 10, 1914, was only the formal acknowledgment that parliamentary government was dead as long as Yuan reigned.

In the larger sense, the events of 1913 represented far more than a setback for the stable development of representative government which Reinsch himself had hoped for. They also threatened the general reform of China's commerce, banking, legal, and administrative systems and tended to discourage needed foreign investment. Moreover, they left a legacy of bitterness and divisiveness that would foster civil war, encourage reactionary elements and militarism, invite foreign intrigue, and divert attention and resources from Chinese development. In fact, having used the proceeds of the Reorganization Loan to put down the Second Revolution, Yuan's treasury was again empty and in need of foreign replenishment.

In the fall of 1913, the United States became the major target of Chinese entreaties. But the Chinese also had misgivings about turning to the United States. The debacle of the American China Development Company was still fresh in their memories. Distrustful of the political designs of the European powers, the Chinese government had granted to that company, which was backed by J. P. Morgan & Co. and other well-known banks and corporations, a concession to build the all important Canton-Hankow Railway, a vital link between south and central China. The company, however, built only a few miles of track and then sold a good part of its shares to Belgian interests. The Chinese were furious and forced the American China Development Company to buy them back.

But the company, uncertain of the value of the concession, turned around, and, in 1905, induced the Chinese government to purchase the concession at a handsome profit to the American investors.

The Chinese also had mixed feelings about the American withdrawal from the Consortium. On the one hand, they believed that without the moderating influence of the United States, the Consortium powers would be far more demanding. On the other hand, the independent policy of the United States offered the possibility of more assistance as well as a chance to play off the inexperienced Americans against the Consortium powers. In any event, the Chinese were desperate for money and anxious to avoid turning to the Consortium for another loan.[38]

*   *   *

China therefore posed a mighty challenge to Reinsch. The Peking post would have tried the most experienced diplomat. Reinsch, however, was an unknown quantity who would have to prove himself not only to the Chinese, but to the foreign powers, American businessmen, and to his own government. Beneath the appearance of a mild, kindly scholar, however, there was an astute, driving fighter, who believed that he carried in his hands the destiny of the United States, China, and the world. During his first month in Peking, Reinsch made a careful survey of Chinese affairs. With the assistance of Hornbeck, Williams, Anderson, Donald, and other members of his emerging Kitchen Cabinet, he concentrated on mastering the intricacies of Chinese and Japanese internal politics and Sino-Japanese relations. He had only begun his study, but, within weeks of his arrival in China, Reinsch was called upon to act.[39]

NOTES TO
CHAPTER IV

1. Clippings in Wilder to Bryan, 3 November 1913, 711. 93/37, DSNA; Reinsch, *An American Diplomat in China* (Garden City, 1922), 8–11. *An American Diplomat* is a condensed version of Reinsch's memoirs, which he originally entitled, "Six Years of American Action in China." Most of the manuscript may be found in Box 15 of the Reinsch Papers, but some pages are scattered in other boxes. The published version will be referred to except where it differs significantly from the original and when there are significant omissions.

2. *Ibid.*

3. Reinsch, *An American Diplomat,* 11–16.

4. *Ibid.*, 17–20; MacMurray to mother, 8 February 1914, MacMurray Papers.

5. For background information on Williams, see his biographical sketch in the Edward T. Williams Papers, Bancroft Library, University of California, Berkeley (hereafter cited Williams Papers).

6. Perhaps because of their clash, Reinsch said little about MacMurray personally in his memoirs. See Reinsch, *An American Diplomat*, 50–51. Also MacMurray to mother, 19 February 1914, MacMurray Papers; Reinsch to MacMurray, 12 January 1918, *ibid*.

7. Reinsch, *An American Diplomat*, 50, 161; Wilder to Reinsch, 15 December 1913, Reinsch Papers; MacMurray to mother, 8 February 1914, MacMurray Papers.

8. Reinsch, *An American Diplomat*, 161; MacMurray to mother, 8 February 1914, MacMurray Papers.

9. Reinsch to Wilson, 5 October 1914, William G. McAdoo Papers, Library of Congress (hereafter cited McAdoo Papers); MacMurray to mother, 8 February 1914, MacMurray Papers; MacMurray to Wilson, 12 September 1914, *ibid*.; Sir John Jordan to Sir Walter Langley, 23 March 1914, Sir John Jordan Papers, FO (Foreign Office) 350/12, Public Record Office, London, England (hereafter cited Jordan Papers, FO and file number); Reinsch, *An American Diplomat*, 12, 48–49; Cyril Pearl, *Morrison of Peking* (Sydney, Australia, 1967), 236; Earl A. Selle, *Donald of China* (New York, 1948).

10. Reinsch, *An American Diplomat, passim.*

11. Reinsch to Bryan, 20 November 1913, 123.R271/12, DSNA; Reinsch, *An American Diplomat*, 4–5.

12. The above analysis is based on the following works: Warren I. Cohen, *America's Response to China: An Interpretative History of Sino-American Relations* (New York, 1971); Tyler Dennett, *Americans in Eastern Asia: A Critical Study of the United States' Policy in the Far East in the Nineteenth Century* (New York, 1963); John K. Fairbank, "'American China Policy' to 1898: A Misconception," *Pacific Historical Review,* XXXIV (November 1970), 409–20; Lloyd Gardner, "A Progressive Foreign Policy, 1900–1921," *From Colony to Empire: Essays in the History of American Foreign Relations,* ed. William A. Williams (New York, 1972), 203–51; Michael Hunt, *Frontier Defense and the Open Door: Manchuria in Chinese-American Relations, 1895–1911* (New Haven, 1973); Delber McKee, *Chinese Exclusion Versus the Open Door Policy 1900–1906; Clashes over China Policy in the Roosevelt Era* (Detroit, 1977); Paul Varg, *The Making of a Myth: The United States and China, 1899–1912* (East Lansing, 1968); Charles Vevier, *The United States and China 1906–1913: A Study of Finance and Diplomacy* (New Brunswick, 1955); Williams, *The Tragedy of American Diplomacy,* chapters 1–2; Marilyn B. Young, *Rhetoric of Empire* (Cambridge, 1968).

13. Press Release, 19 March 1913, 893.51/1335½, DSNA; Arthur J. Brown to Henry P. Davison, 13 January 1913, 893.00/1787, DSNA; Thurlow Reed Barnes to Bryan, 14

March 1913, 893.00/1356, DSNA; Williams to Bryan, 18 March 1913, 893.00/1607, DSNA; Bryan to Williams, 24 April 1913, 893.00/1633a, DSNA; C. E. Scott to Wilson, 1 March 1913, Wilson Papers; House Diary, vol. 1, entries for 9, 14, 15 and 16 March 1913, House Papers; David Cronon, ed., *The Cabinet Diaries of Josephus Daniels 1913– 1921* (Lincoln, 1963), 7–8, 17, 19–20; address of William J. Bryan at the Annual Meeting of the American Asiatic Association, 26 January 1914, *Journal of the American Asiatic Association* (JAAA), XIV (February 1914), 12–13; Vanderlip to Stillman, 21 March 1913, Vanderlip Papers; *New York Times*, 19 and 20 March 1913. For the above analysis, I am also indebted to the following: Israel, *Progressivism and the Open Door*, 106–11; Martin J. Sklar, "Woodrow Wilson, the Six Power Consortium and Dollar Diplomacy: Essays in the Ideology of Modern United States Liberalism in its Period of Emergence" (M.A. thesis, University of Wisconsin, 1960); Williams, *The Tragedy of American Diplomacy*, chapter 2. See also, Link, *Wilson: The New Freedom*, 286–87; Li, *Woodrow Wilson's China Policy*, chapters 2–3; Harley Notter, *The Origins of the Foreign Policy of Woodrow Wilson* (Baltimore, 1937), 230–43; Meribeth E. Cameron, "American Recognition Policy Toward the Republic of China, 1912–1913," *Pacific Historical Review*, II (June 1933), 214–30.

14. *New York Times*, 19 March 1913.

15. Department of State, *Foreign Relations of the United States, 1914* (Washington, 1922), xiv. (Hereafter, references from the *Foreign Relations* series will be cited *FR* and year.)

16. William J. Bryan and Mary Baird Bryan, *The Memoirs of William Jennings Bryan* (Chicago, 1925), 362–63; Williams to Bryan, 11 July 1913, Bryan to Williams, 11 September 1913, 893.51/1457, DSNA; Bryan to H. B. Hollins & Co., 4 June 1913, 893.51/1431, DSNA.

17. Reinsch, *An American Diplomat*, 63.

18. Reinsch to Bryan, 24 November 1913, 893.00/2049, DSNA (author's emphasis).

19. Reinsch, *World Politics*, especially 86, 109, 114–45, 311–18, 325; author's interview with Hornbeck, 20 January 1965; Reinsch, "The Philippines in Its International Aspects," clipping, *Milwaukee Sentinel*, 17 December 1899, Reinsch Papers; Reinsch, "The Development of Commerce and Industry in the Orient," address before the Milwaukee Institute of Bank Clerks, 1907, *ibid.*; clipping, *Chicago Inter-Ocean*, 22 August 1913, *ibid.*; Reinsch to Lansing, 30 December 1915, 893.811/202, DSNA; Hawkins Tapes, 15; Hawkins to author, 21 January 1965.

20. Reinsch, *World Politics*, 87–89, 92–98, 105, 231; Reinsch, "China Against the World"; Reinsch, *Intellectual and Political Currents in the Far East*, 188; Reinsch, "The New Education in China," *Atlantic Monthly*, CIII (April 1909), 515–22; Reinsch address, "The Development of Commerce and Industry in the Orient," Reinsch Papers; Hawkins Tapes, 3.

21. Hawkins Tapes, 3; Hawkins to Reinsch, n.d., Box 1, Reinsch Papers; Hornbeck to Reinsch, 24 January 1912, Hornbeck Papers; Reinsch, *Intellectual and Political Currents in the Far East*, 128, 182, 225–26, 252–71; Reinsch, "A Parliament for China," *Atlantic Monthly*, CIV (December 1909), 790–97; *Milwaukee Journal*, 25 September 1913. Reinsch's views on developments preceding the Chinese Revolution of 1911 should be compared with the excellent analyses in Mary C. Wright, ed., *China in Revolution: The First Phase 1900–1913* (New Haven, 1968).

22. Reinsch, *World Politics*, 194–95; Reinsch, "Cultural Factors in the Chinese Crisis"; Reinsch, "Asia After the Great War," Reinsch Papers; Reinsch, "The Political Psychology of Japan," classroom lecture, 24 March 1905, Hornbeck Papers.

23. Reinsch, *An American Diplomat, passim; Milwaukee Journal*, 25 September 1913.

24. Reinsch to Bryan, 28 November 1914, 793.94/205, DSNA; Reinsch, *An American Diplomat*, xi–xii; Reinsch, "Six Years of American Action in China," Reinsch Papers.

25. Reinsch, "American Love of Peace and European Skepticism"; Reinsch, *World Politics, passim.*

26. Reinsch, *World Politics*, 184; Reinsch, *Colonial Government*, 70; Hornbeck Memo on the Open Door Policy, Box 92, Hornbeck Papers; Hawkins Tapes, 3.

27. Reinsch, *World Politics, passim;* Reinsch, "Russia and England in China," *The Arena*, XXI (January 1899), 75–83; Reinsch, "An Unfortunate Peace," *The Outlook*, LXXXI (16 September 1905), 117–18; Reinsch, "Japan and Asiatic Leadership."

28. Charles A. Beard, *The Idea of National Interest: An Analytic Study in American Foreign Policy* (New York, 1934), 104–12, 183–85; Reinsch lecture, clipping, 1910, vol. 2, Reinsch Papers; Reinsch, "Diplomatic Affairs and International Law, 1910," *American Political Science Review*, V (February 1911), 17–18; *Daily Cardinal*, 20 January 1910.

29. Hawkins to Reinsch, 24 November 1906, Reinsch Papers; Hawkins reports to Reinsch, mostly undated, *ibid.*; Reinsch, "Six Years of American Action in China," *ibid.*; Reinsch, Memo #3, "Spheres of Interest," *ibid.*; Hawkins, "A General Explanatory Note," Reinsch Papers; Hawkins Tapes, 3; author's interview with Hornbeck, 5 January 1965.

30. Reinsch, "Six Years of American Action in China." Compare, Reinsch, *An American Diplomat*, 65–66.

31. Hornbeck to Reinsch, "Notes on the Situation in China," 21 March–8 April 1913, Hornbeck Papers; Wilder to Reinsch, 15 December 1913, Reinsch Papers; editorial, *China Press*, cited in the *New York Journal of Commerce*, 19 December 1913, clipping, *ibid.*; Report of the Annual Meeting of the American Association of China, *JAAA*, XIV (March 1914), 36–37.

32. "Recollections of Willard Dickerman Straight and His Work," Straight Papers; Willard Straight, "China's Loan Negotiations," *Recent Developments in China: Clark University Addresses November 1912*, ed. George H. Blakeslee (New York, 1913), 119–62; Straight, "The Politics of Chinese Finance," *JAAA*, XIII (July 1913), 164–71; editorial, *JAAA*, XV (February 1915), 2; William J. Calhoun, "Address before the American Asiatic Association," 28 May 1913, *JAAA*, XIII (June 1913), 132–38.

33. Williams to Bryan, 21 October 1913, 693.003/44 DSNA; E. T. Williams Diary, 12 November 1913, Williams Papers; Menocal to Straight, 16 August 1913, Reinsch Papers; interview, Reinsch and Chou Tzu-ch'i, 27 November 1913, *ibid.*; Jordan to Langley, 23 February and 8 March 1914, Jordan Papers, FO 350/12; *The Times* (London), 10 January, 14 February, and 16 March 1914.

34. *FR 1912*, 64–65; Straight, "The Politics of Chinese Finance"; clipping, *Japanese Advertiser*, 25 November 1913, Reinsch Papers; Hawkins Tapes, 2, 9; Reinsch, *An American Diplomat*, 61–62.

35. Hawkins Tapes, 2, 9; clippings, *North China Daily News*, 3 November 1913, *Japanese Advertiser*, 25 November 1913, *Peking Daily News*, 10 November 1913, Reinsch Papers; Reinsch, *An American Diplomat*, 61–62.

36. See Wright, ed., *China in Revolution, passim.*

37. According to C. Martin Wilbur, Sun Yat-sen's most recent biographer, the conditions were: "that Nanking be the capital, that Yuan come there to assume the presidency, and that Yuan observe the provisional constitution then being drafted." Wilbur also stresses that virtually all Chinese leaders expected Yuan to be chosen president, if he would join the revolution against the Manchus. Sun's appointment as provisional presi-

dent was therefore understood to be temporary. C. Martin Wilbur, *Sun Yat-Sen: Frustrated Patriot* (New York, 1976), 19–23. See also, Ernest P. Young, "Yuan Shih-k'ai's Rise to the Presidency," *China in Revolution*, ed. Mary C. Wright, 419–42.

38. Williams to Bryan, 11 March 1913, 893.00/1595, 25 April 1913, 893.00/1671, 15 August 1913, 893.00/1887, 21 October 1913, 893.51/1477, 31 October 1913, 893.51/1480, 5 November 1913, 893.00/1795, DSNA; George M. Beckmann, *The Modernization of China and Japan* (New York, 1962), 223–38; Nemai Sadhan Bose, *American Attitude and Policy to the Nationalist Movement in China (1911–1921)* (Bombay, 1970), 1–54; Jerome Ch'en, *Yuan Shih-k'ai,* 2nd ed. (Stanford, 1972), 90–158; Stanley K. Hornbeck, *Contemporary Politics in the Far East* (New York, 1916), 6–16, 37, 70–84; Wilbur, *Sun Yat-Sen,* 19–27, 76–82; Edward T. Williams, *China Yesterday and Today* (New York, 1923), 203, 472–74, 487–91; Wright, ed., *China in Revolution*; George T. Yu, *Party Politics in Republican China: The Kuomintang, 1912–1924* (Berkeley & Los Angeles, 1966).

39. Hornbeck to Hawkins, 24 July 1964, Horatio Hawkins Private Papers (Albany, California); author's interview with Hawkins, 10 August 1971; author's interview with Hornbeck, 20 January 1965; Selle, *Donald of China*, 149.

Chapter V

LOST OPPORTUNITIES FOR AMERICAN ENTERPRISE

The introductions and formal ceremonies, with their hackneyed expressions of historic friendship and mutual interests, were over. By the end of November 1913, President Yuan Shi-k'ai, Premier Hsiung Hsi-ling, Foreign Minister Sun Pao-Chi, and numerous other officials had confronted Reinsch with China's plight and begged him for American assistance. Whether in his chancery or at the presidential palace and the Chinese ministries, Reinsch heard a familiar refrain. China was in desperate financial straits and the powers were strengthening and extending their spheres of influence. To preserve the Open Door and protect its own interests, the United States not only had to move boldly in concert with Great Britain and Germany, it also had to act independently. In return, China would look to the United States for guidance in administrative and constitutional affairs (the Chinese leaders sensed that these were the magic words that Reinsch, Wilson, and all Americans wanted to hear). Bemoaning the failure of Americans to "take their proper place in the development of China," the Chinese also requested American help in industrial matters. The Chinese pledged prompt action and favorable terms to American investors on several pending projects: petroleum development with Standard Oil, the Huai River Conservancy, the Bethlehem Steel contract, and currency reform. They also discussed with Reinsch a broader program of harbor and river improvements, the designation of the British-American Tobacco Company as the selling agent for a proposed Chinese government tobacco monopoly, and a host of other lucrative concessions.[1]

The Chinese officials who quietly approached Reinsch belonged to the short-lived Celebrity Cabinet (or Talented Cabinet) of 1913–1914. These able and resourceful men sought to advance China's interests: to rescue China from near bankruptcy and total dependence on the Consortium; to develop China's integrity from further encroachments; and to regain lost rights. In order to achieve their purpose, they offered a Chinese version of the Open Door and special consideration for the United States. They had serious reservations about turning to America, which had disappointed China on previous occasions and had acted so weakly in dealing with the other powers. And yet China needed some foreign assistance. Besides, the new American minister, unlike his predecessors and the private capitalists who had been offered the same or similar proposals, seemed so responsive and enthusiastic.[2]

Reinsch, indeed, was elated by the Chinese suggestions for an informal Sino-American entente. In one breath, the Chinese proposed to hand over to the United States "more far-reaching opportunities than had been offered to any other nation" at any time. As Reinsch saw it, the United States was being given a unique chance to establish itself as the dominant influence in China, to demonstrate the superiority of American enterprise, to expand American markets and bring profits to American business, and to remove the blemish of the American China Development Company. Here was further proof of Chinese faith in the United States. Here was an opportunity for America to support talented Chinese progressives and modernizers and to render China concrete assistance before it was too late. Here, too, was an excellent device to preserve the Open Door and neutralize the spheres of influence. The Chinese (and possibly the minister's cadre of advisers) suggested the strategy, but Reinsch quickly perceived its usefulness and adopted it as his own. The most effective weapon against the spheres of influence, he informed Bryan on December 2, 1913, "would lie in the acquisition of economic interest in different parts of China."

Reinsch recognized that the proposed initiative was filled with risks. American business might refuse to participate and the American Group might discourage such activity. Washington might withhold support or register opposition. The Chinese might break their promises, interfere with the projects, or merely play the United States against its foreign rivals. Indeed, Chinese officials clearly warned Reinsch that they would be "seriously disappointed if American professions of friendship were to remain without a concrete base." Finally, the powers themselves might retaliate in concert or unilaterally. But Reinsch decided to take the gamble; the stakes were high for both the United States and China and such a golden opportunity might never arise again.[3]

*   *   *

Although accurate and comprehensive surveys were lacking, oil deposits were known to exist in several Chinese provinces and small Chinese companies operated a few wells in Shensi Province. Peking officials now wanted to exploit those resources and to establish a national petroleum industry. The Chinese government also saw an opportunity to exchange a potentially valuable concession for a multimillion-dollar loan. Moreover, the involvement of a well-known American firm, such as Standard Oil, might encourage broad American interest in China.

Standard Oil had become a household word to the Chinese and, along with the YMCA, was often equated, by friend and foe alike, with American influence in China. Foreign competition, however, had forced Standard Oil to mount a counteroffensive. The introduction of the inexpensive *mei foo* lamp and the creation of an efficient distribution system, employing its own specially trained salesmen, helped the company maintain its share of the kerosene market. But the continuing economic and political advantages enjoyed by its rivals combined with the periodic shortages of American oil convinced some Standard Oil officials that it was necessary to establish an integrated petroleum industry in China based on local crude. Furthermore, the Supreme Court's dissolution of the Rockefeller empire left the Standard Oil Company of New York (SOCONY) with a sizeable domestic and foreign marketing network, but no crude. William Edward Bemis, SOCONY's leading marketing executive and director of Standard Oil's resurgence in China, was determined to launch a world-wide search for crude oil. China was high on his list.[4]

The respective needs of the Chinese government and Standard Oil led to exploratory talks during the closing days of the Manchu dynasty. On October 18, 1913, Premier Hsiung Hsi-ling made a concrete offer: Standard Oil could have monopoly rights in Shansi in exchange for a $15 million loan, which would be used to strengthen the Bank of China and to institute currency reform. Chinese insistence that Standard Oil make a large loan and bid against Japanese offers (the Chinese may not have understood that SOCONY was now an independent company with limited resources) led to an immediate impasse. SOCONY refused to play that game. It considered the exploitation of China's oil resources a straightforward business proposition, and it was unwilling to engage in the hazardous, though common, practice of buying concessions or making political loans. In November, the Chinese submitted a revised proposition, providing for a joint Sino-American company that would develop the more attractive fields in Shensi Province. SOCONY's representatives in China agreed to all of the conditions except for a cash advance of two or three million dollars to be secured by the Chinese government's shares in the company.[5]

At the beginning of 1914, while Vice President Bemis was enroute to China, Reinsch decided to involve himself directly in the negotiations. He justified the extensive involvement of the American legation on the grounds that political influence was often necessary to obtain business in China and that Standard Oil's fine reputation was at stake. "With respect to all such matters," Reinsch recalled in his memoir, "I had made up my mind that if any reputable American interest on the ground should desire to engage in some constructive work in industry or commerce, I should extend all the assistance I could properly give. The Standard Oil Company had achieved a position to be proud of." Reinsch therefore tried to prevent misunderstandings and delays, to counter the objections of foreign competitors, and to suggest counterproposals. When a tentative agreement, which he helped to formulate, fell apart because of SOCONY's resistance to making a loan, Reinsch convinced the Chinese that they would be better off dealing with an experienced American firm which had no political aims. And when the Chinese seemed to respond favorably, he persuaded SOCONY's officials to be more generous.[6]

The agreement, signed on February 10, 1914, gave SOCONY one year to explore for oil in certain districts in Shensi and Chihli, during which time the Chinese government promised not to grant oil concessions to any competitors. If commercial deposits were discovered, a Sino-American development company would be chartered in the United States and have an exclusive right, for up to sixty years, to exploit, refine, and market all petroleum produced in those provinces. SOCONY would own 55 percent of the stock in the company; the Chinese would take 37½ percent as payment for the franchise and would have a two-year option to buy the remaining shares. The Chinese government would grant the joint company the right to build pipelines and railroads necessary to transport oil and drilling equipment. It also agreed to acquire control of all land needed for development, and promised to support the company in every possible way. In return, Standard Oil pledged to send its experts immediately and to help China obtain a loan in the United States.[7]

Chinese officials were not only disappointed with the way Standard Oil did business, but they also faced numerous difficulties. Newspaper stories, planted and paid for by Japanese interests and the Asiatic Petroleum Company, charged them with giving away a valuable concession to a foreign company which had no immediate intention of developing it for China's benefit. Foreign powers, especially Japan and Britain, protested and demanded similar rights. Finally, Shensi notables were infuriated because the Peking government had nationalized oil deposits and had taken over the interests of two small companies in their province. To avoid further misrepresentations and to quiet the critics, Reinsch advised the Chinese government to publish the contract and urged Standard Oil to demonstrate good faith by inaugurating the work as quickly as possible. While Roy Anderson placated the ruffled Shensi officials, Reinsch himself persuaded the editor of the *Peking Gazette* to drop his opposition to the enterprise.[8]

Reinsch, meanwhile, quietly rejoiced in this achievement. It accorded perfectly with his plans for development of China and peaceful penetration of American enterprise. For the time being, he had blocked Japanese ambitions and Chinese intrigue. He also thought that the arrangement was equitable. Without investing its own capital, China received a share in the enterprise and a boost in the development of its resources. Standard Oil might obtain large profits as well as an important role in the Chinese economy, but such a result would be warranted by the risks it was undertaking. Moreover, the joint venture might serve as a model for other forms of Sino-American cooperation. But, aware of past American failures and the anger of SOCONY's competitors, Reinsch was determined to leave nothing to chance. He therefore stressed to SOCONY and the State Department that the contract constituted only an opportunity and a legal right, which had to be translated into "actual control of promising oil fields."

With the help of Roy Anderson, who was now employed by Standard Oil, Reinsch prepared a daring blueprint for the establishment of American predominance in the development of China's natural resources. In the provinces already granted, SOCONY should hasten to conciliate local officials and develop the most promising districts with the help of local merchants. If Shensi turned out well, SOCONY should seek similar rights in Shansi and Szechuan; but from the start it should form provincial companies with Chinese businessmen. By providing the capital, the American company would retain control while it enlisted local support and neutralized charges of monopoly and foreign domination. Since Peking was awakening to the value of its oil properties, Reinsch urged SOCONY to send out more geologists to make comprehensive mineral surveys in order to select future enterprises. In addition, SOCONY must work closely with the newly created National Oil

Administration and its director, Hsiung Hsi-ling, by attaching experts to the bureau, sending it frequent reports, and maintaining an important official (Reinsch suggested Bemis) in China, who would be authorized to make decisions. After all, Standard Oil must give the impression that it was working in the interest of China.[9]

During the following months, however, both Standard Oil and the Chinese frustrated Reinsch's plans by proving incapable of forming a real partnership. The Chinese, anxious to improve the terms of the contract, were the first to show bad faith. They failed to assist SOCONY's earnest, if ostentatious, attempts to explore for oil. Moreover, Hsiung secretly negotiated with Belgian interests for a concession that would have prevented the American company from acquiring additional lands adjacent to the Shensi oil fields. Reinsch, Anderson, and MacMurray saw a plot to prevent Standard Oil from fulfilling its agreement in time, thereby returning the enterprise to the international auction block. But the ploy failed because of British objections and the outbreak of World War I.[10]

A greater threat, however, was the disparity of views on the development company, which reflected the different aspirations of Standard Oil and the Chinese. Envisaging the creation of a national oil industry that would produce and market crude oil and refined products, the Chinese wanted the development company to be a large enterprise, capitalized at perhaps $100 million. Standard Oil rejected the Chinese plan, for it naturally had no desire to undermine its profitable distribution business. Instead, it regarded the proposed joint enterprise as a producing and pipeline company, supplying crude to SOCONY which would then refine and market oil products through its own system. Consequently, it foresaw a Sino-American development company which might be initially capitalized at $1 million. Then, as additional capital was needed, the company would borrow money from Standard Oil. Conceived in this manner, Standard Oil would gain access to crude oil in the Far East and it would minimize its capital investment. The Chinese considered SOCONY's plan a preposterous and insulting violation of the spirit, if not the letter, of the original agreement, and pressed for the larger enterprise. Peking could not allow Standard Oil to retain the most profitable part of the operation, nor could it permit the development company to become a mere subsidiary of the American firm. The Chinese demanded a share in all of the profits and a chance to develop Chinese industry and technology.[11]

The negotiations were also complicated by the recurrent delays caused by the need of SOCONY's representatives to refer every question to New York. Reinsch, who continuously pleaded with American companies to send their "big men" to conduct business in China, thought the Chinese correct in demanding that SOCONY send an official with power to make decisions. Warning that foreign rivals were still active, Reinsch bluntly told Bryan, on April 5, 1915, that he would not help the company obtain a further extension of its option unless it changed its methods, sent an authorized representative, and negotiated in the spirit of the 1914 agreement.[12]

Reinsch's telegram jarred SOCONY sufficiently to bring Bemis back to China in June 1915. In a conference with Reinsch, Bemis agreed to discuss the larger project desired by the Chinese, including a national refinery, provided that Standard Oil would be designated as the sales agent for the Sino-American development company. Reinsch considered Bemis's plan reasonable, for SOCONY would protect its organization and share in the marketing profits only through its interest in the joint company. And he thought that it might be acceptable to the Chinese if they were assured a fair share of the profits and the right to control future development. He therefore proposed a provison for an adequate auditing system and an agreement to renegotiate the marketing system when domestic oil constituted 50 percent of SOCONY's sales in China.[13]

Since Reinsch was about to leave for the United States, he also warned Bemis about the complicated political situation in China and the existence of a bitter feud between Hsiung and Chou Tzu-ch'i. Hsiung had never liked Bemis and had conspired with foreign interests against SOCONY; he was now more interested in demonstrating his concern for Chinese interests than in having the project succeed. His appointment as director-general of the National Oil Administration was partly designed to get him out of the cabinet, and he had only limited political influence. Chou, on the other hand, had fathered the project from the start, had often been the only cabinet member to maintain faith in American help-fulness, and shared Reinsch's dream of Sino-American economic cooperation. Reinsch considered him one of the true progressives who ought to be courted and encouraged. Reinsch therefore instructed Bemis to rely on Chou, even if it meant antagonizing Hsiung.[14]

On June 19, 1915, Bemis submitted his plan for the larger enterprise, incorporating Reinsch's modifications of the marketing agreement. However, he proposed that the development company begin business with a capital investment of $7 million Mex. and borrow additional funds from SOCONY at 6 percent interest.[15] The Chinese turned down Bemis's proposal. They were still determined to establish a national refinery immediately and wanted to be free to replace imported oil as rapidly as domestic production would permit. The Chinese vigorously

objected to the small amount of the initial capitalization and contemp-
tuously dismissed the loan provision "as a childish trick to make the
proposed company a debtor to the Standard Oil Company even before it
had gotten started as a going concern."[16]

A crisis was reached at the end of July. With some justification,
Bemis angrily pointed out that the Chinese introduced new terms that
conflicted with the original agreement. He called off the stalemated negotiations on the larger project and, in a burst of temper, Bemis told the
Chinese that, unless they gave him a "square deal," he would "queer" the
Chinese government in the American money market. With MacMurray's
assistance, an understanding was apparently reached on August 5, 1915.
Two days later, however, the Chinese repudiated the agreement, probably because political considerations forced the negotiators to seek better
terms. With MacMurray's cognizance, Bemis postponed further talks
but reserved the company's rights under the agreement of February
1914.[17]

The Chinese now realized that they had gone too far. On August 10,
the Ministry for Foreign Affairs intervened and asked MacMurray to
reopen the negotiations. MacMurray feared exceeding his authority and
did not relish further dealings with Bemis. But the chargé also felt that
he had to avoid another American fiasco in China and to prevent the
enterprise from falling into the hands of America's jealous rivals. Moreover, haste was required to take advantage of Yuan's direct interest in the
matter and Hsiung's declining influence. Furthermore, Chou was planning to retire to a provincial post and his successor might be less friendly
to American interests. MacMurray therefore agreed to help if the Chinese
would negotiate sincerely on the basis of the original Reinsch-Bemis
proposal.[18]

The Chinese accepted MacMurray's terms, but Bemis adopted an
uncompromising attitude and announced plans to return to the United
States. He claimed that the Chinese were merely seeking a face-saving
device to conceal their incompetence and to place the onus for breaking
off the talks on Standard Oil. "They are 'stringing' you," he insisted,
"they are trying to make you, as representing the American Government, believe that it is Mr. Bemis who is responsible for the failure."
MacMurray retorted that if Bemis shut the door, he could only conclude
that it was the American company "which had failed to make good on a
showdown . . . and which had laid itself open to the imputation of not
really having meant business."[19]

Meanwhile, MacMurray urged the State Department to impress
upon Standard Oil the significance of Bemis's decision and suggested

that Reinsch visit the company's headquarters. Reinsch called on SOCONY executives and was told that the negotiations were merely suspended pending further explorations in Shensi. In fact, they later informed the State Department that they were fully satisfied with Bemis's handling of the matter.[20]

Upon his return to Peking, Reinsch found the Chinese filled with bitter disappointment. Despite his preference for Americans, Chou now felt free to negotiate with British and Dutch companies which had been badgering the Chinese for months. Reinsch and MacMurray then requested the State Department to approach other oil companies. However, none of the independents showed any interest and SOCONY was content to leave the matter in abeyance. In April 1917, SOCONY and the Chinese government mutually agreed to cancel the contract of February 1914.[21]

Why did the Standard Oil enterprise fail? The Wilson administration gave its full cooperation and diplomatic support to the extent that it even countenanced a temporary exclusive sales agency for SOCONY.[22] The American legation went much further to ensure its success and to advance Reinsch's larger goal of establishing American predominance in the exploitation of China's resources. Reinsch and MacMurray tendered advice, mediated disputes, coaxed SOCONY, and pressured the Chinese. Reinsch practically wrote the agreement of 1914 and MacMurray had a hand in the final proposals of August 1915.[23]

The Chinese, awakening to the value of their natural resources, proved to be tough bargainers and often played Standard Oil against foreign rivals. On the other hand, Chinese officials practiced outright deception and often made outrageous demands which violated the 1914 agreement with Standard Oil. Chinese political intrigue interfered with the negotiations and sometimes forced Chou, who probably wanted the project to succeed, to take an extreme position. The intervention of President Yuan and the Ministry for Foreign Affairs in August 1915, suggests that some of the intrigue could have been checked. The personality conflicts, emphasized by MacMurray in his dispatches to Washington, further complicated matters. Chou understandably became very bitter with Bemis's behavior, all the more so because he was ridiculed by his colleagues and even twitted by the president. Having lost "face," he took a hard stand in the negotiations to prove that he was not selling out to American exploiters. Bemis also intimated that the "final factor" that influenced his decision to go home was the reported refusal of both Hsiung and Chou to attend his elaborately planned farewell dinner.

Standard Oil, however, must shoulder most of the blame. Bemis labored under severe difficulties: he had to straighten out the company's tangled affairs in north China, protect SOCONY's sales organization, and cope with the Chinese political situation. Most important, since the Chinese venture was largely the result of his enthusiasm, Bemis had to prove to SOCONY that he was correct in risking so much capital and effort. Nevertheless, Bemis magnified the problems. From the beginning of the negotiations he had been overbearing, aloof, defensive, and tactless; he rarely gave the Chinese a chance to clear up misunderstandings and he lost patience with the Chinese manner of bargaining. For the Chinese, the formation of close personal relationships was an essential part of doing business and because of the political infighting it was especially important for preliminary conferences to be informal without committing agreements to paper. In addition, SOCONY resented the intrusion of the American legation and the State Department, failed to confide in American officials and ignored their advice. Moreover, disregarding Reinsch's emphatic warning, Bemis befriended Hsiung and ignored Chou.

Finally, SOCONY terminated the joint enterprise because, by the summer of 1915, it had virtually decided to abandon Bemis's expensive and unsuccessful efforts to locate foreign crude. Thus, in the final stages of the negotiations, Bemis was bluffing and attempted to cast the blame on the Chinese in order to escape both public ridicule and Washington's condemnation. MacMurray suspected as much when Bemis accidentally blurted out, "I won't let them [the Chinese] say they called Mr. Bemis's bluff." Although the company never admitted it, Reinsch correctly concluded from his conversations in New York that SOCONY had decided to confine its Chinese operations to the marketing of imported refined products. Bemis, physically exhausted and broken in spirit, died of a heart attack in November 1915, and SOCONY sought to resolve its problems by acquiring oil-producing companies.[24]

It is unlikely, however, that even the discovery of large oil deposits would have led to a successful joint enterprise. Although Reinsch may have prevented misunderstandings and hastened Yuan's intervention, it is also doubtful if his presence in China during the summer of 1915 would have made any difference. Reinsch's conception of Sino-American cooperation—the marrying of profitable American investment with rapid Chinese development—was simply too advanced for the times and demanded too much of both Standard Oil and the Chinese government, which were absorbed in solving their immediate problems.

*   *   *

A similar fate awaited Reinsch's attempt to rescue the Bethlehem Steel contract. In October 1911, the Chinese government and the Bethlehem Steel Company signed a $20 million agreement to modernize the Chinese navy. Most of the funds were to be spent on the construction of modern naval vessels, thereby ensuring large profits to Bethlehem Steel's armorplate division. But at the insistence of Chinese authorities, a small portion was to be allocated to the improvement of dockyards and arsenals. In order to assist the American company in meeting foreign competition, the Taft administration also agreed to provide secret American naval equipment and to train Chinese naval personnel. Both parties obviously considered the contract as a preliminary agreement and many of the provisions were deliberately left vague. From the start Bethlehem Steel intended to renegotiate the financing provisions, but it wanted first to nail down a Chinese commitment in the face of Chinese orders with British and German firms. China viewed the matter largely in political terms: it desired to involve the United States in the balance of power while belatedly creating a modern navy of its own.[25]

The Chinese Revolution and the ensuing confusion had forestalled the execution of the contract. And by the fall of 1913, when the Chinese repeatedly raised the matter with the American legation, the situation had become vastly more complicated. The United States Department of the Navy had serious reservations about supplying confidential equipment to the Chinese navy, which made Peking anxious to obtain reassurances that the Wilson administration would honor its predecessor's commitments. British maneuvers to obtain the shipbuilding contract forced Bethlehem Steel to send Archibald Johnston, its senior vice president, to China to safeguard the company's interests. In addition, Bethlehem Steel wanted Johnston to substitute payment in Consortium Reorganization Loan bonds for unsecured Chinese bonds, which would be virtually impossible to float in the United States. Meanwhile, Japan's efforts to consolidate its sphere of influence in Fukien Province threatened the most likely site for the contemplated drydock facility. Reinsch and Williams questioned the wisdom of spending so much money on the navy when China had more essential needs. But they decided to support the project because it would boost American export industries, strengthen equal opportunity, and block the revival of the spheres of influence.[26]

To counter Japanese objections, Reinsch and Chou Tzu-ch'i cleverly modified the agreement to provide for the construction of merchant ships convertible into cruisers. These vessels would be used by steamship lines serving the United States and China until Peking might be in a stronger position to launch a regular naval program. Viewing the

Bethlehem Steel contract and the use of naval expenditures as means to increase government revenue (otherwise the navy was a burden on the treasury), the Celebrity Cabinet authorized negotiations with Johnston on the basis of the 1911 contract. In addition, it requested (and Reinsch apparently approved) that Johnston and Commander Irvin D. Gillis, the United States naval attaché in China, go to Fukien to survey potential locations for a naval base and prepare estimates of development costs. But then, after ignoring his correspondence for several weeks, the Chinese informed Johnston that they had decided to postpone implementing the 1911 contract. Internal political problems, China's deepening financial crisis and, above all, Japanese pressure forced the Peking government to abandon plans for both naval vessels and a naval base.[27]

The Japanese, nevertheless, used the opportunity to strengthen their claims to special rights in Fukien, which they based on a vague non-alienation agreement signed in 1898. Japanese agents produced and circulated in China a spurious contract providing for a $30 million loan by Bethlehem Steel to construct a naval base in Fukien. Reinsch alerted the State Department to his suspicions that the contract was a forgery. A quick check indicated that the Chinese had no knowledge of such a contract, which was totally incompatible with the decision of the Peking government to avoid inciting Japan. Reinsch knew that Bethlehem Steel had no real interest in naval base construction since most of the money would go to subcontractors. The authors of the forgery had also been sloppy: Johnston was on his way back to the United States on March 9, 1914, the day the contract was supposedly signed in Foochow.

Reinsch allowed for the possibility of intrigue in the Ministry of Marine, but theorized that the Japanese were behind the contract. He speculated that Japan was either launching a trial balloon to gather further information about the Bethlehem Steel negotiations, or was seeking an excuse to assert "her special interests and rights in the Province of Fukien." Indeed, MacMurray later found irrefutable evidence that the Japanese invented the story of the contract and used an American newspaperman, William P. Giles, to spread the story. And the Japanese motive, as Reinsch correctly guessed, was to find a pretext to insert in the Twenty-One Demands of 1915 a demand for special interests in Fukien.[28]

However, in his desire to accommodate Chinese officials, to maintain American influence, and to block Japanese moves into Fukien and the Yangtze region, Reinsch deliberately failed to inform the State Department about Johnston's survey for the Ministry of Marine. Thus, when he was forced to reply to the formal inquiry made by Japanese

Ambassador Chinda Sutemi, Bryan could deny the authenticity of the contract but he had to acknowledge American involvement in the naval base planning. Bryan also instructed Reinsch to advise the Chinese that the construction of a naval base in Fukien "would be highly objectionable to Japan and would therefore be unwise." It is unclear if the secretary of state acted out of ignorance, naiveté, or a desire to placate the Japanese. In any event, Reinsch was greatly upset by Bryan's acquiescence in Japan's unwarranted pretensions to a sphere of influence in Fukien. It was plainly contrary to the principle of equal opportunity, it endangered American rights and Chinese sovereignty, and it undermined Chinese confidence in the United States. Citing his previous positions on the Open Door, which had been supported by the State Department, Reinsch told Bryan that, unless he received further instructions, he would avoid any action that might compromise the Chinese government.[29]

On the other hand, the State Department ordered Reinsch to protect American interests against British attempts to secure the employment of British naval advisers and shipbuilding contracts. Under no circumstances would the State and Navy Departments tolerate the use of British naval officers, especially if secret equipment were provided on American built ships. The Chinese argued that educational assistance by both British and American officers on separate ships was not incompatible; but they also admitted to Reinsch that the matter had been confused because different Chinese officials had conducted the concurrent negotiations with the United States and Britain. Reinsch correctly divined that the Chinese reasons were two-fold. First of all, they felt they would be in a stronger position to refuse Japanese instructors if they could point to an agreement with Britain than if they turned to the United States alone. In addition, the Chinese were undoubtedly right in questioning the amount of political support they could get from the United States in such a sensitive matter.

United States pressure forced the Chinese to cancel their agreement with the British, but neither Reinsch nor MacMurray could secure a written commitment from Peking that gave the United States an exclusive right to train the Chinese navy. Reinsch still tried to keep the Bethlehem Steel contract alive. Eventually, he recognized the force of China's fears of Tokyo's opposition and the inability of the United States to protect China from Japanese retaliation. Therefore, Reinsch reluctantly concluded that the best thing was to leave the matter in abeyance while he obtained assurances that the Bethlehem Steel contract would take precedence over any other. Despite Bethlehem Steel's desire to arrive at a

more definite arrangement with the Chinese, the State Department concurred in Reinsch's position.[30]

Archibald Johnston blamed both the British and insufficient American diplomatic support for the failure to execute Bethlehem Steel's contract. That interpretation was too simplistic. The situation was complicated by political considerations within China and among the powers.
Reinsch, sometimes supported by the State Department, did his best to
get the business for Bethlehem Steel and, above all, to protect America's
long-range economic interests and China's sovereignty.

*   *   *

Of all of the projects proposed by the Chinese to Reinsch in the fall of
1913, none excited his imagination more than the Huai River Conservancy. For centuries, portions of central China in Honan, Anhui,
Kiangsu, and Shantung Provinces, north of the Huai River and Hungtze
Lake and south of the new bed of the Yellow River, had been ravaged by
repeated floods and subsequent famines. The American National Red
Cross, which had provided famine relief in the afflicted area, sent an
American engineer to China in 1912 to design a plan to prevent future
floods. Charles D. Jameson studied the affected provinces and offered
concrete suggestions for handling the discharge of the Huai and related
streams and for draining lakes and swamps. Subsequently, Jameson
submitted a detailed scheme for financing the project, estimated to cost
$20 million, through a foreign loan, guaranteed by the Chinese govern-
ment and secured by the sale of reclaimed land and benefit taxes in the
conservancy district.[31]

In spite of the moral and political support of the Taft administration, the efforts of the Red Cross to raise a loan in the United States,
general American enthusiasm, and the promise of permanent relief, a
full year passed without any visible progress. The withdrawal of the
United States from the Consortium and the delay in naming a new
minister to China weakened the hand of the Red Cross. At the same
time, Peking's financial stringency combined with the American
Group's growing disinterest in China cast a shadow on the financial side
of the project. The situation encouraged foreign competition, which
appeared in the form of a Belgian syndicate which dangled an attractive
offer before provincial authorities.[32]

Meanwhile, Chinese internal affairs intruded in the person of
Chang Chien. Chang Chien had served as minister of agriculture and
commerce in various Peking cabinets. But he was better known as a
pioneer industrialist, a leading spokesman for gentry rather than gov-

ernment participation in business, and a political power in his native province of Kiangsu. Having in mind both the potential for personal profit as well as relief for his own people, Chang had developed his own ambitious plans for flood control, land reclamation, and agricultural development banks. Typical of the provincial mandarinate, however, Chang was paternalistic, mixed private and public business, feared Peking's tendency to centralize power and resented Western claims to superiority almost as much as demands for foreign control. He therefore regarded Jameson and the Red Cross as interlopers, claimed a preference for Dutch engineers over Americans and encouraged a Belgian syndicate to bid for the financing of the project. And to ensure himself the final voice in the enterprise, Chang secured the creation of the National Water Conservancy Board and his own appointment, in 1913, as director-general.

Red Cross officials and Jameson, however, exacerbated the situation. They regarded Chang Chien as an ignorant obstructionist, a notorious grafter, and a stubborn professional philanthropist. Having left a trail of failures in railroading and mining, Jameson desperately attempted to rescue his tarnished reputation and fortune. He had also offended the Chinese through his overbearing treatment of Chinese subordinates and his disparaging article on China, written for *The Outlook*. It was obvious that Chang and Jameson regarded each other as rivals and were unable to work together. Nevertheless, the Red Cross insisted that the conservancy work be made a national matter, that provision be made for strict financial security, and that Jameson be given full supervision of the project. Red Cross and State Department officials thereby indicated their distrust of Chinese integrity, sincerity, and ability as well as their insensitivity to Chinese internal affairs and their fear that Jameson's removal and the strengthening of Chang's position would enable foreign interests to take over a project that had been identified with American influence and humanitarianism.[33]

By the end of 1913, the outlook for the Huai River Conservancy brightened considerably. The new United States minister was committed to its success and he would serve as a catalyst between the Red Cross and the Chinese leaders, who now favored prompt action by American interests. The Huai River Conservancy—half commercial, half humanitarian—accorded perfectly with Reinsch's belief in the non-political nature of American enterprise in China. It was the essence of concrete and practical American aid which the Chinese desired and needed. Because of the existence of adequate security, it was also a sound business investment for American lenders. Furthermore, it would demonstrate to the Chinese the efficacy of science and technology and would thus serve as a reference point or model for the greater transformation of China. Reinsch stressed the significance of the Huai River project in terms of his vision of a modern, prosperous China. Thus he wrote enthusiastically to Mabel Boardman, the head of the National Relief Board of The American Red Cross:

> I may state to you, as I have said to the Department of State and to the President, that there is no undertaking at present proposed in China which equals in importance and significance the Huai River improvement. . . . The reason for this lies in the fact that the work would be a demonstration to the Chinese mind that through modern scientific methods honestly applied the fundamental conditions of existence may be radically modified. No other enterprise could impress the Chinese mind so vividly with the true meaning of the word PROGRESS. The work would therefore be a model for scientific method and organization as applied throughout Chinese life.

Recalling America's past failures and his own plans for permanent American influence in China, Reinsch hoped that the Huai River Conservancy would vindicate to all "the efficiency of American methods in the organization of large engineering enterprises."[34]

Chang Chien was primarily interested in gaining access to American capital for his projects without incurring American control. Nevertheless, he offered Reinsch American participation in his comprehensive system of river, harbor, and conservancy work (particularly in north China and Manchuria) and development banks. Jameson thought that this grandiose scheme was a ploy by Chang to kill the Huai project, and he feared that Reinsch, a novice in Chinese affairs, would be taken in by Chang's professions of friendship for the United States. Indeed, Chang was still trying to negotiate a loan with Belgian and British syndicates.[35]

Reinsch and Jameson concluded that they had to press the Chinese to give the Huai Conservancy project to the United States. They therefore asked for a twelve- to eighteen-month option, which would give the Americans enough time to raise a loan and organize a construction company. Reinsch played on Chinese fears that the Belgians had ulterior political and economic motives. He also stressed the difficulty in floating a conservancy loan; it was only the humanitarian aspect—the association of the Red Cross—that offered any hope for a loan at a reasonable rate of interest. He coaxed the Chinese and argued every point. And it worked.[36]

On January 14, 1914, after conducting painstaking negotiations with Chang and other officials ("Every sentence . . . had been weighed, every word carefully chosen; . . ."), Reinsch reported to Washington that agreement had been reached on a preliminary contract. The Chinese gave the Red Cross one year to effect a G$20 million loan, with interest fixed at 5 percent, for conservancy work in Kiangsu and Anhui provinces. The loan was secured through the anticipated revenue from the sale of reclaimed land and a conservancy tax on all lands benefited by the work. The American Red Cross would nominate an expert hydraulics engineer to serve as engineer-in-chief. Finally, Reinsch and Chang laid down the principle that all disbursements would require the approval of both the managing director (probably Chinese) and the engineer-in-chief (American).[37]

Reinsch stressed the need for an early decision and asked the State Department for authority to sign the option. He pointed out that the Red Cross incurred no obligation beyond extending its good offices to secure a reputable contractor and competent engineers and to arrange a loan. On the other hand, the Chinese were only partially resigned to a long option and they still doubted the ability of Americans to act decisively. Reinsch also feared that American procrastination, combined with Chinese weakness, would force Peking to yield to foreign pressure. Reinsch knew that the situation was particularly dangerous, for he had found evidence of a Belgian-French-Russian plan to take up the conservancy work as a prelude to demanding railway concessions in central China. This had political overtones as well, for it contemplated linking Siberian lines to the sea through central China and establishing a powerful European sphere of influence. This consideration led Reinsch to suggest somewhat later that the United States obtain rail concessions in the Huai region. But Reinsch's greatest worry was that Americans would simply abandon the project. The withdrawal from the Huai River Conservancy, which had been so prominently associated with America's name, he warned, would be considered "by Chinese and foreigners alike as a renunciation of opportunities to assist in the development of China."[38]

The State Department assured Reinsch that the matter was under serious consideration by the Red Cross and the administration. Mabel Boardman, who had adopted the Huai Conservancy as a personal crusade, had already contacted leading banking houses and had confirmed Reinsch's information that J. G. White & Co. would handle the construction on a cost plus 10 percent basis. She also secured the unanimous approval of the Executive Committee and the International Relief Board for the Red Cross's cooperative role.[39]

In Peking, meanwhile, events progressed faster than Washington realized. Reinsch and Chang had concluded a final draft of the preliminary agreement on January 21, 1914. Reinsch was now in a quandary. He was tempted to sign the agreement immediately to avoid further delays and to preclude any demand to renegotiate the contract. On the other hand, he lacked authority to act on his own. At first he was inclined to proceed unilaterally. Then, nervous about the consequences, he changed his mind. On January 23, 1914, Reinsch wired the text to the State Department and requested power to sign the agreement on behalf of the Red Cross. On January 27 (Peking time), he informed Washington that, unless he was instructed to delay, he would accept the one-year preemption on the following day, when he was to see President Yuan. "Otherwise," he explained to Bryan, "it may be impossible to hold up action conflicting with our best interests in the matter." Reinsch learned of the Red Cross's favorable decision on January 28 (January 27, in Washington); but Bryan's cable did not contain any specific authorization for him to sign the protocol. Although Reinsch may have acted earlier (Reinsch mentions January 27 in his memoir), he reported on January 30, 1914, that he and the Chinese ministers had just signed the Huai River Conservancy memorandum.[40]

In this way, the first phase of the Huai Conservancy negotiations was brought to a successful conclusion. The inability of the Chinese to raise the money elsewhere and their fear of foreign political control certainly made them more willing to accede to the American terms. But Reinsch deserves much of the credit. It was he, rather than Jameson or any other representative of the Red Cross, who negotiated the preliminary agreement. Jameson was still *persona non grata* to Chang and it is doubtful if anyone else could have secured better terms from the Chinese. Reinsch stressed those points as well as the importance of the project to the United States to justify his personal intervention.

In any event, exercising tact, persuasiveness, and occasional pressure, Reinsch obtained a long-term commitment to reserve the business for American interests. To make the loan attractive to American bankers and to keep the borrowing costs as low as possible, Reinsch secured adequate security and a guarantee by the central government. He blocked Chang's attempt to siphon off funds for an agricultural and commercial bank and limited America's initial involvement in conservancy work to the area south of the Great Wall. And to satisfy the Red Cross, Reinsch even won a promise to employ Jameson as an adviser on the project.

Above all, he handled Chang superbly. He won the mandarin's confidence and, arguing that the agricultural bank was premature and unnecessarily complicated the conservancy plan, he persuaded him to postpone it. Reinsch took into account Chang's considerable, though declining, influence in Peking; Chang was on his way out as minister of commerce and agriculture, but he was also director-general of the National Conservancy Bureau. More important, he was a power in Kiangsu, and his support there could be crucial. In addition, Reinsch respected Chang as one of China's devoted economic reformers, an important industrialist and a sincere patriot who wanted to help his people. Reinsch had his own reservations about Chang, but he did not brand him a crook. Rather, he viewed Chang as an old school mandarin who saw political office as personal opportunity, who was loose and devious in financial accounting, who was inclined toward large general programs, and who was ineffectual with the detailed problems of administration.

Reinsch therefore sought to protect American interests and had no illusions about Chinese methods. He maintained that, without disturbing the *amour propre* of the Chinese, Chang and his colleagues could be watched and guided by the American experts in charge of the project. He even argued that the Chinese should participate in the construction company and in subcontracting and that the Americans should make allowance for some "unnecessary expenditures." Only in that way could the Americans obtain the full cooperation of the Chinese and prevent the "organized form of 'squeeze' which would be practiced against any foreign organization not thus allied with the Chinese." That might not sit well with American businessmen, but that was the reality of life in the Orient. On the other hand, Reinsch was just as adamant as the New York bankers in demanding that the final agreement protect the security and the value of the bonds. [41]

But Reinsch must also bear the responsibility for withholding information, acting without authorization, and presenting the State Department and the Red Cross with a *fait accompli*. MacMurray was highly critical of Reinsch's conduct and thought that he had panicked unnecessarily. Clearly, Reinsch took things into his own hands. But that was how he operated when a crucial matter was at stake. In this instance, Reinsch felt that American prestige in the Far East, the reconstruction of China, and the future of the spheres of influence hung in the balance. When it was all over, Reinsch was confident that he had been correct in signing a written protocol committing the Chinese and the Americans to the project. After all, he had nationalized the conservancy work and conciliated Chang, he had fended off foreign rivals, he had gotten a "square deal" for China and he had laid the basis for its economic and technological development. Above all, he had preserved American influence and had given the United States the fullest opportunity to demonstrate what it could do in China.

Furthermore, the Red Cross did not complain or renege; nor did the State Department rebuke him. In fact, both the Wilson administration and the American Red Cross seemed pleased with his achievement and hastened to implement it. Washington endorsed the project and commended the loan to American bankers, though President Wilson entered the caveat that "these good offices would not go to the extent to which some Governments have gone in seeking to enforce the rights of their nationals in the matter of contracts." Moreover, with the cooperation of the administration and the Red Cross, a team of experts was quickly sent to China to make additional surveys and, possibly, to begin directing the engineering work.[42]

The financing of the Huai River Conservancy, however, remained the most difficult problem and, eventually, proved to be insurmountable. J. P. Morgan, Wall Street's leading investment banker, was reluctant to get involved in any Chinese business. But he promised Boardman, the daughter of a prominent Cleveland banker, that he would give the matter serious consideration if the contractors were definitely found, if the bonds were good, and if the market conditions were favorable. Expressing greater optimism, Willard Straight considered the scheme filled with "great promise" and "perhaps . . . the bridge over which we can enter once again upon Chinese business." One of his primary concerns, however, was financing the project through a method that was mutually acceptable to the Chinese and the bankers. Straight appreciated the necessity of "saving China's face." But to reassure the bondholders, he suggested to Reinsch the creation of a foreign-directed Reclamation Service that would administer the hypothecated revenue.[43]

Without dismissing Straight's proposals for issuing the loan, Reinsch countered with an alternative of floating two $10 million installments, each three years apart. Anxious to maintain the interest of the bankers, however, he offered to obtain additional security. Reinsch mentioned the possibility of acquiring the land tax or of having the provinces of Kiangsu and Anhui guarantee the interest payments during the construction stages. He also tried to make Straight's proposal for another foreign-dominated service as attractive as possible to the Chinese and the State Department. He argued that, in addition to collecting the hypothecated revenues, such an organization could introduce other useful work in the Huai River area and elsewhere in China. As expected, the State Department gave the proposal only lukewarm support. In order to make the conservancy work more attractive to the bankers, Reinsch

returned with another suggestion: he would try to get preferential consideration for all rail lines which the Chinese government might want to
build with foreign capital in the Huai region. That would not only protect American interests, but would also lure the bankers who would be
attracted to the more profitable railway concessions. The idea may have
come originally from James A. Thomas, who also suggested it in a letter
to Straight. In a desperate attempt to preserve the enterprise for the
United States, however, Reinsch decided to adopt the methods of his
foreign rivals by proposing the creation of an American sphere of influence in the Huai region as well as the addition of another foreign-
dominated service.[44]

By the end of September 1914, the American engineers completed
their investigations. They reported that the project was entirely feasible
and that the reclaimed land would more than pay for the entire cost of the
work. The preliminary report "makes this enterprise even more attractive than I had anticipated," a jubilant Reinsch wrote to Bryan, and
when executed, "this work will be the greatest credit to the American
name."[45]

The bankers, however, were still unwilling and unable to float a
loan for the entire project, now estimated to cost $30 million. First, the
lingering recession raised doubts that the bankers could sell all of the
bonds in the United States. Then, to make matters worse, Chang Chien
dissented from some of the recommendations of the American experts; if
these were included in the final report, the bankers would probably reject
the entire project. But the overriding obstacle was the shattering effect of
World War I on international finance. The war would make it exceedingly difficult to raise funds for this project and for other enterprises in
China.[46]

The Red Cross therefore concluded that the best solution was to
seek an extension of the option. Reinsch, however, was unwilling to
postpone the matter and persisted in his efforts to obtain financing for the
project. He admitted that conditions were unfavorable, but argued that
smaller amounts could be raised over a period of years as the conservancy
work progressed. "When the European warring nations are spending
every day an amount equal to the proposed loan," he wrote to Boardman,
"it would seem that it should be possible to find this amount for one of
the greatest works of peace and human betterment ever planned." Carrying his appeal directly to Wilson in a personal letter, Reinsch explained
the Chinese viewpoint as well as his own feelings: "America is looked
upon as so rich and powerful that she could accomplish anything she
really desires; and yet this rich and powerful friend is appealed to in vain

to give even the slightest practical assistance to help China to help herself."[47]

Because of its educational and medical work in China, Reinsch and Boardman turned to the Rockefeller Foundation. But they were informed that its relief efforts in Europe and other commitments prevented it from taking an interest in the Huai project. Consequently, the Red Cross, on January 20, 1915, asked Reinsch to obtain a renewal of the option. The Chinese themselves realized that they could not get the money elsewhere and thus they agreed to a one-year extension of the option. The project had largely foundered because of the inability to obtain an American loan, and the immediate prospects were not encouraging.[48]

*   *   *

Ever since China had been opened to Western capital in the 1890s, railroad concessions and railway politics had posed the greatest threats to the Open Door. Railway contracts were valued by the foreign powers and their chosen banking and construction groups for narrow economic reasons: they offered fat profits for construction, materials, and mining development along the right of way, large commissions and discounts for floating the bonds, and markets for industrial goods. They also meant political leverage. This was implemented through provisions for policing the rail lines and by preferential treatment for economic and other concessions in the terminal cities, ports, and the surrounding countryside. In short, they served as the basis for the spheres of influence and became intimately related to international rivalries and alliance systems.

The renewed scramble for railway concessions in the fall of 1913 frightened the Chinese. Even the British, on whom the Chinese often relied to maintain their integrity, adopted a "moderate" policy of sphere of influence. They therefore asked Williams and, later, Reinsch for assistance which would establish the United States as a counterweight, particularly in north China and Manchuria. The Chinese specifically suggested that the United States exercise its option for the Chinchou-Aigun railway, the American alternative to the Knox Neutralization scheme. Under the contract granted in 1909, this major trunk line, stretching across Manchuria from the Liaotung Gulf to the Amur River, was to be financed by the American Group and constructed by the British firm of Pauling & Co. Since London was prepared to respect Russian and Japanese predominance north of the Great Wall in return for their recognition of a British sphere of influence in central China, Pauling & Co.

was willing to accept Japanese financing as long as it received the construction work. The burden therefore fell squarely on the United States. Before leaving Peking, Williams argued that the United States ought to protect this "national asset" and use the opportunity to "reaffirm, in a practical way, the policy of the open door, and endeavor to prevent a return to the dangerous and obnoxious policy of 'spheres of influence.'"[49]

Reinsch grasped the importance of the issue and was prepared to carry out Williams's challenge. But then the Chinese government, the American Group and the State Department proceeded to undermine his efforts. Peking, which was doubtful of American support, hedged on its recognition of American claims. Having no desire to incite Japan and no intention of developing the concession in the near future, American bankers offered either to combine or cooperate with Japanese financial interests. Finally, Washington, which feared it was being placed in the position of "pulling Chinese chestnuts out of the fire in Manchuria," essentially wrote off the three eastern provinces as a Japanese sphere. Consequently, Reinsch was stuck with an empty gesture and the Japanese succeeded, with little difficulty, in blocking America's feeble attempts to develop the concession.[50]

The Wilson administration, however, adopted a different stand on the struggle for equal opportunity in the Hukuang Railways, the all-important trunk system linking Canton with the large and unexploited province of Szechuan via the Yangtze port and industrial center of Hankow. The American Group and its European counterparts floated the $30 million Hukuang Railway loan in June 1911, but local opposition and the Chinese Revolution delayed any work until 1913. To facilitate construction and to minimize jealousies, the Hukuang Loan Agreement of 1911 created "national" sections, in which the work would be directed by a chief engineer from one of the Consortium powers. Nevertheless, the agreement provided for open competition and complete equality of treatment for supply orders and construction contracts. In practice, equal treatment never prevailed since the German chief engineer and especially the British chief engineer favored their nationals and discriminated against American goods. There were several reasons why the American position was so weak. First, the Europeans were backed by powerful financial groups; second, the British and Germans organized purchasing agencies and the Americans and French did not; and third, American standards differed greatly from those used in Europe. Moreover, work had begun on the British section (Canton–Hankow) while the Americans were only beginning to survey their section (Ichang–Kueichoufu) which, incidentally, passed through the most difficult terrain. Here was a matter involving profits for American bankers and manufacturers and, in addition, the principle of the Open Door. Therefore, the American Group, supported fully by the State Department, demanded rigorous adherence to the letter and spirit of the principle of equal opportunity.[51]

Reinsch's initial suggestion that all specifications be standardized was rejected by the British on the grounds that it was too time-consuming and impractical. Further study of the complex problem convinced Reinsch that it was impossible to reach an agreement on standards or on guaranteeing impartiality. Reluctantly, Reinsch concluded that each section would be supplied largely from its own national market. To reduce tensions, therefore, he advised the State Department that without formally acknowledging any "derogation of the ideal of equal opportunity of all sections" the United States should protest "only in the case of such specifications in the indents as are palpably of a merely discriminatory character and not based upon differences of sound engineering methods."[52]

The outbreak of World War I created an entirely new situation. On the one hand, it raised the question of the disposition of the German section. More important to the United States, it prevented the raising of additional funds. Consequently, Reinsch agreed with American bankers and the State Department to concentrate all efforts on the completion of the British section, which would provide a vital link between Canton and Hankow and supply the revenues needed to service the bonds. Under the changed circumstances, Reinsch demanded the removal of the British chief engineer and the withholding of American funds until an agreement was reached on engineering standards. Reinsch also advised that the Chinese, who had not been particularly cooperative, be pressured to insist that the British chief engineer should observe equal opportunity. Toward the end of 1914, the British, who had earlier scoffed at American protests, made conciliatory gestures to Reinsch and Washington. But they did not expect the British chief engineer to back down and the issue remained unresolved. When the Hukuang Railways took on much larger ramifications in 1916 and 1917, Reinsch was more than ready to press the American case.[53]

The Chinese, meanwhile, had formulated their own railway policy, which called for the unification of the disparate lines under the control of the central government and the repurchase of railways and construction rights granted to the foreign powers. In addition, the Ministry of Communications would supervise all future construction in order to create a rational system linking together the different parts of China. Lack of capital and foreign opposition prevented the implementation of these plans and forced the Chinese to enlist foreign assistance. When he headed the National Railway Bureau, Sun Yat-sen designed an extensive system, to be financed by an international underwriting syndicate, which he hoped would spur China's development without conflicting with the rights already granted to the foreign powers. To assist him, Sun appointed George Bronson Rea, an American adventurer in China and editor of the *Far Eastern Review*, as his technical secretary and deputy and gave him full power to negotiate with foreign bankers.[54]

Toward the end of 1913, the Celebrity Cabinet turned the project over to the Bank of Communications, a semi-official financial institution (the Chinese government owned 40 percent of the stock) and the depository for Chinese government railway funds. Given a mandate by the cabinet and Yuan to build a unified railway system with foreign capital and expertise, Rea, now technical secretary for the Ministry of Communications, and Dr. Ch'en Chin-t'ao—recently appointed financial commissioner for the Chinese government—produced a modified version of Sun's plan. They proposed the creation of a Sino-International Construction Company, consisting of the largest construction firms in the United States, Britain, France, and Germany. The company would build an extensive railway system for China and arrange for its financing; it would also grant China a 10 to 20 percent share in the enterprise. The company's rights would be devoid of political implications, interest rates on the loans would be limited, and the routes would be selected by the Chinese.

By the spring of February 1914, Rea and Ch'en had interested Pauling & Co. (British), the Société Construction des Batignolles (French), Philip Holtzmann & Co. (German), and J. G. White & Co. (American) in the project. Reasonably assured of financial backing from their bankers, the representatives of the European construction firms met with Ch'en and Rea in Paris at the end of April and worked out an understanding as to the functions and organization of the Sino-International company. J. G. White, which employed Rea at the time, was given at least six months to arrange financial support and to decide on joining the combination. The Chinese were offered up to a seventh share in the enterprise and most of the loan proceeds would be deposited in the Bank of Communications, the Chinese partner. According to the preliminary understanding, the Sino-International company would finance, construct, and equip ten thousand miles of railway over a twenty-year period. All loans would be floated on an international basis and materials would be purchased in proportion to the amount raised in the various industrial nations. Each firm, however, would construct roughly one-fourth of the rail mileage. The European firms requested that the company be given a preference to build all new foreign-financed railways, but Ch'en subjected this provision to the approval of the Chinese government. To avoid opposition from the powers, only four short lines totalling two thousand miles were planned for the immediate future.[55]

In view of his frustration with the Chinchou-Aigun concession and the strengthening of the spheres of influence, it is not surprising that Reinsch was attracted to the scheme. Indeed, he was so immersed in the entire problem of railway politics and in an attempt to block Japan from getting the Foochow-Nanchang line that he failed to make a thorough investigation of the project and acted on the basis of incomplete information. Reinsch thought it would enable China to plan a comprehensive, well-constructed, and economical railway system based on "the industrial needs of China herself." The introduction of German and American countervailing power would also relieve China of political pressure and undermine the spheres of influence. And it afforded "the last opportunity for Americans to enter and participate in China's economic life on a sufficiently broad basis to keep the door open for future growth."

Reinsch, therefore, hastily placed himself at the disposal of the promoters. At the same time, he cooperated with William H. Donald to secure a railway contract for J. G. White which might later be turned over to the Sino-International company. That was necessary, Reinsch believed, in order to give the United States and J. G. White greater prestige in China and further leverage in the negotiations. To prevent leaks and foreign intervention, Reinsch also delayed informing the State Department about the project until the eve of the Paris meeting in April 1914. But now, insisting that the "last opportunity for Americans to enter the field of China's railway development" should not be lost, Reinsch asked Washington to give the project full diplomatic support and to impress on J. G. White the urgency of its participation.[56]

But neither Wilson nor the State Department would support the proposition. The State Department pointed out that the Sino-International company was effectively asking for a twenty-year monopoly for railway construction in violation of the Open Door and various treaties. The assignment of definite sections might tend to accelerate the division of China into spheres of influence and, in the unlikely event that uniform standards were adopted, they would probably prejudice American manufacturers. The whole idea was inconsistent with the administration's stand on the Consortium and it might very well prompt Belgium, Japan, and Russia to demand admission into the combination. E. T. Williams also observed that J. G. White was known to turn over all of its international business to the London company of the same name. The United States might indeed be forced to support a British firm, which would probably adhere to British standards. Reinsch was therefore instructed to draw the attention of the Chinese government "very earnestly" to the monopolistic features which seemed "to the Department to be inimical to the best interests of China."[57]

Reinsch was stung by Washington's rejection of the plan and by the implication that he favored monopoly. He continued to maintain that the scheme was anti-monopolistic, that it would liberate China from political pressure and that it would encourage the awarding of contracts on a purely competitive basis according to fixed contracts.[58] In any event, the project collapsed in the face of factional rivalry in China, the refusal of Britain and France to admit outsiders into their spheres of influence, and the outbreak of World War I. For several weeks, Rea tried to keep the project alive, but at the end of June he was dismissed as technical secretary and was accused of making improper use of the ministry's letterheads. Embittered and embarrassed, Rea tried to enlist Reinsch's help in clearing his name and collecting his salary. This experience and other factors subsequently caused Rea to turn the *Far Eastern Review* into an organ of Japanese-American cooperation and to denounce Reinsch and his activities.[59]

Reinsch certainly had good intentions. But he should have known better than to get involved in an enterprise that was, at best, doomed from the start. His British counterpart, Sir John Jordan, initially supported Ch'en's mission because he thought that British interests would reap most of the benefits. Upon closer examination, however, Jordan realized that the scheme was hopelessly impractical and that Ch'en was no longer in touch with Peking officials. He therefore advised Whitehall to mobilize British financial and construction interests behind concessions in the British sphere of influence in the Yangtze Valley.

Reinsch, on the other hand, was impulsive in endorsing the Sino-International Construction Company, he was sloppy in not checking out the project more carefully, and he was probably duped by the promoters. He should have realized that the powers would not have tolerated the enterprise unless they stood to benefit from it. They would not abandon their spheres of influence, nor would Japan allow itself to be shut out of future railway construction in China. Furthermore, Reinsch did not take into account the political rivalries in Peking and Ch'en's loss of influence. In fact, as Jordan observed, the Chinese government ignored Ch'en's negotiations in Europe and continued to grant separate rail concessions to the various powers. Despite Rea's known association with J. G. White and the *Far Eastern Review*'s championing of Pauling & Co. over its British competitors, Reinsch also disregarded the personal motives of the promoters. Moreover, while Rea may have been an expert on engineering matters, his political ideas on China were frequently fantastic. Finally, had he kept Washington well informed, Reinsch may have avoided not only his foolish endorsement of this extravagant scheme but a rebuke from his superiors as well.[60]

*   *   *

The list of lost opportunities had grown. Despite Reinsch's efforts, American enterprises succumbed to Chinese duplicity and internal politics and to foreign interference and opposition. At the same time, American business was slow, overly cautious, selfish, and ignorant of Chinese conditions; it failed to make the financial commitment necessary to realize those opportunities. But Reinsch also committed mistakes: he overplayed his hand, exceeded his authority, misled his superiors, and misplaced his trust. He also broke his own rules and adopted the methods of his opponents. He was playing a game, a dangerous game, but the stakes were high and his competitors were ruthless. For the most part, the State Department and American business interests wanted the same things he did. But they were unwilling or unable to make the sacrifices or to take the risks. They may have been right. And yet those experiences were only a hint of what Reinsch was to face in his six years in China.

NOTES TO
CHAPTER V

1. Reinsch to Bryan, 28 November 1913, 893.00/2021, 1 December 1913, 893.00/2049, 2 December 1913, 893.00/2050, DSNA; Reinsch, *An American Diplomat*, 70–76.

2. Patrick John Scanlan, "No Longer a Treaty Port: Paul S. Reinsch and China, 1913–1919" (Ph.D. dissertation, University of Wisconsin, 1973), 49–58.

3. Reinsch to Bryan, 2 December 1913, 893.00/2050, 3 July 1914, 893.00/2152, DSNA; Reinsch, "Six Years of American Action in China," Reinsch Papers.

4. For additional background on Standard Oil's operations in China and the story of its concession, see Noel H. Pugach, "Standard Oil and Petroleum Development in Early Republican China," *Business History Review*, LXV (Winter 1971), 452–55; Ralph W. Hidy and Muriel Hidy, *Pioneering in Big Business, 1882–1911* (New York, 1955), 136–54, 331, 495, 512–21, 528, 547–53. Also see, *New York Times*, 14 and 15 February 1914; Reinsch, *An American Diplomat*, 62. I am indebted to Ms. Betty Hale, Department of Public Relations, Mobil Oil Corporation, for information supplied to me in a letter of 11 September 1972. Standard Oil was commonly called by its trademarked nickname, SOCONY.

5. *New York Times*, 29 March and 5 December 1913; interview between Williams and Hsiung Hsi-ling, 18 October 1913, Reinsch Papers; E. T. Williams Diary, 2 December 1913, Williams Papers; Williams to Bryan, 21 October 1913, 893.451/1477, DSNA; Reinsch to Bryan, 2 December 1913, 893.00/2050, DSNA; enclosures in Reinsch to Bryan, 16 March 1914, 893.6363/4, DSNA.

6. Reinsch to Bryan, 16 February 1914, 893.6363/1, DSNA; Reinsch, "Six Years of American Action in China," Reinsch Papers.

7. Reinsch to Bryan, 16 February 1914, 893.6363/1, DSNA; *New York Times*, 14 February 1914. The text of the agreement may be found in John V. A. MacMurray, *Treaties and Agreements with and concerning China, 1894–1919*, 2 vols. (New York, 1921), II, 1109–13.

8. Reinsch to Bryan, 16 February 1914, 893.6363/1, 24 February 1914, 893.6363/3, 16 March 1914, including enclosure of interview between Japanese Minister Yamaza and Hsiung Hsi-ling, 893.6363/4, DSNA; interview between Sir John Jordan and Hsiung Hsi-ling, enclosed in MacMurray to Lansing, 17 August 1915, 893.6363/20, DSNA; Blake to James Donald, 5 March 1914, Hornbeck Papers; Blake to James Donald, 6 March 1914, Reinsch Papers; Straight to Reinsch, 25 February 1914, Reinsch Papers; *New York Times*, 13 and 20 February 1914; *The Times* (London), 14 July 1914.

9. Reinsch to Bryan, 16 February 1914, 893.6363/2, 16 March 1914, 893.6363/4, DSNA; Reinsch to Bemis, 20 April 1914, RG 84, Records of the Foreign Service Posts of the Department of State, Peking Post file, 863, NA (hereafter cited RG 84, file number, NA); Reinsch to Charles Blake, 28 May 1914, *ibid.*; Anderson to Reinsch, 17 March 1914, Reinsch Papers.

10. Reinsch to Bryan, 2 July 1914, 893.6363/9, 5 April 1915, 893.6363/12, DSNA; Robert Coltman to Reinsch, 27 November 1914, RG 84, Peking Post file, 863, NA; MacMurray to Reinsch, 23 June 1914, Reinsch Papers.

11. Reinsch to Bryan, 5 April 1915, 893.6363/12, DSNA; MacMurray to Lansing, 17 August 1915, with enclosures, 893.6363/20, DSNA.

12. Reinsch to Bryan, 5 July 1914, 893.51/1524, 5 April 1915, 893.6363/12, DSNA; MacMurray to Lansing, 17 August 1915, and enclosure, Bemis to Hsiung Hsi-ling and Chou Tzu-ch'i, 19 June 1915, 893.6363/20, DSNA.

13. Bryan to Standard Oil, 6 April 1915, 893.6363/12, DSNA; Bemis to Bryan, 8 April 1915, 893.6363/13, DSNA; MacMurray to Lansing, 17 August 1915, and enclosures, Reinsch memo, "Suggestions on the Standard Oil Company's Contract," 14 June 1915, MacMurray memos, 21 and 22 July 1915, 893.6363/20, DSNA.

14. MacMurray to Lansing, 17 August 1915, and enclosures, Reinsch memo, "Suggestions on the Standard Oil Company's Contract," 14 June 1915, MacMurray memos, 21 July and 4 August 1915, 893.6363/20 DSNA.

15. Bemis to Hsiung and Chou, 19 June 1915, MacMurray memo, 29 June 1915, enclosed in MacMurray to Lansing, 17 August 1915, 893.6363/20, DSNA. Mexican dollars (or more correctly Mexican pesos) were circulated on a large scale in China and were extensively used in foreign trade. These coins became the standard against which other foreign coins or currencies were valued. Consequently, many contracts between foreign firms or governments and China stipulated amounts in terms of Mexican silver pesos.

16. MacMurray to Lansing, 17 August 1915, and enclosure, MacMurray memo, 21 June 1915, 893.6363/20, DSNA.

17. MacMurray to Lansing, 17 August 1915, and extensive enclosures, 893.6363/20, DSNA; MacMurray to Williams, 5 August 1915, MacMurray Papers.

18. MacMurray to Lansing, 12 August 1915, 893.6363/15, 13 August 1915, 893.6363/17, 20 August 1915, with enclosure of MacMurray memo, 10 August 1915, 893.6363/20, DSNA.

19. MacMurray to Lansing, 17 August 1915, and enclosures, MacMurray memos, 10, 11 and 12 August 1915, 893.6363/20, DSNA.

20. MacMurray to Lansing, 13 August 1915, 893.6363/17, DSNA; Lansing to SOCONY, 14 August 1915, 893.6363/17, DSNA; Lansing to MacMurray, 21 August 1915, 893.6363/17, 25 September 1915, 893.6363/22, DSNA; H. L. Pratt to Polk, 24 September 1915, 893.6363/22, DSNA.

21. MacMurray to Lansing, 23 September 1915, 893.6363/21, DSNA; Reinsch to Lansing, 12 November 1915, 893.6363/24, DSNA; Williams to Trade Advisers, 13 November 1915, 893.6363/24, DSNA; Reinsch to Lansing, 5 April 1917, 893.6363/26, DSNA.

22. Lansing to MacMurray, 26 July 1915, 893.6363/14, DSNA; *New York Times*, 15 August 1915.

23. MacMurray to Williams, 5 August 1915, MacMurray Papers; MacMurray to mother, 16 August 1915, *ibid.*

24. MacMurray to Williams, 5 August 1915, MacMurray Papers; MacMurray to Reinsch, 22 June 1915, Reinsch Papers; MacMurray to Lansing, 17 August 1915, with enclosures, 893.6363/20, DSNA; Reinsch, *An American Diplomat,* 223; *San Francisco Chronicle,* 18 August 1915; *The Mei Foo Shield,* III (January 1927), 106; Betty L. Hale to author, 11 September 1972.

25. F. Huntington Wilson to Calhoun, 12 May 1910, 10216/14, DSNA; Charles Schwab to Calhoun, 22 April 1910, 631.001/139, DSNA. William Braisted has presented an excellent account of the episode in "China, the United States Navy, and the Bethlehem Steel Company, 1909–1929," *Business History Review,* XLII (Spring 1968), 50–66.

26. Williams to Bryan, 9 November 1913, 893.34/107, 11 November 1913, 893.34/109, DSNA; Williams Diary, 2 December 1913, Williams Papers; Reinsch to Bryan, 2 December 1913, 893.00/2050, DSNA; Braisted, "China, the United States Navy, and the Bethlehem Steel Company," 55–56.

27. Reinsch conversations with Chou Tzu-ch'i, 27 November 1913, in Reinsch to Bryan, 893.00/2050, DSNA; Bryan to Reinsch, 3 December 1913, 893.34/110, DSNA; Reinsch to Bryan, 23 December 1913, 893.34/111, 26 May 1914, 893.51/1523, DSNA; Johnston to Reinsch, 23 January 1914, RG 84, Peking Post file, 830, NA; Johnston to Reinsch, 16 July 1914, Reinsch Papers; Braisted, "China, the United States Navy, and the Bethlehem Steel Contract," 56–57.

28. Reinsch to Bryan, 6 May 1914, 893.51/1511, 11 May 1914, attached MacMurray memos of 12 February and 20 July 1920, 893.51/1515, DSNA; G. W. Struble to Hughes, 30 August 1921, 893.34/152, DSNA; MacMurray to Gauss, 10 December 1917, MacMurray Papers; *The Times* (London), 18 and 22 May 1914.

29. Bryan to Reinsch, 7 May 1914, 893.51/1511, 21 May 1914, 893.51/1514, DSNA; Bryan to Chinda, 19 May 1914, 893.345/2a, DSNA; Reinsch to Bryan, 23 May 1914, 893.51/1516, 26 May 1914, 893.51/1523, DSNA; Lansing to Reinsch, 17 April 1914, 893.00/2102, DSNA; Reinsch, *An American Diplomat*, 99–100.

30. Johnston to Schwab, 20 January 1914, 893.34/113, DSNA; Moore to Reinsch, 26 January 1914, 893.34/113, DSNA; Reinsch to Bryan, 30 January 1914, 893.34/114, 31 October 1914, 893.20/33, DSNA; Bryan to MacMurray, 7 July 1914, 893.34/114, DSNA; MacMurray to Bryan, 17 July 1914, 893.20/32, DSNA; Lansing to Daniels, 19 December 1914, 893.20/33, DSNA; Daniels to Bryan, 29 December 1914, 893.20/35, DSNA; Lansing to Reinsch, 4 January 1915, 893.20/115, DSNA; Braisted, "China, the United States Navy, and the Bethlehem Steel Contract," 57–66.

31. Knox to Calhoun, 16 May 1911, 893.811/44a, DSNA; Jameson to General George Davis, 30 July 1912, in 893.811/75, DSNA; Jameson, "Preliminary Report on the Huai River Conservancy," 893.811/67, DSNA; minutes of the Executive Committee of the American National Red Cross, 1 June 1911, American National Red Cross Papers, Washington, D.C. (hereafter cited Red Cross Papers and file number where indicated); Mabel Boardman to editor, *New York Times*, 8 February 1914.

32. Davis to Boardman, 17 September 1912, 898.5, Red Cross Papers; Boardman to Davis, 19 September 1912, 898.5, *ibid.*; Jameson to Davis, 3 and 13 June and 19 December 1913, 898.5/08, *ibid.*; Davis to Jameson, 26 March 1913, 898.5/2, *ibid.*; Jameson to Boardman, 2 December 1912, 898.5/08, *ibid.*; Boardman to Taft, 14 October 1912, 898.5/08, *ibid.*; Bland to Boardman, 4 January 1913, 898.5/2, *ibid.*; Huntington Wilson to Calhoun, 20 September 1912, 898.811/74, DSNA; Davis to Bryan, 9 July 1913, 893.811/89, DSNA; Israel, *Progressivism and the Open Door*, 133–35.

33. Chang Chien, "Conservancy Work in China, Being a Series of Documents and Reports" (Shanghai, 1912), in 893.811/82, DSNA; Chang Chien, "Report and Estimate of the Huai Ho Conservancy Bureau," 898.5/08, Red Cross Papers; Williams to Knox, 1 June 1911, 893.811/49, DSNA; Williams to Bryan, 20 June 1913, 893.811/88, DSNA; Davis to Bryan, 9 July 1913, 893.811/89, DSNA; Boardman to Moore, 26 July 1913, 893.5/08, Red Cross Papers, 29 August 1913, 893.811/92, DSNA; Jameson to Davis, 13 May, 13 June, and 9 December 1913, 898.5/08, Red Cross Papers; Davis to Jameson, 26 March 1913, 898.5/2, Red Cross Papers; Boardman to Wilson, 12 July 1913, 898.5/08, Red Cross Papers; Jameson to Williams, 26 July 1913, RG 84, Peking Post file, 881, NA; Jameson, "Wanted—A Master of Men," *The Outlook*, XCVIII (15 July 1911), 577–83; Bashford to Reinsch, 2 January 1914, Reinsch Papers; interview, Reinsch and Chang Chien, 23 December 1913, Reinsch Papers; Samuel C. Chu, *Reformer in Modern China: Chang Chien 1853–1926* (New York, 1965); Israel, *Progressivism and the Open Door*, 134–35.

34. Reinsch to Bryan, 2 December 1913, 893.00/2050, 23 January 1914, 893.811/

104 and /109, DSNA; Reinsch to Davis, 19 December 1914, 893.811/184, DSNA; Reinsch to Boardman, 27 November 1914, Wilson Papers; Reinsch to Wilson, 29 November 1914, *ibid.*; *FR 1914,* 98; Reinsch to Straight, 24 March 1914, Reinsch Papers.

35. Reinsch to Bryan, 2 December 1913, 893.00/2050, 19 December 1913, 893.811/01, DSNA; Jameson to Davis, 9 December 1913, 898.5/08, Red Cross Papers; Reinsch, *An American Diplomat*, 70–72; Scanlan, "No Longer a Treaty Port," 58–61.

36. Reinsch to Bryan, 19 December 1913, 893.811/98 and 101, DSNA; Davis to Bryan, 23 December 1913, 893.811/100, DSNA; Moore to Reinsch, 26 December 1913, 893.811/100, DSNA; Jameson to Davis, 19 December 1913, 898.5/08, Red Cross Papers.

37. Interview, Reinsch and Chang Chien, 23 December 1913, Reinsch Papers; Reinsch to Bryan, 14 January 1914, 893.811/102, 3 February 1914, 893.811/112, DSNA; Jameson to Davis, 19 December 1913, 898.5/08, Red Cross Papers; Reinsch, *An American Diplomat*, 81–82. The text of the preliminary agreement may be found in *FR 1914,* 102. The agreement stipulated that the loan was to be made in gold (G) dollars.

38. Interview, Reinsch and Chang Chien, 23 December 1913, Reinsch Papers; Reinsch to Bryan, 19 December 1913, 893.811/101, 14 January 1914, 893.811/102, 20 January 1914, 893.811/103, 23 January 1914, 893.811/104 and /109, DSNA; Jameson to Davis, 9 December 1913, 898.5/08, Red Cross Papers.

39. Bryan to Reinsch, 19 January 1914, 893.811/102, 21 January 1914, 893.811/103, DSNA; *FR 1914*, 99–102; de Forest to Boardman, 19 January 1914, 898.5/01, Red Cross Papers; Boardman to de Forest, 20 January 1914, 898.5/01, *ibid.*; minutes of the Joint Meeting of the International Relief Board and the Executive Committee, 27 January 1914, *ibid.*

40. Reinsch to Bryan, 23 January 1914, 893.811/104, 27 January 1914, 893.811/105, 30 January 1914, 893.811/106, 3 February 1914, 893.811/112, DSNA; Bryan to Reinsch, 26 January 1914, 893.811/104, DSNA; Moore to Wilson, 4 February 1914, Wilson Papers; Reinsch, *An American Diplomat*, 81–82. MacMurray, who was highly critical of Reinsch's conduct, is the chief source for Reinsch's decision to sign the agreement without authorization. See MacMurray to mother, 19 February 1914, MacMurray Papers. Reinsch's Log Book gives 30 January 1914 as the date he signed the memorandum on behalf of the Red Cross. See Reinsch Log Book, entries, January 1914, Hornbeck Papers.

41. Interview, Reinsch and Chang Chien, 23 December 1913, Reinsch Papers; Reinsch to Bryan, 20 January 1914, 893.811/103, 23 Janaury 1914, 893.811/104 and /109, 3 February 1914, 893.811/112, 17 February 1914, 893.811/115, DSNA.

42. Reinsch to Bryan, 14 January 1914, 893.811/102, 23 January 1914, 893.811/109, 19 February 1914, 893.811/110, DSNA; Bryan to Reinsch, 18 March 1914, 893.811/119a, DSNA; Moore to Wilson, 4 and 11 February 1914, Wilson Papers; Boardman to Wilson, 11 February 1914, Wilson Papers, 11 June 1914, 893.811/152, DSNA; MacMurray to mother, 19 February 1914, MacMurray Papers; minutes of the Executive Committee of the American National Red Cross, 22 April and 9 June 1914, Red Cross Papers; *FR 1914*, 99–100, 105.

43. Straight to Boardman, 21 January 1914, Elihu Root Papers, Library of Congress; Straight to Reinsch, 25 February 1914, Reinsch Papers; Straight to Thomas, 24 March 1914, Straight Papers; Boardman to Moore, 28 July 1914, John B. Moore Papers, Library of Congress.

44. Straight to Reinsch, 25 February and 25 March 1914, Reinsch Papers; Reinsch to

Straight, 24 March and 21 April 1914, *ibid.*; Straight to George Caseneve, 11 February 1914, Straight Papers; Straight to Thomas, 24 March 1914, *ibid.*; Reinsch to Bryan, 24 March 1914, 893.811/123, 31 March 1914, 893.811/122, DSNA; Lansing to Reinsch, 22 April 1914, 893.811/122, DSNA.

45. Reinsch to Bryan, 31 October 1914, Reinsch Papers; William Sibert to Davis, 26 August 1914, in 893.811/153, DSNA; *FR 1914*, 110–19.

46. Straight to Reinsch, 24 March 1914, Reinsch Papers; Straight to Bland, 24 March 1914, Straight Papers; Straight to Thomas, 24 March 1914, *ibid.*; Chang Chien to Mac-Murray, 21 July 1914, in 893.811/177, DSNA; MacMurray to Boardman, 18 August 1914, 898.5/2, Red Cross Papers; Davis to Kai Fu Shah, 14 October 1914, 898.5/08, *ibid.*; Chang Chien to Kai Fu Shah, 1 October 1914, 898.5, *ibid.*; Gen. George Davis to A. P. Davis, 21 December 1914, 898.5/2, *ibid.*; *FR 1914*, 114–19.

47. Reinsch to Bryan, 31 October 1914, Reinsch Papers; Reinsch to Boardman, 27 November 1914, Wilson Papers; Reinsch to Wilson, 28 November 1914, *ibid.*; Reinsch to Davis, 19 December 1914, 893.811/184, DSNA.

48. Reinsch to Judson, 27 November 1914, Reinsch Papers; Judson to Reinsch, 19 January 1915, *ibid.*; Bryan to Lansing, 22 December 1914, 893.811/167, DSNA; Boardman to Reinsch, 9 January 1915, 898.5/2, Red Cross Papers; Gen. George Davis to A. P. Davis, 21 December 1914, *ibid.*

49. Interview, Williams and Chang Chien, 29 October 1913, Reinsch Papers; Williams to Bryan, 31 October 1913, 893.77/1311, 12 November 1913, 893.77/1303, 13 November 1913, 893.77/1306, 18 November 1913, 893.77/1319, DSNA; Reinsch to Bryan, 893.00/2050, 26 May 1914, 893.51/1523, 14 April 1914, 893.77/1366, DSNA; Menocal to Straight, 14 November 1913, Reinsch Papers; memo by J. D. Gregory, "Respecting Railway Construction in China," 1 March 1914, 10247/f10247/14, Foreign Office 371/1945, Public Record Office, London, England (hereafter, the unpublished records from the British Foreign Office will be cited by file number, and FO group or volume number).

50. Reinsch to Bryan, 16 February 1914, 793.94/192, DSNA; Reinsch to Lansing, 5 May 1916, 793.94/1528, DSNA; Straight to Bland, 24 March 1914, Straight Papers.

51. Fiedler to Bryan, 18 November 1913, 893.77/1308, DSNA; Moore to American Group, 21 November 1913, *ibid.*; Moore to Reinsch, 2 December 1913, 893.77/1312, DSNA; Osborne to American Group, 10 March 1914, 893.77/1337, DSNA; Menocal to H. T. S. Greene, 17 March 1914, 893.77/1351, DSNA; Lansing to Reinsch, 9 October 1914, 893.77/1416, DSNA; Straight to Charles Whigham, 2 September 1913, Straight Papers.

52. Reinsch to Bryan, 17 March 1914, 893.77/1350, 28 December 1914, 893.77/1413, DSNA; memo of interview, Reinsch and Liang Tun-yen, 13 June 1914, in 893.77/1379, DSNA; Williams to Trade Advisers, 4 August 1914, 893.77/1388, DSNA; Jordan to Grey, 24 March 1914, 13025/f4291/14, FO 371/1940.

53. Bryan to Reinsch, 9 November 1914, 893.77/1423, DSNA; Reinsch to Bryan, 11 November 1914, 893.77/1426, DSNA; Lansing to Reinsch, 25 February 1916, 893.77/1515, DSNA; Reinsch to Lansing, 3 March 1916, 893.77/1520, DSNA; *FR 1916*, 150–53; Jordan to Grey, 3 February 1915, plus enclosures and minutes, f26198/15, FO 371/2328.

54. Scanlan, "No Longer a Treaty Port," 161–62; Li, *Wilson's China Policy*, 178–79.

55. Memorandum of a Meeting Held in Paris, 22 April 1914, in 893.77/1433, DSNA; Herrick to Bryan, 25 April 1914, 893.77/1358, DSNA; Reinsch to Bryan, 20 April 1914, 893.77/1355, DSNA; Ch'en to Pauling & Co., 16 April 1914, Reinsch

Papers; Rea, "Memorandum Concerning the Organization of an International Construction Company for the Financing, Construction and Equipment of Railways in the Republic of China," for W. H. Page, 26 May 1914, *ibid.*; Jordan to Langley, 8 February 1914, Jordan Papers , FO 350/12; Langley to Jordan, 11 March 1914, Jordan Papers, FO 350/11; *The Times* (London), 13 March 1914; Scanlan, "No Longer a Treaty Port," 162–67.

56. Reinsch to Bryan, 20 April 1914, 893.77/1355, 5 May 1914, 893.77/1365, DSNA; Bryan to Reinsch, 6 May 1914, 893.77/1365, DSNA; Selden to Lansing, 9 May 1914, 893.77/1367, DSNA; Donald to Reinsch, 12 March 1914, Reinsch Papers.

57. Williams memos, 2 April 1914, 893.77/1355, 8 May 1914, 893.77/1366, DSNA; Bryan to Reinsch, 16 May 1914, 893.77/1366, DSNA; Lansing to Reinsch, 20 May 1914, 893.77/1371, DSNA; Lansing to J. G. White, 15 May 1914, 893.77/1367, DSNA.

58. Reinsch to Bryan, 18 May 1914, 893.77/1371, DSNA; Reinsch to Bryan, 13 June 1914, with enclosure, interview, Reinsch and Liang Tun-yen, 13 June 1914, 893.77/1379, DSNA; Rea to J. G. White, 31 May 1914, 893.77/1379, DSNA; Rea memo for Page, 26 May 1914, Reinsch Papers.

59. Selden to Rea, 22 June 1914, Reinsch Papers; Ch'en Chin-t'ao to Rea, 29 June 1914, *ibid.*; Rea to Ch'en, 20 June 1914, *ibid.*; Rea to Reinsch, 3 October 1914, *ibid.*; Reinsch to Wilson, 6 June 1914, in 893.77/1379, DSNA; interview, Reinsch and Liang Tun-yen, 13 June 1914, in 893.77/1379, DSNA; Reinsch, *An American Diplomat*, 100–01; Li, *Wilson's China Policy*, 180–81.

60. Jordan to Gregory, 23 March 1914, Jordan Papers, FO 350/12; Jordan to Langley, 23 March 1914, *ibid.*; Jordan to Grey, 26 January 1914, and FO minutes, 5887/f5887/14, FO 371/1943, 24 March 1914, and FO minutes, 13125/f10247/14, FO 371/1945.

Chapter VI

TRANSFORMING
CHINA

Yuan Shih-k'ai's favorite metaphor gave Reinsch an instant clue to the man who ruled China. "As you can see," Yuan frequently repeated, "the Chinese Republic is a very young baby. It must be nursed and kept from taking strong medicines like those prescribed by foreign doctors." Those words, uttered during Reinsch's first lengthy interview with the Chinese president left a sour taste in his mouth and chilled his hopes for China's political development and modernization. To begin with, the transformation of China's ancient society posed insurmountable problems. But Yuan's patrimonial attitude combined with the legacy of recent political events raised a serious question as to whether the changes begun at the end of the nineteenth century and continued during the Revolution of 1911 could not only be consolidated but also extended.[1]

At this critical juncture in its history, China faced far-reaching alternatives: the unity of the nation versus its division; continued independence and administrative integrity versus direct foreign domination and partition; the tendency of its political institutions to lean either in the direction of Russo-Japanese absolutism or United States republicanism; and the question of whether its legal and educational systems would evolve under the influence of Anglo-American or Euro-Japanese influence. "Under these circumstances," Reinsch wrote in one of his earliest comprehensive surveys, "it is of great moment whether the Chinese government will remain free, with the assistance of influences friendly to the development of China's nationality, to preserve the unity of the Chinese State and to develop its institutions; or whether its financial distress, combined with the plottings of a revolutionary opposition, will deliver it into the hands of those who are less favorable to the growth of China's national life."[2]

China seemed to look at the United States as a model for its political and economic system and Reinsch thought this tendency should be encouraged. He recognized that the "vast masses of the Chinese people are so very different from the people of the United States in their conditions of life and in all other inherited tendencies that any direct transfer and adoption of foreign institutions and methods are scarcely to be looked for." Still, he maintained, "in the temper of approaching public questions, in the practical spirit of work, and through technical experience, a great influence may be exercised."[3]

This desire to transform China along American lines, however, raised all sorts of irresolvable dilemmas. Where did one draw the line between influence and interference? How far could the United States support Yuan, his successors, and the existing power structure within China? What should America do about the political opposition? How much of progressive America was applicable to China? How did one mobilize the United States government and private American institutions in this effort? What would be the response of competing ideologies and foreign rivals? And how could the United States cope with them without involving itself in a major war and turning China into a battleground? In the course of his six years in China, Reinsch groped for answers to these questions. But one thing he was certain of from the outset: "Whether the exertion of such influence will be possible will, however, depend in large measure not so much upon the abstract excellence of American principles and methods, but upon the actual position which America will occupy in the next few years as a factor in Chinese development—commercial, financial and political."[4]

*   *   *

The plain fact was that while Yuan Shih-k'ai was not necessarily the master of China, he was clearly its dictator. On May 1, 1914, Yuan promulgated a revised provisional constitution which was prepared by his hand-picked Constitutional Compact Conference and based largely on a draft prepared by Frank J. Goodnow, the American constitutional adviser. It established a presidential system of government and gave the chief executive a ten-year renewable term of office, an absolute veto, and extensive powers in all matters of foreign affairs, defense, appointments, and finance. The constitution created an elected legislature and an appointed council of state, but both lacked real power to check the president. Yuan also forged ahead with his plans to restore the empire and establish his own dynasty. He granted audiences to his subjects, assumed the role of protector of the Confucian faith and, on December 23, 1914, worshipped heaven at the Altar of Heaven, a prerogative of the Chinese emperor. Meanwhile, Yuan cleverly cultivated the foreign powers and the foreign press. Convinced, for the most part, that Yuan offered the only hope for internal stability and protection for foreign investments, they generally endorsed his regime.[5]

Although Yuan made occasional obeisance to republican principles, Reinsch had few illusions about his views and occasionally he depicted the president in unflattering terms. "He is, first of all, a man of authority, a military leader of great personal influence over his followers, who views political action and institutions primarily in their bearing upon the maintenance of authority," he informed Bryan. Yuan's methods represented all the vices of Chinese politics—personal rule, unscrupulousness, corruption, and vindictive action against all opponents. Yuan was an autocrat, who had inherited the forms of republican government from the revolution, but who had nothing but contempt for what they stood for. He had no knowledge of or appreciation for the "commonwealth principle of government" and no perception of the value of parliamentary bodies as a basis of public authority. "Political opposition to the Head of State is confused with disloyalty, or even treason, to the State itself," Reinsch observed after his early encounters with Yuan.[6]

Nor did Yuan's regime bring about the promised administrative and financial reforms. The Peking government was disrupted by a bitter split over the question of restoring the monarchy, between the northern militarists, headed by Tuan Ch'i-jui, and the Cantonese or Communications clique, led by Liang Shih-yi. The old pattern of corruption and opportunism persisted and the composition of the cabinets deteriorated after the fall of the Celebrity Cabinet. The Peking government lived from day to day with an empty treasury and it was dependent on the foreign administered Customs Service and Salt Gabelle, loans and cash advances.

Yuan's power was largely illusory and superficial. His large army, which was the source of his power, was not only a drain on China's meager financial resources, it was also largely ineffective. Yuan's authority rested entirely on his military organization and the loyalty of his commanders, an inadequate basis for any regime. Indeed, financial stringency forced Yuan to invest the provincial military leaders with the title of *tutuh*, or military governor. Since they were expected to maintain themselves without much financial support from Peking, the *tutuhs* became increasingly independent of the central government and laid the basis for the regional empires that characterized the warlord period in China.[7]

And yet, there was another side to the picture, one that forced Reinsch and the Wilson administration to support Yuan Shih-k'ai. Reinsch never embraced the president with the enthusiasm of such Americans as Jeremiah Jenks, W. W. Rockhill, or the editors of the *Journal of the American Asiatic Association*. Nevertheless, Reinsch developed a certain admiration and respect for Yuan. Unlike most Chinese leaders, he appeared to be a man of decision and vision. While this was largely untrue, Reinsch frequently described Yuan as an administrator who had abandoned the role of military commander to build a new China; and he saw him in terms akin to Goodnow's "progressive conservative." Moreover, Reinsch believed that Yuan's desire to centralize power might hasten China's orderly development and internal reform. Most of China's true reformers actually favored decentralization, but Reinsch reinterpreted their aims largely in American progressive terms. "The reform movement in China," he told an audience at the University of Chicago in 1915, "seeks not so much parliamentary government as the development of a strong central government in a country where formerly the central government performed none of the functions which the idea of administration suggests."[8]

More important, Yuan symbolized the stability which was desperately needed to contain foreign interference, to encourage American investment, and to modernize China. Reinsch and policy makers in Washington desired to foster democracy and constitutional government. But since they placed a high premium on continuity and order, they were stuck with Yuan. Reinsch interpreted the promulgation of the Goodnow Constitution not as "a definite reaction against democracy, but rather as an assumption of those powers necessary to enable the Central Government to bring about the only conditions under which constitutional development can be safely and profitably fostered, namely conditions of national cohesion and internal tranquility."[9]

There was also the fact that at the time there was no acceptable alternative to Yuan. "The really serious feature of the situation," E. T. Williams had lamented, "is that the peace of the whole country seems to depend upon this one man." Reinsch agreed with practically all other Americans in China that Sun Yat-sen was not a viable choice. At best, Reinsch regarded Sun as an impractical, albeit well-meaning, Chinese patriot. Nonetheless, Sun's revolutionary activity and intrigue would once more reduce the country to a civil war that would threaten China's very existence. Furthermore, Reinsch also considered Sun a dangerous opportunist who, out of desperation and naiveté, would betray his beloved country to its greatest enemy, Japan. Reinsch therefore distinguished between Sun and his older followers (whom he discounted as potential leaders of China) and the "more modern-minded" element in the Kuomintang "who desired to adopt the best institutions and practices of the West, but who did not favor violent measures." Toward the latter group, which included such close friends as C. T. Wang, Reinsch displayed great sympathy. And he continued to encourage the moderates in the Young China Movement, who, in turn, looked to him for help. Still, there could not be any public or even indirect withdrawal of support from Yuan Shih-k'ai. That would only provide an opening for the militarists, hungry for power and booty, the monarchists, waiting in the wings to reestablish the Manchu dynasty, and the foreign powers, anxious for any opportunity to extend their influence.[10]

Finally, Reinsch was forced to admit that there was some strength in Yuan's argument that China was not ready for full parliamentary government. Returning to his earlier position after a few months in China, Reinsch warned about the dangers of transplanting foreign institutions and emphasized the evolutionary transformation of the Chinese political system. Reinsch thought that Goodnow's ideas were a little too conservative and lodged too much power in the hands of the central government. Still, he believed that Goodnow's constitution was a reasonable foundation on which to build representative government in China. And since the Chinese had no conception of government as a commonwealth of the people, Reinsch conceded that an emperor might be needed in order for the government to collect taxes and maintain order. By March 1914, in fact, Reinsch was leaning toward a constitutional monarchy that included a viable parliamentary body representing the most powerful, wealthy, and intelligent citizens. Such a solution would mesh with Chinese traditions, would give a voice to the progressive elements in Chinese society, would base representation on interests rather than numbers, and would promote stability and evolutionary change.

Nevertheless, Reinsch never completely abandoned his hope for the development of democracy in China. As late as 1919, after witnessing turmoil and disintegration for almost five years, Reinsch still maintained that the underlying sense of equity and the Chinese concept of "li" (doing that which is right and fitting) fostered the natural evolution of democracy in China. Reinsch criticized Yuan's press regulations, promulgated on April 2, 1914, for discouraging frank discussion of issues and infringing on freedom of the press. Naively, Reinsch used every opportunity to educate Yuan as to the value of parliamentary government; he stressed that a parliament even of limited function was necessary to conciliate the middle class as well as the educated Chinese. Their support and confidence were needed in order to prevent them from turning to revolutionary activity. Reinsch argued that strong political parties could appeal to the patriotism of the Chinese people and would also enable the National Assembly to assist in defending the nation and its political integrity. And he tried to demonstrate how a representative body could be used to bridge the gap between Peking and the provinces.[11]

Reinsch also tended to side with the Communications clique against the militarist dominated Anhui clique. Although personally venal and largely indifferent to political forms, Reinsch believed that men such as Liang Shih-yi, Chou Tzu-ch'i, and Chang Chien were more progressive and cosmopolitan than any other group in China. They seemed to appreciate modern business methods and desired to cooperate with American financiers and industrialists. They talked about organizing Chinese life and strengthening China economically. But these eminently practical men were also attracted by the opportunities for lucrative profits and greater security that would flow from their association with Americans. Since they often held portfolios in various Chinese cabinets and often controlled the important Ministry of Communications, Reinsch thought that they could cement lasting Sino-American ties and facilitate the negotiations for important contracts. Ironically, these men frequently worked against American interests and may have retarded the efforts "to modernize China within a democratic framework." Reinsch was aware of their shenanigans, their dependence on government connections for their apparent success, and their lack of sympathy for the aims of Young China. Nevertheless, he continued to work with them and excused their behavior as typically Chinese. While his assessment of these men contained elements of truth, Reinsch tended to judge them, as well as Yuan Shih-k'ai, in terms of how they might serve American interests and how they fitted his own image of China's needs.[12]

Yuan naturally ignored Reinsch's advice. But Reinsch was unable to abandon him. There was too much at stake: China's independence and freedom of development, the balance of power in the Far East, and the survival of American philanthropic, educational, and business interests. Nor did the Wilson administration offer any alternatives. When Reinsch asked Washington for official guidance on the attempt to make Yuan president for life, the State Department acknowledged his excellent report and disregarded the probing questions he raised.[13]

Instead, Reinsch found himself apologizing to the State Department for Peking's actions. The Chinese government desired to "profit by American experience," and the president wanted to "give the Government a more truly representative character," he explained to Bryan in July 1914. However, the fear of revolutionary intrigue drove it to "assume an ultra-conservative, if not reactionary attitude." Similarly, Reinsch was forced to defend Yuan to the American public and to reassure businessmen as to the stability of the Chinese government. "I think that the position of the republic may be regarded as quite secure," he told a *New York Times* correspondent. "President Yuan Shih-K'ai has a resolute grasp of the situation. His determination to enforce a stable government is supported by the ardent wish of the vast majority of the Chinese people for a long era of peace and industrial activity." Reinsch also insisted that the safety of American investments was not compromised by China's internal problems. Either conditions would improve and China would embark on an era of economic progress or, in the event of national bankruptcy, the administration of the country would be taken over by the powers which would protect legitimate obligations. "It would seem that on neither alternative would the substantive rights of investors be affected," he argued in convoluted fashion, "although, of course, the recurrence of unrest or the changes connected with a transfer of authority might be the source of incidental difficulties and expense."[14]

Reinsch insisted, however, that this confidence in China and moral support to Yuan's government had to be supplemented with concrete assistance. The Chinese did not ask the United States to underwrite China completely or to render direct political support, he hastened to add, but only to do its share to prevent China from "falling under the complete dominance of forces not favorable to her national development." Over the next ten years, Reinsch's monologue acquired an increasingly apocalyptic tone. The failure of American capital, industry, and commerce to give "that comparatively slight assistance which the situation called for" would eventually place American action in China "on a far more modest basis than present possibilities promise." It would cause China to lose faith in the United States and would also confirm the propaganda of the other foreign powers that America's much vaunted good will was meaningless. Moreover, Reinsch warned with prescience that "China may soon find itself in a position where it would be impossible for her to choose her friends." Once China's affairs were under the control of other powers, an attempt would be made to destroy American influence in China—moral as well as economic—and to generate antipathy toward the United States. On the other hand, fulfillment of the generous concessions China granted to Americans, coupled with loans, would bring many good things: the destruction of the spheres of influence, the establishment of American business methods, the stimulation of China's modernization, and the development of administrative reforms and republican institutions.[15]

In 1914, Reinsch thought that American participation in banking and currency reform was the kind of direct financial assistance that China so desperately needed. The Chinese had made considerable progress in establishing a standard monetary system, but there remained in circulation millions of irredeemable and virtually worthless notes issued by various banks and provincial military leaders. Yuan had sought a large foreign loan that would enable the Bank of China, opened in 1912 under the control of the Ministry of Finance, to eliminate the dangerous paper and to issue a new national currency backed by sufficient metallic reserve. In the fall of 1913, the Chinese had simultaneously approached the United States and the Consortium for a currency loan, playing them against each other for the best possible terms. Tight money conditions in Europe, the Consortium's political motives, and Standard Oil's refusal to make a loan forced the Chinese to rely on Reinsch's promise to help them find the money in the United States.[16]

Suddenly, on March 7, 1914, Guion M. Gest, a New York contractor who was touring China with his family, signed an exclusive seventy-five-day option to arrange a $30 million forty-year loan in the United States. Reinsch had helped Gest in the negotiations, but he quickly pointed out that the security was inadequate and the term of the option was too short. In addition, the Gest option said nothing explicit about the supposed purpose of the loan—the creation of a metallic reserve to back the new Bank of China currency and institute comprehensive currency reform. That would have to be spelled out in the final agreement. Reinsch, moreover, deliberately associated banking reform with currency reform in order to gain support for the Gest loan at home and in the hope that the Chinese would seek American help in both areas. As it then stood, the option essentially provided for an administrative or political loan to bail out Yuan's government. There was also a question as to whether currency reform had been made part of the Reorganization Loan. In that event, a currency loan would be unavailable to Americans in spite of their traditional interest in the matter. But Reinsch insisted that "the field is still open for a resumption of the American interest in Chinese currency reform and in a currency loan."

Despite these problems, Reinsch considered the option as "a basis on which to negotiate" and commended the project to the State Department as a "signal service to the Chinese Government." The reform would strengthen the central government, stimulate economic development, establish confidence between the business classes and the government, assist in the floating of domestic loans, and relieve China of "possible inroads connected with financial pressure from without." Simultaneously, Reinsch asked Straight for help and informed him that Gest would present the matter to the American Group. Disregarding China's backwardness, Reinsch fell back on the argument, which he and other friends of China used frequently, that the per capita debt of China was small. Reinsch also distinguished between the bankruptcy of the Chinese government, which could occur through the "worst administrative incompetence," and that of the Chinese nation, which was impossible because of its vast resources. If that was not sufficiently reassuring to the bankers, Reinsch added that he could get additional taxes to cover the interest charges.[17]

Gest was well received at the State Department. But, as Reinsch expected, he found little encouragement on Wall Street.[18] Reinsch, meanwhile, had to contend with the imminent expiration of the Gest option and the ongoing Chinese negotiations with the Consortium for a currency loan. The Peking government also faced another financial crisis, as approximately $40 million in short-term gold obligations were about to fall due. The Five Power Consortium intimated that it would refund those debts, but only if it were given the currency loan "accompanied by a degree of control" which the Chinese found unacceptable.

Reinsch tried to get the Chinese to recognize the link between banking and currency reform. Liang Shih-yi, who had negotiated the Gest option, "concurred" with Reinsch's statement that the Bank of China loan would result in the issuance of new notes that would "inevitably lead to currency reform conditions." But Liang pointed out that the Ministry of Finance now handled the matter and that a long-term option would require a preliminary advance—most of which was likely to be wasted or wind up in the pockets of Chinese officials. Reinsch then turned to the minister of finance. Chou Tzu-ch'i told Reinsch that the Chinese government would continue to resist terms that were inimical to its interests, but he also indicated that China expected American assistance. "The next few months will show whether there are any friends left to China," Chou pointedly remarked.[19]

Reinsch eventually obtained an extension of the Gest option through August 15. But the Chinese made it clear to Reinsch that he had to make good. Reinsch therefore launched another strong appeal both for the Bank of China loan and for assistance in redeeming China's short-term debts. Reinsch addressed the State Department in the strongest terms: "The actual test has now come whether the Government will have to capitulate and put itself entirely in the hands of the Five Power Group monopoly, or whether independent sources of support will be opened which will enable the Chinese to overcome this last great difficulty."[20]

The outbreak of World War I eliminated competition from the Consortium and Liang Shih-yi succeeded in floating several large domestic loans. However, upon his return to China in the fall of 1914, Reinsch learned that the Chinese had renewed their efforts to secure a large administrative loan (about G$50 million) and had commissioned Roy S. Anderson to conduct negotiations in the United States. Faced with the new threat posed by Japan's occupation of Shantung, Reinsch intervened on behalf of the Chinese with a direct appeal to President Wilson. "I cannot fully express to you the seriousness of the situation," Reinsch declared to Wilson. "China is at the parting of the ways. Whether her destiny is to be one of peaceful and orderly development along the lines of constitutional freedom and self-government, or whether she is torn asunder in civil conflict and international intrigue: this depends in no small measure upon whether active assistance can be given to the Chinese at the present time in effectively organizing the activities of her national life."[21]

Wilson acknowledged the "capital and immediate importance" of Reinsch's suggestions, which he planned to discuss with his advisers. During the following months, the Wilson administration supported Gest's attempts to raise a $15 million short-term loan as well as a loan of from $100 to $200 million to reform the banking and currency system which was now entrusted to B. Howell Griswold, Jr. After an interview with Frank J. Goodnow and Griswold, who represented the banking house of Alexander Brown & Sons, Wilson delivered his strongest statement to date in support of American loans to China.[22]

It was so ironic. After denouncing the practices of the Consortium, Reinsch and Wilson now supported enormous political loans. They proceeded to endorse the hopeless efforts of promoters who knew little about China's internal affairs or America's lending capability and who were primarily interested in the commissions. They allowed themselves to be bullied by the Chinese who had only limited bargaining power. Even more revealing, the proceeds of the loans would be used to maintain an increasingly autocratic and corrupt regime which was unresponsive to the reform impulses that were germinating within China. But here was their dilemma. If they failed to assist Yuan's regime or even helped to topple it, they might open the door to internal disorder and ensuing foreign intervention. That might destroy the Chinese nation as well as American interests. In the end, they rationalized their way through by associating Yuan with China and by concentrating on the greater challenge to China itself. For Reinsch, it was always the last opportunity for America to save China. They were also eternal optimists—hopeful that

American money and moral influence would bring about progressive change and make republicans out of Yuan Shih-k'ai and his coterie.

*   *   *

While Peking's political turmoil and financial plight often overshadowed other problems, Reinsch also addressed himself to the larger question of China's adjustment to the twentieth century. Reinsch stated the problem as follows:

> How will a non-political society based on family cohesion and on cooperative arrangements in economic life, resting directly on the soil through the predominance of agriculture, dealing always in concrete personal relationships—how will it react when brought in contact with the abstract ideas, principles, and institutions of the West? Particularly how soon will it be able to make laws instead of selecting men through experience and natural development of qualities of leadership; how soon will it learn to enforce commands by penalties instead of using methods of moral suasion and compromise? . . . The question is will our ideas act merely as a dissolvent acid reducing Chinese society to disorganization and confusion leaving nothing but purely materialistic motives behind? or will Western ideas and institutions constitute nuclei for new growth and organization using the materials furnished by Chinese past development but not destructive of the same? The question is whether China will have to pass through our intensely competitive stage of development or whether its social and cooperative basis may be maintained together with a higher organization of its general social efficiency.[23]

Reinsch admitted that these were big issues. He worried that Westernization would erode the moral and social fabric of Chinese civilization and society, which he so greatly admired and respected; he feared that industrialization would destroy the beautiful Chinese artistry and handicrafts—the silks, porcelains, carpets, and bronzes—which he prized and collected, and throw thousands of artisans out of work. And yet machine industries—such as cottons and iron—had to be established. "The modern industrial spirit should not crush out the old industries of China," he lectured, "but should assist them by giving them a more perfect organization and securing them a market." Reinsch, however, was confident that China could make great strides in solving these problems. China would also need friendly outside guidance, which he was prepared to give either on a personal basis or through others.[24]

First, the Chinese must change some of their basic attitudes. Reinsch wanted to see the idea of commonwealth permeate China: leaders must learn to trust their people and must become concerned with their needs; the people, in turn, must acquire the art of selecting capable leaders; confidence must be established between the government and the business community; grandiose plans must give way to simple, practical action; the Chinese must adopt Western scientific methods and technical efficiency.

Turning to the building of the basic infrastructure of a modern economy, Reinsch stressed the priority of the transportation sector. China needed a standardized national railway system that was built for sound economic, rather than political, reasons. Although he personally leaned toward a publicly regulated private system, Reinsch thought that the Chinese might prefer a state-owned railway system. He also strongly advocated the construction of good macadamized roads. Reinsch saw the potential of garnering a large market for American goods. But he was primarily motivated by the need to unite China and the opportunity to provide jobs for millions of unemployed workers. Reinsch failed to obtain a major road-building contract, but he was directly responsible for the road-building program around Peking and in a few other provinces.[25]

Reinsch considered modern banking one of the most important and promising fields of endeavor. China needed, in particular, commercial and investment banks such as those suggested by Chang Chien, but operating under sound, efficient, and experienced Western methods. Reinsch maintained that such institutions would attract large amounts of Chinese capital, currently being hoarded or loaned at usury, which could then be used to finance commercial and industrial enterprises.[26]

Similarly, Reinsch singled out China's need to adopt the modern corporation and commercial law codes. The word of a businessman was sacred. But Chinese business largely consisted of short-term partnerships, which were frequently dissolved after accounts were settled and profits divided on the Chinese New Year. The temporary nature of these arrangements as well as the personal interference by the partners made these ventures ill suited for large-scale enterprises. "Considered from the point of view of the upbuilding of China as an efficient modern community and society, in fact from the point of view of national independence and permanence," Reinsch declared, "there is perhaps no more urgent need than that the true character of the corporation and impersonal credit and responsibility should be realized—that it is just as important to be faithful to the corporation as to a partnership, that it is just as wrong to steal from a large body of people whose rights are represented by a government or a corporation, as it is to steal from an individual." Reinsch therefore emphasized that the Chinese would learn to adopt American methods through American participation in such projects as the Huai River Conservancy and joint Sino-American enterprises.[27]

Reinsch naturally devoted much attention to the field of education. He appreciated the enormous task of educating China's large, intelligent population with the limited resources at its disposal. He assigned to the Chinese university the difficult role of mediator between Western and Eastern knowledge; he hoped it could preserve Chinese civilization while it taught Western science and technology.[28] Reinsch took a special interest in the problems of Chinese students who had studied abroad. Whether they acquired a purely theoretical Western education or a highly advanced technical training, these individuals felt cut off from traditional Chinese society and generally could not find useful or responsible work. Reinsch served as their counselor and criticized the Chinese government for failing to make the most of their education for the benefit of China.[29]

Reinsch felt that these needs justified the appointment of an educational attaché at the American legation in Peking. Such an expert, he argued to the State Department, could advise the Chinese on education policy, work with the returned students, assist Chinese scientific societies in the preservation of Chinese antiquities and arts, support the efforts of the YMCA, and address Chinese cultural organizations and educational institutions. While the designation of an educational attaché accorded perfectly with his view of the broad scope of modern diplomacy, Reinsch was further stimulated by the example of the German legation. Nevertheless, neither Williams nor Lansing felt there was sufficient need for such an officer and turned down Reinsch's recommendation.[30]

Despite his other concerns, Reinsch rarely found it possible to turn down speaking invitations, and he actively promoted the establishment of Sino-American clubs. He was a founder of the Chinese Political Science Association and took special interest in its work. It was an important organization because it linked China to scientific activity abroad, it developed Chinese intellectual life, and it stimulated Chinese nationalism by advancing the knowledge of China's traditions, problems, and achievements. "In addition," he declaimed, "it stands for the standardizing of methods of observation in political and social action, bringing to bear upon these methods the rigid criteria of scientific exactness." Reinsch was also responsible for the building of a library in Peking; it was small, yet served as a model for others.[31]

Reinsch was also concerned about the improvement of administration and the training of younger officials. In January 1916, he submitted a plan for employing foreign experts incorporating ideas used later in the Peace Corps and Point Four programs. Foreign experts would be assigned to work closely with Chinese officials in organizing municipal services, river conservancy, techniques of railway management, tax bureaus, and other administrative matters. In some cases, foreigners possessing certain valuable skills might be employed directly as engineers, mint assayers, and health experts, but they would always serve in subsidiary positions. In all cases, the aim would be to train the Chinese to take over the work themselves as quickly as possible. This was a major departure from the Chinese Maritime Service, where foreigners occupied responsible positions and the Chinese were confined to low-paid clerical and menial jobs. It was important, however, that foreign experts be engaged in useful work. To ensure that the most qualified men were selected and also to avoid political appointments, Reinsch suggested that the Chinese approach such organizations as the Carnegie Endowment or the "great institutions of learning and technical associations."[32]

Reinsch himself turned repeatedly to American foundations and educational institutions for help in transforming China. In his view, there were no limits to Sino-American cooperation; nor were such efforts superfluous. It was all part of Reinsch's integrated strategy to expand American action in China and to advertise the greatness of American institutions to the Chinese public. "It is my opinion," he argued to Dr. Wallace Buttrick, president of the China Medical Board, "that it will make a great deal of difference not only to the future of China, but also to her relations with the world and with ourselves in particular, as to whether educational forces may be liberated so as to give the Chinese mind an opportunity to develop, or whether through lack of adequate knowledge or through untoward influences the educational development of this great people is to be turned into narrow channels." Reinsch asked the China Medical Board to establish a model school in China. He called upon the Carnegie Endowment to fund a reference library in Peking (the absence of which handicapped government officials as well as students), a chair of international law at Peking University, a permanent home for Peking's China-American Club, and subsidies for the *Chinese Social and Political Science Review.*[33]

Reinsch certainly disappointed Chinese officials who relied on him to get American loans, to fulfill the generous concessions they had granted American businessmen, and to obtain United States action against their enemies. Nevertheless, they recognized that he was a "friend" of China and an idealist, who took a broad view of affairs and opposed nineteenth-century colonialism. It was the first time, V. K. Wellington Koo reminisced, that a foreign diplomat "not only understood the injustice of the situation" but also tried to carry out his convictions as far as he could go. A professional diplomat himself, Koo recalled: "He impressed us as being a sort of scholar-diplomat—not the professional career man."[34]

In his official dealings with the Chinese, Reinsch always tried to be fair. Reinsch was a gentleman and did not threaten as other foreign ministers did. He appreciated the Chinese method of negotiating and was willing to establish close ties with officials over many cups of tea. He was frequently critical of the way his countrymen negotiated and sometimes admitted when they were wrong or made excessive demands on the Chinese. Even Reinsch's critics thought well of him. One unfriendly minister stated: "There was a sort of congeniality existing between us. I could reason with him, and he was reasonable. He could see my point of view and so could I. . . . In the case of Dr. Reinsch, I only wished that he would give me a longer time to argue out the case with him."[35]

But Reinsch also demanded that the Chinese observe American treaty rights and vigorously defended American claims to equal opportunity. Thus, when the lieutenant-general of Charhar denied the right of the Mongolian Trading Company to trade in Mongolia, Reinsch persisted in the negotiations until he received what he wanted for the American firm. He complained when the Chinese failed to stand up to the British in the conflict over the Hukuang Railways. When Peking apparently allowed several provinces to impose illegal inland taxes which interfered with the free flow of commerce, Reinsch advised the State Department to withhold its consent to the stamp tax in order to secure total Chinese compliance with American treaty rights concerning likin. In fact, Reinsch occasionally overreacted to the Chinese failure to observe the Open Door. Reinsch also believed that extraterritoriality had to be maintained. But he did not think that it should be expanded; nor should it interfere with China's attempt to reorganize its society.[36]

* * *

Reinsch's ideas and actions regarding China's political, economic, and social transformation were frequently contradictory and inchoate. On the one hand, he displayed sensitivity to the turmoil within China and wished the Chinese well as they struggled to establish parliamentary government and to develop their economy and resources. Reflecting his understanding of the difficulties inherent in modernization, as well as his humanitarianism and anti-colonialism, Reinsch appreciated and supported the Chinese desire to shape their own destiny. Unlike many foreigners, Reinsch hesitated to impose foreign fiscal control on the Chinese government. On the other hand, Reinsch showed ambivalence toward the survival of democracy and republicanism in China and expediently abandoned the cause of parliamentary government in the face of Yuan's ambitions. Meanwhile, he naively lectured Yuan on the elements of parliamentary democracy and patronizingly singled out the United States as the proper model for China to emulate. Contrary to the theory that he propounded, Reinsch seemed to lose sight of the enormous gulf separating Chinese and American civilizations when he tried to implement plans for China's rapid modernization.

Three interrelated factors help to explain these inconsistencies. First, Reinsch never developed a rigorous, clear-cut concept or definition of Chinese modernization.[37] He equated it largely with industrialization, parliamentary government, nationalism, scientific education, and an abandonment of certain traditional attitudes; but he also expected that these Western experiences would be Sinified, or married to Chinese developments and traditional values. However, Reinsch's limited knowledge of China, his dislike of certain Chinese traits (inefficiency and the tendency toward corruption), and the absence of a non-Western model (or a recent social revolution) prevented him from devising a workable equation. Second, since he was floundering about, Reinsch fell back on the model that he knew well and greatly admired—progressive America, an efficient, highly industrialized, democratic capitalist society imbued with the spirit of commonwealth. In addition, Reinsch joined his contemporaries in believing that the United States had to export its values and institutions, as well as its goods and capital, in order to expand American influence. Third, Reinsch worried about drawing American investments to China, preventing internal chaos and revolutionary change, and containing foreign intervention and influence. Increasingly, the threat of Japanese imperialism colored his policies and behavior.

Consequently, Reinsch relied on the American experience and supported an autocratic, corrupt regime which did not share his vision, but which seemed to promise continuity and stability. Reinsch's sincerity somehow enabled him to retain a degree of credibility within the Young China Movement, even though he continued to defend Yuan, the Communications clique, and the succession of warlords who claimed the presidential chair in Peking. He was uncomfortable, even distressed, about the whole thing. But he felt trapped in his determined effort to save China, safeguard American interests, and check foreign encroachment and competition.

NOTES TO
CHAPTER VI

1. Reinsch, *An American Diplomat,* 1–7.
2. Reinsch to Bryan, 3 July 1914, 893.00/2152, DSNA.
3. Reinsch to Bryan, 16 March 1914, 893.00/2101, DSNA.
4. *Ibid.*
5. Interview, Reinsch and Yuan, 24 November 1913, in Reinsch to Bryan, 1 December 1913, 893.00/2049, DSNA; *FR 1913*, 82–86; *The Times* (London), 7 July 1914; *San Francisco Chronicle,* 4 May 1914.
6. Reinsch to Bryan, 1 December 1913, and enclosure, 893.00/2049, 15 March 1915, 893.00/2102, DSNA; Reinsch, *An American Diplomat*, 1–7; Ch'en, *Yuan Shih-k'ai, passim*.
7. The above synthesis is based on Williams to Bryan, 31 October 1913, 893.51/1480, DSNA; Reinsch to Bryan, 15 March 1914, 893.00/2102, 14 April 1914, 893.00/2116, 2 July 1914, 893.00/2150, DSNA; *FR 1913*, 188–89; Reinsch, *An American Diplomat*, 53–58; Beckmann, *The Modernization of China and Japan*, 224–25; Bose, *American Attitude and Policy to the Nationalist Movement in China,* 79–83; Ch'en, *Yuan Shih-k'ai,* 160–62.
8. Reinsch, *An American Diplomat,* 5–7; clipping, *Chicago Herald,* 17 July 1915, Reinsch Papers; Goodnow to Butler, 18 May and 17 June 1914, Frank J. Goodnow Papers, The Johns Hopkins University Library, Baltimore, Maryland.
9. Reinsch to Bryan, 16 March 1914, 893.00/2101, 5 May 1914, 893.011/15, DSNA; *FR 1914*, 42–43; Li, *Wilson's China Policy,* 139–40, 143.
10. Williams to Bryan, 1 April 1913, 893.00/1628, DSNA; Reinsch to Bryan, 2 July 1914, 893.00/2150, 25 November 1914, 893.00/2238, DSNA; Sun Yat-sen to Wilson, 20 November 1914, Wilson Papers; Bryan to Tumulty, 2 December 1914, *ibid.*; Reinsch, *An American Diplomat,* 43; Hawkins Tapes, 3; Bose, *American Attitude and Policy to the Nationalist Movement in China,* 82–83; Li, *Wilson's China Policy,* 144–45.
11. Reinsch to Bryan, 1 December 1913, 893.00/2049, 16 March 1914, 893.00/2101, DSNA; *FR 1914*, 42–44; Reinsch, "Chinese Society in Relation to Its Environment," n.d., Reinsch Papers; Reinsch, MS, "Foundation Principles of Government," 1919, *ibid.*; Pugach, "Embarrassed Monarchist: Frank J. Goodnow and Constitutional Development in China, 1913–1915." Reinsch misunderstood and misused the term "li," which really referred to ritual behavior and implied an authoritarian structure. It was not a basis for democracy and egalitarianism.
12. Reinsch to Bryan, 2 July 1914, 893.00/2150, DSNA; Reinsch, "Six Years of American Action in China," Reinsch Papers; Reinsch, *An American Diplomat, passim;* Albert Feuerweker, *China's Early Industrialization: Sheng Hsuan-Huai (1844–1916) and Mandarin Enterprise* (Cambridge, Mass., 1958), 251.
13. Reinsch to Bryan, 16 March 1914, 893.00/2101, DSNA; Lansing to Reinsch, 17 April 1914, *ibid.*
14. Reinsch to Bryan, 1 December 1913, 893.00/2049, 16 January 1914, 893.03/9, 29 January 1914, 893.01/10, 16 March 1914, 893.00/2101, 3 July 1914, 893.00/2152, 24 November 1914, 893.00/2237, 25 November 1914, 893.00/2238, DSNA; *New York Times,* 26 July 1914.
15. Reinsch to Bryan, 16 March 1914, 893.00/2101, 3 July 1914, 893.00/2152, DSNA; Reinsch to Wilson, 5 October 1914, McAdoo Papers.
16. *FR 1913*, 189–91; *FR 1914*, 62–64; Ch'en, *Yuan Shih-k'ai,* 148–50.
17. Reinsch to Gest, 10 March 1914, RG 84, Peking Post file, 851.6, NA; Reinsch to

Bryan, 23 March 1914, including Preliminary Agreement between Liang Shih-yi and Guion M. Gest, 893.516/27, 13 June 1914, with enclosures, 893.516/32, DSNA; Williams to Bryan, 893.516/26, DSNA; *FR 1914*, 64; Reinsch to Straight, 21 March 1914, Reinsch Papers.

18. Bryan to Reinsch, 29 May 1914, 893.516/27, DSNA; Straight to Reinsch, 30 June 1914, Reinsch Papers.

19. Reinsch to Bryan, 16 May 1914, 893.51/1513, 13 June 1914, with enclosures, 893.516/32, 2 July 1914, 893.00/2150, 6 July 1914, 893.51/1524, DSNA.

20. Reinsch to Bryan, 13 June 1914, with enclosures, 893.516/32, 2 July 1914, 893.00/2150, 3 July 1914, 893.00/2152, DSNA; MacMurray to Bryan, 10 July 1914, 893.516/31, DSNA.

21. Lansing to MacMurray, 5 August 1914, 893.00/2152, DSNA; Reinsch to Wilson, 5 October 1914, McAdoo Papers.

22. Wilson to Reinsch, 9 November 1914, Reinsch Papers; Gest to Bryan, 26 March 1915, 893.51/1571, DSNA; Bryan to Gest, 27 March 1915, *ibid.*; Bryan to Wilson, 3 May 1915, Wilson Papers; Wilson to B. Howell Griswold, 8 June 1915, *ibid.*; Li, *Wilson's China Policy,* 169–70.

23. Reinsch, "Chinese Society in Relation to Its Environment," n.d., Reinsch Papers.

24. *Ibid.*; Reinsch speech, "The Present Needs of China—in Industrial and Social Life," May 6, [?], Reinsch Papers; Reinsch, MS, "Foundation Principles of Government," *ibid.*

25. Reinsch address, "The Advantages and Disadvantages of State Control of Railways," 31 May 1914, *ibid.*; Hollington K. Tong, "Dr. Reinsch: A Popular American Minister," clipping, *Millard's Review,* 13 September 1919, *ibid.*; Reinsch, *An American Diplomat*, 163–64.

26. Anderson to Reinsch, 17 March 1914, Reinsch Papers; Reinsch to Lansing, 28 December 1915, 893.516/40, DSNA; Gauss to MacMurray, 31 August 1915, RG 84, Peking Post file, 885, NA; *FR 1917*, 114–15. See Chapter XIII for a discussion of Reinsch's involvement in Sino-American banking.

27. Reinsch speech, "The Present Needs of China—in Industrial and Social Life," Reinsch Papers; Reinsch, "The Attitude of the Chinese towards Americans," *Annals of the American Academy of Political and Social Science,* XCIII (January 1921), 7–13; Reinsch, *An American Diplomat,* 380.

28. Reinsch speech at St. John's University, 3 November 1913, clipping, *North China Daily News,* 4 November 1913, Reinsch Papers; Reinsch Commencement Address at the University of Peking, 1 June 1915, in 123.R271/32, DSNA; Reinsch to Buttrick, 1 December 1915, 124.93/16, DSNA.

29. Reinsch to Butler, 10 February 1914, Chinese Affairs, C12-157, CEIP Papers; Reinsch address, "The Chinese Political Science Association," 16 February 1916, Reinsch Papers; author's interview with V. K. Wellington Koo, 24 February 1965, New York.

30. ·Reinsch to Bryan, 25 January 1915, and comments of Williams and Lansing, 124.93/15, DSNA; Reinsch, "Six Years of American Action in China," Reinsch Papers; Reinsch, *An American Diplomat,* 144.

31. Memo of conversation, Reinsch and Yuan, 20 January 1916, in 893.01/88, DSNA; Reinsch speech at the "British-American Evening," 8 December 1917, Reinsch Papers; Tong, "Dr. Reinsch: A Popular American Minister."

32. Memo of conversation, Reinsch and Yuan, 20 January 1916, and Reinsch memo, "On the Use of Foreign Experts," in 893.01/88, DSNA.

33. Reinsch to Buttrick, 1 December 1915, 124.93/16, DSNA; Reinsch to Williams,

19 January 1918, Reinsch Papers; Reinsch to James Brown Scott, 5 December 1916, *ibid.*; Reinsch to Butler, 10 December 1914, Chinese Affairs, C12-108, 17 January 1918, Chinese Affairs, C12-157, CEIP Papers; Jordan to Grey, 14 April 1914, 10/18964/14, FO 371/1947.

34. Author's interview with Koo, 24 February 1965.

35. *Ibid.*; Tong, "Dr. Reinsch: A Popular American Minister."

36. MacMurray to mother, 19 February 1914, MacMurray Papers. For Reinsch's handling of the disputes involving the Chinese mining regulations of 1914 and the stamp tax, see *FR 1914*, 119–39; *FR 1915*, 216–31.

37. For an excellent discussion of the terminology of modernization, see John H. Kautsky, *The Political Consequences of Modernization* (New York, 1972).

Chapter VII

THE JAPANESE NEMESIS: WORLD WAR I AND THE TWENTY-ONE DEMANDS

During his first six months in China, Reinsch crossed swords with all of the major foreign powers. But it was Japan that emerged as the chief nemesis of the United States and China and the primary threat to the Open Door. Japan assisted the rebels during the summer of 1913, used the Nanking troubles to augment its permanent military forces in China, and seemed to take advantage of every weakness in Chinese political and social life. It extended its Manchurian sphere of influence into Inner Mongolia and Jehol and advanced its claim to special rights in Fukien. Then, to London's chagrin, Tokyo sought to enlarge the Anglo-Japanese Alliance into an economic pact in order to obtain British capital for its enterprises in China. At the same time, it attempted to gain admission to the Yangtze Valley. Britain rejected both initiatives, but Japan pressed ahead by acquiring control of the financially troubled Hanyehping Company, China's largest iron and coal complex, and demanded that Peking grant Japanese capitalists railway concessions in central China. The accession of the Okuma government led to a relaxation in tension between China and Japan as the Japanese premier propounded his policy of cooperation among Oriental peoples. Reinsch, however, regarded this rhetoric, and subsequent references to a Japanese Monroe Doctrine as euphemisms for Japanese domination of China and the elimination of all foreign rivals.

Meanwhile, American conflicts with Japan became more frequent and serious. Japan protested the Standard Oil contract, expressed displeasure with the Huai River Conservancy agreement, blocked the Chinchou-Aigun Railway and infringed on American trademarks. Japanese efforts to undermine the Bethlehem Steel contract alerted Reinsch to Tokyo's intentions and methods and eliminated any residue of his earlier sympathy for Japan. In a frank exchange with the Japanese minister in March 1914, Reinsch objected to the repeated insinuations in the Japanese press that every American enterprise was directed against Japan. On the other hand, the Japanese were sensitive to the mildest criticism of their activities, such as appeared when Japan concluded the Hanyehping loan.

Thus, as Reinsch prepared to leave Peking to spend the summer of 1914 in Europe, he offered a decidedly pessimistic analysis of the international situation in the Far East. The Open Door was under siege. Little did he realize, however, the grave crisis that loomed on the horizon.[1]

*   *   *

The outbreak of World War I shattered the delicate balance of power which had operated in China for many years. Japanese military forces landed in Shantung and quickly seized the entire Tsinan-Tsingtao Railway (Germany's chief economic interest in the province) as well as the German leasehold. Fearful of a Japanese-German rapprochement, which was cleverly cultivated by Tokyo, and concerned with protecting their spheres of influence, the Allies were forced to accede to further Japanese demands during the war. Japan was given a virtual free hand in the Far East and was determined to make the most of it.[2]

American policy makers agreed that the preservation of the status quo was desirable, if not necessary, for the protection of American interests and China's integrity. The United States sounded out the other powers on some form of joint action to maintain China's neutrality and integrity, but their inability to go beyond expressions of sympathy brought Washington's intervention to a halt. The United States, Counselor Robert Lansing stated in an often-quoted dispatch, wanted to reassure China of American friendship, "but the Department realizes that it would be quixotic in the extreme to allow the question of China's territorial integrity to entangle the United States in international difficulties."[3]

Reinsch, ironically, was in Europe to attend the Lucerne Conference when the great catastrophe, which the Carnegie Endowment for International Peace had labored to prevent, erupted in full force. As Reinsch passed through the United States on his way back to China, Bryan asked him to submit an analysis of the Far Eastern situation. The tone of Reinsch's memorandum, dated August 27, 1914, was moderate. Reinsch declared that Japan's return of Kiaochau would promote friendly relations between China and Japan, which the United States need not fear as long as the Open Door was observed. However, unlike Lansing's forthcoming bargain, Reinsch insisted that the United States should not compromise any of its rights or China's integrity; nor should it publicly recognize Japan's special interests on any part of the Asian mainland. "By protecting our rights we shall also protect those of China," he explained. Nevertheless, Reinsch advocated the bold use of America's economic power if Japan exceeded its legitimate interests. "Japan should understand," he declared, "that the capital which she will necessarily require for the development of her economic enterprises at home and on the continent of Asia, can be secured from America, only if her policy in China is one of fair treatment, not of armed conquest."[4]

When Reinsch returned to Peking on September 30, 1914, he was besieged by troubled Chinese officials, led by Minister of Communications Liang Tun-yen, who looked to America for salvation. Fully aware of the State Department's position, Reinsch told them that China would have to exercise "self control" and rely on a "just arrangement" at the end of the war. Reinsch also assured the new Japanese minister, Hioki Eki, of America's good will toward Japan's legitimate enterprise. But he reminded him that Americans were entering China "by their own right."[5]

By the end of November, however, Reinsch's attitude hardened. First of all, the "Manchurianization" of Shantung had begun. Japanese leaders began to deny their former commitment to hand over Kiaochau to China and used the occupation of the railway to extend Tokyo's influence in Shantung. Moreover, Reinsch sensed that a major Japanese démarche was imminent. He was still unable to determine whether Japan planned to use its economic influence or its political and military power. But the time was propitious. Europe was preoccupied with the war and China was weak and rife with unrest.[6]

Reinsch therefore maintained that the United States had to carry the burden of maintaining the status quo in the Far East. The interests of the United States were then unimportant compared with Britain's. But Reinsch stressed that "the traditions of American policy, the efforts and sacrifices of two generations of Americans at work in China, the trusteeship of intimate confidence which the Chinese place in America and, above all, the need which our country will have in the future of continued free access to China and of mutual friendship with its peoples" made the disposal of Shantung "a matter far from indifferent to Americans." Reinsch also felt that America had to demonstrate that its friendship was not "a bubble which vanished before any concrete facts, such as the violation of China's neutrality," as its foreign rivals delighted to point out to Peking officials.

China's enforced submission to Japan, the paralysis of the Chinese government, and the appeals of Chinese officials moved Reinsch to seek positive American action. Reinsch also felt that the Chinese were justified in expecting the United States—"rich and powerful beyond measure in the minds of the Chinese"—to help them maintain their independence and sovereignty. As they had encouraged American activities, "looking upon them as a safeguard to their own national life, . . . the Chinese hope and expect as a minimum that Americans would not allow themselves to be excluded by political intrigue or by other means from their share in the development and activities of China."

Furthermore, Japan failed to appreciate America's forbearance and its "simple, direct, open and straightforward policy." That was unfortunate, for Japan was vulnerable. "If the United States should really enter upon a policy of trying to block the development of Japan, and should utilize the hostility of China and the latent but serious fears of Great Britain, Russia and more especially of Canada and Australia, the results might indeed be very damaging to Japan," he observed to Bryan.

Reinsch therefore prescribed a stout defense of American rights in China and forceful opposition to any special preferences in railways and other public concessions. Second, he called upon Americans to take advantage of the unusual opportunities that were offered to them and which "will pass away forever," unless they were promptly utilized. Reinsch also believed that the United States could obtain the concerted action of the other powers, especially Britain, against the "Manchurianization of Shantung." Finally, Reinsch held the door open for a frank understanding with Japan. America would not begrudge Japan's legitimate enterprises and prosperity. In return, Tokyo had to recognize that Washington had responsibilities to its own citizens and that Americans are in China "for their own purposes and of their own rights." On the other hand, Reinsch opined, it would be "futile and dangerous" to yield anything concerning "our present position and interests in China; such yielding would not result in feelings of gratitude, but would be taken as a sign of weakness and would simply make way for other attempts to walk over us."[7]

*   *   *

Reinsch accurately divined Japan's intentions. On the evening of January 18, 1915, Japanese Minister Hioki Eki arrogantly presented the Twenty-One Demands to President Yuan Shih-k'ai. Thinly veiled threats accompanied this diplomatic insult. Hioki also enjoined the president to maintain strict secrecy about the demands and the subsequent negotiations.[8]

The Twenty-One Demands were divided into five groups. The first required China to accept any arrangement that Japan made concerning German rights and interests in Shantung and to recognize Japan's prior claim to all rail and industrial concessions in the province. The second group demanded Chinese recognition of Japan's predominant position in South Manchuria and Eastern Inner Mongolia, including the use of Japanese advisers and new railway concessions. Under the third section, China would consent to the eventual conversion of the Hanyehping Company into a joint Sino-Japanese enterprise. China was also to pledge that the company would not dispose of any of its interests without Japanese approval nor allow outsiders to work at mines neighboring those owned by the company. With Fukien primarily in mind, the fourth group required that Peking not cede or lease to a third power any harbor, bay, or island along the China coast. The fifth group contained the most far-reaching and dangerous demands. Among other things, it called for the employment of "influential" Japanese advisers in political, military, and financial affairs, the purchase of fixed amounts of munitions from Japan, a Japanese veto over all foreign industrial contracts in Fukien, and several major railway concessions in central China.[9]

The Chinese were stunned. China's armed forces could not resist Japan's proven military might and the European powers could not render any direct assistance. America might be encouraged to defend its own rights against Japanese encroachments and might conceivably arrange joint action with the other powers. Otherwise, the Chinese were limited to ascertaining Japan's specific intentions, practicing the ancient art of procrastination, and mobilizing world opinion against Japanese aggression.[10]

Consequently, the Chinese commenced negotiations with the Japanese on February 2, 1915. Hioki pressed for rapid acceptance of the entire list of demands. But the Chinese delegation, headed by Foreign Minister Lu Tseng-tsiang, refused absolutely to discuss the demands affecting Chinese sovereignty, especially Group V, and argued for the separate discussion of each point. In time, the Chinese showed a willingness to concede the less obnoxious demands relating to Shantung and Manchuria. For the next three months, the negotiations labored on, punctuated by further Japanese threats and additional Chinese concessions.[11]

Reinsch learned of the crisis on January 22, when one of the Chinese ministers confided to him, "almost in tears," that Japan had made serious demands which threatened China's independence. On the following day, Reinsch was given a more complete oral account of the Japanese

document and was told that there were twenty-one points. Subsequently, Reinsch kept in touch with the progress of the negotiations through
the nightly visits of Wellington Koo, counselor in the Ministry of
Foreign Affairs, who made his way into the Chancery by means of the
back door. In addition, Reinsch was supplied with reports by numerous
Chinese officials and by William H. Donald. However, the cautious
Chinese waited several weeks before giving him a complete written copy
of the demands, the substance of which was already generally known in
China and the United States.[12]

Reinsch recognized immediately the extent and danger of the
Japanese démarche; sooner, in fact, than British Minister John Jordan.
Calling it "the greatest crisis yet experienced in China," Reinsch believed that the demands threatened China's independence, American
interests, and the entire Open Door policy.[13] Without interfering with
the formal "integrity, sovereignty, and independence of China," Japan
was seeking to control China's administration and economic development. It intended to use its consolidated position in Manchuria, Shantung, and Fukien to extend its influence throughout northern, central,
and southern China. Group V, moreover, would give Tokyo complete
control over China's military, political, and fiscal affairs and make China
a vassal state.[14]

Reinsch argued that Japan was seeking more than temporary advantages or a fair share of the concessions which the other powers had
previously denied it. Rather, Japan's current behavior was part of a larger
scheme to dominate the Far East. "The most disquieting feature of this
situation," Reinsch warned early in the crisis, "is that since the appetite
of the Japanese masses grows with the expansion of power it seems hopeless to expect inner restraint or limitation on the aggressive policy of that
nation, which bids fair to continue until it comes against a dead wall of
sufficiently powerful resistance from without."

He also stressed that, because of the long history of Japanese-
American antagonism, American interests would suffer more than those
of most nations from Japan's vast increase in influence. "The good will
and sincere friendship which the Chinese people have for Americans
would no longer be free to manifest itself," Reinsch predicted; "Americans could engage in enterprises in China only at the sufferance of another
government, and the friction inevitably resulting would tend to feelings
of hostility between Americans and Japan."[15]

Finally, Reinsch found Japanese methods almost as disquieting as
the substance of the demands. The imposition of secrecy and the threat of
armed intervention exemplified the worst forms of power diplomacy and

Machiavellianism. Even though it was a sovereign nation, China was so intimidated that it feared consulting other friendly powers. With the cooperation of British censors, Japanese diplomats tried to suppress news reports of the astounding Japanese démarche. Furthermore, when the details of Group V became widely known, Japan explained that they were merely "wishes" or "suggestions." The Japanese made only a casual distinction to the Chinese and they demanded that Peking concede the entire list.[16]

Reinsch hesitated to do anything that might imply a United States commitment to intervene. But taking advantage of the legal ramifications of the various international treaties, he did, in fact, offer advice to the Chinese in the guise of his "carefully weighed opinion" and his impressions of the "tactical situation," as it developed from week to week. Reinsch encouraged the Chinese to prolong the negotiations in order to buy time for other governments to protest and for China's friends to arouse world public opinion; he told them to concede small points, to be as specific as possible, and to grant those things which the other powers could demand under the most favored nation clause. Above all, he cautioned the Chinese to stand firm against Group V. There would be a day of reckoning at the end of the European war, and China must be careful not to compromise itself too much.[17]

Reinsch realized that the Chinese would have to bear most of the burden of limiting the Japanese demands. Still, he believed that China should enlist the influence of Britain, press the United States to defend its rights and, ignoring the injunction of secrecy, publicize the demands. When it became apparent that London and Washington were reluctant to act, Reinsch and the Chinese concluded that publicity was their only ready weapon. They quickly worked out an arrangement: Koo and other officials kept Reinsch abreast of the progress of the negotiations, which the minister then leaked to friendly, reliable foreign correspondents. The Chinese also found ways of releasing details directly to Chinese and foreign newspapermen. Their collaboration not only succeeded in turning world public opinion against Japan, but also enabled the United States and other powers to question Japan about the demands, and eventually forced Tokyo to admit their existence.[18]

Meanwhile, the response of British and American policy makers caused Reinsch profound disappointment. A turn to London seemed natural. Japanese designs on the Yangtze Valley and their misuse of the Anglo-Japanese Alliance greatly upset the British. In any event, of all the powers only Britain had some leverage on Japan. "All aspects of the crisis indicate that the British Government holds the key to the situation," Reinsch advised the State Department. And if London was unwilling to cooperate, Reinsch pointed out that "the friendly characters of American neutrality" and the "coercive power of supplies" might be used to strengthen Washington's hand. In fact, primarily concerned with protecting their commercial interests in the Yangtze during the war, British policy makers debated whether "effacement" or cooperation with Japan was the best strategy to buy time. To the chagrin of the Chinese, Jordan advised them "to be conciliatory and run no risks."[19]

Washington's response was far more frustrating and disconcerting. The Far Eastern crisis in 1915 produced the first serious tensions, misunderstandings, and exchanges of recriminations between the American minister and Secretary of State Bryan. The State Department believed that Reinsch was too deeply involved in advising the Chinese and that he was responsible for the disclosure of confidential information to the press, especially the contents of important official notes to Tokyo. Reinsch may have exceeded the bounds of propriety in offering friendly advice to the Chinese and leaking the progress of the Sino-Japanese negotiations to the press. But there is no evidence that he was responsible for the disclosures that troubled Washington. Both the Chinese and the Japanese used the same tactic when it suited their purposes. Nevertheless, Reinsch became very defensive and stoutly denied Bryan's imputation of misconduct. Reinsch also expressed dissatisfaction that he was not being properly informed of all developments in the crisis.[20]

Reinsch was primarily upset by Washington's apparent indifference to Japanese aggression and its acquiescence in the Japanese position. For those like Reinsch who wanted the United States to intervene strongly, the Twenty-One Demands intruded at an inopportune time. The administration, Wilson above all, was immersed in the submarine issue and the ongoing Mexican affair. Although the president was concerned with Japanese intentions and the threat to the Open Door, he thought that, in the present instance, any direct advice to China would excite Japanese hostility and do more harm than good. Wilson wrote Reinsch that he would play the part of China's prudent friend, "watching the situation carefully and ready to step in at any point it is wise to do so."[21]

During the early stages of the crisis, therefore, Far Eastern policy making was largely in the hands of Bryan. Bryan agreed that, if Reinsch and the press were accurate, China's integrity and equal opportunity were seriously threatened. But American differences with Japan, especially the California land question, made Bryan extremely reluctant to antagonize Japan. Reflecting his pacifism, Bryan also adopted the position that since China and Japan were neighbors, "it is of vital importance that they should be neighborly and a neighborly spirit cannot be expected if Japan demands too much and China concedes too little." Bryan's failure to appreciate the consequences of some of the demands and his implicit faith in the assurances of the Japanese ambassador, particularly that Group V did not exist or had been withdrawn, revealed his ignorance of Far Eastern matters as well as his general naiveté. "I trust the Japanese Ambassador," Bryan wrote on a memorandum charging Tokyo with deliberately misleading the United States.[22]

Nevertheless, Bryan thought that the United States ought to take advantage of the opening provided by Japan's admission of the existence of Group V to comment on their effect on China's integrity, the Open Door, and America's treaty rights. Wilson, who may have been influenced by Reinsch's cable of February 18, strongly concurred. "I think those views can be made very weighty and conclusive," he replied to the Secretary of State. "We shall not have uttered a more important state paper."[23]

Within the State Department opposition quickly developed to Bryan's intended reply on the grounds that it was too weak and that, if confined to Group V, it would give the impression that the United States did not object to the rest of the demands. E. T. Williams would not protest the demands regarding South Manchuria, but he wanted to use the opportunity to obtain assurances that Japan would discontinue its discriminatory practices against American trade. He also believed in the veracity of Reinsch's reports and agreed with the minister that the United States, as "custodian" of the Open Door, had both an obligation and a practical need to protect its legitimate interests and assist China.[24]

Robert Lansing, counselor in the State Department, was more concerned about the protection of American commercial interests than China's integrity. He also thought that the United States should insist on a *quid pro quo*. Lansing therefore used the opportunity provided by Wilson's request for a comprehensive review of American Far Eastern policy and Bryan's proposed note to put to paper his ideas for a bargain with Japan. The United States would recognize that Japan had "special interests" in South Manchuria, Inner Mongolia, and Shantung. In return, Japan would promise not to protest the alien land legislation, as long as it was not confiscatory, and reaffirm the principle of equal opportunity even in those areas where Japan possessed "special interests."[25]

The important American note of March 13, 1915, largely drafted by Lansing, represented a compromise of the varying viewpoints in the administration. There was to be no formal bargain and Wilson and Bryan agreed to postpone any reference to the alien land legislation. Wilson objected to any formal recognition of Japan's special interests, but the note implied as much in the significant passage that would later haunt American policy makers: "The United States frankly recognizes that territorial continuity creates special relations between Japan and these districts." The note's basic tone was conciliatory in that the United States acquiesced in Groups I, II, IV. On the other hand, the United States presumed that Japan would not seek to monopolize trade and investments in China or use its special preferences to discriminate against American commerce. The note restated the validity and relevance of various Chinese treaties, the Open Door notes, and the Root-Takahira Agreement. It also gave a broad construction of the Open Door by declaring the right of the United States to claim similar rights in the development of Fukien and other provinces. Finally, it dwelt on the severity of Group V and its incompatibility with China's political independence. The note appeared to make major concessions to Japan while reserving American rights and freedom to intervene in the future.[26]

Considering the serious threat to Chinese independence and to American interests, Reinsch's initial response to the Japanese démarche had been surprisingly cautious and pragmatic. His recommendations were moderate and reasonable. His dispatches emphasized the reality of the situation and lacked the moral fervor and pleading that characterized his later diplomatic correspondence. But by the middle of February, Reinsch exhibited impatience and irritation with Washington and he adopted a more aggressive posture.

From his vantage point in Peking, Reinsch concluded that China required stronger diplomatic support. The Chinese were increasingly apprehensive that submission to Japan's demands would encourage Tokyo to press for others. The Japanese, in fact, orchestrated their tough stand at the bargaining table with intimidating movements of troops and naval vessels. Plainly, Japan sought China's acceptance of the more dangerous demands contained in Group III and Group V, which it had still failed to communicate in their entirety to the other powers. Moreover, Reinsch found it increasingly difficult to avoid encouragement of the Chinese toward the possibility that the United States would intervene for the sake of friendship and international justice.[27]

Therefore, when the Japanese informed the Chinese negotiators, on February 18, 1915, that they would have to discuss all of the Twenty-One Demands, Reinsch cabled Wilson inviting his "personal attention to the proposals which affected the rights and legitimate prospects of Americans in China." During the following weeks, Reinsch hammered away at this theme with increasing intensity, particularly since Washington persisted in accepting the Japanese distinction between demands and "wishes." In his lengthy dispatch of March 6, 1915 (his important "571"), Reinsch, finally armed with a copy of the demands presented to Yuan on January 18, compared them point for point with the list which the Japanese minister had recently given him. Japanese ambition and duplicity were now fully evident.[28]

Bryan's well-intentioned but clumsy mediation effort at the end of March further infuriated Reinsch and moved him to action. The Japanese ambassador had convinced Bryan of the need to calm Japanese fears that the United States planned to establish a naval base or coaling station on the Fukien coast. Viscount Chinda Sutemi also persuaded Bryan that some of the demands contained in Group V were reasonable. Consequently, Bryan told United States ambassador to Japan George Guthrie on March 26 that he could inform the Japanese government that the United States would approve a Sino-Japanese agreement withholding from any foreign power the right to build a naval base or harbor improvement along the coast of Fukien. Bryan also suggested further compromises regarding railway concessions in Fukien and the "requests" relating to arms and advisers.[29]

Reinsch was astounded by Bryan's naiveté. He warned that Bryan's suggested compromises would destroy China's administrative independence without assuring peace. He insisted that Group V must be totally eliminated. "Any version of them," he later explained in his memoirs, "would tangle, would more inextricably snarl, the already complicated relationships of foreign powers in China, and choke all constructive action." Reinsch also reported how the Japanese propaganda machine had disparaged American action in order to undermine Chinese confidence in the United States. Japanese newspapers claimed that Bryan was under the influence of Viscount Chinda, and so it appeared in the Far East. Reinsch feared that when the Chinese learned about Bryan's proposals to Guthrie—and they would surely be told by the Japanese—they would feel betrayed by the United States. If Washington did not plan to take positive action, he remarked in his telegram of March 30, it would be more expedient to pursue a course of "passive acquiescence rather than to intervene in such a manner as could scarcely fail to cause revulsion of Chinese feeling against the United States and put an end to our influence here and our opportunities either of assisting the Chinese government or of preserving our own rights in China." Meanwhile, Reinsch informed Bryan, he would take "appropriate steps" through friendly Chinese to prevent the spreading of misrepresentations.[30]

Reinsch's telegram of March 30 caused Wilson "a good deal of concern" and indicated clearly that a different view prevailed in Peking. Shortly afterward, Reinsch's "571" arrived at the State Department and that was followed by his dramatic plea of April 14 for the United States to disassociate itself publicly from the "unconscionable demands of Japan." This series of messages initiated a new phase of policy making. A chastened Bryan tried to made amends by telling Reinsch that his advice to Guthrie would be divulged only "in case of inquiry" and by adopting a tougher stand against Japan during the following weeks. Embarrassed because he had already conveyed his suggestions to the Japanese ambassador, Bryan did not tell Wilson of his predicament and transferred the note to Japan from the official files to his personal papers. In fact, Wilson personally took over the direction of Far Eastern policy and, because of his stand on the submarine issue, Bryan was on his way out as secretary of state.[31]

Reinsch's persistence, supported by protests from American merchants in China and the United States, finally brought him a fair hearing in Washington. "We shall have to be very chary about seeming to concede the reasonableness of Japan's demands or requests either, until we get the whole of the situation in our minds by hearing from Peking as well as from Tokyo," Wilson told Bryan. It also fired Wilson's determination to be as active "as circumstances permit."[32]

Subsequently, Reinsch was instructed to issue a statement to the effect that the United States had not surrendered any of its treaty rights or "abated one iota of its friendly interest in all that concerns the industrial and political welfare of China."[33] Increasingly concerned about the implications of Group III and the discrepancies between the demands presented to China and the other powers, Wilson instructed Bryan to have a "very candid talk" with Chinda. "I think that you will be justified in showing him that we take it very seriously and are very much concerned, seeing in such things a very decided infringement of the principle of the open door and also of China's administrative and economic integrity," the president told his secretary of state.[34]

The administration's tougher stand became evident during Bryan's frank and somewhat heated conversation with Chinda on April 27. Bryan delivered a forceful expression of America's dissatisfaction with the increase of Japanese troops in China. The secretary of state pointed out Japan's failure to distinguish for the benefit of the Chinese between demands and requests. He also suggested that there was no justification for Tokyo's insistence on the joint ownership of the Hanyehping Company. Bryan hinted further that the United States might feel compelled to make public the correspondence dealing with the Twenty-One Demands. He observed that American silence had led to unjustified speculations and misrepresentations of American policies and views and that the private nature of the negotiations prevented the United States from conferring with China.[35]

Meanwhile, the Sino-Japanese negotiations in Peking reached their climax. On April 26, as a prelude to an ultimatum, Hioki presented the Chinese with a revised list of the demands. There was no retreat from the demands regarding Manchuria, Shantung, Eastern Inner Mongolia, and the Fukien coast. The Hanyehping Company was to be converted into a Sino-Japanese company and China had to pledge that it would not make it a government enterprise, but the demand for control of the surrounding mines was dropped. Group V was formally withdrawn, but most of the demands were to be embodied in a separate Chinese note to Japan. Reinsch quickly pointed out that the withdrawal of Group V left "the substance of the demands unaffected." He also stressed the emptiness of Japan's promise to return Tsingtao at the end of the war: Japan would still be entrenched in Shantung through its ownership of the railway and mines, its preference in industrial matters, and the grant of a settlement to be selected by Japan.[36]

Forewarned by Reinsch, Bryan critically analyzed the revised demands. Bryan understood that Japan was not included in the non-alienation provision regarding the Fukien coast and that Tokyo was still pressing for most of Group V. In particular, he recognized the potential danger of a Japanese sphere of influence in the Yangtze should Britain permit the construction of Japanese railroads in central China. It would be better to advise China to built its own railroads with money borrowed from general loans and "not by mortgage of particular property," he told Wilson. "I think our capitalists will loan money on China's credit and if our capitalists will loan on this security other capitalists will be compelled to loan on the same terms. This will make China's loans national, like the loans of other governments, and relieve her of the danger which follows in the wake of these concessions." Bryan dwelt on many of these points when he presented a formal American note to Chinda on May 5. He also expressed concern that Japan was preparing to deliver an ultimatum to China and was putting its armed forces on a war footing.[37]

On May 6, Reinsch confirmed that the Japanese legation had an ultimatum in its hands and would present it to the Chinese on the following day. Bryan immediately sent notes to China and Japan requesting both governments to continue the negotiations in a friendly and patient manner until an amicable solution could be reached. Simultaneously, he instructed American ambassadors in Britain, France, and Russia to inquire if those governments would join with the United States in counseling moderation upon Japan.[38]

Reinsch had finally received just about all he could expect from the Wilson administration. But it came too late. On the afternoon of May 7, Japan submitted its ultimatum, accompanied by military movements, and required China's unconditional acceptance by 6 P.M. on May 9. The final Japanese terms followed closely those conceded by the Chinese on May 1, 1915, and, with the exception of industrial matters in Fukien, Group V was postponed. In fact, the Chinese had expected an ultimatum and it probably made Yuan's capitulation easier. On May 25, 1915, this chapter of Japanese encroachment in China came to an end when the two powers exchanged notes and protocols confirming Peking's submission to the terms contained in Tokyo's ultimatum.[39]

*   *   *

Japan therefore accepted less than total victory. Britain's belated intervention in the final phase of the crisis, especially Foreign Minister Edward Grey's note of May 3, may have tipped the balance in favor of the moderates as well as those Japanese leaders who continued to value the Anglo-Japanese Alliance.[40] But Chinese resistance to the most egregious demands, an aroused world public opinion, and the change in the American position also influenced the outcome of the crisis. And in these matters, Reinsch played a useful, if not significant, role.

At the beginning of the crisis, Reinsch had reached the same conclusion as the Chinese on the nature of the Japanese démarche and devised a similar strategy to deal with it. Unlike his British counterpart, Sir John Jordan, Reinsch never told the Chinese that their cause was hopeless. Although Jordan favored a somewhat stronger British response than Whitehall adopted, he personally believed that China was largely "to blame for its weakness and might is right in these days."[41] Instead, Reinsch helped to stiffen the Chinese resolve and encouraged them to draw out the negotiations. Then, having won the confidence of the Chinese, he helped to unmask Japanese duplicity to the rest of the world. The efforts of Reinsch and the Chinese thereby denied Japan an early and easy victory, broke the web of Japanese secrecy, aroused world opinion against Japanese aggression, and bought time. In this way, they enabled the British and American governments to confront Tokyo with the concealed demands and, eventually, to object to the most flagrant threats to Chinese independence and their own interests. Indeed, Reinsch's most important contribution was to educate American policy makers to the seriousness of the Japanese initiative with his perceptive analysis of the immediate dangers and implications for the future.

Reinsch never expected the United States to intervene on a major scale. But he hoped that it would at least avoid compromising its own rights along with China's independence. Despite initial setbacks and disappointments, Reinsch succeeded in getting his message through to Washington by the middle of April. Two days after China accepted the Japanese ultimatum the United States made another effort to protect its position by falling back on its traditional rights and interests in China. In the historically important note of May 11, 1915, the United States declared to China and Japan that it would not recognize any agreement which impaired the rights of the United States, the political or territorial integrity of China, or the Open Door. Reflecting Bryan's optimism that Americans would lend money to China, the Wilson Administration seemed more determined than ever to encourage independent American economic activity in China.[42]

Throughout the crisis Reinsch generally acted thoughtfully, cautiously, and realistically. It was only in April, when Reinsch feared that the American position in China would be permanently compromised, that his correspondence rang with an impassioned tone decrying Japan's "unconscionable" demands. Even MacMurray, who was often critical of his chief's excesses, believed that, with the exception of the "few lapses into 'sob-stuff,'" Reinsch had handled the situation "admirably." The usually restrained professional diplomat waxed indignant over Washington's failure to read Reinsch's telegrams carefully, the State Department's apparent indifference to the threat of American rights and interests, and Bryan's gullibility.[43]

*   *   *

Japan now turned its attention to consolidating its position in China. Continued Chinese weakness, European preoccupation in the war, and America's limited interests would encourage Japan to take advantage of every opportunity to extend its recent gains; nor would there be any retreat from the long range objective of establishing Japanese hegemony in East Asia. Reinsch shared the growing feeling of many Americans in China that Japan was waging "a Cold War against the United States." The Twenty-One Demands made Reinsch a determined foe of Japan. It convinced him of the need to watch every Japanese move and to strengthen the American position in China.[44]

NOTES TO
CHAPTER VII

1. Williams to Bryan, 15 August 1913, 893.00/1887, DSNA; Reinsch to Bryan, 29 November 1913, 893.00/2021, 26 May 1914, 893.51/1523, 12 June 1914, 793.94/196, 29 June 1914, 893.00/2149, DSNA; memo of conversation, Reinsch and Yamaza, 12 March 1914, in 893.00/2102, DSNA; Robert J. Gowen, "Great Britain and the Twenty-One Demands of 1915: Cooperation versus Effacement," *Journal of Modern History,* XLIII (March 1971), 76–85.

2. Li, *Wilson's China Policy,* 91–100; Griswold, *Far Eastern Policy,* 176–85; Thomas E. LaFargue, *China and the World War* (Stanford, 1937), 7–25; Gowen, "Britain and the Twenty-One Demands," 83; Frank W. Iklé, "Japanese-German Peace Negotiations during World War I," *American Historical Review,* LXXI (October 1965), 62–75; Sadao Asada, "Japan and the United States, 1915–25" (Ph.D. dissertation, Yale University, 1963), 10–12, 23. See also, Madeline Chi, *China Diplomacy, 1914–1918* (Cambridge, Mass., 1970), 1–27; Ian Nish, *Alliance in Decline: A Study in Anglo-Japanese Relations, 1908–1923* (London, 1972), 115–31.

3. *FR 1914, Supplement (Supp.),* 161–211; *Foreign Relations: The Lansing Papers, 1914–1920,* 2 vols. (Washington, 1939), I, 1–5 (hereafter cited *FR: Lansing Papers*); Bryan to MacMurray, 3 August 1914, 763.72111/4, 29 September 1914, 763.72/995, DSNA; Li, *Wilson's China Policy,* 91–100; Griswold, *Far Eastern Policy,* 176–85; Link, *Wilson: The Struggle for Neutrality,* 193–94; Ernest May, "American Policy and Japan's Entrance into World War I," *Mississippi Valley Historical Review,* XL (September 1953), 279–80.

4. Reinsch, "Informal Memorandum on China and Japan Submitted at the Suggestion of the Secretary of State," 27 August 1914, 793.94/356, DSNA.

5. Reinsch to Bryan, 2 October 1914, 763.72/1181, DSNA, 31 October 1914, Reinsch Papers; *FR 1914, Supp.,* 182–83, 192–93, 197; Reinsch, *An American Diplomat,* 124–26. Patrick Scanlan points out that the Chinese were divided on whom to turn to for help. He sees two groups: one, consisting of members of Yuan's old *mu-fu,* had become disenchanted with the promises of American support and decided not to antagonize Japan; the other, including such new *mu-fu* officials as Liang Tun-yen, looked to Reinsch and America for help. See Scanlan, "No Longer a Treaty Port," 102–3.

6. Reinsch to Bryan, 25 November 1914, 893.00/2238, 28 November 1914, 793.94/205, 22 December 1914, 793.94/216, DSNA; *FR 1914, Supp.,* 204; Reinsch, *An American Diplomat,* 127–28. Reinsch's dispatches in November-December 1914 indicate that he had a pretty good idea of the alternatives available to Japan. Yet, Scanlan states that Reinsch did not have "the slightest inkling of Japan's next move." See Scanlan, "No Longer a Treaty Port," 109.

7. Reinsch to Bryan, 31 October 1914, Reinsch Papers, 28 November 1914, 793.94/205, 22 December 1914, 793.94/216, DSNA; Reinsch, *An American Diplomat,* 126–28.

8. Reinsch to Bryan, 26 January 1915, 793.94/211, DSNA; *FR 1915,* 132; Reinsch, *An American Diplomat,* 129–31. For accounts justifying Japan's actions, see LaFargue, *China and the World War;* Kikujiro Ishii, *Diplomatic Commentaries* (Baltimore, 1936), 85–92.

9. *FR 1915,* 99–103; Reinsch, *An American Diplomat,* 133–34.

10. Author's interview with Koo, 24 February 1965.

11. *Ibid.;* Reinsch to Bryan, 26 January 1915, 793.94/211, DSNA. The course of the

negotiations may be followed in *FR 1915* and in the memoranda entitled, "Sino-Japanese Negotiations," scattered in the Reinsch Papers, especially in Box 15. These memoranda were probably prepared by Donald for Reinsch's use.

12. Reinsch to Bryan, 15 February 1915, 793.94/257, DSNA; *FR 1915,* 79–80; Tsai T'ing-kan to Reinsch, 29 April 1915, RG 84, Peking Post file, 800, NA; Reinsch, *An American Diplomat,* 132; Hawkins Tapes, 3; author's interview with Koo, 24 February 1965. For early newspaper stories, see *New York Times,* 24 and 27 January 1915; *San Francisco Chronicle,* 27 January and 7 February 1915.

13. Reinsch to Bryan, 24 January 1915, 793.94/210, 10 February 1915, 793.94/257, DSNA; *FR 1915,* 79–87; Reinsch, *An American Diplomat,* 131–32.

14. Reinsch to Bryan, 10 February 1915, 793.94/257, 31 March 1915, 793.94/216, 5 April 1915, 793.94/284 and /344, DSNA; Reinsch, *An American Diplomat,* 133.

15. Reinsch to Bryan, 26 January 1915, 793.94/211, 29 January 1915, 793.94/256, 1 February 1915, 793.94/219, 10 February 1915, 793.94/257, 31 March 1915, 793.94/216, 5 April 1915, 793.94/284 and /344, DSNA; *FR 1915,* 118–24; Reinsch, *An American Diplomat,* 131–32.

16. Reinsch to Bryan, 15 February 1915, 793.94/259, 6 March 1915, 793.94/292, DSNA; Bryan to Reinsch, 24 February 1915, 793.94/236, 6 April 1915, 793.94/284, DSNA; *FR 1915,* 79–111; Reinsch, *An American Diplomat;* Selle, *Donald of China,* 156.

17. Reinsch to Bryan, 27 January 1915, 793.94/214, 10 February 1915, 793.94/257, DSNA; *FR 1915,* 122; Reinsch, "Six Years of American Action in China," Reinsch Papers; Reinsch, *An American Diplomat,* 132–34, 143–44; author's interview with Koo, 24 February 1965.

18. Reinsch to Bryan, 1 February 1915, 793.94/219, DSNA; Reinsch, "Six Years of American Action in China," Reinsch Papers; Reinsch, *An American Diplomat,* 144; author's interview with Koo, 24 February 1965; Koo to author, 29 June 1965; Selle, *Donald of China,* 156.

19. Reinsch to Bryan, 24 January 1915, 793.94/210, 26 January 1915, 793.94/211, 27 January 1915, 793.94/214, 1 February 1915, 793.94/219, DSNA; House to Wilson, 7 May 1915, Wilson Papers; Jordan to Langley, 26 January 1915, Jordan Papers, FO 350/13; Gowen, "Britain and the Twenty-One Demands," 86–92.

20. Reinsch to Bryan, 22 March 1915, 793.94/264, 12 April 1915, 793.94/293, DSNA.

21. Wilson to Bryan, 27 January 1915, Wilson-Bryan Correspondence, Microcopy T-841, reel 3, NA; Wilson to Reinsch, 8 February 1915, Wilson Papers; Curry, *Woodrow Wilson and Far Eastern Policy,* 113–29; Link, *Wilson: The Struggle for Neutrality,* 267, 271ff.

22. Bryan to Wilson, 22 February 1915, 793.94/240, DSNA, 25 March 1915, Bryan Letterbooks, Bryan Papers; Williams memo and Bryan comment, 15 February 1915, 793.94/225, DSNA.

23. Bryan to Wilson, 22 February 1915, 793.94/240, DSNA; Wilson to Bryan, 24 February 1915, *ibid.*

24. Williams to Bryan, 25 January 1915, 793.94/498, DSNA, 2 February 1915, Wilson Papers, 26 February 1915, 793.94/240, DSNA; Williams memos, 27 January 1915, 793.94/211, 15 February 1915, 793.94/225, DSNA.

25. Lansing Desk Diary, November 1914–May 1915, Robert Lansing Papers, Library of Congress (hereafter cited Lansing Papers); Lansing to Bryan, 1 March 1915, 793.94/240, DSNA; Burton F. Beers, *Vain Endeavor: Robert Lansing's Attempt to End American-Japanese Rivalry* (Durham, 1962), 36–42.

26. *FR 1915*, 105–11; Robert Lansing, *War Memoirs of Robert Lansing: Secretary of State* (New York, 1935), 283; Beers, *Vain Endeavor*, 41–45.

27. Reinsch to Bryan, 9 February 1915, 793.94/224, 15 February 1915, 793.94/231 and /259, DSNA; *FR 1915*, 97–98, 122; "The Sino-Japanese Negotiations," 8 February 1915, Reinsch Papers.

28. Reinsch to Bryan, 13 March 1915, 793.94/250, DSNA; *FR 1915*, 98–104; Reinsch, *An American Diplomat*, 136.

29. Wilson to Bryan, 16 March 1915, 793.94/267½, DSNA, 24 March 1915, Bryan Letterbooks, Bryan Papers; Bryan to Wilson, 22 and 25 March 1915, Bryan Letterbooks, Bryan Papers; Bryan to Reinsch, 1 April 1915, 793.94/275, DSNA; *FR 1915*, 111–15; *FR: Lansing Papers*, II, 412.

30. Reinsch to Bryan, 30 March 1915, 793.94/275, 14 April 1915, 793.94/294, DSNA; *FR 1915*, 116–27.

31. Wilson to Bryan, 24, 30 and 31 March and 14 April 1915, Bryan Letterbooks, Bryan Papers; Bryan to Wilson, 9 April 1915, T-841, reel 3, NA; Bryan to Reinsch, 1 April 1915, 793.94/275, DSNA, 9 April 1915, Bryan Letterbooks, Bryan Papers; Reinsch to Bryan, 14 April 1915, 793.94/294, DSNA; Link, *Wilson: The Struggle for Neutrality*, 288–95, 308; Paola E. Coletta, *William Jennings Bryan, II: Progressive, Political and Moral Statesman 1909–1915* (Lincoln, 1969), 234.

32. Wilson to Bryan, 14 April 1915, Bryan Letterbooks, Bryan Papers, 16 April 1915, 793.94/292. DSNA; Williams to Bryan, 13 April 1915, 793.94/292, DSNA.

33. Bryan to Reinsch, 15 April 1915, 793.94/294, 16 April 1915, 793.94/333c, DSNA; Bryan to Wilson, 14 April 1915, T-841, reel 4, NA.

34. Bryan to Wilson, 5 April 1915, Bryan Letterbooks, Bryan Papers, 16 April 1915, 793.94/292, DSNA; Wilson to Bryan, 16 April 1915, 793.94/292, DSNA.

35. Bryan to Chinda, 27 April 1915, T-841, reel 4, NA; Wilson to Bryan, 27 and 28 April 1915, Bryan Letterbooks, Bryan Papers; Coletta, *William Jennings Bryan, II*, 234; Link, *Wilson: The Struggle for Neutrality*, 296–97.

36. "The Sino-Japanese Negotiations," 22 and 26 April 1915, Box 14, Reinsch Papers; *FR 1915*, 127, 131–40.

37. Wilson to Bryan, 5 May 1915, T-841, reel 4, NA; Bryan to Chinda, 5 May 1915, *ibid.*; *FR: Lansing Papers*, II, 418–22.

38. Wilson to Bryan, 6 May 1915, T-841, reel 4, NA; *FR 1915*, 143; *FR: Lansing Papers*, II, 422–23.

39. Reinsch to Bryan, 9 May 1915, 793.94/341, DSNA; *FR 1915*, 143–45, 148–56, 159–204; Reinsch, *An American Diplomat*, 144–49; Gowen, "Britain and the Twenty-One Demands," 101–5.

40. Langley to Jordan, 12 and 26 May and 15 June 1915, Jordan Papers, FO 350/184; Gowen, "Britain and the Twenty-One Demands," 101–5.

41. Jordan to Langley, 26 January, 15 February, and 6 May 1915, Jordan Papers, FO 350/13.

42. Reinsch to Bryan, 4 May 1915, 793.94/376, DSNA; Bryan to Wilson, 8 May 1915, 793.94/392½, DSNA; *FR 1915*, 144–46; *FR: Lansing Papers*, II, 424, 426; Beers, *Vain Endeavor*, 46–48.

43. MacMurray to mother, 3 March, 14 March, and 4 May 1915, MacMurray Papers; MacMurray to Williams, 2 May 1915, *ibid.*; MacMurray to Wilson, 5 April 1915, RG 84, Peking Post file, 800, NA.

44. Asada, "Japan and the United States," 23; Hawkins Tapes, 15.

Madison, Wisconsin, 1910–1911, across the street from the Reinsch house. Paul Reinsch, extreme left; Alma Reinsch, extreme right; daughter Claire, second from right; rest of children are friends of Claire. By permission of Library of Congress.

Arrival in Shanghai,
November 1913,
Paul Reinsch and daughter
Claire, disembarking.
Courtesy of
Mrs. Claire Reinsch Cadura.

Preparing to start on
a long ricksha ride from
Tsinghua College, January 1914,
Paul and Alma Reinsch.
Courtesy of
Mrs. Claire Reinsch Cadura.

Minister Reinsch inspecting the United States Marine Guard, Peking. No date.
Courtesy of Mrs. Claire Reinsch Cadura.

Paul S. Reinsch, side veranda of Minister's residence, Peking. No date. By permission of Library of Congress.

Chapter VIII

MAKING
THE OPEN DOOR
WORK

In March 1915, Reinsch requested permission from the State Department to make an extended summer trip to the United States. He wanted to visit his mother and to attend to numerous personal and business matters in Madison. In order to maintain his academic ties, Reinsch intended to lecture at the University of Wisconsin and the University of Chicago. In addition, Reinsch had agreed to address the American Association for the Advancement of Science in San Francisco on August 8, 1915, in connection with the Panama Pacific International Exposition. Reinsch also told a Japanese reporter that he was exhausted and he hoped that the long sea voyage would enable him to rest and recover his strength. His primary purpose, however, was to generate American interest in China so that the Open Door could function as Reinsch and his predecessors had conceived it. He therefore planned to review the Far Eastern situation with President Wilson and the State Department and to confer with America's business leaders.[1]

* * *

Peking was not an easy post for the serious diplomat. There was so much going on in that vast country, and China experienced one crisis after another during Reinsch's tenure. The Peking post was unique in that consular officials reported directly to the American legation rather than to Washington. Special effort, skill, and patience were also required to deal with the Chinese and win their confidence. Reinsch quickly learned that it was unwise to confine his relations to the Ministry of Foreign

Affairs. Responsibility was often divided and various ministries negotiated with foreign representatives on matters that came within the purview of their departments. The factional conflicts further complicated negotiations and demanded a thorough knowledge of Chinese internal politics. In addition, Reinsch realized that the Chinese preferred to conduct business informally, avoiding the cumbersome machinery of diplomatic notes and *procès verbaux*. Memoranda were prepared only when matters were finally concluded. Operating in this fashion, Reinsch achieved great success in his negotiations with dozens of individual ministers, including some of the more venal politicians, the militarists, and the pro-Japanese clique.[2]

But Reinsch unnecessarily added to his burden. In typical fashion, he wrapped himself in his work. Reinsch never kept regular hours in the Chancery, and he could often be found there well past midnight writing long, comprehensive dispatches, many of which were never read in Washington. He tried to make the legation the center for every aspect of human activity—economic, political, military, cultural, and educational. Reinsch also recognized that Peking was not China and he yearned to make extensive tours through the countryside. First the press of business and later political considerations prevented him from carrying out his plans. For the time being, Reinsch contented himself with a careful study of the reports submitted by his special agents and the consular officers in the field. Reinsch worked closely with his consuls, especially Consul-General Thomas Sammons in Shanghai, communicated to them his zeal for economic expansion, and took a personal interest in them.[3]

Like every chief of mission, Reinsch faced a steady stream of visitors: Chinese officials, members of the diplomatic corps, foreign dignitaries, businessmen and tourists bearing letters of introduction from their congressmen or friends in government positions. Reinsch was gracious to all of them. He spent hours listening to the most harebrained schemes offered by casual tourists who were totally unfamiliar with Chinese affairs and business conditions in the United States. From time to time, MacMurray sarcastically observed to his mother, Reinsch developed plans for the "regeneration of this effete political entity," because someone staying at the Grand Hotel des Wagon-lits claimed that he could raise a multimillion dollar loan that would save China. In his search for personal fortune, Reinsch had been enticed by a prospectus or a tempting deal. Now, in his desire to develop China and expand American influence, Reinsch entertained and supported impractical propositions from promoters and commission seekers—the Gests, Reas,

Philip Mansons—to his subsequent frustration and embarrassment. With some truth, MacMurray described Reinsch as "credulous and gullible as a blue-eyed babe."[4]

Reinsch was also a poor administrator. He failed to organize the operations of the Chancery and to keep his subordinates properly informed. MacMurray traced his inability to influence Bemis to Reinsch's refusal to confide in him. Reinsch seemed incapable of delegating responsibility, even though MacMurray and other members of the staff were competent and anxious to relieve the minister of many duties. Instead, Reinsch wasted precious hours rewriting dispatches, deleting words from telegrams to save a few cents, and handling routine matters which should have been given to the secretaries.

Even more serious, MacMurray believed, was Reinsch's failure to consult the State Department on policy matters not explicitly covered by instructions. Pointing to his own experience in Washington, MacMurray advised Reinsch that the State Department was disposed to sanction all but the most unreasonable recommendations made by its representatives abroad, but that they "run a big risk of breaking their necks by omitting the formality of submitting their plans in advance." Insisting on his "plenipotentiousness," as MacMurray called it, Reinsch spurned suggestions that he consult his superiors and counted on the department's support, just as his friends used to back him up in Madison.

MacMurray attributed much of Reinsch's behavior to his excessive idealism and to his fear of his responsibilities; "and among all his fears the most dreaded is that of seeming to be afraid." It was true that Reinsch felt that he had to prove himself to American businessmen, Washington officials, and the Chinese. Reinsch also felt that he had a mission to make the Open Door work and to save China. Only his personal intervention would sway the Chinese and win their confidence; only his personal conferences or correspondence with American leaders and businessmen would win their support. He was the man of the hour; he was "Mr. Citizen-Fixit."

MacMurray tended to be suspicious of all inexperienced political appointees. Concerned about protecting United States interests and prestige and instinctively loyal to his superiors, MacMurray worried about Reinsch's excesses, errors, and usurpation of authority. Supremely confident in his own abilities, he resented Reinsch's reliance on his Kitchen Cabinet. This situation produced almost continuous conflict between the minister and his first secretary. From time to time, MacMurray complained to Reinsch and things temporarily improved. But then Reinsch lapsed into his old ways, forcing MacMurray to sulk, to vent his feelings in long letters to his mother, or to withdraw into his own special project—a massive collection of Chinese treaties and agreements.

In August 1916, however, MacMurray exploded when things took a turn for the worse upon his return from a leave of absence in the United States. MacMurray was bitter because he had been ignored in the formulation of policy for the Lee Higginson loan and the Siems-Carey contracts. This lack of confidence, MacMurray wrote to Reinsch who was vacationing at Peitaiho, hurt "my *amour propre*," it impaired the usefulness of the legation, and it demoralized the staff. MacMurray did not think it was deliberate, he told Reinsch, but was due to "a particular habit of mind in which you happen for some reason to be, which imposes upon your dealings with your subordinates the constraint of some subconscious feeling that nothing is really done unless you do it yourself, and that (conversely) a thing is completed and achieved and done with when you have personally taken cognizance of it. Will you take it amiss if I venture the suggestion that no organization can 'carry on' on so personal a theory?" Relations improved somewhat afterwards. But, in a personal letter, Lansing delicately inquired if the reports reaching the department were true. Reinsch felt that his actions required no justification, but he fell back on the peculiar Chinese situation to explain his method of operation.[5]

And yet, Reinsch's work bore results. The former university professor had obtained numerous concessions for American interests and had fought hard to protect them against foreign intrigue and Chinese connivance. More important, he created a feeling of optimism for Americans in China, and he gave the impression that the United States was a major force in the Far East. Just four months after Reinsch's arrival in China, Thomas Sammons reported that "the most flattering expressions come to me regarding your work at Peking on behalf of extending American interests in China. Apparently much more is being accomplished than has ever been the case heretofore." Straight expressed his own appreciation as well as that of the minister's "friends at 27 Broadway" for obtaining the Standard Oil contract. "We have followed your activities with great interest and wish to congratulate you most heartily upon what you have accomplished." And in November 1914, President Wilson lauded Reinsch "on the way in which your work is developing and on the manner in which you are handling it."[6]

Reinsch was undoubtedly pleased by this flattery as well as by his success in getting concessions for American interests. But he was plainly dissatisfied with the actual amount of American investment, the absence of loans to rescue the Chinese government, and the decline in American exports to China between 1913 and 1915, which was partially attributable to the war.[7] What went wrong? Why was the economic stake of the United States in China so small?

Reinsch knew that American businessmen were discouraged by China's political and financial instability and the interference of the other foreign powers. But he argued that they were not serious deterrents. His own faith in the China market remained unshaken. "The longer I live in China," he told reporters in Berlin in 1914, "the more I am impressed by its vast possibilities as a market for American commerce and trade."[8]

He also believed that the Wilson administration had amply demonstrated its support for foreign expansion by reforming the tariff and banking system, by streamlining the Department of Commerce and by persuading Congress to appropriate funds to support ten commercial attachés, one of whom would be headquartered in Peking. Washington had supported most of Reinsch's early projects, and the minister felt that he was carrying out the president's policies in China. There was potential for future conflict. Reinsch felt that the Wilson administration sometimes failed to respond quickly enough during major crises, notably the Twenty-One Demands, and to resist every challenge to American rights and China's sovereignty. Most serious was the fact that neither Wilson nor the State Department could ever accept Reinsch's underlying premise—that China would eventually become the center of international affairs. For the present, however, the dialogue between Reinsch and Washington continued.[9]

Rather, Reinsch cast most of the blame on American businessmen. They were ignorant of opportunities in China, timid and short-sighted, notoriously backward in their techniques, and indifferent to the national interest. American capitalists had "seen" South America and were ready to invest there, but China seemed "too distant and strange to them." Working through Straight and other friends, Reinsch tried to induce the "big" men of American finance "to see the situation themselves. It is one that is eminently attractive to the American spirit of enterprise," he reminded Straight. "As you know, the opportunities that exist at the present time will not last long, and it is of the highest importance that we should now take a more important position here before things have set and crystallized as to make entry next to impossible." On the other hand, when American businessmen did come to China, they ruined valuable concessions because they failed to appreciate Chinese sensitivities or methods of negotiations. They made petty and excessive demands which antagonized the Chinese and destroyed America's good name; or else company officials at home repudiated or changed signed contracts. Concerned with the shortage of men well qualified to work overseas, Reinsch suggested that the State Department cooperate with leading American universities to establish training programs and that the Department of Commerce institute a clearing house for foreign employment.[10]

Reinsch repeatedly denounced Wall Street's excessive demand for government protection. In his exchanges with Reinsch, Straight emphasized the difficulties faced by the bankers in disposing of their commitments, especially to Americans who were unaccustomed to buying foreign securities. "The man in the street regards China as a heathen land, full of revolutions and capable of defaulting on its bonds," Straight explained to Reinsch. "He feels, therefore, that he should be assured that the American Government would protect his investment in case China did not meet her obligations." Reinsch agreed that, to a point, the bankers had legitimate grounds for worry. He also recognized the need to exempt foreign enterprise from the provisions of the antitrust laws. "Nothing will help us more than a banking syndicate for foreign commerce in which individual banks at home could participate in large numbers," he responded to Straight. But Reinsch still maintained that American bankers conceived their role too narrowly which prevented them from rendering greater assistance to American industry's bid for foreign markets and to Washington's effort to exert influence abroad. In fact, Reinsch placed the blame for discouraging American enterprise in China squarely on the House of Morgan. Morgan, he felt, was still sulking because of Wilson's withdrawal from the Consortium; it also feared losing control of American activity in China.[11]

A decade earlier, Reinsch had been critical of the immaturity of American business operations in South America. Now he discovered that American business was simply unprepared to function as required by modern conditions and the Chinese environment. Throughout China, there were no American commission houses or import-export organizations. With the exception of a few large firms (such as Standard Oil and British-American Tobacco), most American trade was handled by foreign, mainly British and German, trading companies.[12] Similarly, American banking facilities were practically non-existent. The International Banking Corporation (IBC), under the control of J. P. Morgan, was the only American bank in China; it confined its business to foreign exchange and commercial paper transactions and it failed to provide the leadership for American enterprise that other foreign banks offered to their nationals. The withdrawal of the Pacific Mail Steamship Company in 1915 meant that no American line operated regular service to China. In addition, all of the channels of publicity and news gathering were controlled by other nations. Consequently, Americans were forced to rely on the services of other nations, which added to their costs and denied them profitable business. It also placed American enterprise at the mercy of competitors and affected United States freedom of action. That was forcefully demonstrated when Britain easily enforced the blacklist of American firms dealing with Germany.[13]

Therefore, Reinsch maintained that the Open Door had not failed. Americans had never really tried to implement the strategy as envisioned by Hay and other policy makers. Nor could the United States tolerate this dangerous state of affairs much longer. The United States had to combine the advanced methods of its competitors with the American capacity for broad action and its enterprising spirit. American overseas expansion required systematic and expert planning, coordination and cooperation, and attentive consideration to national needs. Reinsch thereby made an explicit connection between the progressive program at home and American overseas expansion. Both proceeded from the conditions of the modern industrial age which required systematic action by large, efficient organizations, supervised by the national government, and acting in the general interest. Reinsch spelled it out in his address to the American Society for the Advancement of Science:

> In this capacity for broad action, in this experience of dealing easily with the vast interests and activities, there lies the real qualification of Americans to take a lead in upbuilding the economic organization of countries in the Pacific area. It is pioneer work which requires, however, the experience of men accustomed to handle large affairs according to the most severe tests of modern efficiency. There is no room for adventurers here.[14]

Reinsch insisted that if American business promptly established a large and broad economic interest, the United States could still influence Chinese affairs and could, itself, win handsome profits. Within six months after his arrival in China, Reinsch submitted a five-point program to the State Department, which was subsequently published in the *Daily Consular and Trade Reports* and excerpted in leading American newspapers.[15]

Reinsch first called for the immediate appointment of capable commercial attachés who would coordinate the activities of diplomatic and consular officials and guide American manufacturers and merchants to trade and investment opportunities. Second, Reinsch stressed the need for American commission houses for, "only by creating its own organs of distribution can our manufacturing industry hold its own in a market like China." Taking his cue from the British and Germans, Reinsch then advised the organization of sales agencies, exempted from the antitrust laws, to represent a number of manufacturers and assist them in marketing their goods. Fourth, Reinsch emphasized the importance of long-range investment, the lack of which was responsible for the failure of American trade to develop more rapidly in China. "Commerce no longer develops alone," he continued to insist, "but it is so closely bound up with investment that the two must be constantly associated." Speaking to the point made by Straight and Morgan, Reinsch argued that Americans would place their surplus capital in the hands of efficient and responsbile investment companies.

The greatest need, however, was the establishment of adequate banking facilities in the Far East. And since individual banks were not ready to engage in foreign operations on a large scale and Morgan was unwilling to take the lead, Reinsch proposed that a new broadly based syndicate be organized to advance the national interest. "With your encouragement," he stated to Wilson, "they are ready to come forward." Reinsch further assured the president that such an institution need not be monopolistic. In fact, since it would require government support and it would represent the financial energies of the entire nation, he suggested that the banking syndicate assume a quasi-public character. And once such a group was in operation and American interests were entrenched in China, Reinsch intimated that a new consortium might be constituted under American leadership.[16]

By the spring of 1915, Reinsch decided that he had to go to the United States to put this program into effect. Reinsch had missed seeing Wilson in the summer of 1914, and he believed that the president's active support was essential. "Opportunities are offered for *your* administration," he wrote to Wilson in March 1915, "to lay the foundation of a great development of American enterprise in the Far East—a development which will soon be a life necessity to our industries and for which future ages will give their thankful recognition." He also had to reach the "big" men of American finance and industry.[17]

Moreover, Reinsch believed that several enterprises deserved his personal attention. Among old business, the Huai Conservancy project and the Standard Oil contract required immediate action. An exciting new venture, a Sino-American steamship company, had to be nurtured.

In the spring of 1915, Reinsch brought together a group of Chinese investors, led by Liang Shih-yi, and a fairly small American shipping company, represented in China by Philip Manson.[18] In the face of the Morgan monopoly, it was necessary to organize a new banking group. At that very time, Selwyn W. Tait was in China exploring the field for Frank Vanderlip, president of National City Bank, and other business firms. Reinsch was also in touch with the Siems-Carey Construction Company, a reputable and experienced outfit based in St. Paul, which expressed genuine interest in railway projects in China. In addition, Reinsch was working on the formation of a Sino-American bank and a plan for Americans to take over the Belgian concession for the Lanchou-Haichou Railway.[19]

The time was also propitious for the United States to establish its dominance in the Far East. The outbreak of the war, coinciding with the opening of the Panama Canal, presented the United States with unique advantages and opportunities. Reinsch understood that America was fast becoming the financial and commercial center of the world. The Orient would soon recover its former place in the minds of New England and New York merchants while the newer Pacific ports would boom. The day was not distant, he told the delegates to the Panama Pacific International Exposition, when the Pacific Ocean would become a broad highway of trade. Moreover, Europe's involvement in the war combined with the breakdown of the Consortium left the investment field to the United States. And should the powers object or interfere, Reinsch suggested that the United States withhold loans from the Allies until they agreed to abide by the Open Door policy. Reinsch welcomed Anglo-American cooperation in the Far East, but he was unwilling to accept a secondary position in relation to Great Britain, particularly when economic supremacy was within the reach of the United States.[20]

Confident of his power of persuasion and aware of the good impression he made in public, Reinsch felt that he was the man of the hour. Armed with blueprints, designed in collaboration with Julean Arnold, the new commercial attaché, and Thomas Sammons, the consul-general at Shanghai, Reinsch set out on the long transpacific voyage.[21]

*   *   *

Reinsch arrived in Seattle on July 3, 1915, and immediately wired the White House asking for an appointment with the president to lay before him "several matters of the highest importance." Reinsch then went on to St. Paul, where he discussed contemplated railway projects with William F. Carey and Chester Siems, who would figure prominently in his plans for China. Reinsch arranged to discuss the matter with them in New York and Washington, and Carey and Siems became frequent travelling companions as Reinsch crisscrossed the continent.[22]

In Madison, Reinsch, suffering from physical and nervous exhaustion, became seriously ill and was forced to enter a hospital for medical treatment. Reinsch's recuperation took longer than expected and he was forced to cancel his appointment with the president scheduled for July 22. As soon as he recovered his strength, Reinsch composed a letter to Wilson, in which he defined the problem of Sino-American relations: "Shall China, hitherto bent on peaceful industry and genuinely friendly to us, be forced into a militarist policy and into a position where she will not be free to manifest good will toward the U. States?" Reinsch then offered his prescription. "It seems to me," he told Wilson, "that the only promise of safety for the future lies in attempting to do certain concrete things—to develop every individual American interest in China quickly and with energy while there is yet time; to oppose at every point all attempts to establish an exclusive policy; and to have if possible a clear understanding with Gt. Britain and Russia as to means for averting the common danger." Furthermore, Reinsch stated the Chinese needed reassurance by word and deed that "will preserve their sense of dignity of their country."[23]

Reinsch also asked if another interview could be scheduled before August 2, when he had to leave for his West Coast speaking engagements. Wilson expressed his regrets over Reinsch's illness, but indicated that other commitments ruled out another appointment. The president also replied sympathetically to Reinsch's letter of July 25, and promised to keep in touch with the minister. Reinsch was crushed because he believed that a personal exchange with the president could be instrumental in obtaining energetic administration support for his program.[24] Nevertheless, he did confer with numerous State and Commerce Department officials at the end of July. He was particularly pleased with his conversations with Lansing, who thoroughly favored "giving to American enterprise in China every possible support and encouragement."[25]

The outlook improved, however, when, on August 14, the State Department asked him to report to Washington for consulations on the monarchical movement in China, the breakdown in the Standard Oil negotiations, and several other problems involving American enterprise, Reinsch's return to Washington enabled him to see Wilson. In the course of a long conference at the White House on August 18, the *Baltimore Sun* reported, Reinsch told the president that the United States government must encourage American financiers to go into China in order to prevent Japan from monopolizing China's resources and to keep the Open Door functioning. Before the meeting was concluded, Reinsch apparently obtained assurances from Wilson and Lansing that the government, without acting as a guarantor, would ask American business leaders to "open their purses to the Chinese government."[26]

Further deliberations with officials in Washington led to the announcement by Dr. Edward E. Pratt, chief of the Bureau of Foreign and Domestic Trade, that the departments of State and Commerce had worked out an aggressive plan with Reinsch to develop "an American vested interest in China that will insure to the United States a fair share in that country's trade and be powerful enough to take care of itself in the complicated political and commercial situation there." Pratt specifically mentioned the need for a well-capitalized American bank.[27]

Reinsch had also been discouraged by his initial conferences with business leaders in New York, Philadelphia, Detroit, and Chicago. He found a disproportionate willingness to invest in South America, which portended that after the war Americans would turn south and ignore China. J. P. Morgan, "being deeply occupied with matters of European finance," showed only faint interest in China and dampened the enthusiasm of other banking houses in New York. The heads of the three largest locomotive manufacturers in the United States (Baldwin Locomotive, American Locomotive, and American Car and Foundry) were anxious to develop China as a market for railway equipment. Alba B. Johnson, president of Baldwin Locomotive, endorsed the idea of general selling agencies representing groups of industrial firms, but he indicated that the antitrust laws and the need for long-term credits would frustrate such plans.[28]

And yet, by the time Reinsch left for China, things started to jell. J. P. Morgan & Co., United States Steel, Baldwin Locomotive, and National City Bank agreed to create an agency to foster American trade and investments in China. Anxious to begin business, the combination decided to take over Anderson, Meyer & Co., a general export-import house with long experience in and numerous branches throughout China.[29]

More significant, Lee Higginson & Co., one of the nation's leading banks, with offices in Boston and New York, offered to negotiate with Peking for a $15 million loan and to create a regular market for Chinese securities. In return, the bank expected to be appointed China's fiscal agent in the United States and to have a prior option on all general bond issues floated in America. Reinsch approved the terms and argued to the State Department that no monopoly was contemplated and that the arrangement would be advantageous to China. The State Department did not object and instructed MacMurray to sound out the Chinese government.

But MacMurray hesitated to act because he had not been adequately informed about Reinsch's negotiations in the United States. He was uncertain if National City, represented by Tait, was cooperating with Lee Higginson in the venture; or if National City was only considering the Sino-American bank proposal and the Belgian railway project. The State Department was equally confused and asked Reinsch to submit a full report of his conferences with American interests "so that intelligent action may be taken." Reinsch replied that Tait's negotiations would not interfere with the loan as his principals were primarily interested in the railway project. But then he cryptically added that "should they seriously take up the first matter [i.e., the loan] the other capitalists would shift to other enterprises." Still, he was inclined to use the "Lee firm who are ready to act." Reinsch obviously was trying to cover every possibility in order to nail down at least some American commitments. In the process, however, he left Washington and Peking thoroughly confused. Eventually, the matter was straightened out and in November 1915, the Chinese government granted the fiscal agency to Lee Higginson.[30]

National City Bank's bold and imaginative plans held out the most promise for America's future in China. Led by its dynamic president, Frank A. Vanderlip, National City was on the verge of launching a movement to capture overseas business and to establish itself as the leading American financial institution in the Orient. Vanderlip had a vision of America's postwar supremacy and wanted to "co-ordinate all the vital forces that are looking towards foreign finance."

Therefore, when Reinsch stepped into Vanderlip's New York office, he was able to capture the banker's imagination. "I am particularly indebted to you for having stimulated and brought to a head my interest in China," Vanderlip later thanked Reinsch, "and beg to assure you that it is our desire to cooperate in any work which will help you put American interests in China on a strong and permanent foundation." Vanderlip agreed that China held out great opportunities, but the astute banker was pessimistic about China's political stability. Shortly after seeing Reinsch, Vanderlip confided to James Stillman, chairman of National City: "There is of course more business there than in all South America together, if conditions are ever ripe for getting into that situation, which I am not sure of."[31]

Nevertheless, concrete results flowed from their conversations. Vanderlip advised Reinsch that National City planned to establish a branch in China and shortly afterward it bought control of the International Banking Corporation. After Reinsch introduced Siems and Carey to Red Cross officials, the contractors agreed to take up the Huai River Conservancy work provided they could obtain the necessary financing. Reinsch then brought Siems and Carey together with Vanderlip in New York, and the parties decided to form a construction and engineering concern that would undertake large-scale projects in China. Eventually two companies were organized: the China Corporation and the Siems-Carey Railway and Canal Company.[32]

But the crowning achievement was the formation of the American International Corporation in November 1915. AIC was an expression of the movement to rationalize and expand American foreign trade and investment. It would evaluate, select, finance, and operate the most promising overseas ventures. In the process, it would issue its own collateral debentures which, unlike the original securities, would find a ready market in the United States. Since American products would be used whenever possible, it would also tend to stimulate American exports. Vanderlip retained the chairmanship of AIC, but succeeded in filling the board of directors with the titans of American finance and industry. Straight, who had left Morgan earlier in the year, because his ideas were ignored and the firm would not make him a partner, was named vice president. He handled delicate negotiations in Europe as well as overseeing AIC's Far Eastern operations.[33]

*   *   *

Reinsch returned to China in September pleased with the results of his mission. His visit had coincided with and had helped to crystallize the burgeoning interest of government and business leaders in the rationalization and expansion of American foreign enterprise. The Wilson administration had endorsed the strategy and projects that Reinsch had developed. With certain modifications, Wilson seemed to be returning to Dollar Diplomacy.[34]

During the next few months, AIC and its associated firms quickly built up an organization in China headed by Ernest T. Gregory, the manager of the Peking branch of National City (IBC). Roy Anderson was employed as an adviser and troubleshooter; he provided valuable assistance to AIC while he continued to work closely with Reinsch. In December 1915, William F. Carey, to whom Reinsch took an immediate liking, arrived in China "not only to negotiate, but to start work." Reinsch also resumed his correspondence with Straight, who denied the rumors that he was trying to displace him as minister to China.[35]

And yet Reinsch was haunted by the feeling that American business would repeat the same mistakes. He was particularly afraid that it would timidly submit to foreign pressures at the expense of national interests. One hint came in Straight's quick rejection of Reinsch's suggestion that the United States complete its section of the Hukuang Railways. Straight replied that, in view of the Hukuang Agreements, the United States could not proceed on the Ichang-Chengtu line without the prior approval of the American Group and the other foreign syndicates.[36]

More revealing was Wall Street's acquiescence in Britain's ruthless enforcement of the Trading-with-the-Enemy Act. British authorities forced American companies to discharge German employees and to discontinue handling German goods before they would permit the use of British, and even Japanese, shipping and banking facilities. With good reason Reinsch suspected that British authorities were inspired "by a desire to monopolize Sino-American trade for British firms to the exclusion of German and Austrian concerns as much as by the demands of the war effort."

Reinsch was furious—all the more so because he saw the war as an opportunity to expand American economic power and to force the other powers to observe the Open Door. Reinsch asked the State Department to register a strong diplomatic protest, but he thought that Wall Street, which was financing the war for England, might be more successful in influencing London. Reinsch also asked Straight to strengthen the backbone of IBC, which was so intimidated that it refused to extend its services to Americans who incidentally did business with Germans or Austrians. "It is pitiable to contemplate," Reinsch exploded, "that the International Banking Corporation, far from acting as an independent support for American trade in this matter, has made itself the instrument for the enforcement of British regulations."[37]

But the bankers, who profited from the war trade, saw things through a different lens. Do you not agree, Straight asked Reinsch, "that inasmuch as nonconformity with these regulations would merely mean that our people would be black-listed and get no business at all, it is perhaps better not to kick hard against the bricks? A stone wall is a stone wall and half a loaf is better than no bread. It is perhaps cowardly to argue from the point of expediency, but I confess that I see no other way out at the moment." Moreover, Straight also believed that the time had come to lay the basis for long-range cooperation between the United States and the other industrial nations. AIC, therefore, could not antagonize the Allies or give the impression that it was trying to "pick things off the bargain counter" during the war.[38]

Reinsch was far more alarmed by the growing support in the United States for Japanese-American cooperation. It was an old idea, but, in 1915, Japanese leaders actively courted the United States. The British had rejected Tokyo's suggestion of an economic entente and the Japanese needed foreign capital to finance their ambitious plans in China. The Japanese also feared that the United States might take advantage of its financial strength and Chinese preference for American capital to build up a strong independent position in China. By 1916, in fact, Japan wanted to work with the United States and opposed the British suggestion that America rejoin the Consortium. As it was understood in Tokyo, Japanese-American cooperation meant procuring American capital to finance Japanese development at home and the exploitation of Chinese resources. In effect, American capital would become an instrument of Japanese expansion in East Asia.[39]

The idea horrified Reinsch, but he tried to be polite and noncommittal when the *Hochi Shimbun*, one of Japan's leading newspapers, asked his views on Japanese-American cooperation in June 1915. Reinsch replied that it was a matter for capitalists of both nations to decide. However, since there were so many opportunities all over China, "it might be better for China's development for individuals of all nations to exert themselves freely."[40]

Reinsch was deeply worried by the visit of Baron Shibusawa Eiichi to the United States in the fall of 1915. Shibusawa met with Vanderlip, Straight, and a host of leading American bankers and industrialists. Both in his private conversations and public statements, the Japanese financier frankly encouraged Americans to put their money in Japanese hands for investment in China. Reinsch, Donald, and other friends of China worked diligently to counter Japanese propaganda that Shibusawa had convinced American businessmen of the advantages in allowing Japan to wield political influence while Americans supplied the capital. Reinsch confronted Straight with reports that he had publicly endorsed the idea "that we might come into China in the wake of some other country," and impressed upon him the dangers inherent in the proposal. "You must have been misrepresented in this," he wrote hopefully to Straight, "because I know that you know that we can do things in China on our strength and reputation on better terms than anyone else can get them for us, if our people will only take hold. We are under no need of proctorship except our own. In fact, whatever we might do to support any other Power's plans here would soon be turned to our disadvantage."⁴¹

Straight replied that the matter had been left open for future discussion, but reassured Reinsch that Baron Shibusawa was "certainly not warranted in stating that we had made a blanket agreement for cooperation." Straight had no illusions about the Japanese interpretation of cooperation and realized that a close Japanese-American understanding would prejudice the American position in China. He sought to find a middle ground where American interests could benefit without upsetting the Chinese or the Japanese. Straight had lost his old antagonism toward Japan; he admired Japanese foresight and intelligence and concluded that cooperation with Tokyo "might very well be profitable for us." On the other hand, Straight had become disgusted with China's inability to set its house in order. "We love our China but our Chinese friends seem to be so persistently inept and incorrigibly foolish, that I don't believe that they can ever work out their own salvation, nor do I believe they will ever let their friends do it for them," he confided to J. O. P. Bland. "The world is a rather hard master, and God does not seem particularly anxious to help those who cannot help themselves."

Britain's temporary acquiescence in Japanese expansion, China's weakness, and Washington's uncertain support convinced Straight that there was no sense in deliberately antagonizing Japan. "After my years in Korea and Manchuria," he explained to Reinsch, "I am not inclined to kick too hard against the bricks unless I am sure that I can wear hobnailed boots instead of tennis shoes, and if we can't kick we can certainly try to gain our purpose in some other way." Consequently, Straight told Reinsch, AIC would proceed slowly and cautiously. It could engage in industrial enterprises, such as the Grand Canal project, and commerce. But until the impact of the European war became clearer, AIC must avoid large loans to the Chinese government, which would certainly arouse Tokyo and might also endanger Chinese and American interests.⁴²

While Straight and Vanderlip piloted AIC to limited cooperation with Japan, their outlook gained adherents in New York and Washington. But Reinsch held firm and pointed out the shoals. He refused to give up on China and he pressed ahead with his campaign to establish a strong independent American position in China. Following up Reinsch's visit, George E. Anderson, the consul-general at Hong Kong, and Julean Arnold toured the United States in 1916, spreading the gospel of American opportunities in trade and investment. Reinsch also admonished Vanderlip that "this is practically the last opportunity for Americans to enter upon enterprises in China on a large scale and on a favorable footing. For indeed, were we not to make good this time the Chinese would be delivered into the hands of our competitors, and no amount of work and inevitable wailing in future years could make up for the lost advantage."[43] Reinsch correctly predicted the outcome. Nevertheless, he desperately tried to hold back the tide.

NOTES TO
CHAPTER VIII

1. Reinsch to Bryan, 5 March 1915, 123.R271/29, DSNA; "An Interview with the American Minister," by the *Hochi Shimbun*, Reinsch Papers; Reinsch, "Six Years of American Action in China," *ibid*.

2. Reinsch, "Six Years of American Action in China," Reinsch Papers.

3. Reinsch to Bryan, 24 February 1914, 123.R271/14, DSNA; Reinsch, "Six Years of American Action in China," Reinsch Papers; John V. A. MacMurray, "Dr. Paul S. Reinsch," *American Consular Bulletin,* V (May 1923), 150–51; Norwood F. Allman, *Shanghai Lawyer* (New York, 1943), 34–35.

4. MacMurray to mother, 8 and 18 February 1914, 9 March 1915, MacMurray Papers.

5. MacMurray to mother, 19 February, 9 March, 13 March, and 6 October 1914, 3 March 1915, 7 August and 4 September 1916, MacMurray Papers; MacMurray to Reinsch, 28 August 1916, Reinsch Papers; Lansing to Reinsch, 20 September 1917, *ibid*.

6. Sammons to Reinsch, 6 March 1914, Reinsch Papers; Straight to Reinsch, 25 February 1914, *ibid*.; Wilson to Reinsch, 9 November 1914, *ibid*.

7. Reinsch, *An American Diplomat, passim.* In 1914, American investments in China totalled $49.3 million and represented only 3.1 percent of total foreign investment in China. By comparison, the figures for Britain were $607.5 million (37.7 percent) and for Japan $219.6 million (13.6 percent). C. F. Remer, *Foreign Investments in China* (New York, 1933), 76, 265.

8. E. V. Douglas to Reinsch, 26 June 1915, RG 84, Peking Post file, 610, NA; Reinsch to Straight, 21 March 1914, Reinsch Papers; *New York Times*, 26 July 1914.

9. Wilson to William C. Anderson, 2 February 1914, Wilson Papers; Wilson to Reinsch, 9 November 1914, Reinsch Papers; Wilson to McAdoo, 9 November 1914, McAdoo Papers; *FR 1914*, xii–xiv; Edward E. Pratt, "Government Aids to Foreign Trade: What the New Bureau of Foreign and Domestic Commerce Is Doing for American Business," *Cleveland Plain Dealer,* 4 July 1915.

10. Reinsch, "Six Years of American Action in China," Reinsch Papers; Reinsch to Straight, 24 March and 21 April 1914, *ibid*.; Reinsch to Lansing, 12 November 1915, 893.6363/24, DSNA, 11 February 1916, RG 84, Peking Post file, 610, NA; *FR 1915*, 216; Reinsch, *An American Diplomat,* 95–107, 223.

11. Straight to Reinsch, 25 March and 30 June 1914, Reinsch Papers; Rea to Reinsch, 12 October 1914, *ibid*.; Reinsch to Wilson, 5 March 1914, in Daniel J. Gage, "Paul S. Reinsch and Sino-American Relations" (Ph.D. dissertation, Stanford University, 1939), 597–98.

12. In Manchuria, Mitsui Bussan Kaisha was the sole agent for such leading American firms as General Electric, American Locomotive, and Swift & Co. In China proper, much of American trade was handled by Arnhold Karberg & Co. (German), Shewan, Tomes & Co. (British), and Anderson, Meyer & Co. (Danish). See Reinsch, "American Handicaps in Reaching Chinese Trade," *Daily Consular and Trade Reports,* 20 August 1914; Reinsch to Bryan, 3 July 1914, 693.11/13, DSNA; P. S. Heintzleman to Lansing, "Report on Political and Economic Conditions in the Mukden Consular District," 31 December 1915, 893.00/2345, DSNA; Straight to Reinsch, 25 March 1914, Reinsch Papers.

13. Reinsch to Lansing, 5 November 1915, 800.8890/128, DSNA; Reinsch to Lee Higginson, 21 December 1915, 893.51/1604, DSNA; Wilder to Bryan, 29 July 1913, RG 84, Peking Post file, 851.6, NA; Reinsch, "Summary of an Address on the Future

Economic Development of the Pacific Area," n.d. [August 1915], Reinsch Papers; Hawkins Tapes, 9; Millard to Crane, 21 January 1913, Crane Papers; Walter Rogers to Crane, 25 June and 8 August 1917, *ibid.*

14. Reinsch, "Summary of an Address on the Future Economic Development of the Pacific Area," Reinsch Papers; Reinsch to James A. Farrell, 9 February 1914, RG 84, Peking Post file, 610, NA.

15. Reinsch to Bryan, 3 July 1914, 693.11/31, DSNA; Reinsch, "American Handicaps in Reaching Chinese Trade"; clippings, *New York Times*, 23 August 1914, *New York Commercial*, 21 August 1914, Reinsch Papers.

16. Reinsch to Bryan, 3 July 1914, 693.11/31, DSNA; Reinsch, "American Handicaps in Reaching Chinese Trade"; Reinsch to Straight, 21 April 1914, Reinsch Papers; clipping, Reinsch remarks, *Milwaukee Journal, ibid.;* Reinsch, "Six Years of American Action in China," *ibid.*; Reinsch to Wilson, 5 March 1915, in Gage, "Paul S. Reinsch," 597–98; MacMurray, "Dr. Paul S. Reinsch," 138.

17. Reinsch to Wilson, 5 October 1915, McAdoo Papers, 5 March 1915, in Gage, "Paul S. Reinsch," 597.

18. The venture ended in failure. Manson proved to be another incompetent, profit-seeking promoter. Reinsch was so embarrassed and disappointed by the fate of this enterprise that he made no mention of it in his memoirs. The episode is covered fully in Noel H. Pugach, "American Shipping Promoters and the Shipping Crisis of 1914–1916: The Pacific & Eastern Steamship Company," *The American Neptune*, XXXV (July 1975), 166–82.

19. Reinsch to Bryan, 7 April 1915, 166.083/1, DSNA; Rea to Reinsch, 12 October 1914, Reinsch Papers; C. A. Severance, 9 June 1915, *ibid.*; clipping, *China Press*, 1 July 1915, in Sammons to Lansing, 1 July 1915, RG 84, Peking Post file, 610, NA.

20. Reinsch to Straight, 24 March 1914 and 12 February 1916, Reinsch Papers; Reinsch speech at a luncheon given by the manager of Standard Oil in China, 21 June 1915, *ibid.*; Reinsch, "Summary of Address on the Future Economic Development of the Pacific Area," *ibid.*; Reinsch to Bryan, 13 April 1915, 893.51/1580, DSNA; Reinsch to Wilson, 25 July 1915, Wilson Papers.

21. Sammons, Annual Report on Commerce and Industries for 1914, Shanghai District, 24 May 1915, RG 84, Peking Post file, 610, NA; Sammons to Reinsch, 8 October 1915, 793.94/201, DSNA; Julean Arnold, "Memo for Minister Reinsch re Suggestions for American Trade Activity in China," 2 June 1915, Reinsch Papers.

22. Reinsch to Tumulty, 3 July 1915, Wilson Papers; Reinsch, "Six Years of American Action in China," Reinsch Papers.

23. Reinsch to Tumulty, 20 July 1915, Wilson Papers; Reinsch to Wilson, 25 July 1915, *ibid.*

24. Reinsch to Wilson, 25 July 1915, *ibid*; Wilson to Reinsch, 31 July 1915, *ibid.*

25. Reinsch, "Six Years of American Action in China," Reinsch Papers.

26. Lansing to Reinsch, 14 August 1915, *ibid.*; *Baltimore Sun,* 19 August 1915.

27. *New York Times,* 22 August 1915; *San Francisco Chronicle,* 23 August 1915.

28. Alba Johnson to Reinsch, 20 July 1915, Reinsch Papers; Reinsch, "Six Years of American Action in China," *ibid.*; Reinsch to Lansing, 30 August 1915, 693.11/36, DSNA.

29. Reinsch to Lansing, 30 August 1915, 693.11/36, DSNA; Vilhelm Meyer to MacMurray, 31 August 1915, RG 84, Peking Post file, 610, NA.

30. Reinsch, "Six Years of American Action in China," Reinsch Papers; MacMurray to Lansing, 16 August 1915, 893.77/1478, 23 August 1915, 893.51/1595, DSNA; Lans-

ing to MacMurray, 19 August 1915, 893.77/1478, and 893.51/1595a, DSNA; Lansing to Reinsch, 24 August 1915, 893.77/1478, DSNA; Reinsch to Lansing, 29 August 1915, 893.77/1481, 30 August 1915, 693.11/36, 13 November 1915, 893.51/1596, DSNA.

31. Vanderlip to Stillman, 27 August and 8 and 29 October, 1915, Vanderlip Papers; Vanderlip to Reinsch, 12 January 1916, Reinsch Papers.

32. Reinsch to Lansing, 30 August 1915, 693.11/36, DSNA; Rea, memo, May 1917, 893.811/257, DSNA; "American International Corporation," *Far Eastern Review,* XIII (March 1917), 370–71.

33. Vanderlip to Stillman, 8 and 29 October 1915, Vanderlip Papers; "Purposes of AIC," undated memorandum, *ibid.*; Straight to Davison, 1 November 1915, Straight Papers; "Diary for the Perusal of Whitney Straight Esquire . . .," *ibid.*; *New York Times,* 24 November 1915; "American International Corporation," 370–71; George T. Mazuzan, "Our New Gold Goes Adventuring: The American International Corporation in China," *Pacific Historical Review,* XLIII (May 1974), 212–32; Henry N. Scheiber, "World War I as Entrepreneurial Opportunity: Willard Straight and the American International Corporation," *Political Science Quarterly,* LXXXIV (September 1969), 486–511.

34. Clipping, article by David Lawrence, *New York Evening Post,* 27 June 1916, Reinsch Papers.

35. Reinsch to Straight, 15 January 1916, Reinsch Papers; Straight to Reinsch, 28 February 1916, *ibid.*; Vanderlip to Reinsch, 12 January 1916, *ibid.*; Reinsch to Vanderlip, 17 May 1916, Vanderlip Papers; Straight to Davison, 1 November 1915, Straight Papers; Reinsch, *An American Diplomat,* 207.

36. Reinsch to Straight, 12 February 1916, Reinsch Papers; Straight to Reinsch, 21 June 1916, *ibid.*

37. Reinsch to Lansing, 28 December 1915, RG 84, Peking Post file, 300, NA; Lansing to Reinsch, 24 January 1916, 763.72112/2035, DSNA; Reinsch to Straight, 12 February 1916, Reinsch Papers; *FR 1915, Supp.,* 610; *FR 1916, Supp.,* 330.

38. Straight to Reinsch, 21 June 1916, Reinsch Papers; Straight to House, 17 May 1916, Straight Papers; Straight to Roosevelt, 25 March 1916, *ibid.*; "Diary for the Perusal of Whitney Straight Esquire. . . , *ibid.*; Straight to Vanderlip, 11 September 1916, Vanderlip Papers; Israel, *Progressivism and the Open Door,* 132–51; Scheiber, "World War I as Entrepreneurial Opportunity," 486–511.

39. Straight to Bryce, 2 December 1916, Straight Papers; Guthrie to Lansing, 1 August 1916, 793.94/538½, DSNA; Asada, "Japan and the United States," 25–27.

40. "An Interview with the American Minister," by the *Hochi Shimbun*, Reinsch Papers.

41. Reinsch to Straight, 15 January 1916, Reinsch Papers; Reinsch to Vanderlip, 17 May 1916, Vanderlip Papers; Reinsch to Lansing, 9 March 1916, RG 84, Peking Post file, 610, NA; *Seattle Post-Intelligencer,* 4 April 1916.

42. Straight memo for Vanderlip, 26 November 1915, Vanderlip Papers; Straight to Reinsch, 28 February 1916, Reinsch Papers; Straight to McKnight, 14 March 1913, Straight Papers; Straight to Bland, 3 November 1916, *ibid.*; Straight to Bryce, 2 December 1916, *ibid.*; Straight to Polk, 26 March 1917, Frank Polk Papers, Yale University Library (hereafter cited Polk Papers).

43. Arnold to Reinsch, 1 November 1916, Reinsch Papers; Arnold to Redfield, 14 December 1916, RG 40 (Records of the Department of Commerce), 70801/105, NA; *Seattle Post-Intelligencer,* 6 and 10 April 1916; *San Francisco Chronicle,* 17, 22, and 28 September 1916; Reinsch to Vanderlip, 17 May 1916, Vanderlip Papers.

Chapter IX

YUAN SHIH-K'AI'S MONARCHICAL SCHEME AND THE LEE HIGGINSON LOAN

The Twenty-One Demands had only delayed Yuan's plans to establish a new dynasty. The settlement of the crisis set the stage for the flowering of the monarchical movement during the summer of 1915. In a desperate effort to regain power, Liang Shih-yi and the Cantonese clique (the old Communications party) seized the leadership of the movement from the Anhui party, by convincing Yuan they could manage the enterprise more successfully and discreetly. To give the movement the sanction of American constitutional expertise, Frank J. Goodnow, president of Johns Hopkins University, but still on retainer as constitutional adviser to the Chinese government, was recalled to Peking. Unaware of how he was being used, Goodnow prepared a memorandum which advocated a constitutional monarchy under certain stipulated conditions. The final element was the formation of the Ch'ou An Hui (the Peace Planning Society), which agitated for a return to the monarchy under its cover of an educational group concerned with China's future. As foreign and domestic opposition began to surface in September, the monarchists temporarily slowed their campaign. But Yuan's subsequent decision to realize his ambitions ultimately plunged China into civil war and undermined Reinsch's plans for China.[1]

*   *   *

Reinsch was caught by surprise. He had earlier reported on Yuan's imperial inclinations and the extent of monarchical sentiment in China. But, accurately gauging the potential internal and foreign opposition,

Reinsch seriously doubted that an attempt would be made to restore the empire. In his conversations with President Wilson and State Department officials as well as in his public statements during the summer of 1915, Reinsch therefore discounted the rumors reaching America and dismissed Goodnow's memorandum as mere academic discussion. At the request of MacMurray and the State Department, Reinsch delayed his departure for China so that he could review the political situation in San Francisco with Wellington Koo, the new Chinese minister to Mexico. Pointing to Goodnow's memorandum, Koo hinted that something was afoot. But he also tended to confirm Reinsch's assessment of the obstacles facing the restoration and declared that "Yuan himself was very doubtful." Consequently, Reinsch was dismayed and embarrassed when he learned that Koo had been assigned to prepare the ground in the United States for Yuan's assumption of the throne.[2]

By the time Reinsch returned to Peking at the end of September, the monarchists had regained their confidence and had announced plans to submit the question to a national referendum. Reinsch was plainly disappointed with his progressive friends and greatly disturbed by the monarchical scheme. He regarded it as a serious setback for constitutional government and reform. Moreover, it came at a most inopportune time. It threatened to frighten American financiers and industrialists, just when they seemed ready to enter China on a large scale. In the lull after the Twenty-One Demands, when China should have concentrated on strengthening itself with American help, Reinsch wrote in his memoirs, "the Chinese had immediately embarked on this doubtful political enterprise, consuming precious energies and money. The sums spent on military expeditions, in favorably attuning doubtful military leaders, and in the creation of the alleged unanimous consent through a popular vote, had been thrown away."

Reinsch candidly told the plotters that the movement would not be welcomed in the United States and he lectured them on the need to demonstrate accelerated political reform and freedom of discussion. However, as long as American interests were safe from internal disorder and foreign interference, he saw no alternative but to acquiesce in Yuan's misguided adventure and to hope for the best. Washington concurred.[3]

The situation changed dramatically when, on October 27, 1915, Japan invited the other major powers to send a joint note advising Yuan to suspend the monarchical movement. Reinsch cabled that any attempt to stop the movement while elections were in progress for the Convention of Citizens' Representatives would only create confusion and unrest. Japan, he observed, was seeking the position of "a maintainer of Peace of the Far East" in return for guarding foreign interests; it was also trying to assert against China the role of "protector without whose assent and assistance no important action may be taken." If Washington felt that it had to communicate its views to Peking, Reinsch continued, it must be done independently. He further advised that should Japan use any disturbances as a pretext to intervene, the United States should exercise its right to be consulted "and throughout act as a co-guarantor of security here."[4]

With Reinsch's warning in hand and Japanese duplicity fresh in his memory, Wilson instructed Secretary of State Lansing to tell Britain and Japan that it would be a breach of China's sovereignty to interfere as long as foreign interests were safe. Nevertheless, Wilson agreed that Peking should be advised in a friendly way that its interests might be compromised "unless the present changes can be guided with a very firm and prudent hand."[5] Reinsch reported that the Chinese appreciated the American position and that "at no time has America enjoyed greater popularity among the Chinese than at present." On the other hand, the Chinese resented Japan's claim to a vital interest in China's domestic affairs, which implied "a claim of virtual suzerainty."[6]

With one eye on Japan and the other powers, Yuan, on December 11, 1915, accepted the verdict of the national referendum. He announced plans for the formal promulgation of the empire and his own glorious enthronement. Minimizing the contrived nature of the election and the extent of official intimidation, Reinsch recommended that the United States recognize the empire as soon as it was proclaimed. At the same time, he cautioned Washington that the withdrawal of several American naval vessels to Manila might encourage the Japanese to intervene in the event of trouble. He therefore requested that the American squadron be brought up to full strength in Chinese waters "as demanded by the fulfillment of our responsibilities in China, so as to avoid a situation extremely dangerous to ourselves, to foreigners and to China herself." Lansing supported Reinsch's recommendations and, on December 21, instructed him to extend United States recognition to the empire, provided there was no serious organized opposition.[7]

*   *   *

On Christmas Day, 1915, a well-planned and executed revolt was launched in distant Yunnan, which then spread throughout the southern provinces. A hodgepodge of constitutionalists, republicans, remnants of the Kuomintang, opportunistic generals, and military governors, advocates of provincial autonomy, and a variety of dissidents found a vague common ground in their opposition to Yuan's personal ambitions and dictatorial rule. Yuan attempted to regain control of the rebellious provinces, but his loyal troops performed poorly in Szechuan and generally showed little inclination to fight. Meanwhile, Feng Kuo-chang, Tuan Ch'i-jui, and other members of the Anhui clique, who resented being upstaged by the Cantonese clique, sat on the sidelines. Having alienated the military governor of Kwangsi and fearing the defection of other provinces, Yuan bowed to defeat.

After conferring with Vice President Li and his former lieutenants, Hsu Shih-ch'ang and Tuan Ch'i-jui, Yuan issued a decree on March 22, 1916, abolishing the empire and blaming himself for China's turmoil. He then appointed Hsu minister of state, initiated peace moves with the south and offered southerners and republicans several important cabinet posts. At the same time, he continued his secret negotiations for an American loan in case his peace offers were rejected and a long civil war ensued.[8]

As Reinsch had expected, this was not enough to satisfy the rebels who demanded Yuan's retirement. The fighting continued and more provinces declared their independence. The president made one final effort to maintain China's unity and to keep at least the title of his office. He turned over administrative power to a reconstituted cabinet dominated by the Anhui faction and appointed Tuan premier; he decreed that the cabinet be responsible to Parliament, which was to be elected within three months; and he transferred control of the army to the Board of War, retaining only a household guard under his personal command.

Yuan's concessions settled nothing. While disorder and confusion reigned throughout China, the Anhui and Communications cliques vied for power in Peking. In May 1916, the Anhui leaders drove their rivals from the cabinet, but the Cantonese men retained some influence because of their financial expertise and their control of the national banks. At the same time, Tuan and Feng advanced their respective claims to succeed Yuan and jockeyed for the support of the militarists. In an attempt to resolve the question and to unify the loyal provinces, representatives of the northern military governors and commanders assembled in Nanking at the end of May. But the conference was quickly adjourned because of the inability of the delegates to agree on the succession and the unwillingness of the provinces to give financial and moral support to the Peking government. Meanwhile, southern leaders refused to talk peace until Yuan resigned. Consequently, a resumption of major fighting and a protracted civil war cast a dark shadow over China's future.[9]

Yuan's abortive monarchical scheme produced other serious repercussions. Japan interfered by sheltering revolutionaries, lending money and supplying arms to the insurgents, and encouraging Fukien provincial leaders to declare independence. In an attempt to sow discord, the Japanese legation informed the Chinese government that Reinsch was in contact with revolutionaries in Shanghai.[10] Far more disconcerting were Tokyo's continuing attempts to force the European powers to grant it a controlling voice in Far Eastern affairs. The Japanese also tried to make China financially dependent on Tokyo by playing on the ambitions of the various political factions. Reinsch was also nervous because the pro-Japanese Ts'ao Ju-lin was appointed minister of communications, which gave him an opportunity to dispense favors to Tokyo. Finally, as a means of destroying the credibility and credit of the Peking government, the Yokohama Specie Bank refused to turn over the surplus from the salt revenue.[11]

The civil war also threatened American financial assistance to China. Reinsch had high hopes for Lee Higginson's involvement in Chinese affairs. It marked the entry of a new major bank, which had none of the unpleasant memories that plagued other Wall Street houses. Its appointment as fiscal agent for the Chinese government promised continuous influence in Chinese economic life, a regular system for floating Chinese securities, and long-range planning for China's financial needs.[12]

However, Lee Higginson's fiscal agency encountered problems from the outset. Because of delays and omissions in the transmission of messages between the United States and China, the bank had accepted the agency on the false assumption that it included industrial and administrative loans. Reinsch believed that the bank should have waited for clarification before committing itself and agreed with the Chinese that the agency covered only administrative loans. Following this misunderstanding, rival factions in Peking separately approached American banks for loans to rescue the national banks from imminent collapse and to keep the Chinese government afloat. Liang Shih-yi and the Communications clique negotiated with Lee Higginson through Gest, while the Anhui clique and the minister of finance turned to Guaranty Trust of New York.[13]

Then, on March 20, 1916, two days before Yuan's cancellation of the monarchy, Reinsch asked the State Department to advise American bankers to postpone all loan negotiations pending clarification of China's internal affairs. It was a painful decision for Reinsch, particularly since he had labored so hard to interest American banks in Chinese loans.

Because of his continued support for Yuan's regime, it is doubtful if Reinsch was influenced by Liang Ch'i-ch'ao's direct appeal of February 28, 1916. "I beg to suggest," the former minster of justice and presently the ideological leader of the revolution wrote to Reinsch, "that such a scholar of your understanding and reputation for whom I cherish great respect, should observe the present situation not so much with the eyes of a diplomat, but with the far-sighted mind of an impartial judge and to interpret current events in the sense of a just and constitutional struggle on the part of the people against the tyranny and personal government of Yuan Shih-k'ai." In any event, Reinsch informed the State Department, the opposition had grown in "extent and import" and, regardless of the success of the revolutionaries, a general loan might tarnish America's democratic image and endanger its long-range interests in China.[14]

Misunderstanding Reinsch's motives, the State Department warned the minister not to dictate the terms of the loan. A petulant Reinsch retorted that, without indicating a lack of confidence in the central government or implying support for the rebels, it was essential to avoid the impression that the United States was encouraging Peking's military operations. The declaration of independence by Kwangtung, he wisely pointed out, made it "inexpedient" either to grant or advertise general American loans "until financial conditions are again upon a normal basis free from the dangers of associating them with partisan antagonism." Subsequently, the State Department agreed that, in view of the continued fighting and defection of provinces, it would be difficult to persuade the bankers to make a loan except on conditions injurious to China's credit.[15]

Anxious to get its foot into China ahead of its rivals, Lee Higginson ignored Reinsch's advice. On April 3, 1916, the bank made an advance of $1 million and four days later signed an agreement to float in the United States $5 million in three-year, gold treasury notes of the Republic of China. But in the middle of April, Lee Higginson suddenly postponed the loan. Reinsch's advice combined with the disintegration in China finally made an impression on the bank.[16]

*   *   *

Reinsch was greatly troubled by the turn of events. During the first half of 1916, he searched feverishly, almost frantically, for some means to maintain China's unity, the international status quo, and American influence. In the process, Reinsch intervened directly in Chinese internal affairs, submitted changing and sometimes contradictory advice to Washington, and compromised his own beliefs and policies.

Reinsch never abandoned his hope for constitutional and administrative reform in China. But he did not view the political struggle in Liang Ch'i-ch'ao's terms: republic or monarchy, the rule of law versus the rule of men, right versus might. To Reinsch, "the imminent issue" was the unity and administrative integrity of China. Peking, "the central government," represented continuity, stability, and a loosely defined legitimacy. Although they were not men of the highest caliber, Yuan, Liang Shih-yi, Chou Tzu-ch'i, even Tuan and Feng, were at least known quantities. The motley group of rebels, on the other hand, included bloodthirsty militarists, "demagogues" like T'ang Shao-yi, and a host of questionable characters whom neither Liang Ch'i-ch'ao nor Sun Yat-sen could control. Nor did they have a common policy beyond ousting Yuan from power. "If there were evidence of the existence of a large republican party, governed by definite views of public policy, and led by responsible and able men," Reinsch opined to Lansing, "everyone would desire to have them given a chance to establish and maintain their ascendance in the Government, but no such organization has thus far made its appearance." Since Peking had the only "adequate organization at present in sight," there was no alternative but to support Yuan and his successors. Moreover, any attempt to withdraw support from Peking would only "encourage the opposition and give scope to unfavorable outside influences."[17]

Reinsch therefore did everything in his power to prop up Yuan's crumbling regime. He advised prompt recognition of the empire and took an optimistic view of Yuan's position during the early weeks of the revolt. He underestimated the strength and determination of the opposition and dismissed the revolutionary movement as a "personal revolt" against Yuan "of a few prominent and able military leaders." In February 1916, he was forced to admit that a strong undercurrent of "ill will" against Yuan was beginning to "surface here and there." But he also argued that Yuan could still establish a strong empire and block foreign interference if he would only "make a definite and conclusive declaration of policy, including the firm establishment of an honest and straightforward constitutional system." In fact, Reinsch became impatient with Yuan's timidity in putting down the rebellion and, in a heated exchange on February 16, 1916, he admonished the president for his failure to initiate political and economic reforms.[18]

Reinsch was also unhappy with the sudden cancellation of the monarchy on March 22, 1916. He thought that created uncertainty and strengthened the Anhui clique, led by Hsu Shih-ch'ang and Tuan Ch'i-jui, who had advised that action in their attempt to wrest power from the Cantonese party. Despite the involvement of the Cantonese clique in the monarchical plot, Reinsch still regretted their fall from power. "The Cantonese leaders have impressed the foreign representatives here, and in fact, have proven themselves to be men of real capacity for organization and personal efficiency," he explained to Lansing. "They had not originally been active in the monarchical movement, but had taken it out of hands of others and pushed it with energy and success until foreign interference changed the course of events." Many of the Cantonese men were his personal friends and he feared that the militarists would attempt to execute or banish them. On the other hand, Reinsch disliked most of the Anhui leaders, especially Ts'ao Ju-lin. He doubted if American economic interests would fare as well in their hands and worried about the growing militarist influence in China. Nevertheless, he soon argued for American support to the Anhui government as the only practical means of insuring stability and preventing foreign intervention.[19]

Increasingly, Reinsch tried to shape the course of Chinese political development. He encouraged the formation of a ruling coalition composed of the Cantonese faction, Liang Ch'i-ch'ao's Chinputang party, the moderate wing of the Kuomintang, and the competent military governors of central China. Such a combination, he thought, might be powerful enough to restore unity and give China positive, reform government. To this end, Reinsch put the American legation at the disposal of the various factions. He sent the American military and naval attachés to Canton and the Yangtze region to gather information. Donald and Anderson, with Reinsch's knowledge and probably acting under his direction, went to Shanghai to arrange an understanding between the north and the south. Reinsch operated under a strange illusion, if he thought he could create a government to his liking. In any event, the KMT in Shanghai, led by T'ang Shao-yi, refused to make peace until Yuan resigned.[20]

Through the end of May, Reinsch hoped that Yuan could be retained as the nominal head of state, thereby lending stability to the central government. But the failure of the Nanking Conference convinced him that Yuan's resignation and Li's succession offered the only viable solution to the immediate political crisis. Li was certainly not the best choice for the presidency. He was not a strong figure and he had no influence over the northern militarists. He would also require immediate and ample foreign financial support. Nevertheless, Li's assumption of the presidency would imply a deference to constitutional forms and might set the stage for renewed talks between the warring factions.[21]

Meanwhile, Reinsch groped for an effective and feasible formula to cope with the Japanese menace. Although domestic discontent had sparked the rebellion, Reinsch increasingly blamed Tokyo for China's political turmoil. On April 1, 1916, Reinsch suggested a joint démarche of the powers which combined an agreement to maintain the status quo during the war with a demand that China protect foreign life and property. Two days later, Reinsch proposed an American caveat, similar to that of May 11, 1915, reserving to the United States the right to challenge any infringement of its rights at the end of the war. He also suggested joint international control of Chinese finances, a reversal of Reinsch's declared position. Reinsch's hastily drawn recommendations offered little guidance to troubled policy makers in Washington. When the Allies ignored American feelers, the Wilson administration ruled out unilateral political intervention. But the State Department kept under consideration Reinsch's suggestions for independent economic action and international control of Chinese finances, possibly through a revived consortium.[22]

Reinsch also tried to enlist British support. Britain still commanded considerable prestige in Peking and it still possessed the largest foreign economic stake in China. Even though he generally ignored the British minister's advice, Yuan turned to Jordan more often than to Reinsch. Nor could Japan totally ignore the interests and sensibilities of its ally. Reinsch therefore consulted frequently with Sir John Jordan and more than once hinted that "an Anglo-American combination would act as a solvent of political difficulties and bring much good to China." But British policy makers, including Jordan, adopted a policy of expediency at this point; they were primarily concerned with protecting and advancing their trade and were willing to subordinate and sacrifice China to the winning of the war. Jordan therefore maintained a noncommittal attitude toward Reinsch and fought off his "flattering attentions."[23]

Consequently, Reinsch was forced to fall back on America's economic power. At the end of April, Reinsch asked Lee Higginson to issue the $5 million loan and encouraged William F. Carey to sign a preliminary agreement for a $10 million loan, secured by the mining tax, which would presumably be floated by AIC.[24] This was merely the prelude. In his urgent telegram of May 27, 1916, Reinsch requested two large American loans. The first, for $15 million, was designed to rehabilitate and strengthen the two national banks, which had been forced to suspend specie payment. Reinsch also asked for a $13 million loan to enable the central government to carry on its normal functions. It would be secured by the land tax, which would be reorganized under American supervision in a manner similar to the successful Salt Administration.[25]

Reinsch was no longer deterred by the expected protests of the south. He felt that it was more important to prevent the imminent collapse of the Peking government, which was likely if the Yokohama Specie Bank continued to withhold the surplus revenues. In addition, the United States had to justify China's faith in America, particularly in view of Peking's recent generous railway and canal concessions to AIC and Siems-Carey. The Chinese obviously expected a *quid pro quo* in the form of a loan. "As in the past, the nations which have been most prominently engaged in the development of Chinese resources, have also come to the assistance of the Chinese Government, when the latter was in need of replenishing its financial resources," he declared to Lansing; "so today, when the European Nations, on account of the war, are unable to take their accustomed part in financial affairs in China, the Chinese Government must look to Americans to supply, or assist in supplying, the needs on the foreign financial markets."

Reinsch's case, however, rested primarily on the threat to the balance of power in the Far East and America's future interests in China. Japan was then offering a $30 million silver loan in return for an exclusive fiscal agency for foreign loans. Because the European war prevented Allied action in China, the United States had the responsibility to prevent Chinese dependence on Japan. An immediate moderate investment, he argued, would save the hundreds of millions that would be necessary in the future to rescue China from Japan's grasp. Japan's "menacing ambitions," Reinsch maintained, still rested on a "slender basis and could be held in check by display of active interests in China." Nor did Reinsch rule out American cooperation with the other powers, including Japan, on the basis of a frank understanding of the Open Door principles. "The issues involved," he insisted, "exceed those in Europe in ultimate importance"—unless "the abandonment of our position in China and of Chinese independence is required by other weighty considerations." In that event, Reinsch asked for a candid statement from Washington and a comprehensive reassessment of American foreign policy.[26]

After making this appeal, Reinsch left for Peitaiho, the seaside resort favored by the foreign community seeking to escape Peking's blistering summer heat. There, on the afternoon of June 6, 1916, Reinsch received a brief coded telegram from MacMurray: "Pan [Yuan Shih-k'ai] is dead." Reinsch hurried back to Peking on the night train. The Allied ministers had already received assurances from Premier Tuan Ch'i-jui that Vice President Li would be allowed to succeed as president without interference. On the following day, Li Yuan-hung quietly took the oath of office.[27]

Reinsch recognized that the crisis was by no means over, and on June 15, 1915, he repeated his appeal for American loans. "Unless a decision is made now American opportunity will be irrevocably lost," he cabled the State Department. "It is not necessary for Americans to assert primacy or to antagonize anyone, but simply to make use of the right which still exists to participate in Chinese affairs on an equal and independent basis." Reinsch again insisted that he had to know where Washington stood and he demanded "an immediate decision of policy, whether of inaction or of independent or joint financial assistance."[28]

Things were not so simple. The Chinese loan proposals revealed a bitter dispute on Wall Street. The American Group was not particularly anxious to reenter Chinese finance; yet it resented the intrusion of Lee Higginson and its success in obtaining the fiscal agency. It also feared that this novice in Chinese affairs would issue loans without adequate security, thereby depressing the Hukuang and Reorganization Loan bonds. Moreover, the American Group desired to avoid irritating Japan and was still wedded to the cooperative policy. It pointed out that under the terms of the loan agreement of 1913, the Sextuple Group had an option for all administrative loans until June 1917, or until the balance of the Reorganization Loan was floated.

Lee Higginson meanwhile pressed its case upon the State Department and the financial community. It, alone, had loaned money to China, the bank argued, and it possessed the fiscal agency. By the end of June, however, Lee Higginson, now allied with Guaranty Trust, admitted that it could not act independently. Lee Higginson's ability to market Chinese securities was badly damaged by the appearance of articles in the *New York Times* and the *Christian Science Monitor* (probably planted by Japanese agents), which deliberately discredited the Peking government. In addition, J. P. Morgan & Co. blocked Lee Higginson in its attempt to find other Wall Street underwriters for the Chinese bonds. Lee Higginson therefore offered to join the American Group, to float the loan in cooperation with other Wall Street banks, or to turn over its option to the Consortium, making it a part of a second reorganization loan. Although the American Group had not fully made up its mind on reentering Chinese finance, it agreed, on June 27, to sound out the British Group on making an immediate advance of $2 million which would be followed by larger loans floated by a revived consortium.[29]

The State Department fully appreciated the seriousness of the situation and had endorsed Reinsch's loan requests to the bankers. "The results of Japanese aggression in Manchuria show what we may expect elsewhere," Lansing observed to Wilson. The secretary of state also feared that the conflict between American bankers might enable Japan to "secure the prize." The State Department therefore concluded that the best solution lay in a combination of all American interests. A consensus was also emerging in the department that the loan should be internationalized in order to preserve the status quo and prevent Japanese obstruction. In the event of delays, however, Wilson and Lansing preferred a straight American loan by Lee Higginson and Guaranty Trust. The administration was edging back to the cooperative policy, but it still reserved the option of independent American action.[30]

Reinsch and the Chinese became apprehensive when they learned that the American Group planned to reenter the Consortium. Reinsch granted that under certain circumstances, and subject to certain reservations, a degree of American cooperation with other national groups was necessary. But fearing a repetition of American indifference and impotence, Reinsch first wanted assurances that American bankers would assert themselves sufficiently to prevent Japanese predominance. In particular, he insisted that the bankers' agreement provide for an American chief inspector of the land tax. To safeguard Chinese and American interests, Reinsch also believed that independent action had to accompany cooperation. He therefore called upon Lee Higginson to complete its $5 million loan.[31]

By the end of July, it became clear that a Consortium loan could not be arranged. Determined to prevent unilateral Japanese action, the State Department asked the American Group to consider an immediate $4 to 5 million advance to China. In its reply, the American Group rehearsed the history of its involvement in Chinese finance and indicated that it was in no hurry to reenter that business. However, it might reconsider its position if the State Department made a specific request. The Wilson administration preferred to have an enlarged American Group float the loan, but it was not ready to satisfy Morgan's terms.[32]

An independent loan by Lee Higginson–Guaranty Trust, AIC–National City, or some combination of these institutions, therefore offered the only means of delivering prompt American assistance to the hard-pressed Chinese government. In August, Lee Higginson and Guaranty Trust tentatively agreed to float a five-year, $5 million loan, issued at 92 (a discount to the bankers of eight points) and secured by the mining tax. For the moment, Reinsch was optimistic and took the occasion to suggest that the United States should try to disarm Japan and satisfy its special interests in Manchuria. "If international cooperation could be developed, if the American group could continue to negotiate with a view to undertaking reconstruction loans with other groups, and if Japan could have some assurance of financial assistance in the Manchurian economic enterprises," Reinsch remarked, "the edge would be taken off any animosity engendered by American progress."[33]

Reinsch spoke too soon. Morgan tried to bully Lee Higginson into dropping the loan by pointing out that it had made a bad deal. More important, China's turmoil gave Lee Higginson "cold feet." And when the State Department refused to collect the security in case China defaulted, Lee Higginson decided to drop the loan. In reprisal, the Chinese cancelled the fiscal agency. Reinsch was very disappointed. The proposed involvement of American financiers, especially Lee Higginson, he told the State Department, was "significant and even decisive in determining the internal development of this country and its political relationship not only with the United States, but with other countries, in matters closely affecting the American policies of Chinese integrity and the 'open door.'"[34]

*   *   *

Yuan's death and Li's succession to the presidency gave China a brief respite during the summer and early fall of 1916. Parliament was convened on schedule, the cabinet was approved after careful parliamentary scrutiny of each individual member, and Feng Kuo-chang was elected vice president without a bitter fight. For a month or so, Parliament actually conducted its business in responsible fashion. In addition, the Ministry of Finance and the Bank of China were in the competent hands of Dr. Ch'en Chin-t'ao and Hsu Un-yuen, both foreign-educated and sympathetic to American commercial and industrial involvement in China.

But the political calm was superficial and Reinsch's optimism was frayed. President Li inherited from Yuan Shih-k'ai semi-independent military governors (*tuchuns*) and a revitalized demand for provincial autonomy, bitter political partisanship and suspiciousness, and an empty treasury and an insolvent Bank of China. Li was well intentioned and devoted to constitutional government, but he was also politically and personally weak and inept.

Indeed, by the end of the year, the tenuous peace between the various factions in Parliament—the Kuomintang, the Chinputang, and the Peiyang (the militarist party)—began to crumble. In an attempt to assert its power, Parliament refused to approve a $5 million loan negotiated by the minister of finance with Japanese interests; this was no cause for joy, for American loans and concessions concluded in 1916 faced a similar threat. A complete deadlock between Tuan's cabinet and the Kuomintang-controlled Parliament loomed on the horizon. In addition, the truce between Premier Tuan and President Li was very fragile. Although the militarists had thus far acted with surprising restraint, Reinsch warned that they were ready to seize power if Li's government fell or if their position were threatened. The KMT was equally nervous. Reinsch learned from reliable sources that the KMT, which was little inclined to compromise and feared a confrontation with the militarists, was preparing for secession and the establishment of an independent government south of the Yangtze.[35]

In the meantime, the Japanese threat appeared in a different, but to Reinsch equally disturbing, guise. Supported by Japanese financial leaders who demanded a more liberal China policy instead of naked force or dubious political pressure, the government of Terauchi Masatake was preparing a new strategy of peaceful economic penetration. Following a visit to China in the summer of 1916, Nishihara Kamezo organized a syndicate composed of the industrial Bank of Japan, the Bank of Korea, and the Bank of Formosa, which would soon funnel funds from the Japanese government in the form of grants and loans in return for Chinese cooperation and Japanese control of China's natural resources. Taking advantage of China's political dissension and financial woes, the Japanese courted almost all Chinese factions, especially the militarists. Indeed, in September 1916, the Japanese minister to Peking proffered a large loan, secured by the land tax which would be placed under Japanese control. The Japanese intended to share the loan with the Allies and even the Americans, but they first wanted the Chinese to deal with them.

For the time being, the Chinese evaded the Japanese offer by turning to the Consortium for a $50 million loan, secured by the salt revenue, and then to American bankers. Within a few months, however, the Chinese were persuaded that a policy of friendship and cooperation was within certain limits desirable, if not necessary, and they welcomed Nishihara's money. While Ts'ao Ju-lin and the New Communications clique favored a close relationship with Japan, there were many other Chinese leaders who thought it was possible to arrange a temporary understanding with Tokyo without sacrificing China's independence. Reinsch appreciated China's financial plight and grudgingly admitted the inevitability of increased Japanese financial and economic activity. But, as he noted in a revealing cable on September 5, 1916, he still hoped to find enough American financial support so that China "could also accept aid from Japan without placing itself in such a position of complete dependence as would make impossible [the] safeguarding of

Chinese national rights together with general international interests in arranging the details of a new understanding with Japan concerning Manchuria."[36]

In October 1916, Reinsch decided to write directly to President Wilson to apprise him of the deteriorating situation in China and to appeal for stronger administration support for his efforts. The fate of the Siems-Carey contracts and the need for an American loan to China were very much on his mind. But, in fact, everything had gone sour since he had seen the President in 1915. The men upon whom Reinsch had depended to bring stability, reform, and development to China—Yuan and the Communications clique—had disappointed him and had passed from the scene. Their ambition drove China into civil war, invited Japanese interference, and frightened away American investors. They also forced Reinsch to compromise his principles: in the name of China's integrity and survival, Reinsch intervened in China's internal affairs and advocated the use of political loans. They fell anyway, and their successors did not inspire the same confidence or express the same desire for American influence. In the meantime, American bankers failed to seize the opportunity to become the financiers of China and to reorganize China's administrative and tax systems. Simultaneously, the very men who promised to take the initiative in China—Vanderlip and Straight—betrayed him and American interests to Japan, the greatest menace to the United States and China.

Reinsch therefore had little to show for his efforts. He therefore offered the following somber analysis to Wilson:

So China is in danger of being wrecked and the wreckers hope to reconstruct her political and economic life in their own interest. For such a contingency we have to be prepared. It would be a great good fortune for China and the world if as the trusted friends of China we could prevent this wrecking: and it would not require much national assistance (not more money in fact, than one day's expenditure in this war) if that were accompanied with construction work such as the Chinese would be glad to have us do. Nor would it be necessary to play a lone hand only to accord some *support* so that they might not be utterly delivered to the mercy of their pursuers.

If such action is not taken the only alternative left will be the creation in China of some form of international control; and our task will be to find means to prevent the just interests of America from being ignored or excluded.[37]

*   *   *

A few weeks later, upon Wilson's reelection, Reinsch volunteered to resign, if that would assist the president in carrying out his foreign policy. Reinsch's offer was probably intended only as a courtesy; it was the kind of letter that was expected of all political appointees at the end of an administration. Reinsch certainly did not feel that his work was done. But it did give Wilson an opportunity to change his representative in Peking and to reevaluate his Far Eastern policy. Several months earlier, in fact, Reinsch had pointedly asked Washington if it desired to reassess its commitment to China and the Open Door.

But Wilson never seriously thought of revising America's traditional policy toward China or of reexamining the assumptions on which it was predicated. As much as ever, the Wilson administration was wedded to the Hay Doctrine. "I believe that I am expressing the feeling of the Secretary of State when I say that we have the greatest confidence in your discretion and judgment and should be very sorry to lose you in time when clear heads and steady hands are so absolutely necessary," Wilson replied to Reinsch. In January 1917, Charles Crane's suggestion that Reinsch be moved to Washington as third assistant secretary of state interested Wilson. And yet, Wilson told Crane, "I should hesitate to remove him from a post for which it would be so extremely difficult to find a substitute." Reinsch therefore remained in Peking, until he felt betrayed by his president.[38]

NOTES TO
CHAPTER IX

1. *FR 1915*, 46–60; memo of interview, Arnold and Chou Tzu-ch'i, 26 August 1915, RG 84, Peking Post file, 800, NA; Reinsch, *An American Diplomat*, 23–28, 171–75; *New York Times*, 16 and 30 August 1915; Bose, *American Attitude and Policy to the Nationalist Movement in China*, 96–98; Ch'en, *Yuan Shih-k'ai*, 159–72; Pearl, *Morrison of Peking*, 313; Pugach, "Embarrassed Monarchist," 499–517.

2. Lansing to Reinsch, 14 and 19 August 1915, Reinsch Papers; Reinsch, *An American Diplomat*, 171; *Baltimore Sun*, 19 August 1915; *San Francisco Chronicle*, 18 August 1915.

3. Reinsch to Lansing, 11 October 1915, 893.01/49, DSNA; *FR 1915*, 61–69; Reinsch, *An American Diplomat*, 175–78, 187; Hawkins Tapes, 4.

4. Reinsch to Lansing, 28 October 1915, 893.01/41, 11 December 1915, 893.01/56, DSNA; *FR 1915*, 69–76.

5. Lansing to Reinsch, 28 October 1915, 893.01/30, DSNA; *FR: Lansing Papers*, II, 426–29; *FR 1915*, 76–77.

6. Reinsch to Lansing, 28 October 1915, 893.01/41, 19 November 1915, 893.01/62, DSNA; *FR 1915*, 78.

7. Reinsch to Lansing, 9 November 1915, 893.01/46, 17 December 1915, 893.00/2330, DSNA; *FR 1915*, 77–79; Reinsch Log Book, 18 December 1915, Hornbeck Papers; Ch'en, *Yuan Shih-k'ai*, 172–78.

8. *FR 1916*, 179–88; *San Francisco Chronicle*, 23 and 25 March 1916; Ch'en, *Yuan Shih-k'ai*, 179–88; Joseph Levenson, *Liang Ch'i-ch'ao and the Mind of Modern China* (Cambridge, 1959), 176–81.

9. *FR 1916*, 65–86; Reinsch, *An American Diplomat*, 188–90; Ch'en, *Yuan Shih-k'ai*, 189–92.

10. Reinsch to Lansing, 9 March 1916, 893.00/2377, DSNA; Guthrie to Lansing, 17 April 1916, 893.00/2378, DSNA; memo of conversation, Williams and Koo, 19 April 1917, 893.51/1641, DSNA; *FR 1916*, 51–84; Raymond Tenney to Reinsch, 11 May 1916, RG 84, Peking Post file, 800, NA; Reinsch to Captain I. Newell, 11 May 1916, *ibid*.

11. Reinsch to Lansing, 15 January 1916, 793.94/500, 18 April 1916, 893.51/1635, 28 April 1916, 893.51/1643, DSNA; *FR 1916*, 76–77; Jordan to Langley, 29 February 1916, Jordan Papers, FO 350/15; Ch'en *Yuan Shih-k'ai*, 176–78.

12. Reinsch, *An American Diplomat*, 187.

13. Reinsch to Lansing, 20 March 1916, 893.51/1609, 21 March 1916, 893.51/1622 and /1610, 27 March 1916, 893.51/1613, DSNA; Lansing to Reinsch, 25 March 1916, 893.51/1612a, DSNA.

14. Reinsch to Lansing, 20 March 1916, 893.51/1609, DSNA; Liang Ch'i-ch'ao to Reinsch, 28 February 1916, Reinsch Papers; Reinsch, *An American Diplomat*, 187.

15. Lansing to Reinsch, 6 April 1916, 893.51/1617, DSNA; Reinsch to Lansing, 7 April 1916, *ibid.*; memo of interview, Williams and Koo, 18 April 1916, 893.51/1641, DSNA.

16. Reinsch to Lansing, 14 April 1916, 893.01/97, 19 April 1916, 893.01/96 and 893.51/1635, DSNA; Lee Higginson to Lansing, 15 April 1916, 893.51/1629, DSNA; *FR 1916*, 128–33.

17. *FR 1916*, 51–84; Reinsch, *An American Diplomat*, 189–90; Liang Ch'i-ch'ao to Reinsch, 28 February 1916, Reinsch Papers.

18. *FR 1916,* 59–66; Reinsch, *An American Diplomat,* 184–86; memo of conversation, Reinsch and Yuan, 16 February 1916, in 893.01/90, DSNA.

19. *FR 1916,* 77–82; Reinsch, *An American Diplomat,* 188–90; memo of conversation, Williams and Koo, 18 April 1916, 893.51/1641, DSNA.

20. Reinsch to Lansing, 3 April 1916, 793.94/508, DSNA; memo of conversation, Williams and Koo, 18 April 1916, 893.51/1641, DSNA; Sammons to Reinsch, 7 June 1916, 893.00/2453, DSNA; MacMurray to Reinsch, 5 June 1916, RG 84, Peking Post file, 800, NA.

21. Reinsch to Lansing, 2 June 1916, 893.51/1645, DSNA; *FR 1916,* 82–89.

22. Reinsch to Lansing, 1 April 1916, 793.94/507, 3 April 1916, 793.94/508, DSNA; Wilson to Lansing, 7 April 1916, 793.94/516½, DSNA; Li, *Wilson's China Policy,* 155–59.

23. Jordan to Langley, 1 February, 14 March, and 16 April 1916, Jordan Papers, FO 350/15; Jordan to Grey, 26 May 1916, f49/101131/16, FO 371/2645; Madeline Chi, *China Diplomacy,* 69.

24. Reinsch to Lansing, 16 April 1916, 893.51/1638, 27 April 1916, 893.00/2384, 28 April 1916, 893.51/1643, 27 May 1916, 893.51/1644, 17 May 1916, 893.51/1650, DSNA; Jenks to Vanderlip, 14 May 1916, Vanderlip Papers.

25. Reinsch to Lansing, 27 May 1916, 893.51/1644, DSNA.

26. *Ibid.*; Reinsch to Lansing, 2 June 1916, 893.51/1645, DSNA.

27. Reinsch, *An American Diplomat,* 192–93; *FR 1916,* 84.

28. Reinsch to Lansing, 15 June 1916, 893.51/1652, 26 June 1916, 893.51/1657, DSNA; *FR 1916,* 84–85.

29. Williams memos, 21 June 1916, 893.51/3009, 26 June 1916, 893.51/1696, 18 August 1916, 893.51/1697, 19 August 1916, 893.51/1694, DSNA; Lansing to Wilson, 15 June 1916, 893.51/1652, DSNA; Phillips to Lansing, 6 July 1916, 893.51/1665, DSNA; Lansing to Reinsch, 27 July 1916, 893.51/1652, DSNA; J. P. Morgan to Morgan Grenfell, 27 June 1916, 893.51/1665, DSNA; cables from AIC (New York), 3, 17, 25, 27, and 30 June, and 1 and 2 July 1916, Reinsch Papers; Phillips to Polk, 12 July 1916, Polk Papers.

30. Williams to Reinsch, 1 June 1916, Reinsch Papers; Lansing to Reinsch, 27 June 1916, 893.51/1652, DSNA; Lansing to Wilson, 15 June 1916, *ibid.*; Williams memo, 26 June 1916, 893.51/1696, DSNA; Lansing to Polk, 3 July 1916, 893.51/1692½, DSNA; Phillips to Lansing, 6 July 1916, 893.51/1665, DSNA; Lockhart to Lansing, 6 July 1916, 893.51/1665, DSNA; Phillips to Polk, 12 July 1916, Polk Papers.

31. Reinsch to Lansing, 26 June 1916, 893.51/1658, 28 June 1916, 893.51/1660, 29 June 1916, 893.51/1661, 29 June 1916, 893.51/1663, 15 July 1916, 893.51/1667, DSNA; Reinsch to Lee Higginson, 14 July 1916, 893.51/1676, DSNA.

32. Polk to Frederick Allen, Charles Stone, J. P. Morgan, et al., 21 July 1916, 893.51/1667a, DSNA; Williams to Lansing, 11 August 1916, 893.51/1670, DSNA; *FR 1916,* 134–38.

33. Reinsch to Lansing, 9 August 1916, 893.51/1673 and /1674, DSNA; Williams to Lansing, 11 August 1916, 893.51/1670, DSNA.

34. Williams memos, 14 August 1916, 893.51/1702, 18 August 1916, 893.51/1697, 19 August 1916, 893.51/1694, DSNA; Lee Higginson to Adee, 6 September 1916, 893.51/1687, DSNA; Lee Higginson to Reinsch, 21 August 1916, 893.51/1679, DSNA; Reinsch to Lansing, 22 August 1916, 893.51/1678, 1 September 1916, 893.51/1683, 16 September 1916, 893.51/1678, DSNA; Lansing to Reinsch, 31 August 1916, 893.51/1678, DSNA.

35. Memo of interview, Reinsch and Li, 29 June 1916, Reinsch Papers; Reinsch, "Six Years of American Action in China," Reinsch Papers; Reinsch, *An American Diplomat*, 198–204; Anderson to Straight, 3 October 1916, RG 84, Peking Post file, 800, NA; Reinsch to Wilson, 14 October 1916, *ibid.*; *FR 1916*, 85–98; O. Edmund Clubb, *20th Century China* (New York, 1964), 61–62.

36. Reinsch to Lansing, 5 September 1916, 793.94/519, DSNA; *FR 1916*, 90–96; Jordan to Grey, 5 September 1916, f183716/16, FO 371/2652; Frank C. Langdon, "Japan's Failure to Establish Friendly Relations with China in 1917–1918," *Pacific Historical Review*, XXVI (August 1957), 245–58; Scanlan, "No Longer a Treaty Port," 192–201, 234–36.

37. Reinsch to Wilson, 14 October 1916, RG 84, Peking Post file, 800, NA.

38. Reinsch to Wilson, 11 November 1916, Wilson Papers; Wilson to Reinsch, 27 December 1916, *ibid.*; Crane to Wilson, 20 January 1917, *ibid.*; Wilson to Crane, 23 January 1917, Ray S. Baker Papers.

Chapter X

BETRAYAL
AND SUBVERSION

Private initiative and investment plus government support and encouragement yielded profits, foreign markets, and American influence. The United States government had an obligation to provide the structural framework and to defend American treaty rights so that private enterprise could raise and deploy American capital abroad and compete successfully for trade and concessions. But the major burden fell on American merchants, manufacturers, and bankers to seize the overseas opportunities that awaited them. It was assumed that American businessmen, searching for profits and conscious of the need to expand American influence, would rise to the challenge. American policy makers had operated on the formula since the 1890s. It was the basis of the Open Door strategy, of Dollar Diplomacy. Reinsch had been raised on it and believed in its validity. It underlay his entire program in China. "It is my purpose," he declared to Frank Vanderlip, "that the foundation of American enterprise in China shall be deeply and firmly laid."[1]

But what should the United States do when American private enterprise failed to come through? What if it subverted the diplomatic objectives of the United States government and the efforts of its diplomatic representatives? What if it even betrayed America's friends and made common cause with its rivals? In that event, should the United States government discipline the offenders, find others to do the job, or engage directly in foreign economic operations? American policy makers have wrestled with these questions throughout this century—from the shenanigans of the American China Development Company to the recent activities of the giant multinational firms. It also became Reinsch's most frustrating dilemma. And because they were so important to his plans, the American International Corporation and its associated firms hurt him the most. Reinsch could condemn AIC's betrayal, but he could not subvert American private enterprise. Instead, Reinsch turned to other interests, outside Wall Street, for help in salvaging American influence in China. He also precipitated a showdown with Japan, which he blamed for much of the problem.

* * *

Faced with the expiration of the Red Cross option, Reinsch and Mabel Boardman made another valiant effort to obtain a loan for the Huai River Conservancy in the fall of 1915. AIC alone expressed interest in the project. However, Yuan's monarchical scheme and fear of Japanese retaliation made AIC exceedingly cautious. It therefore requested Reinsch to secure an extension of the option and to arrange for a representative of Siems-Carey to discuss the matter with the Chinese. Reinsch was embarrassed to ask the Chinese for another extension. He was even more disturbed by Vanderlip's deference to Japan. "Fortunately, the political situation has not yet undergone such radical changes that American capitalists need ask permission of their competitors before engaging even in new business with China," Reinsch replied with unconcealed irritation. But he also realized that he had no choice. He had to keep the Huai River project alive and under American control. The Chinese agreed to a four-month extension, subject to the condition that AIC finance the clearing and restoration of the Grand Canal from the Yangtze to Techow.[2]

AIC accepted the terms and directed Carey and Gregory to negotiate a contract. Reinsch facilitated their work, but stayed in the background in order to avoid charges of political interference. Instead, he relied upon Anderson to guide Carey and Gregory and on Chou Tzu-ch'i and Liang Shih-yi to influence the Chinese negotiators. The talks resulted in the signing of two agreements: The South Grand Canal of Shantung Province Seven Percent Improvement Loan (April 19, 1916) and the Huai River Conservancy Grand Canal Improvement Loan (May 13, 1916). With Reinsch's assistance, Carey also signed an agreement with the Ministry of Communications, which provided for the Siems-Carey Construction Company to build 1,500 miles of railways in central and south China. Carey then departed for the United States to obtain ratification of the various contracts. He also carried an informal agreement for a $10 million political loan, secured by the mining tax.[3]

Reinsch was excited. The terms of the canal and railway contracts, he observed, "were the most favorable ever obtained by any foreign firms for a loan in China." In fact, Reinsch thought that the terms in the Grand Canal agreement were "almost too severe for China." The railway contract was especially significant because it gave Siems-Carey a share of the profits (25 percent) during the life of the bonds and a voice in the technical management of the railroads. "The American management," Reinsch pointed out, "will actually have a free hand to introduce efficient and scientific means of management, and a real opportunity will be afforded to show what Americans trained in handling similar problems at home can do by way of giving China a well managed and efficient railway system." In addition, the American canal and railway concessions would serve to neutralize the foreign spheres of influence. To be sure, the Chinese were using the Americans as a foil against Japan and the other powers. The hard-pressed Chinese also expected loans (from Lee Higginson as well as from AIC) in return for their exceptional generosity. Nevertheless, the soundness of the security and the overall benefits required AIC to ratify the contracts and to begin work immediately.[4]

It was too good to be true. AIC ignored Reinsch's warning that the clearing of the Grand Canal be started in Kiangsu, pending clarification of German and Japanese preferential rights in Shantung. AIC preferred to begin in Shantung because preliminary work had been done in that section and provincial authorities had signed a separate agreement. AIC also demanded modifications in the contracts that would make the bonds more marketable: among other things, it wanted an extra ½ percent service charge for the canal bonds and a separate guarantee by the Kiangsu provincial authorities. Finally, AIC reduced the proposed loan to $2 million, hedged it with all sorts of conditions, and then abandoned it completely because of the need for a full understanding with the American Group.[5]

Reinsch was appalled by AIC's insensitivity to Chinese feelings, its ignorance of Chinese affairs, and its timidity. AIC's insistence on renegotiating the contracts—on trivial matters, for the most part—occurred during a political transition in China. Li had just assumed the presidency and different men occupied the various ministries. Hsu Shih-ying, who headed the important Ministry of Communications and represented the New Communications clique, was not particularly friendly to American interests. In addition, the revised contracts might have to be submitted to the 1913 Parliament, which might not approve them.

Had the original contracts been accepted by AIC, Reinsch told

Lansing, it would have been easy to obtain modifications at a later date. But American bankers attached to minor points "an importance beyond their real consequence." The demand for a guarantee by the Kiangsu authorities would only affront the central government and invite provincial and foreign interference without strengthening the security. Therefore, AIC merely opened the door to complications and delays. In the process, AIC embarrassed Reinsch and underminded Chinese faith in the United States.[6]

Reinsch complained bitterly to the State Department and AIC. Here was further proof that something was "radically wrong" with the way Americans handled foreign business. "The Chinese here are accustomed to deal with men who can say that a thing can be done or that it cannot be done and who can also give assurances that it will be done," he scolded Vanderlip. While other foreigners took into account long-range and national considerations, Americans still lacked an organization "which was broadly representative so as to look upon all parts of Chinese commerce and finance in their interrelation." Therefore, unless they decided to abandon China completely, American businessmen would have to change their methods. Americans might succeed in modifying their contracts this one last time, but never again would the Chinese let them get away with it. In the future, Reinsch warned, "American concerns attempting to do business in China should definitely make up their minds as to what they want and what they can grant before the main contract is finally signed."[7]

Reinsch might fume at AIC, but he could not subvert American capital. The State Department also ordered him to cooperate with AIC in getting the changes in the contracts. That was not an easy matter. "The displeasure of the Chinese knew no limit," Reinsch later noted, "and it seemed as if the entire negotiations might have been in vain." Reinsch did his best to mollify the Chinese. He justified AIC's actions on the basis of sound business practices and pointed out that American capital was not as experienced as the big European banking firms. He also encouraged the Chinese to create the best climate for American business, for out of it "would naturally grow a readiness to afford financial support." The Chinese did not dispute Reinsch's arguments, "but felt themselves confronted by a condition, not a theory." Pressed to the wall, Peking had to reopen the negotiations and accede to most of the demands. But the Chinese also exacted a price. In the supplementary railway agreement signed on September 29, 1916, the Chinese reduced the rail mileage to 1,100 miles and Siems-Carey's share of the profits to 20 percent.[8]

But this was only the beginning of Reinsch's troubles. The foreign rivals of the United States soon objected to the railway and canal concessions and AIC sabotaged the efforts of Reinsch and the State Department to defend American rights in China. On August 8, 1916, the Russian minister to China protested the selection of the Fengchen–Ninghsia line as one of the Siems-Carey railways. Reinsch's conversations with Prince Koudacheff convinced him that the Russian protest was really designed to forestall Chinese colonization in Mongolia and that the United States need not fear vigorous opposition to the railway concession itself. Nevertheless, he believed it was necessary for the United States to adopt a firm stand with the Chinese government and to hold a protest in reserve. Lansing agreed and, on August 12, 1916, instructed Reinsch to "take measures to safeguard American interests."[9]

AIC, however, ordered Carey not to proceed with the Fengchen–Ninghsia line until the Russian protest was settled. "As far as the American International Corporation is concerned," Charles Stone informed Lansing, "we do not wish to become involved in political controversies between the Chinese and Russian Governments." The Russians (and later the Japanese in the Grand Canal matter) indicated that AIC could enter their spheres of influence as long as they recognized their predominance. Straight and his Wall Street colleagues recognized that they could not formally accept such claims. On the other hand, they felt that they could not rely on Washington for political support in the Far East and that China would be humiliated in its attempt to balance the United States against the other powers. In addition, AIC was contemplating joint ventures with Russia and Japan in Manchuria and was converted to the cooperative policy. Straight therefore told the Russian ambassador in Washington that AIC did not care for the line in question and would seek a substitute.[10]

Reinsch was livid with rage. "Never was the ground cut from under any one exerting himself to safeguard the interests of others as was done in this case," he wrote in his memoirs. He denounced AIC's cowardice and selfishness; he also warned that AIC jeopardized American interests and China's sovereignty and encouraged the other powers to remonstrate. The Chinese government had actually promised Carey that it would assume responsibility for answering the Russian protest and indicated that it would feel compromised if AIC hesitated in the face of Russian opposition. "Were this statement known in China," Reinsch alerted the State Department, "it would involve great prejudice to the opportunities of the Corporation and to the American rights."[11]

Subsequently, France and Britain protested against the proposed

Siems-Carey railways in Kwangsi, Hunan, and Hupei. The British, in fact, called upon the United States to recognize that a reversion to spheres of influence had actually taken place. But at the same time, Britain and France invited American participation in railway construction, subject to the recognition of their claims. The British were particularly anxious to secure American financing and to amalgamate the Siems-Carey concessions with their own. In other words, the Allies wanted the best of all worlds while they were tied up in the European war: American money to advance construction of their lines, neutralization of the Siems-Carey concessions, and recognition of their spheres of influence.

In view of the desirability of completing the Canton–Hankow and other major trunk lines, Reinsch welcomed genuine cooperation. He saw an opportunity to demonstrate America's ability to handle large projects, to settle the issue of discrimination in the Hukuang Railways, and to strengthen Anglo-American ties. But Reinsch would not allow these considerations to compromise his defense of the Siems-Carey concessions or the American position on the Open Door. He believed that the time had arrived to obtain from Britain, France, and Russia a reaffirmation and redefinition of the Hay notes. He wanted a clear statement that extended equal opportunity to investments and distinguished between "specific rights in particular undertakings" and "general rights of priority or of exclusive interest in any region in China." In effect, he asked the powers to recognize that the situation had changed since 1900: the United States was going to assume a much larger role in Far Eastern affairs and the days of formal spheres of influence were over.

The State Department concurred in Reinsch's analysis and denounced the revival of spheres of influence in formal notes to the British and French governments. "We should urge that the real interests of the great western powers demand an undivided China, open on equal terms to the commercial and industrial enterprises of all nations," Williams declared in a departmental memorandum, "and we ought to ask their acceptance of an interpretation of the 'Open Door' policy that will secure this." In his memoranda to the British and French governments, Lansing tried to secure such a statement, which he preferred to vague offers of cooperation. But he did not press the point on the Allies and nothing came of the effort.[12]

Far more disconcerting was the fate of the Huai River–Grand Canal project. Without any warning, Straight cabled Gregory and Carey that AIC had agreed in principle to co-sponsor the Grand Canal loan with Japanese banking interests led by the Industrial Bank of Japan. He directed AIC's representatives to obtain Chinese approval and to facilitate the negotiation of a final agreement with the Peking government. The only alternative to Japanese-American cooperation, he reminded them, was Japanese control and development of the project. Japan had already protested the Grand Canal project on the grounds that it had inherited prior German rights in Shantung. But Tokyo actually wanted Japanese-American cooperation rather than the exclusion of AIC. Confronted by almost certain financial loss if it proceeded independently, AIC agreed to admit the Japanese. Consequently, on March 8, 1917, AIC signed an agreement with the Industrial Bank of Japan, which provided for a joint $6 million loan to dredge the Grand Canal: $3.5 million would be floated in New York, the rest in Tokyo. Despite AIC's assertions that it would not act without Chinese approval, AIC presented Peking with a *fait accompli*.

Americans in China, as well as the Chinese themselves, were astounded. Knowing full well Chinese hostility toward Japan and Reinsch's insistence on independent American action, Carey, Gregory, and Warren Austin, then a young attorney working for AIC, protested AIC's decision to Straight. They feared that Reinsch might withdraw his support from AIC and that the Chinese might refuse to approve the railway contract that was still pending in Peking.[13]

Reinsch could hardly contain his anger. Wall Street again demonstrated its timidity and, because of its failure to sound out Peking, its inexcusable bad manners. "It is to be doubted if the nationals of any other country would have acted in this manner," he reflected in his memoirs. Reinsch believed that cooperation was, in general, premature. But the choice of Tokyo as a partner and New York's subservience to its political objectives could only destroy China's confidence in the United States. Moreover, the Huai River–Grand Canal enterprise was intimately identified with American humanitarianism and non-political support for China; it was considered a touchstone for American organizing ability and engineering talent. "It would have been impossible," he fumed, "to find a more unsuitable project enterprise for cooperation. Should the Chinese learn that it is proposed to carry the Japanese into Kiangsu on the backs of Americans their indignation will be without limit, resulting in great danger to American interests in general and universal antagonism to the International Corporation."[14]

After advising the Chinese to accept joint financing, Reinsch received the crowning blow. In April 1917, Reinsch learned that the agreement with the Industrial Bank of Japan also provided for joint management and construction. "The withholding of this important informa-

tion until the Chinese should have bound themselves to an arrangement
which they supposed related only to financial matters is so disingenuous
that the exact effect of such tactics upon the Chinese cannot be foretold
aside from the fact that they will surely be disastrous to the standing of
the Corporation in the eyes of the Chinese. . . ."[15]

In retaliation, Reinsch suggested that AIC be informed that the
United States government would support its enterprises in China "only
on the condition and to the extent that they are fully and frankly communicated in advance to the Department and are approved by it."
Reinsch also hinted that the legation would refuse to pressure the
Chinese into accepting the agreement. But the minister was overwhelmed by the growing sentiment in Washington favoring cooperation. While it advised AIC to find another enterprise for Japanese-
American cooperation, the State Department informed Reinsch that the
matter was between the bankers and the Chinese and instructed him not
to interfere with the AIC-Japanese negotiations.[16]

Reinsch could not let the State Department and AIC off the hook so
easily. In an angry telegram, dated April 24, 1917, Reinsch castigated
AIC for tying the hands of the Chinese government. Pointing to the
endless difficulties encountered in the Hukuang Railways, Reinsch also
questioned the feasibility of cooperation. More important, he told the
State Department that it was inaugurating a fundamental and dangerous
change in American Far Eastern policy. In essence, Washington was supporting Japan's political aims in China and Japanese interests at the expense of American business. It would be impossible, he noted, for independent American firms to challenge the Japanese-American syndicate
"supported by all the political agencies of the Japanese Government."[17]

Reinsch vented his feelings, but it was an empty gesture. Reinsch
could not sabotage American economic expansion. He knew that he
would have to help pull AIC out of the "disastrous muddle" which it had
created. Nor could he abandon China to Japan. In his conversations with
Chinese officials, Reinsch emphasized that the Americans would retain
financial control. He treated AIC's action as a minor matter and explained that it was common for banks to place part of their bond issues in
other markets. The Chinese were furious and felt that AIC was guilty of a
breach of trust. Nevertheless, they were reconciled to Japanese participation; they knew that if the negotiations failed, Tokyo would demand a
takeover of the entire enterprise. "What can we do?" the Chinese premier
replied to Reinsch. "The corporation has tied our hands." Consequently,
a new agreement for the Grand Canal improvement was signed by Carey
and Hsiung Hsi-ling on November 20, 1917. Despite several advances

on the Japanese-American loan, however, the Grand Canal project, like the Siems-Carey railway concessions, never materialized.[18]

AIC probably believed that it was making a practical adjustment to the new "realities" in East Asia. It was clear that the Allies and especially Japan, aware of the enormous resources of American capital, would resist an American "invasion" of their spheres of influence. The Chinese themselves were accepting money from Japanese interests as part of an accommodation with Tokyo, which rendered Reinsch's moralistic appeals and condemnations somewhat vacuous. Moreover, the State Department, pressed by Straight and other Wall Street bankers as well as by the exigencies of the war, was in the process of returning to the policy of cooperation and America's reentry into the Consortium.

On the other hand, it is difficult to justify AIC's cynical disregard of Chinese sensitivities and America's overall interests, its selfish and timid submission to the spheres of influence, or its failure to consult with the State Department and Reinsch before establishing *faits accomplis*. It is true that, in 1916–1917, the State Department's positions revealed confusion and vacillation. Basically, however, the Wilson administration continued to support independent American action and a broader conception of American rights under the Open Door. Within certain limits, a well-coordinated effort on the part of Wall Street, the State Department, and the United States legation in Peking might have indeed strengthened the position of American interests in relation to the other powers without trying to exclude them entirely from China.

*   *   *

During the fall of 1916, just when the future of American enterprise in China looked grim and Peking's financial situation appeared critical, a glimmer of hope radiated from Chicago. The Continental and Commercial Trust and Savings Bank agreed to float a $5 million gold loan, secured by the Tobacco and Wine Public Sales Tax. The proceeds were eventually to be used for industrial purposes, but the immediate intent was political—to rescue the Bank of China and the Bank of Communications. In the agreement, signed in Washington on November 16, 1916, the Chicago bank was also granted an option on future loans up to $25 million.[19]

For the moment, Reinsch was jubilant. The loan was quickly floated and oversubscribed. Although much more money would be needed to put the national banks on a firm foundation, an important step had been taken in strengthening the credit of the Chinese government.

Reinsch also saw an opportunity to implement a plan, once discussed with the British-American Tobacco Company, to reorganize the tobacco industry and to rationalize the government revenues derived from it. In any event, the Chicago bank was creating a new security that could be used to support future loans. Finally, Reinsch was pleased that a large Western bank, independent of Wall Street and London, had taken an interest in China.[20]

In its haste to conclude the loan, however, Continental and Commerical Trust and Savings failed to scrutinize the security for the loan. Shortly afterwards, the French minister protested that the same taxes had been pledged for a French loan. In response to Reinsch's inquiries, the Chinese minister of finance argued that the tax placed on the manufacture of tobacco and spirits had been granted to the French while the sales tax on these products, which were distributed under government license, served as the security for the American loan. The minister of finance later admitted to Reinsch that the distinction was artificial. Nonetheless, Reinsch maintained that the security was sufficient to cover both the French and American loans. But to protect the American bank, and to cover the contemplated $25 million loan, Reinsch obtained a promise from the Chinese that they would add additional revenues and appoint an American expert to systematize the administration of the wine and tobacco taxes.[21]

Meanwhile, the Consortium maintained that the Chicago loan was administrative in nature, hence in conflict with the Six Power Agreement. Although the argument had merit, Reinsch saw an opportunity to extend the interpretation of the Open Door and to prevent Chinese dependence on Japan. He therefore insisted that the Chicago loan was entirely outside the scope of the Reorganization Loan of 1912. To avoid complications, Reinsch urged the Chinese to use the money for industrial purposes. Then, if the Chinese succeeded in maintaining their position that the loan did not conflict with Peking's obligations to the Consortium, part of the proceeds from the larger loan might be used for administrative purposes, such as the disbandment of troops.[22]

Washington's response was very heartening. Lansing authorized Reinsch to tell the ministers representing the Consortium powers that any strained construction of existing agreements, or any attempt to exclude American bankers from a fair participation in China, "would meet with very decided resistance from this Government." The administration's strong stand forced the powers to accept the Chicago loan as American business. And fearful of Japanese independent action, the British and the French expressed their strong desire for the reentry of the

American Group into the Consortium for the purpose of making another reorganization loan.[23]

Pleased with the success of its first venture into Chinese finance and pressed by the Chinese and Reinsch, the Chicago bank was tempted to pursue the larger loan. But now it had to contend with Japanese opposition. The Japanese offered Peking officials an immediate ¥10 million loan on the condition that they would break off negotiations with the American bank. Then, after the Chicago loan was wrecked, the Japanese planned to offer participation to the more pliable New York bankers. Reinsch sounded the tocsin: "I regret to report such manifestations of an attempt covertly to abridge American opportunities and to make our action dependent on Japan. . . . Unfortunately some persons in the United States appear to be walking into a trap. Continued prompt independent action on our part is necessary to assure our position which is inherently very strong."[24]

But the Japanese found an ally in Ts'ao Ju-lin and the New Communications clique, and they moved quickly to take advantage of Peking's financial stringency and Tuan Ch'i-jui's growing conflict with President Li. In January 1917, a Japanese banking syndicate concluded a ¥5 million loan with the Bank of Communications. It was the first of the Nishihara loans, through which Tokyo cemented friendly relations with Tuan and his allies—the Peiyang party, which provided military support, and the New Communications clique, which supplied the necessary money and experts to run the Peking government. In the bargain, Japan received generous concessions and predominant influence in Peking, while Tuan and his followers obtained loosely controlled funds to bolster their military power, to buy political support, and to finance their bureaucratic-capitalist enterprises. Because they strengthened Japan's position and endangered American interests, these developments alarmed Reinsch, who increasingly denounced the corrupt gang and lackeys of Japanese imperialism in Peking. In fact, Yuan and the old Communications clique were not very different; but Reinsch did not condemn them as severely since they seemed to favor American influence and to oppose Japanese expansion.[25]

Japan's initiatives also caused consternation in Washington. Lansing thought that it might be necessary to resist Japan at this point, but also worried about overextending the United States in China. "I am disposed to believe that the more we yield to Japan the more we shall be asked to yield and that a firm stand upon our undoubted rights will compel a modification of Japanese demands upon China," he declared to Wilson. "But if we decide to insist upon our rights in this matter the

Chinese will expect our assistance in case Japan should attempt to intimidate it."[26]

Time was running out for independent American action. Continental and Commercial Trust and Savings read the Japanese signals and decided to postpone the larger loan until the situation was clarified. To remain in business in China, John J. Abbott conceded to Williams, American bankers would have to work with Japan. On January 31, 1917, in fact, Abbott visited the State Department in order to ascertain the administration's position on Japanese-American cooperation and the extent to which it would support independent American activity. These questions, and the dilemmas they raised, were then under review by the State Department. Williams's cautious reply reflected the department's indecision and nervousness. In principle, the chief of the Far Eastern Division advised Abbott, the department did not object to Japanese-American cooperation. It felt, however, that Americans should not solicit it, since that might imply an American recognition of Japanese predominance. Williams reminded the banker that the administration would not approve contracts which established monoply or political control. He also felt safe in declaring that the State Department would always support the right of Americans "to loan money to China without asking the permission of other Powers."[27]

In March 1917, the American Group in association with the Consortium also tried to head off the Chicago bank loan by proposing a supplementary reorganization loan of approximately $50 million. The loan would be secured by the surplus salt revenues and the land tax; the latter would be administered under the supervision of a Japanese chief inspector. Unless the United States reentered the Consortium, Straight pointed out to the State Department, China's integrity would be menaced and Japan would act alone without America's restraining influence. The Wilson administration was very worried by the prospect of a separate Japanese loan and Japanese control of the land tax, but it was forced to postpone a decision on the American Group's request. Wilson had not yet made up his mind regarding the rejoining of the Consortium and he was then wrestling with the question of entering the war.[28]

The Chicago bank was in a quandary. On the one hand, it was afraid to challenge Japan, but it also was reluctant to give up its stake in China. It is also likely that the Chicago bank saw its option as a means of gaining entry into the American Group and shedding its pro-German image. The Chicago bank therefore asked for an extension of its option and announced that it was sending Abbott, a personal friend of Reinsch from his Madison days, to China. Reinsch replied that the Chinese minister of finance was unwilling to extend the exclusive option, but he would allow the bank a reasonable amount of time to investigate the situation. Abbott left for China in March 1917, with full powers to negotiate as Reinsch had insisted. The talks proceeded amicably. Abbott first secured additional security for the bank's original bond issue and its option for the larger loan. But the renewal of China's political turmoil, among other factors, prevented the conclusion of a definite loan agreement before Abbott sailed for home.[29]

*   *   *

By the end of 1916, Reinsch concluded that he had to obtain clarification of the interrelated questions of international cooperation and the status of the spheres of influence under the Open Door. Recent developments—China's political and financial difficulties, Japan's aggressive ambitions and its success in blocking independent American action, Wall Street's timid obeisance to the spheres of influence and its susceptibility to Tokyo's serenade of cooperation, and the State Department's vacillation and uncertain support—threatened Reinsch's entire program and turned his thinking to a diplomatic showdown. Primarily for tactical reasons, but also because of Bryan's dangerous concessions to Japan in March 1915, Reinsch focused on Manchuria.[30]

Reinsch did not oppose all forms of cooperation. To be sure, he still believed that the United States had a unique relationship with China, which he expected would continue even after it rejoined the Consortium. He also maintained that, under prevailing circumstances, any special understanding with Japan would confuse and demoralize the Chinese. In addition, he felt that America's withdrawal from the Consortium had prevented it from becoming an instrument of exploitation. Similarly, the success of the United States in obtaining concessions had forced the Entente Powers to invite the American Group to rejoin the Consortium and had compelled Japan to offer Americans participation in joint enterprises.

Rather, Reinsch objected to premature cooperation. He argued that the United States first had to acquire sufficient experience, confidence, and concessions so that it could protect its own interests and China's welfare and thereby allow Americans "to enter into the give-and-take of business and cooperation with others on equal footing." Reinsch granted that even now limited cooperation on specific enterprises might in "certain cases be desirable." Indeed, during the summer of 1916, Reinsch endorsed the sharing of the Lee Higginson loan with other nations, possibly through the Consortium, provided that the "American partners assert themselves sufficiently in determining the common policy."

In general, Reinsch preferred to work with Britain. But since it was necessary to conciliate Japan, he would also accept selected joint enterprises with Tokyo on a basis of "absolute parity." Above all, such cooperation must not signify American acquiescense in Japanese special privileges, political rights, or spheres of influence. To do so would be "suicidal," Reinsch warned, "because the exclusiveness inherent in any such policy of political dominion would very soon react to the defeat of every principle of American policy in the Far East." Eventually, the United States would rejoin the Consortium, or, better yet, it would fashion a new international organization. That day was coming sooner than Reinsch expected. In any event, he stressed that American partici- pation in the Consortium could be permitted only if it served the na- tional interest and only if the American Group "were strong enough to enforce proper respect for its point of view and not merely to become an attachment to the policy of others."[31]

Given Reinsch's concern with protecting America's long-range interests and China's independence as well as his frustration with the past performance of American business, his position was theoretically sound and logically reasoned. On the other hand, there was clear evidence that Wall Street would not challenge the spheres of influence and that it would rejoin the Consortium without preconditons. Nor had the State Department indicated that it would support a major démarche, which Reinsch had hinted at since the summer of 1916. Reinsch ignored these realities and, probably expecting that Washington would come to his rescue in the end, decided to act unilaterally. He now looked for an issue on which he could draw the line and establish American principles for cooperation. He found it in the Ssupingkai–Changchiatun Railway, which the Chinese had granted to Japan in a secret agreement signed in December 1915.

On January 3, 1917, Reinsch dropped his carefully prepared bomb- shell on Japanese Minster Hayashi Gonsuke. Reinsch began by express- ing his willingness to entertain specific suggestions for cooperation. But, he added, "it could hardly be expected that Americans would be so childlike, in view of the fact that they had an enviable and independent position in China, as to commit themselves to an understanding that in the future they would always cooperate with some outsider." Then, under cover of requesting information about the Ssupingkai–Chang- chiatun Railway, he daringly suggested that the American Group or some other combination might want to participate in the financing and construction of the line. If the Japanese were really sincere about cooperation on a business basis, "and without any implication of special political rights," Reinsch later explained to Lansing, "it would seem that a more fitting field of cooperation would be that of railway construction in South Manchuria, in respect to which our nationals possess actual rights [the Chinchou–Aigun]. An opportunity would thus be given to the Japanese to reconcile with ours the rights which they appear to have obtained secretly in disregard of our prior claims, instead of ousting us from those rights in Manchuria and simultaneously claiming the privilege of cooperating with us in our canal projects as a matter of comity." A week later Reinsch urged the United States to secure from the powers a reaffirmation of the principles of China's integrity and equal opportunity "and that specifically they agree not to seek in China any general or local exclusive preferences or territorial rights but will continue to respect the complete freedom of the Chinese Government and people in the choice of means for the economic development of any part of China." In others words, Reinsch wanted to obtain a general agreement that the day of spheres of influence was over.[32]

Hayashi was stunned by the minister's blunt initiative, but Reinsch did not press the matter. On January 20, 1917, Hayashi replied that the bonds for the railway concession had already been floated in Japan and that the line had been specifically granted to Japanese interests in October 1913. In any event, as a result of the Twenty-One Demands, Japan had secured from China "a general preferential right concerning railway investments in South Manchuria and eastern Inner Mongolia."[33]

Reinsch felt that Hayashi's note on January 20 required an immediate response. It was of the utmost importance, he told Lansing on January 30, 1917, that Japan understand two things: first, the United States has not recognized Japan's so-called "special position" in Manchuria, except those rights derived from particular or specific grants or concessions; second, that Japan must offer cooperation in their enterprises as well as those held by Americans. If the United States adhered to this position, Reinsch advised Lansing, it might be possible to arrange a bargain with Japan: the United States might give a "more specific recognition" of Japan's "special position" in Manchuria, but in return Tokyo must share the wealth of Manchuria with America and refrain from seeking special rights in China proper. Reinsch, like Lansing, was willing to concede the reality of Japan's primacy in Manchuria; but he insisted on an equivalent. "To recognize the existence of such 'a special position' without getting some such assurances as are mentioned above, would be to make to Japan a gratuitous concession—a gift—

instead of giving the transaction a form under which the recognition and tolerance of the position aimed at by Japan would be made to yield results, both for the protection of American trade and of Chinese independence."[34]

Alarmed by Reinsch's challenge, Tokyo instructed its ambassador in Washington to press its proposals for cooperation and Japan's claim to special interests in Manchuria and Shantung. In his conversations with Lansing on January 25, 1917, Viscount Chinda Sutemi also tried to discover if Reinsch had acted on his own or under direction from the State Department. Lansing declared that the United States welcomed cooperation as long as it was free of political motivation, and for this reason the administration was still opposed to America's reentry into the Consortium. The State Department, he added, recognized that "Japan had special interests in Manchuria," but not in Shantung. Lansing also admitted that Reinsch had acted on his own initiative. Wilson endorsed Lansing's positions. Williams, however, told the secretary that Reinsch's actions could be justified on the basis of departmental instructions concerning cooperation on the Grand Canal and Straight's conversations with the Japanese on joint action in Manchurian railway construction.[35]

Reinsch was furious when he learned that Lansing had conceded that "the Department recognizes that Japan has special interests in Manchuria." He pointed out that the secretary of state had undermined his interpretation of Japanese rights (i.e., that were limited to specific concessions), and contradicted the American caveat of May 11, 1915. Reinsch reiterated his belief that Japan considered its claim to a "special position" in Manchuria so important that it would "undoubtedly be disposed to make concessions by way of assurances as to China proper." Reinsch testily asked whether the department was instructing him to abandon his position and was giving up America's claim to rights in Manchuria under the "most favored nation clause." Lansing knew that Reinsch was right. Somewhat embarrassed, the secretary of state explained that in using the term "special interests," he had in mind only specific railway concessions and Japan's lease of the Kwantung Peninsula, thereby confirming Reinsch's interpretation. He also specifically approved Reinsch's advice to American citizens, "to the effect that they can fully engage in business in Manchuria."[36]

For the moment, the matter rested in a draw. The American position had been compromised, but the damage might yet be repaired. Tokyo recognized this and it would soon try to win from Washington a more explicit recognition of its "special position" in China. Reinsch was also increasingly nervous and disheartened. His attempt to establish a large, pervasive American economic influence in China—the program launched in the summer of 1915—had fallen apart. The very capitalists he had counted on were subverting his efforts. In addition, the State Department had equivocated in defense of American rights and had not backed him up when it really mattered. Nevertheless, Reinsch stood firm in his determination to implement the Open Door and to broaden its interpretation.

NOTES TO
CHAPTER X

1. Reinsch to Vanderlip, 17 May 1916, Vanderlip Papers.

2. Boardman to Vanderlip, 28 October 1915, *ibid.*; *FR 1915,* 214–15; *FR 1916,* 103–06.

3. Anderson to Reinsch, 28 February 1916, Reinsch Papers; *FR 1916,* 103–19, 181, 183–88; Reinsch, *An American Diplomat,* 209–14; MacMurray, *Treaties and Agreements,* II, 1287–1324. The following railway lines were enumerated, but were subject to change: Hengchoufu (Hunan Province)–Nanking (Kwangsi); Fengchen (Shansi)–Ninghsia (Kansu); Ninghsia (Kansu)–Lanchowfu (Kansu); Chungchow (Kwangtung)–Lu Hwei (Kwangtung); Hangchow (Chekiang)–Wenchow (Chekiang).

4. Reinsch to Lansing, 17 April 1916, 893.811/213, 21 April 1916, 893.811/215, 17 May 1916, 893.51/1650, 24 May 1916, 893.811/219, DSNA; Adee to AIC, 16 May 1916, 893.811/217, DSNA.

5. Reinsch to Lansing, 13 October 1916, 893.811/234, DSNA; Lansing to Reinsch, 15 June 1916, 893.811/226a, DSNA; Straight memo for Vanderlip on China, Vanderlip Papers; *FR 1916,* 120–22.

6. Reinsch to Lansing, 19 June 1916, 893.811/226, 26 June 1916, 893.811/229, 13 October 1916, 893.811/234, DSNA; *FR 1916,* 121–22; Reinsch, *An American Diplomat,* 214–16; Reinsch, "Six Years of American Action in China," Reinsch Papers; Scanlan, "No Longer a Treaty Port," 192–201.

7. Reinsch to Vanderlip, 17 May 1916, Vanderlip Papers; Reinsch to J. H. Perkins, 6 September 1916, RG 84, Peking Post file, 610, NA; Perkins to Reinsch, 8 July 1916, Reinsch Papers; Reinsch, "Six Years of American Action in China," *ibid.;* Reinsch to Lansing, 13 October 1916, 893.811/234, DSNA; Reinsch, *An American Diplomat,* 212–16.

8. Reinsch to Lansing, 13 October 1916, 893.811/234, DSNA; *FR 1916,* 192–97; Anderson to Reinsch, 14 August 1916, Reinsch Papers; Reinsch, "Six Years of American Action in China," *ibid.*; Reinsch, *An American Diplomat,* 214–16; Austin to Straight, 4 October 1916, RG 84, Peking Post file, 800, NA; MacMurrary, *Treaties and Agreements,* II, 1321–24.

9. Reinsch to Lansing, 23 August 1916, 893.77/1553, 10 November 1916, 893.77/1564, DSNA; *FR 1916,* 188–92, 198–210; Reinsch, *An American Diplomat,* 219–21.

10. Reinsch to Lansing, 10 November 1916, 893.77/1564, DSNA; *FR 1916,* 191–92, 198; Straight to Polk, 4 December 1916, Polk Papers; Straight to Bland, 13 November 1916, Straight Papers; Straight to Reinsch, 30 October 1916, Reinsch Papers; *New York Times,* 17 December 1916; Mazuzan, "Our New Gold Goes Adventuring," 223–24.

11. Reinsch to Lansing, 26 October 1916, 893.77/1560, 10 November 1916, 893.77/1564, DSNA; Arnold to Redfield, 30 November 1916, RG 40, 70801/105, NA; Reinsch, *An American Diplomat,* 222.

12. Minutes on Hillier telegram, 22 December 1916, 263767/f12458/16, FO 371/2652; *FR 1917,* 183–203; Williams memo, undated, 893.77/1608, DSNA; Williams to Lansing, 14 May 1918, Breckinridge Long Papers, Library of Congress (hereafter cited Long Papers); Paul Clyde, "Railway Politics and the Open Door in China, 1916–1917," *The American Journal of International Law,* XXV (October 1931), 642–56.

13. AIC to Gregory, 27 December 1916, 893.811/254, DSNA; Straight to Bland, 13 November 1916, Straight Papers; Straight to Reinsch, 2 February 1917, Reinsch Papers;

Reinsch, *An American Diplomat,* 217; *FR 1916,* 123–28; *FR 1917,* 208–14; Henry W. Berger, "Warren Austin in China, 1916–17," *Vermont History,* XL (Autumn 1972), 257–59; Mazuzan, "Our New Gold Goes Adventuring," 227–30.

14. Reinsch, "Six Years of American Action in China," Reinsch Papers; Reinsch, *An American Diplomat,* 217–18; *FR 1917,* 162–207.

15. Reinsch to Lansing, 14 April 1917, 893.811/256, DSNA; Carey to Straight, 3 February 1917, RG 84, Peking Post file, 881, NA; *FR 1917,* 207–16; *FR 1917, Supp.* I, 402.

16. Williams to Lansing, 4 January 1917, 893.811/238, DSNA; Lansing to Wilson, 17 January 1917, 893.51/1746a, DSNA; *FR 1917,* 208, 215.

17. Reinsch to Lansing, 24 April 1917, 893.811/259, DSNA; Reinsch, *An American Diplomat,* 219.

18. Reinsch to Lansing, 17 April 1917, 893.811/260, DSNA; *FR 1917,* 209, 215, 219–31; Reinsch, *An American Diplomat,* 218–19.

19. Lansing to Reinsch, 8 September 1916, 893.51/1705, DSNA; Reinsch to Lansing, 15 September 1916, 893.51/1707, DSNA; Koo to Reinsch, 12 January 1917, RG 84, Peking Post file, 851, NA; *FR 1916,* 138–43; MacMurray, *Treaties and Agreements,* II, 1337–45.

20. Reinsch to Lansing, 20 March 1916, 893.51/1621, 8 December 1916, 893.51/1729, DSNA, 16 January 1917, RG 84, Peking Post file, 851, NA; *FR 1916,* 222, 236.

21. Reinsch to Lansing, 29 November 1916, 893.51/1735, 8 December 1916, 893.51/1729, DSNA, 16 January 1917, RG 84, Peking Post file, 851, NA; *FR 1916,* 143–45.

22. Reinsch to Lansing, 8 December 1916, and enclosure, 893.51/1729, DSNA; *FR 1916,* 143–49; *FR 1917,* 114–15.

23. Wilson to Lansing, 3 December 1916, 893.51/1718½, 6 December 1916, 893.51/3010, DSNA; Lansing to Wilson, 4 December 1916, 893.51/3010, and 893.51/1715, DSNA; Williams to Lansing, 4 December 1916, 893.51/1715, DSNA; Lansing to Reinsch, 5 December 1916, 893.51/1716, DSNA; Reinsch to Lansing, 23 December 1916, 893.51/1722, DSNA; *FR 1916,* 146, 148–50.

24. Lansing to Wilson, 17 January 1917, 893.51/1746a, DSNA; *FR 1917,* 114–16, 121.

25. Reinsch to Lansing, 26 January 1917, 893.00/2565, DSNA; *FR 1917,* 122; Madeline Chi, "Bureaucratic Capitalists in Operation: Ts'ao Ju-lin and His New Communications Clique, 1916–1919," *Journal of Asian Studies,* XXXIV (May 1975), 675–86.

26. Lansing to Wilson, 17 January 1917, 893.51/1746a, DSNA.

27. Memo of conversation, Williams and Abbott, 31 January 1917, Long Papers; Abbott to Williams, 8 February 1917, 893.51/1746, DSNA.

28. Straight to Polk, 26 March 1917, Polk Papers; Abbott to Williams, 8 February 1917, 893.51/1746, DSNA; *FR 1917,* 126–30.

29. Abbott to Williams, 8 February 1917, 893.51/1746, DSNA; Abbott to Reinsch, 4 June 1917, RG 84, Peking Post file, 851, NA, 30 June 1917, Reinsch Papers; memo of conversation, Long and Abbott, 10 July 1917, Long Papers; *FR 1917,* 124–25, 128–33.

30. Reinsch to Lansing, 5 September 1916, 793.94/519, 19 December 1916, 793.94/553, 26 January 1917, 893.00/2565, DSNA; Reinsch, *An American Diplomat,* 23; Reinsch, "Six Years of American Action in China," Reinsch Papers.

31. Reinsch to Lansing, 28 June 1916, 893.51/1660, 9 December 1916, 893.51/1731, DSNA; Reinsch to Straight, 15 January 1916, Reinsch Papers; Reinsch to Vanderlip, 17 May 1916, Vanderlip Papers; MacMurray, "Dr. Paul S. Reinsch"; *FR 1917,* 285–86.

32. *FR 1917*, 161–70; Reinsch, "Six Years of American Action in China," Reinsch Papers.

33. *FR 1917*, 170–72.

34. *FR 1917*, 171–72.

35. Memo of conversation, Lansing and Chinda, 25 January 1917, and attached comments by Wilson and Williams, 893.51/1743, DSNA; *FR 1917*, 171.

36. Lansing to Reinsch, 16 April 1917, 793.94/560, DSNA; *FR 1917*, 173–74, 182–83

Chapter XI

ANOTHER CHANCE:
CHINA AND
WORLD WAR I

For Reinsch, as for so many of his contemporaries, World War I represented a monumental failure of modern civilization. Reinsch harkened back to the pre-war years when he joined other sane men in the search for a peaceful world order based on mutual cooperation and a viable international law. In a personal letter to President Wilson, dated January 4, 1915, Reinsch suggested that the United States attempt to mediate the conflict along the following lines: a return to the territorial *status quo ante*; the payment of an indemnity by Germany and its allies, which would increase with the duration of the fighting; a pledge by the Allies to reduce military expenditures; and the strengthening of the Hague Court with an executive supported by the armies and navies of the Allied Powers. "As I am setting these things down, I realize their triteness and the great difficulty in the way of their realization," he admitted to Wilson; yet he was hopeful that the good offices of the United States and other neutrals "exercised in this direction at the right time," might bring an end to the bloodshed.[1]

Despite charges that he was pro-German, Reinsch clearly sided with the Allies and blamed the Central Powers for starting the war. Reinsch justified America's involvement in the war in the highest terms; he defended the use of force to establish a global "Commonwealth" and the establishment of a "more efficient and beneficial organization of civilized life." The attacks on his sympathies, and later his loyalties, were instigated by personal enemies, opponents of his China policies, and nationals of the Allied Powers, who were easily excited by wartime events and embittered by the freedom of action enjoyed by the neutrals.

Reinsch's maligners drew upon a large body of specious and circumstantial evidence: his German ancestry, his friendship with German Minister Paul von Hintze, his humanitarian solicitude for German and Austrian prisoners, and his refusal to be carried away by Allied propaganda and war hysteria.[2]

Reinsch linked the Chinese question to "the possibility of rehabilitating justice as a controlling force in human affairs after the war is over." But the European conflagration affected China directly in much more concrete ways. European financiers were forced to withdraw from the Far East and American capital decided that the wartime trade was more profitable and safer than direct investments in China. Even more important, the war removed most of the restraints on Japanese ambitions and enabled Tokyo to launch a frankly aggressive program of continental expansion. Furthermore, from 1915 on, Japan was increasingly successful in obtaining international sanction for the predominant position it had gained in Chinese affairs. Thus, Japan blocked two efforts by Yuan Shih-k'ai to protect China's integrity by bringing Peking into the war on the side of the Allies. The Chinese, meanwhile, grew resentful of America's pious professions of support and began to make realistic compromises with Japan.

Pained by these developments and worried that China might be used as a field for "compensations," Reinsch insisted, on January 10, 1917, that China be represented at the peace conference or at a special conclave on the Far East. Washington sympathized, but could promise nothing. Germany's announcement of unrestricted warfare, however, reopened the question of Chinese participation in the war and raised the possibility of placing China under America's protective wing.[3]

*   *   *

On February 4, 1917, a mild sunny Sunday afternoon, Reinsch was lunching at the suburban cottage of Dr. George Morrison when a messenger informed him that a very important cable had just arrived from Washington. When he arrived back at the legation, Reinsch found Secretary of State Robert Lansing's circular of February 3 (Washington time) addressed to the diplomatic representatives in neutral countries. The secretary of state instructed Reinsch to inform the Chinese government that the United States had severed relations with Germany and to invite Peking to associate itself with the American action. As no further explanation followed, Reinsch assumed that Washington was engaged in a serious effort to apply pressure on Germany. After conferring with his staff at the legation, Reinsch decided to try to prevail upon the Chinese government to break relations with Germany. Later that evening, in separate conferences with President Li and Premier Tuan, Reinsch delivered the State Department's note and urged them to make a quick decision. Neither Li nor Tuan responded with much enthusiasm. They feared, above all, that acceptance of the American invitation would bring Japanese reprisals. Furthermore, the president worried that mobilization would strengthen Tuan and the militarists.[4]

Undeterred by this cool reception, Reinsch conferred all through the night with members of the legation staff and his Kitchen Cabinet. They agreed to launch an all-out campaign to persuade the Chinese government to break relations with Germany, and carefully chartered their strategy. In his colorful, though basically accurate, account which appeared in the *Saturday Evening Post*, Sam Blythe described the effort as a "straight-out drive, a Flying Wedge of muscular and determined American citizens who drove China relentlessly over the line of self-sufficiency and into world affairs." Reinsch, whom the newspaperman called "a real American as well as a real diplomat," stood at the "apex" of the "wedge." Behind him were Anderson, Donald, Morrison, Dr. John C. Ferguson, and two newspapermen, Charles Stevenson Smith and Blythe himself. They were assisted by some members of the minister's official staff, though the legation was largely bypassed, and certain Chinese officials, especially Admiral Tsai T'ing-kan and members of the Young China party. These men pooled their influence and their knowledge of Chinese affairs to bring pressure upon selected political leaders and important groups. Reinsch was "indefatigable." For five days he argued with Li, Tuan, Minister of Finance Ch'en Chin-t'ao, and numerous other officials that China's involvement in the war would unify the nation, strengthen its position at the peace conference, and protect Chinese interests.[5]

The persistent efforts of the Anglo-American team soon yielded results. The resistance of the older generals folded, Tuan wavered, and Li, still opposed to China's involvement in the war, let it be known that he would accept the cabinet's decision. Before giving its consent, however, the cabinet first asked for certain assurances: full Chinese participation at the peace conference; financial assistance to enable China to contribute to the war effort; and safeguards against foreign control of Chinese resources, military forces, and arsenals. Reinsch asked Washington to meet these requests, but at this critical moment cable communications between the United States and China were interrupted.[6]

Reinsch was in a quandary. Peking would act, but only with positive American assurances. The Germans were caught off guard and the

Japanese minister was absent from Peking. Delay would mean obstruction, and probably defeat.

Smarting from his recent reverses, Reinsch read into Lansing's circular his hope that the administration had finally decided to put real meaning into its repeated professions of support for China's integrity and the Open Door. He also gambled that Washington "would act in a manner consonant with its position as a powerful Government in its relations with those who gave support and associated themselves in carrying through a policy of fundamental importance." And so, Reinsch began to rationalize. In view of the hundreds of millions of dollars already advanced to the Allies, it did not seem possible that the United States could refuse China's moderate requests. By associating China with American action, it would also be possible to strengthen China materially, to stabilize the political situation, to restore America's prestige, to assure China a seat at the peace conference, and to put an end to the "vicious use which Japan has hitherto been able to make of its control of the balance of power." Finally, by basing Chinese international politics on the same grounds as the submarine question, the United States could bolster China's rights and the case for international justice and security.[7]

After considerable deliberation and much soul-searching, Reinsch decided to act unilaterally. In his carefully drafted note of February 7, 1917, Reinsch informed the Chinese that he was recommending to the United States government that it provide funds for the purposes required by the Chinese government and suspend the Boxer indemnity payments. He also assumed the responsibility of assuring the foreign minister that the United States would uphold Chinese control over its military establishment and general administration. At the same time, Reinsch refrained from making any direct commitments. Reinsch pointed out that the nature of American assistance would have to be decided by various administrative bodies in Washington and might require congressional approval. He hedged still further by making American help contingent upon China's complete and direct association with Wilson's invitation to the neutral nations.[8]

Reinsch's note combined with a long morning session with the cabinet induced the Chinese government to send a formal protest to Berlin and to pledge that Peking would sever relations with Germany if the United States declared war. Although this fell short of total Chinese association with American action, Reinsch concluded that it was the best that could be obtained in view of China's fear of Japan. Reinsch and his colleagues hailed the Chinese decision as a significant break with China's traditional isolationism and a victory for the younger republicans and intellectuals against the old mandarinate and the military. They also took satisfaction in the fact that now the nervous Allied representatives could endorse the *fait accompli*.[9]

This was the most striking example of Reinsch's tendency to use unorthodox methods and to take unauthorized action. Although he made his commitments to the Chinese as vague and conditional as possible, Reinsch imposed upon the United States government at least a moral obligation to help China. With considerable justification, contemporaries in China and in the United States condemned Reinsch's precipitous action. And in view of the political turmoil and increased Japanese influence that followed, many historians have subsequently criticized Reinsch's daring intervention. It is also doubtful if the Chinese took Reinsch's assurances as seriously as he believed and if they acted solely because of Reinsch's persuasion and arguments. It is more likely that Reinsch served as a useful catalyst for those Chinese who had been thinking of involving China in the war in order to gain specific benefits for their country and to play off the powers against each other.[10]

Reinsch, however, prepared a strong defense. Considering the circumstances and the interruption of communications, Reinsch thought that he had acted judiciously and in accordance with American diplomatic objectives. He reminded the State Department that its instructions of February 3 were given without qualification. "As the success of the policy depended upon prompt action by neutrals," he countered, "I felt obliged to secure *within the sphere* of this Legation the action desired and did secure it." Reinsch was less that truthful when he declared to Lansing, and reaffirmed in his memoirs, that the men involved "acted spontaneously with the sole connecting link of a common purpose." But even though Reinsch and his associates put unremitting pressure on Chinese officials, their actions hardly resembled the coercion employed by the other foreign powers. "I could not find that he [Reinsch] had done more than state, without secret, the American point of view," Richard Child reported to Colonel Edward House. "The weight given his opinions by the Chinese is to his credit."[11]

The State Department was far from pleased. Lansing's brief, but carelessly phrased, circular of February 3 certainly did not contemplate American assistance in return for concurrent action by the neutrals; nor did it take into account the peculiar circumstances existing in China. With the restoration of telegraphic communications, Lansing curtly warned Reinsch not to offer any assurances to China and, in view of Japan's sensitivities, told him to advise prudence upon Peking.[12]

Reinsch apparently never delivered the State Department's message to the Chinese. First of all, he faced the prospect of a humiliating personal and diplomatic defeat. During the following weeks, he was embarrassed by Chinese reminders of their loss of confidence in the United States because of AIC's betrayal and Washington's failure to fulfill Reinsch's assurances. Second, Reinsch still hoped to persuade the administration to grant China the assistance it requested. He admitted that China's failure to identify itself completely with the American note of February 3 freed the United States from any technical obligation. But he implored the State Department not to rebuff China after it had committed itself to American leadership at the risk of inviting Japanese displeasure and control of its military resources. China's association with the United States in the war, he reiterated in his frequent appeals, was still the best means to protect the interests of all the powers and to prevent total Chinese dependence on Japan. On February 14, 1917, Reinsch wrote directly to Wilson and requested the State Department to submit all telegrams on the subject to the president. He also emphasized the importance of his personal consultations with Wilson and the State Department in order to formulate "a co-ordinated constructive policy of action."[13]

But the administration still declined to confirm Reinsch's assurances to the Chinese and virtually repudiated the minister's actions. The administration wanted to preserve China's integrity and equal opportunity and the international status quo. It continued to support the Chicago Bank loan, even though it expected Japanese opposition. On the other hand, Washington saw no good reason to hasten China's involvement in the war or to bid against the Entente Powers or Japan for China's adherence. And since the United States was not yet a belligerent, it could not guarantee China a seat at the peace conference. But the administration's overriding concern was that Japan would be provoked into demanding control of China's arsenals and armed forces—the very thing that the United States wanted to avoid. In that event, Washington would be confronted with the "practical inability" to aid China "if serious opposition should be offered to such assistance." Reinsch believed that a limited amount of American assistance would suffice to contain Japan and strengthen China. The administration concluded that the United States lacked the capability to meet determined Japanese opposition, especially when the United States gave priority to the war in Europe. "What she has asked through Reinsch has not been unreasonable," Wilson observed, "but can we count on the Senate and our bankers to fulfill any expectations we may arouse in China?"[14]

*   *   *

On March 14, 1917, the Chinese government severed relations with Berlin. For Reinsch, however, it was a Pyrrhic victory. The Chinese acted in the hope of extracting concessions and money from the Allies and cancelling China's obligations to Germany. Having secured secret pledges of support from the Entente Powers to support its demands at the peace conference, Japan now pressed China to declare war and waved a ¥20 million loan as an inducement. Equally disturbing was the renewed struggle for power which delayed the Chinese declaration of war until August 1917.

On one side stood the militarists led by Premier Tuan, the Chinputang and the pro-Japanese clique centered in the New Communications party. They favored an immediate declaration of war as a means of abolishing the provisional constitution and assuming power in a new Peking government. The president and the Kuomintang-dominated Parliament opposed any further involvement in the war precisely because it would strengthen the northern militarists. The unity of China hung in the balance, for any attempt by the militarists to seize power would force the Kuomintang to lead a secessionist movement. A fragile truce between Tuan and Li lasted until May. At the end of April, Tuan assembled the *tuchuns*—the semi-independent military governors—in Peking. He secured a vote of confidence and then planned to stage a *coup d'état* in May. Convinced that Tuan could no longer be trusted, Li courageously fired him. Tuan and the northern *tuchuns* gathered in Tientsin where they formed a provisional government and seized control of the railway in an attempt to isolate Peking.[15]

Reinsch believed that the bulk of the men in Parliament favored, or could be persuaded to support, China's entry into the war under American auspices if they received assurances that the militarists would not take advantage of the situation. On the other hand, Reinsch was incensed that the militarists coined political capital out of their fictitious identification with the Allied cause while they destroyed constitutional government and welcomed Japanese money and influence. And yet Reinsch recognized that the militarists had the "only powerful organization in China" and had to be "reckoned with in any settlement to be made." Reinsch also saw, or wanted to see, Tuan as the "savior of China"—the strong, honest, patriot who would unite the various factions and bring peace and stability to China. Although Reinsch was aware of Tuan's many weaknesses, his indolence, ignorance, and stubbornness, he considered him a moderate who could be weaned from the reactionary *tuchuns*. In order to improve his relations with the *tuchuns*, Reinsch entertained them in his home on April 29, 1917, and congratulated them for supporting the war against Germany. And in a frank interview on May 9, Reinsch naively encouraged Tuan to seek the cooperation of the younger republicans in Parliament who sympathized with his war policy.[16]

Based on this analysis, Reinsch suggested to the State Department, on May 11, 1917, that a Chinese declaration of war coupled with formal pledges by the powers to guarantee China's integrity would solve China's political problems. Such a program, he argued, would eliminate the war issue from Chinese politics and might pave the way for a reconciliation between President Li and the moderate militarists led by Tuan. On June 2, 1917, Reinsch warned that only "a united mediation of the powers might save the situation."[17]

Reinsch's advice confirmed the view in the State Department that some form of intervention by the United States and the other powers was warranted. On June 4, 1917, Lansing instructed Reinsch to tell the Chinese minister for foreign affairs, as well as the militarists in Tientsin, that the United States considered China's entry into the war secondary to the principal need to maintain "one central, united and responsible government." At the same time, the State Department requested Britain, France, and Japan to send identical representations to Peking.[18]

Reinsch welcome the department's note and delivered it on June 7, 1917. In doing so, he made an explicit connection between the note of June 4 and the invitation of February 3. In a personal statement, Reinsch added that no matter "how much the United States wanted the cooperation of China in the war," which America conceived as a struggle for democrary, "it did not desire to bring this about by using the political dissensions or working with any one faction in disregard of Parliament."[19]

Britain and France declined to join the American effort because they wanted an immediate Chinese declaration of war. Japan was openly hostile and denounced the American note as a deliberate interference in Chinese affairs. Tokyo was piqued because it had not been consulted before Reinsch delivered the note and used the occasion to reassert its claim to paramount economic and political interests in China. The Japanese press declared that Reinsch was the chief intriguer and savagely denounced him for taking unilateral action. Although Reinsch was accustomed to Japanese propaganda attacks, he nevertheless sought vindication. The State Department subsequently directed the American embassy in Tokyo to deny the charges. Lansing also told the Japanese ambassador in Washington that the United States had just as much right as Japan to express an opinion to the Chinese government.[20]

The Chinese, Reinsch reported, appreciated the American intervention. "The effect produced by the note," he maintained as late as August 24, 1917, "has been to emphasize in the minds of the Chinese of all parties and of all provinces the primary importance of subordinating all other wishes to the maintenance of national unity and of representative institutions." In fact, the American note had no practical effect on China's political turmoil. In a desperate move to thwart the *tuchuns,* President Li called in General Chang Hsun, the military governor of Anhui, a notorious bandit and pronounced monarchist. Chang Hsun demanded the dissolution of Parliament and, on June 12, 1917, the helpless president complied. Three weeks later, Chang Hsun proclaimed the reconstitution of the Manchu empire and installed Pu Yi as emperor. Recognizing his mistake, Li turned over his office to Vice President Feng, appointed Tuan premier, and then took asylum in the Japanese legation. The Manchu restoration, however, was short-lived. On July 12, Tuan's army recaptured Peking.[21]

Tuan formed a new government composed of strong men from the northern militarists, the Chinputang, and the New Communications clique. Then, with the assistance of Nishihara's generous loans, Tuan pressed ahead with his policy of unifying China by force. Meanwhile, the warlords used the war to enrich themsleves and to strengthen their power in the provinces. Nor could the pro-Japanese group be ousted for fear of incurring Japanese wrath and retaliation. Even though he was willing to accept a degree of Japanese influence; Tuan soon discovered that his position was precarious. He proved to be a poor facsimile of Yuan Shih-k'ai.

These developments forced the southern republicans and the remnants of the Kuomintang to flee to Canton, where they established the National Military Government in September 1917. Sun Yat-sen was the nominal leader of the southern government, but real power resided with Lu Yung-t'ing, the *tuchun* of Kwangsi and Kwantung. The southern government subsequently declared war against Germany and claimed that it was the legitimate government of China. But, as Reinsch frequently observed, there was little difference between Canton and Peking. Extortion of the peasantry, public corruption, and authoritarian rule prevailed in the south as well as in the north.

Reinsch's strategy to use China's involvement in the war as a means of strengthening China, protecting American interests, and neutralizing Japan's influence had therefore backfired. Nor did his meddling in Chinese politics produce the hoped-for coalition of moderate militarists and republicans. China was split in two, and when it suited their purposes, northern and southern *tuchuns* sent their swelled armies into rather bloodless battle. Reinsch refused to consider recognition of the Canton government, for fear that it might endanger the integrity of China. He therefore participated in the charade of maintaining the legitimacy of the Peking government and continued to express the hope that Tuan's "professions in favor of representative institutions . . . will be lived up to." For Reinsch, however, the sinister and growing influence of Japan was the most disquieting feature of the Chinese situation.[22]

*   *   *

On August 14, 1917, the Peking government declared war on Germany. Shortly afterwards, the Chinese asked for some $200 million in loans and grants to equip and transport an army to Europe as well as to carry out administrative and currency reforms. Although Reinsch was disturbed by the size of the request and Peking's simultaneous approach to the Consortium for a reorganization loan, he warned Washington that a complete rebuff "would be most detrimental to the interest and influence of the Associated powers." Besides, he argued, the United States still had a moral obligation to help and to strengthen China. But his overriding concern was to steer China "beyond earshot of the financial sirens that were luring her upon the Japanese rocks."[23]

In September 1917, Reinsch proposed to the State Department an aid program totalling approximatley $100 million. He suggested projects that would stimulate China's development and enhance American influence as well as those that would mobilize China's resources for direct use in the war. "The materials are all here," he explained to Lansing. "It is only the organization that is required." Predicting an imminent world-wide shortage of foodstuffs, Reinsch allocated $25 million for the systematic development of Chinese agriculture. Reinsch then recommended that $20 million be spent on Chinese shipyards and arsenals.[24]

Third, Reinsch endorsed the Chinese offer to send forty thousand troops to Europe, though he thought that $5 million would suffice at the start. Not only would that help the war effort, Reinsch noted, it would raise China's standing in the world, strengthen China's identification with the American cause, and engender salutary changes in China's internal affairs. He further suggested that Tuan, who was ousted from the premiership by the Communications party in the fall of 1917, head a special commission that would coordinate the war effort and perhaps even lead the Chinese army in Europe. This was actually a ploy on

Reinsch's part to make Tuan independent of the reactionaries and thereby enable him to "become the trusted leader China needs." Reinsch also hoped that the creation of the commission and the preparation for the Chinese military missions to Europe would channel the energies of the militarists into constructive paths and divert their attention from a contemplated invasion of the south. Indeed, in December 1917, Peking established the War Participation Bureau and named Tuan its director. Reinsch then argued that if the United States rejected immediate financial assistance for Tuan's bureau, "the progressive leaders in the China war policy will seem to be disavowed and will be weakened in the face of all influence which will be brought to bear to turn China against the Allies."[25]

At the heart of Reinsch's program was a $30 million loan for the completion of the Canton–Hankow Railway. Reinsch maintained that this project would unify China politically and economically, stimulate its industrial and commercial development, and force Britain and France to waive their objections to the Siems-Carey railways. Recalling the blot of the American China Development Company, Reinsch declared that "no other act would signally contribute to the national and war efficiency of China and forever redeem [the] American reputation originally compromised in connection with the Canton railway."[26]

Finally, Reinsch advocated American participation in a currency reform loan. It was not in his original package. He was forced to add it because Japan offered to take up the currency loan, independently, or in conjunction with the Consortium, on the condition that Baron Sakatani Yoshiro be appointed financial advisor to the Chinese government. Moreover, the expiration of the Consortium's option on October 15, 1917, would leave Japan free to conclude a loan on its own terms. With State Department backing, Reinsch secured an extension of the option to April 15, 1918. But the determination of the minister of finance to conclude a loan with Japan forced Reinsch to demand the prompt appointment of a qualified American representative and an early decision to join in the currency loan.[27]

Because of the corruption, dissension, and growing Japanese influence in China, Reinsch now insisted upon strict accountability. He opposed any general advances against loans, which would be squandered or pocketed by the militarists and would also arouse resentment in the south. As an additional safegard, he proposed that a commission of American experts go to Peking to work out the details of the aid program and that the Chinese government be required to communicate all of its obligations to the Allies and to make the information public. In addition, American help should be tied explicitly to the principles stated in the notes of February 3 and June 4. "According to the method pursued," Reinsch admonished Washington, "this loan will tend either to unify China and prepare her for efficient national action, or furnish the means for corruption and civil strife in an effort of the dominant faction to fasten its power upon the country. If applied with foresight, the loan will greatly strengthen the policies for which the United States is contending."[28]

Reinsch's aid program was predicated on the assumption that the United States government would give credits and loans to China on the same basis as Washington assisted its co-belligerents in the struggle against Germany. He also left the door open for private American investment and hoped that the Chicago bank would issue the $25 million loan. However, China's request for a reorganization loan and Japan's willingness to undertake currency reform forced Reinsch to accept American participation in a reorganized consortium as a last resort as long as the United States was free to extend independent private and government assistance. Explaining his apparent about-face, Reinsch pointed to the past failures of American enterprise in China and the need to maintain the balance of power in the Far East. "If, during the last three years, American financiers had taken a strong interest in China," he chided Lansing, "constructive Republican elements would have been strengthened so as to assure free development. This opportunity has now passed away forever. Only by joining in the councils with other friendly nations will it be possible for the United States effectively to push its influence not only in behalf of efficient popular Government, but safeguarding of American interests."[29]

The State Department sympathized with Reinsch's objectives and found his aid program reasonable. "We can yet prevent much injury to ourselves and the world if we will but come to China's assistance," Williams told Lansing. The State Department also viewed the Canton–Hankow project as an excellent means to restore American prestige and to destroy the spheres of influence. "This would put the United States in control of one of the largest railway systems in the world and would establish a great commercial and industrial field of operation divorced from political authority," Breckinridge Long declared in a memorandum for the president. The State Department originally conceived of an American credit "as a substitute for the Consortium loan" and shared Reinsch's worry that Japan might use a currency reform loan as a means of extending full control over China's financial and monetary systems. While American financing of currency reform would manifest American helpfulness to China, Lansing explained to Secretary of Commerce William Redfield, "the political point of view" always predominated. In the following months, therefore, the State Department spearheaded a drive to win the president's approval and the support of other departments for large-scale financial assistance to China.[30]

In December 1917, the State Department outlined a revised aid program around two loans to China. The United States government would lend China $50 million for military purposes and work on the Canton–Hankow Railway. Second, the United States would provide $100 million toward the currency loan made in association with the Consortium. That would be a private banking loan and would require the formation of a new American group.[31]

By the fall of 1917, most policy makers in the State Department had concluded that the cooperative policy offered the only means of securing American interests and maintaining the balance of power in China. Tokyo's determination to proceed with the currency loan and Britain's acquiescence in a Japanese advance left the United States no choice. Reinsch gave his approval to America's reentry into the Consortium and observed that immediate American participation might dispose Japan to delay its loan advance. To prevent the United States from carrying the British and French share, the Japanese made an advance of £1 million in January 1918. Faced with this *fait accompli,* the State Department recommended to Wilson the formation of a new American group. In the meantime, Wall Street indicated its interest in returning to the field and Lee Higginson and Continental and Commercial Trust and Savings agreed to join the American Group and even to assume the leadership of the syndicate.[32]

Although he had not yet made up his mind about America's reentry into the Consortium, Wilson approved the State Department's plan in principle. The War Department supported the loan to China and, despite the difficulties in equipping and transporting a large Chinese army, the dispatch of 100,000 Chinese troops to France. Redfield not only gave his immediate endorsement, but also urged that a direct government loan be made to China and he criticized the Treasury Department for dragging its feet. Indeed, it was the Treasury that stymied the State Department's efforts.[33]

Secretary of the Treasury William G. McAdoo had been lukewarm about the China loans from the start. The Treasury Department raised one objection after another: the United States government lacked the authority to make the loan for the Canton–Hankow Railway and arsenal improvements; China was a bad risk and the money could be utilized more advantageously elsewhere; there was no immediate need for a currency loan and further study of the matter was necessary. Above all, the Treasury Department emphasized that it would be unwise to allow the currency loan to compete with the sale of Liberty Bonds.

These arguments, however, probably concealed the Treasury's desire to foster cooperation with the Entente Powers and Japan and to support the old American Group against the new entries into Chinese finance. The Treasury Department knew that Tokyo opposed the war loan which was designed to strengthen China; it may also have tried to soften the State Department's opposition to the appointment of a Japanese financial adviser. And stressing the helpfulness of the Wall Street banks in floating Liberty Bonds, McAdoo and other Treasury officials asserted that "the feelings of the members of the old group would be hurt and that they might refuse to co-operate if the leadership were given to the western bank."[34]

The loans to China were temporarily stalled. The State Department, however, kept the matter alive and reassured a very disappointed Reinsch that it was working on his proposals for American assistance. "The American people have lost none of their friendship for China and the American Government cherishes China's goodwill even more than in the past," Lansing wrote to Reinsch. He also alluded to the department's difficulties in getting the Treasury's approval and the cooperation of the Allies, the shortage of shipping, and the enormous demands on the financial resources of the United States. "The real reason why so little is done in response to your representations is not the indifference of the Department," Williams explained. "Action is prevented by the necessity for consultation and agreement with other Departments."[35]

Reinsch, meanwhile, was recovering from the jolt administered by the Lansing-Ishii Agreement. Reinsch had watched the visit of Viscount Ishii Kikijiro to the United States in the fall of 1917 with great apprehension. Reinsch's confrontation with Hayashi over Japanese rights in Manchuria, the State Department's failure to consult Tokyo before sending its June 4 note, and Japan's success in extracting pledges of support from the Entente Powers made the Japanese anxious to obtain American recognition of Japan's special position in China. On June 15, 1917, the Japanese ambassador to the United States asked Lansing to confirm Bryan's statement, in the American note of March 13, 1915, that "territorial contiguity creates special relations" between Japan and South Manchuria, Eastern Inner Mongolia and Shantung." The Japanese memorandum, however, referred to the "paramount" economic and political interests of Japan in China. In the conversation that followed,

Lansing carelessly concurred "with the deep sense of the memorandum," though he used the term "special" rather than "paramount" interests. The secretary of state thereby missed the point that Ambassador Sato Aimaro had linked Japanese economic and political interests and had applied them to all of China

When Reinsch learned about the Japanese note, he quickly observed that Tokyo was claiming a protectorate over China. Should such a claim be accepted by the United States, "it would arouse a storm of indignation" in China. The attempt to make use of Bryan's incidental note, he warned, showed that "the Japanese are overreaching themselves in an effort to secure their object while the war lasts." Realizing his mistake, Lansing, in his formal reply of July 6, 1917, took issue with the Japanese interpretation of the American position; he strongly denied that the United States had permanently renounced its rights in Manchuria and Shantung and carefully distinguished between "special" and "paramount" interests.[36]

The question was still unsettled when Ishii arrived in the United States on his special wartime mission. Lansing was determined to obtain a reaffirmation of the Open Door policy before Ishii departed; Japan's special ambassador was amenable as long as the document advanced Tokyo's purposes. The formula which they signed on November 2, 1917, was, in the words of Burton F. Beers, "a declaration of divergent aims." The United States and Japan declared their adherence to the Open Door (which was specifically defined to include equal opportunity for both commerce and industry) and their respect for the territorial integrity of China. In a secret protocol, the two nations also pledged themselves to refrain from taking advantage of the war to upset the status quo in China. But the key section, and its most dangerous feature, proclaimed the doctrine that "territorial propinquity creates special relations between countries." Consequently, the United States recognized that Japan possessed "special interests in China, particularly in the part to which her possessions are contiguous."[37]

Washington now paid the price for failing to inform Reinsch of the negotiations and for Lansing's faith that the Japanese would abide by the understanding to release the Lansing-Ishii Agreement simultaneously on November 6–7, 1917. In order to score a diplomatic and propaganda triumph, the Japanese minister, on November 4, told the Chinese Foreign Ministry, the Allied ministers, and the press that the United States had recognized Japan's special interests in China. In releasing the text of the notes to the press, the Japanese deliberately translated special interests as special *position* or *paramount* influence. In the course of a routine conversation at the Japanese legation, on the evening of November 4, Hayashi also read a summary of the notes to a stunned Reinsch. Attempting to maintain his poise, Reinsch managed a reply without revealing his ignorance of the Japanese-American negotiations.[38]

Reinsch hurried back to the legation and dashed off an irate telegram to Washington. "While I understand that the reasons which prompted this momentous decision are confidential," he sarcastically noted, "I have the honor to ask whether at the time of the publication of this note you desire me to present to the Chinese officials any explanation of this action which so profoundly affects their interests and which at first sight appears a reversal of American policy in China." Reinsch was justifiably angry. He felt embarrassed in trying to explain the meaning of the notes to the Chinese and helpless in refuting the Japanese interpretation.

Two days later, Reinsch received a copy of the notes from the State Department. But he believed that it was too late to rectify Washington's error and the ensuing damage. Although Reinsch later corrected the Japanese translation, Tokyo succeeded in leaving the impression that America had abandoned China and that no practical assistance could be expected from Washington. The notes strengthened the pro-Japanese clique and reinforced the Japanese position in Shantung. For Reinsch, the Lansing-Ishii Agreement became a prime example of the evils of secret diplomacy.[39]

*   *   *

Throughout the winter and spring of 1918, Reinsch carried on his campaign for concrete assistance to China, even though its disorganization and corruption galled him. During his visit to the United States in 1918, he made no effort to defend the Peking regime and he disassociated himself from the "corrupt clique manipulated by military reactionaries," which threatened China's existence. "I am enclosing a depressing report on the present situation in China," Reinsch told Wilson in February 1918. "There is much that is good, strong and promising here . . .; but we must recognize the full extent of the evil before we can do anything helpful." Precisely because there were still 350 million Chinese who looked to America as a model and friend, the United States had to remain an active force in the Far East. "It is my hope that the impulse for free government in China may not die for want of encouragement from the liberal nations and because of obstruction from other sources," Reinsch continued. "I know that you feel that our ideals and our safety are bound up with a free, self-governing China." Reinsch also reminded Lansing of the importance of maintaining the "enviable reputation of the American name in China. This may in the future be one of our greatest national assets, because after this war the situation in the Far East will undoubtedly loom larger and larger in the attention of the whole world. Quietly to preserve our own in this field and to build further for the future is my aim."

There were other weighty considerations. While the prospects of sending a military expedition to Europe dimmed, the Bolshevik Revolution raised the possibility that Chinese troops would be needed in Siberia and for policing the Chinese Eastern Railway. The prolongation of the war into 1919, he argued, would definitely require the use of Chinese manpower and resources. Reinsch still believed that China's participation in the war might unify the nation and lead to constructive work.[40]

Above all, Reinsch was influenced by the growing Japanese menace to American interests and China's independence. Each week brought news of another so-called "industrial loan," which was coupled with additional concessions to Japan. Ironically, a large share of Japanese money and military supplies flowed through the War Participation Bureau, which Tuan used to bolster his power in Peking and to prepare for a major offensive against the south. Furthermore, Japan's unilateral advance for currency reform and its continued pressure for the appointment of Baron Sakatani as China's financial czar forced Reinsch to secure another six-month extension of the currency loan option. He then pressed the State Department for the immediate formation of the American Group, arguing that "the power to maintain our position in financial and industrial work in China will be a prime necessity for American industry after the war."[41]

In May 1918, Reinsch alerted the State Department to yet another challenge to an established American interest in China. The Chinese minister of finance was in the process of negotiating for a loan to meet military expenses that would be secured by the wine and tobacco revenues and which contemplated a Japanese director for a planned Chinese government tobacco monopoly. The consummation of such an arrangement, Reinsch pointed out, would add another lien to the security pledged for American and French loans; it would undermine the Chicago bank's option, eliminate the British-American Tobacco Company as a major factor in the China market, give the Japanese-owned East Asia Tobacco Company a virtual monopoly in China, and hand over to Tokyo control over revenues that were potentially larger than the salt tax. "It is hoped that without detracting from the effort made necessary by the war," Reinsch wired Lansing, "the relatively insignificant financial means will be accorded to prevent exclusion of American enterprise from China."[42]

But that was not all. The Japanese were using the most unscrupulous methods to poison Chinese life. They incited insurrections, encouraged banditry, introduced morphia, abetted financial corruption, and misled the press. During the fall of 1917, the Japanese established a civil administration along the Shantung Railway and in the following months they extended it to cities beyond the railway zone. This action, coupled with the introduction of Japanese immigrants throughout the province, implied that Japan intended to remain indefinitely in Shantung. Finally, Japanese intervention in Siberia underscored Tokyo's ambition to dominate all of East Asia.[43]

Reinsch's Siberian policy was initially based on his opposition to Bolshevism and the need to maintain a strong, independent Russian government that would continue to aid the Allied war effort. His program emphasized economic assistance, stability, and adequate publicity to advertise America's benevolent motives. However, at the beginning of June 1918, Reinsch called for ten thousand American troops as part of a joint military intervention in Siberia. To some extent, Reinsch hoped to overthrow the Bolsheviks and to "resurrect at least Siberia as an Allied factor" in the struggle against Germany. But the Japanese threat was largely responsible for converting Reinsch to military intervention.[44]

From the onset of the crisis, Reinsch had worked to counter Japanese activities and misrepresentations of American intentions. By backing Semenov and the arch-reactionaries, Japan had in fact launched an independent policy. Simultaneously, Tokyo pressured Peking to accept joint Sino-Japanese occupation of the Trans-Siberian and Chinese Eastern Railways. This resulted in a secret exchange of notes on March 25, 1918, which provided for military cooperation between the two nations. And on May 16 and May 19, secret military and naval agreements were signed which specified the form of cooperation. The agreements applied only to Siberia and on the surface contained nothing that impinged on Chinese sovereignty. Nevertheless, they showed the strength of the pro-Japanese faction and lessened the chances for a Sino-American concert. "It is apprehended the agreement will be used to prevent any free cooperation between China and the other allies in the present war," Reinsch informed the State Department, "and to limit any action which China may take distinctly to cooperation under Japanese leadership."[45]

Siberia, then, was further proof of Japan's evil designs and aggressiveness. By 1918, Reinsch's view of Japan had undergone a radical transformation. Japan was no longer simply a dangerous competitor. It inherited the mantle of Prussianism; Tokyo was the enemy of liberal democracy and the source of all future strife in the world. Reflecting on his years in China, Reinsch concluded that Japan had been pursuing a deliberate policy of domination in East Asia. Only its tactics had changed. Nor were Japan's aims purely economic; Reinsch pointed out that every concession had been obtained by military and political pressure and intrigue. Reinsch admitted that he had leveled a harsh indictment against Japan but he felt that it was fully justified. "Fundamentally friendly to the Japanese as my published expression[s] show," he explained to Frank Polk on the eve of the Paris Peace Conference, "I have been forced through the experience of five years to the conclusion that the methods applied by the Japanese military masters can only lead to evil and destruction and also that they will not be stopped [by] any consideration of fairness and justice but only through the definite knowledge that such action will not be tolerated." Should the United States fail to check Japan on all fronts, he warned, "there will be created in the Far East the greatest engine of military oppression and dominance that the world has yet seen. Nor can we avoid the conclusion that the brunt of the evil results will fall on the United States."[46]

Intervention in Siberia, the establishment of a civil administration in Shantung, the monopolistic concessions won by Japanese interests, and the numerous other signs of "Yellow Prussianism" convinced many in the State Department that Tokyo sought hegemony in Asia. And yet, Washington wished to avoid unwise "pin-pricks on Japan." However, Japan's attempt to secure control of currency reform and especially the wine and tobacco taxes forced the State Department to insist that the Treasury reconsider the Chinese loans. On June 4, 1918, Breckinridge Long presented a revised program based entirely on private financing. American bankers would independently lend China $25 million for administrative purposes (the loan to be secured by the wine and tobacco taxes) and $30 million for the completion of the Canton–Hankow Railway. They would also join with Japanese capitalists in advancing funds for currency reform. "This program," Long told the Treasury Department's representative, "would put Japan and the United States into China as partners in connection with the currency loan and would give the United States the influence that would arise from the tobacco loan and railway loan. These two enterprises in which American capital would be interested being thus an offset to various loans made by interests exclusively Japanese." Although he was still opposed to Chinese loans on fiscal grounds, McAdoo informed Lansing that he would permit them "on the basis of the diplomatic point of view which you regard as of great importance."[47]

Lansing thereupon asked Wilson to approve the plan which contemplated the formation of a new American group and required assurances of government support. Wilson quickly gave his endorsement and the State Department invited a broadly representative group of bankers to form a new American syndicate and to make the proposed loans. The bankers responded favorably, but suggested that all of the loans be internationalized, which entailed the creation of a new Four Power Consortium. Long and arduous negotiations would now be necessary to draw up the ground rules for the Second Chinese Consortium and to obtain the approval and cooperation of the Chinese. The United States had finally decided to reenter the field of Chinese finance, but it was too late to have any impact on the deteriorating situation in the Far East.[48]

*   *   *

Reinsch's long struggle to implement his war policy had failed. As late as June 1919, Reinsch maintained that "a great opportunity was missed when China had broken off relations with Germany. The very least recognition of her sentiments, support and efforts on our part would have changed the entire situation," he insisted in his letter of resignation. "But while millions upon millions were paid to the less important of the countries of Europe not a cent was forthcoming for China. This lack of support drove Tuan and his followers into the arms of the pro-Japanese agents. Instead of support we gave China the Lansing-Ishii note (as interpreted by Japan)." Similarly, while Reinsch later admitted that he had misjudged Tuan's abilities and qualities, he continued to regret the failure to bring him and President Li together in the spring of 1917. For more than a year afterwards, Reinsch nursed the hope that Tuan might be united with the progressive political elements in China.[49]

To some extent, Reinsch's bitterness was justified. For while the State Department agreed with his analysis and often encouraged him to defend the Open Door, it made only a half-hearted effort to implement the minister's strategy and to obtain the necessary support of Great Britain. Moreover, the Wilson administration never really gave careful consideration to Reinsch's dispatches or to the Far East in general. Washington was simply too engrossed with European affairs. Finally, without first consulting Reinsch, Lansing rushed to sign an agreement with Ishii, a step he later regretted.

On the other hand, Reinsch was less than truthful and was overly optimistic in expecting miracles from American assistance to China in 1917 and 1918. The British, for their part, dismissed the plan to send Chinese troops to Europe as impractical, if not ridiculous. Japan would have put up stern resistance to meaningful American intervention. Above all, it is doubtful if American money would have made much of a difference; the Chinese, first, would have to work out their own salvation. Indeed, reflecting his disgust with the situation in China, Reinsch declared in an unusually frank conversation with pro-Japanese Minister of Finance Ts'ao Ju-lin on June 10, 1918:

> For my part I cannot believe that any amount of foreign money can soundly establish the authority of the Government of China, as China is too large a country with too enormous a population for that; moreover, the population will accept only an authority which has moral claims to recognition. Is it possible that a group of statesmen could boldly declare that the finances of the country did not warrant any further internal hostilities; that peace must be restored and that thereafter finances must be managed so as to give support to the regular military arrangement and to constructive public enterprise?

That was impossible, Ts'ao replied candidly, as long as Peking's authority was not established by force of arms. And to achieve this goal, Tuan and the Communications clique would continue to take money from Japan because "the common experience in China has been that American financiers are too slow, they never come to the point."[50]

Reinsch despaired. Either China's internal turmoil would fester indefinitely, or as Ts'ao suggested, Japanese-American financial cooperation might enable Peking to establish unity and order.[51] Frustrated and disappointed, Reinsch hoped that the peace conference in Europe would offer a better solution.

NOTES TO
CHAPTER XI

1. Reinsch, *An American Diplomat*, 105; MacMurray, "Dr. Paul S. Reinsch," 151; Reinsch to Wilson, 4 January 1915, Wilson Papers.

2. Reinsch to Wilson, 4 January 1915, Wilson Papers; Reinsch, Thanksgiving Day Address, 29 November 1917, in Reinsch to Lansing, 15 December 1917, 123.R271/64, DSNA; Rea to Wilson, 1 June 1917, 893.00/2585, DSNA; Hawkins Tapes, 7, 10; von Hintze to Reinsch, 11 February 1917, Reinsch Papers; Jordan to Langley, 10 and 14 November 1914, Jordan Papers, FO 350/12; MacMurray, "Dr. Paul S. Reinsch."

3. Reinsch to Wilson, 25 July 1916, Wilson Papers; Reinsch to Lansing, 10 January 1917, 763.72119/461, DSNA; Long to Williams, 3 February 1919, Long Papers; Reinsch, *An American Diplomat*, 105–7; *San Francisco Chronicle*, 20, 22, 23, and 27 November 1915; author's interview with Wellington Koo, 24 February 1965; Chi, *China Diplomacy 1914–1918, passim*.

4. Reinsch, *An American Diplomat*, 241–59; *FR 1917, Supp.*, I, 414–16; J. B. Powell to Reinsch, 8 February 1917, Reinsch Papers; J. Paul Jameson to Reinsch, 9 February 1917, *ibid.*; B. L. Putnam Weale, *The Fight for the Republic of China* (New York, 1917), 310–18; Werner Levi, *Modern China's Foreign Policy* (Minneapolis, 1953), 148; Robert Pollard, *China's Foreign Relations 1917–1931* (New York, 1933), 8–9.

5. Reinsch, *An American Diplomat*, 241–59; Reinsch Diary, 1917, Reinsch Papers; Samuel Blythe, "The First Time in Five Thousand Years," *Saturday Evening Post*, 28 April 1917, 28–34; Selle, *Donald of China*, 197–203. Selle gives Donald the credit for charting the campaign.

6. Reinsch, *An American Diplomat*, 245–47; *FR 1917, Supp.*, I, 401–2; Blythe, "The First Time in Five Thousand Years."

7. Reinsch, *An American Diplomat*, 247–48; Reinsch to Lansing, 6 February 1917, 763.72/3230, 8 February 1917, 763.72/3270, 12 February 1917, 763.72/3301, DSNA; Reinsch to Wilson, 14 February 1917, Wilson Papers; *FR 1917, Supp.*, I, 401–4, 415–16.

8. Reinsch, *An American Diplomat*, 249–50; *FR 1917, Supp.*, I, 403–4, 416–17.

9. Reinsch to Lansing, 10 February 1917, 763.72/3289, DSNA; *FR 1917, Supp.*, I, 404, 407–8, 417–18; Reinsch, *An American Diplomat*, 251–55; Weale, *Fight for the Republic of China*, 315–18.

10. *New York Times*, 29 April 1917; Beers, *Vain Endeavor*, 96–97; Griswold, *Far Eastern Policy*, 199–203; Levi, *Modern China's Foreign Policy*, 148; Scanlan, "No Longer a Treaty Port," 238–47.

11. Reinsch's emphasis. Reinsch to Lansing, 13 March 1917, 763.72/3501, DSNA; Reinsch Diary, 1917, Reinsch Papers; *FR 1917, Supp.*, I, 414–18, 453–54; Reinsch, *An American Diplomat*, 241–59; Richard Child to House, 7 June 1917, Wilson Papers; Hawkins Tapes, 2; Blythe, "The First Time in Five Thousand Years."

12. Lansing to Reinsch, 10 February 1917, 4 P.M., 763.72/3245, DSNA; Lansing to Wilson, 10 February 1917, 763.72/3270, DSNA; Wilson to Lansing, 10 February 1917, 763.72/3275, DSNA; *FR 1917, Supp.*, I, 408, 410–11; *New York Times*, 29 April 1917; Chi, *China Diplomacy*, 118–19; Russell Fifield, *Woodrow Wilson and the Far East* (New York, 1952), 64–65; Griswold, *Far Eastern Policy*, 200–3.

13. Reinsch to Wilson, 14 February 1917, Wilson Papers; Reinsch to Lansing, 21 February 1917, 763.72/3372, 1 March 1917, 763.72/3697, 9 March 1917, 763.72/3852, 13 March 1917, 763.72/3501, DSNA; *FR 1917, Supp.*, I, 408–9, 412–14, 418–21.

14. Williams to Lansing, 14 February 1917, Long Papers, 1 March 1917, 763.72/

3372, 12 March 1917, 893.51/1755, DSNA; Wilson to Lansing, 9 February 1917, 763.72/3275½, DSNA; Lansing to Wilson, 10 February 1917, 763.72/3270, DSNA; unsigned memo, 20 March 1917, 893.51/2008, DSNA; Polk to Wilson, 10 March 1917, 763.72/3538½,DSNA; Lansing to Reinsch, 16 February 1917, 763.72/3372, 2 March 1917, 763.72/3397, 12 March 1917, 763.72/3397, DSNA; *FR 1917, Supp.*, I, 410–11, 419–20; Fifield, *Wilson and the Far East*, 65, 70–71; LaFargue, *China and the World War*, 92–94.

15. Reinsch to Lansing, 13 April 1917, 763.72/3817, and /4612, 12 March 1916, 763.72/5179, DSNA; Reinsch Diary, 8 May 1917, Reinsch Papers; Reinsch, *An American Diplomat*, 260–68; *FR 1917*, 46–48; *FR 1917, Supp.*, I, 412, 418, 420, 425–30, 433–37, 445–51; Chi, *China Diplomacy*, 122–24; Pollard, *China's Foreign Relations*, 26–33.

16. *FR 1917*, 46, 51–55; *FR 1917, Supp.*, I, 445–51; Reinsch to Lansing, 27 June 1918, 893.00/2866, DSNA; Reinsch, "Six Years of American Action in China," Reinsch Papers; Reinsch, *An American Diplomat*, 242–43.

17. Reinsch to Lansing, 11 May 1917, 763.72/4568, DSNA; *FR 1917*, 46–48, 50–51.

18. Williams comment, 12 May 1917, 763.72/4568, DSNA; Williams to MacMurray, 2 June 1917, MacMurray Papers; memo of conversation, Long and Koo, 4 June 1917, Long Papers; *FR 1917*, 48–50.

19. *FR 1917*, 55–57, 100–1; Reinsch, *An American Diplomat*, 268; *New York Times*, 8 June 1917.

20. Reinsch to Lansing, 11 June 1917, 893.00/2602, 14 June 1917, 893.00/2614, DSNA; excerpt from *Asahi*, 4 July 1917, in 893.00/2681, DSNA; clipping, *New York World*, 17 June 1917, Reinsch Papers; *FR 1917*, 60–63, 68–78; Reinsch, *An American Diplomat*, 269; Lansing, *War Memoirs*, 288–89.

21. Reinsch to Lansing, 4 July 1917, 893.00/2648, 15 July 1917, 763.72/5850, DSNA; Reinsch Diary, 14 July 1917, Reinsch Papers; *FR 1917*, 77–102.

22. Reinsch to Lansing, 13 July 1917, 893.00/2669, 15 July 1917, 763.72/5850, 3 August 1917, 763.72/6173, 18 September 1917, 893.51/1822, 28 October 1917, 893.51/1823, 10 November 1917, 893.51/1826, 3 December 1917, 893.00/2750, 27 June 1918, 893.00/2866, DSNA; Anderson to Reinsch, 27 January 1918, Reinsch Papers; Reinsch, "Six Years of American Action in China," *ibid.*; Long Diary, 27 October 1917, Long Papers; Long memo, 29 October 1917, *ibid.*; author's interview with Koo, 24 February 1965; Chi, *China Diplomacy*, 137–40; Pollard, *China's Foreign Relations*, 32–33.

23. Reinsch to Lansing, 7 September 1917, 893.51/1804, 24 September 1917, 893.51/1809, 12 December 1917, 763.72/8122, 20 December 1917, 763.72/8360, 20 December 1917 (personal letter), 763.72, DSNA; *FR 1917, Supp.*, I, 454–55; Reinsch, *An American Diplomat*, 286–87.

24. Reinsch to Lansing, 16 September 1917, 893.51/1807, 20 December 1917, 763.72, 11 February 1918, 893.00/2767, DSNA.

25. Reinsch to Lansing, 16 September 1917, 893.51/1807, 2 October 1917, 763.72/7080, 7 November 1917, 763.72/7562, 30 November 1917, 763.72/8360, 12 December 1917, 763.72/8122, 23 December 1917, 763.72/8262, DSNA, 12 October 1917, 12 February 1918, Reinsch Papers; *FR 1918*, 82–88.

26. Reinsch to Lansing, 16 September 1917, 893.51/1807, 16 November 1917, 893.77/1647, DSNA; *FR 1917*, 194.

27. Reinsch to Lansing, 11 October 1917, 893.51/1819, 12 October 1917, 893.51/1821, DSNA; Reinsch to Wang Ta-hsieh, 20 October 1917, 893.51/1828, DSNA; *FR 1917*, 149, 152–53.

28. Reinsch to Lansing, 15 September 1917, 893.51/1806, DSNA, 16 September 1917, 893.51/1807, 28 September 1917, 893.51/1822, 15 December 1917, 763.72/ 8146, DSNA; *FR 1917, Supp.*, I, 454–55; *FR 1917*, 142–43; *FR 1918*, 83–84.

29. *FR 1917*, 135–36, 142–43; Reinsch, *An American Diplomat*, 296–97.

30. Williams to Lansing, 10 August 1917, 893.51/1794, 6 September 1917, 893.00/2700, DSNA, 13 April 1918, Long Papers; Lansing to Reinsch, 20 September 1917, 893.51/1807, 24 January 1918, 763.72/8784, DSNA; Lansing to McAdoo, 19 September 1917, RG 39 (Records of the Department of the Treasury, Bureau of Accounts), China, 130.00, NA; memo for Wilson, 20 October 1917, Long Papers; Williams to Long, 23 January 1918, 893.51/1869, DSNA; Williams memo, 16 February 1918, Long Papers; Lansing to Wilson, 11 February 1918, *ibid.*; Long to Lansing, 12 February 1918, 893.51/1894, DSNA; Lansing to Redfield, 11 January 1918, Long Papers.

31. Lansing to McAdoo, 15 December 1917, RG 39, China, 130.00, NA; Long to Leffingwell, *ibid.*; Lansing to Wilson, 11 February 1918, Long Papers.

32. Lansing to Wilson, 25 June 1917, Letterpress, RG 59, DSNA; Williams memo for Lansing, 26 June 1917, Long Papers; Long to Lansing, 4 August 1917, *ibid.*; Williams to Lansing, 10 August 1917, 893.51/1794, DSNA, 30 April 1918, Long Papers; Long memos, 30 July and 29 October 1917, Long Papers; Williams to Long, 29 October 1917, *ibid.*; Reinsch to Lansing, 2 November 1917, 893.51/1824, 10 November 1917, 893.51/ 1826, 20 November 1917, 893.51/1835, DSNA.

33. Lansing to Wilson, 11 February 1918, Long Papers; Newton Baker to McAdoo, n.d., RG 39, China, 130.00, NA; memo by Acting Chief of War College Division, 9 October 1917, 763.72/10259, DSNA; Redfield to Lansing, 16 January 1918, RG 40, 76338, NA; Lansing to Reinsch, 26 December 1917, 763.72/8262, DSNA.

34. McAdoo to Wilson, 4 September 1917, Wilson Papers, 27 September 1917, Polk Papers; memos of conversation, Long and Albert Strauss, 24 November 1917, 22 January 1918, Long Papers; McAdoo to Lansing, 10 December 1917, 21 January 1918, RG 39, China, 130.00, NA, 21 January 1918, 893.51/1869, DSNA; Strauss to McAdoo, 19 December 1917, RG 39, China, 130.00, NA; Long to Lansing, 22 January 1918, Long Papers; Williams memo, 23 January 1918, 893.51/1869, DSNA.

35. Lansing to Reinsch, 24 January 1918, 763.72/8784, 29 January 1918, 793.94/ 665, DSNA; Williams to Reinsch, 16 February 1918, Reinsch Papers.

36. *FR 1917*, 77–78, 260–63; *FR: Lansing Papers*, II, 431; Lansing, *War Memoirs*, 288–89; Beers, *Vain Endeavor*, 107–8; Asada, "Japan and the United States," 32–33.

37. *FR 1917*, 264–65, 273; Lansing to Reinsch, 29 January 1918, 793.94/665, DSNA; Nelson T. Johnson, "Japanese Interpretation of the Lansing-Ishii Agreement," memo for the United States Delegation to the Washington Conference, 500A41a/119, DSNA; Lansing memo on the Lansing-Ishii Agreement, 3 October 1921, Lansing Papers; MacMurray to Hornbeck, 22 December 1932, Hornbeck Papers; Hornbeck to Phillips, 29 May 1936, *ibid.*; Beers, *Vain Endeavor*, 115–19.

38. Reinsch to Lansing, 30 April 1918, 893.00/2838, DSNA; *FR 1917*, 265–69; Reinsch, *An American Diplomat*, 307–8; Long to Williams, 21 February 1918, Long Papers.

39. *FR 1917*, 265–66, 268, Sammons to Reinsch, 10 November 1917, 793.94/6216, DSNA; Reinsch to Lansing, 30 April 1918, 893.00/2838, DSNA; Reinsch, *An American Diplomat*, 307–16; Reinsch, *Secret Diplomacy: How Far Can It Be Eliminated?* (New York, 1922), 199.

40. Reinsch to Wilson, 12 February 1918, Reinsch Papers; Reinsch to Lansing, 20 December 1917, 763.72, 12 February 1918, 893.00/2480, DSNA; *FR 1918*, 83–93,

222–26; Reinsch address to the Milwaukee City Club, 3 September 1918, clipping, *Milwaukee Journal,* 4 September 1918, Reinsch Papers.

41. Reinsch to Lansing, 10 January 1918, 893.51/1863, 18 January 1918, 893.51/ 1868, 7 February 1918, 893.51/1882, 8 April 1918, 893.51/1888, 13 April 1918, 893.51/1890, 27 April 1918, 893.51/1893, 17 May 1918, 893.51/1895, 24 June 1918, 893.51/1928, DSNA; Williams memo, 26 February 1918, 893.51/1877, DSNA; *FR 1918*, 107–8.

42. Reinsch to Lansing, 28 May 1918, 893.51/1897, 5 June 1918, 893.51/1902, DSNA.

43. Reinsch to Wilson, 7 June 1919, 123.R271/101, DSNA; Reinsch to Lansing, 20 December 1917, 862a.01/8, 13 February 1918, 862a.01/10, DSNA; Wilson to Lansing, 16 February 1918, 862a.01/10, DSNA.

44. Reinsch to Lansing, 17 December 1917, 861.00/1138, 18 February 1918, 861.00/1112, 19 February 1918, 861.00/1124, 10 April 1918, 861.00/1571, DSNA; Reinsch to Lansing, 6 December 1917, and Long's penciled comments, Long Papers; Reinsch to Long, 6 September 1918, Reinsch Papers; *FR 1918, Russia,* II, 5, 9, 158–62, 181, 189, 206–7; Betty M. Unterberger, *America's Siberian Expedition 1918–1920: A Study of National Policy* (Durham, 1956), 28, 60; William A. Williams, "American Intervention in Russia 1917–1920," *Studies on the Left,* III (Fall 1963), 24–48.

45. Reinsch to Lansing, 19 February 1918, 861.00/1124, 7 April 1918, 793.94/672, 18 May 1918, 793.94/681, DSNA; *FR 1918, Russia,* II, 54–55, 133, 141, 147–48, 158–62, 231; Reinsch, *An American Diplomat,* 451–52; MacMurray, *Treaties and Agreements,* II, 1407–15.

46. Reinsch to Lansing, 19 October 1918, 893.00/2893; Reinsch to Polk, 12 December 1918, 893.77/1696, 23 January 1919, 893.51/2145, 30 April 1919, 893.00/2838, DSNA; Reinsch to Wilson, 7 June 1919, 123.R271/101, DSNA; *FR: The Paris Peace Conference, 1919,* II, 522–23.

47. Lansing to Reinsch, 9 April 1918, 893.51/1888, 7 May 1918, 893.51/1849a, 23 May 1918, 893.51/1895, DSNA; Williams to Long, 20 May 1918, 893.51/1895, DSNA; Long memo, 8 June 1918, 893.51/1897, DSNA; Polk to Reinsch, 8 June 1918, 893.51/ 1897, DSNA; Lansing to Morris, 27 June 1918, 893.51/1897, DSNA; Redfield to Lansing, 15 June 1918, RG 40, 76338, NA; McAdoo to Lansing, 23 May 1918, 893.51/1898, DSNA; memo of conversation, Strauss and Long, 5 June 1918, RG 39, China, 130.00, NA; Strauss memo for Leffingwell, 8 June 1918, *ibid.*; "Proposed Loan for China," memo by the Far Eastern Division, 18 June 1918, *ibid.*

48. *FR 1918*, 171–99.

49. Reinsch to Wilson, 7 June 1919, 123.R271/101, DSNA; Reinsch to Lansing, 27 June 1918, 893.00/2866, DSNA.

50. Conversation between Reinsch and Ts'ao Ju-lin, 10 June 1918, in Reinsch to Lansing, 27 July 1918, 893.51/1940, DSNA; Chi, *China Diplomacy,* 143–45.

51. Conversation between Reinsch and Ts'ao Ju-lin, 10 June 1918, in Reinsch to Lansing, 27 July 1918, 893.51/1940, DSNA.

CHAPTER XII

THE LAST YEAR
IN CHINA

China's distintegration and Japan's successes began to overwhelm Reinsch by the end of 1917. Reinsch's exhausting pace, the strain of the war effort, and progressive and painful growth of his brain tumor brought him to the edge of a complete physical and mental breakdown. They made him tense and impatient and may have also distorted his judgment. During the summer of 1917 he baldly announced to an American visitor that when he spoke the word China would declare war "on the side of America and not of Japan, as Japan is assiduously seeking." During the following months, Reinsch toyed with the idea of provoking a confrontation with Tokyo. Confiding his innermost thoughts to Breckinridge Long, Reinsch wrote in December 1918:

I have the feeling that America does not sufficiently realize the critical importance for our own future welfare and safety of decisions to be made with respect to the Far East. Unless these decisions are right, we shall not be able to live in peace. I sometimes feel that it is my duty to be more insistent and to do something striking and that would attract attention to the dangers here, of course entirely on my own responsibility and possibly with the result of temporarily inviting great disapproval. It may yet be necessary for me to act in this way, although I consider things very carefully. Even in its most emphatic form, of course, my action would be such that any possible bad effects would come entirely to myself, and to no one else. The point is, that I fear, between us, that a solution on general principles will not be effective unless a definite warning is given which will put an end to a great many unconscionable and intolerable things which are going on at the present time.

Reinsch kept his head and remained circumspect. But he was at the end of his tether and he was prepared to sacrifice himself, if that became necessary, for the interest of the United States, China, and world peace.[1]

In July 1917, however, illness forced Reinsch to turn over the legation to MacMurray for about three weeks. By February 1918, he had again worked and worried himself to the point of collapse and his physician advised immediate rest and a change of scene. Reinsch therefore requested permission to tour American consulates in south China. The State Department approved, but asked him to delay his departure because of the political situation in Peking. By March, he could not wait any longer. Accompanied by his family and private secretary, LaMotte Belin, Reinsch spent twelve days touring the Philippines and on their return trip the group stopped at the American consulates at Amoy, Swatow, Shanghai, and Tsingtao. Reinsch regained his strength, but the mood of his last year in China remained somber.[2]

Nevertheless, Reinsch decided that he had to make another heroic effort to awaken American businessmen and policy makers to the importance of China. Twice in 1917 the State Department rejected Reinsch's requests to visit the United States on the grounds that it was "more important that you remain in China at present." Finally, on June 21, 1918, Reinsch was instructed to come to the United States for conferences with the Department of State. In preparation for his contemplated trip, Reinsch resumed his correspondence with Vanderlip and Straight. "I hope that with all the attention which war activities require," he pleaded with Straight, "nevertheless American capitalists will reserve that relatively small, almost insignificant share of attention which will keep American interests in the Far East alive and protect the future there."[3]

Reinsch landed at Victoria, British Columbia, on July 23, 1918. He had a number of conferences with Lansing, Undersecretary of State Frank Polk, and Breckinridge Long, the pro-Chinese third assistant secretary of state. He also managed to get two interviews with the president, during which they discussed Chinese political and financial affairs and specific courses of American action in Siberia.[4] Pointing to the importance, along with the war effort, of extending American economic influence in China, Reinsch urged the War Trade Board, the War Industries Board, and the Department of Commerce to relax the export regulations so as to allow China some coal and rolling stock in order to keep its railways in operation. "The strongest reason for a favorable action in releasing at least a moderate amount of railway materials at the present time for use in China," he wrote upon his return to Peking, "is that whenever American standards have once been used on any one of the Chinese railways, the argument that they are not suitable, which had constantly been advanced in the past by the representatives of other nations, can no longer be made. They will be established for all times; and though this does not imply that all materials will continue to be furnished by America it will certainly assure to American manufacturers more complete equality of opportunity than they have hitherto enjoyed."[5]

In New York, Reinsch conferred with representatives of National City, J. P. Morgan & Co., Guaranty Trust, Kuhn Loeb, Chase National, General Electric, American Locomotive, AIC, Siems-Carey, and a host of other firms. He emphasized the priority of railroad construction and the importance of expanding banking facilities. He maintained that, if Americans were ready to commit large amounts of capital, they could still obtain major concessions, safeguard China from looting and foreign influence, and assure the United States a large and growing market for its expanded industrial capacity.[6]

On the surface, Reinsch's trip went smoothly. Commerce officials seemed anxious to push for American trade and investments in China, Wilson expressed agreement with Reinsch's views on Chinese finance, and business leaders in New York listened approvingly to Reinsch's arguments. "The reception they have all accorded me this time," he reported to his wife, "has made me feel very good as they made sure that I have their confidence and respect." E. T. Williams's impending departure from the State Department for a teaching position at the University of California also led Reinsch to cultivate the support of Breckinridge Long. It was the first time that the scholar-diplomat had met the thirty-seven-year-old Missouri attorney and Wilsonian politician. But out of their many conferences and informal get-togethers, a close friendship was formed. The third assistant secretary lacked real influence. Yet his pro-Chinese inclinations made him an important ally. Moreover, Long became Reinsch's sounding board and confidant. "I write to you," Reinsch declared to Long, "because I know you understand these matters and are anxious that our future shall be kept as free as possible from this great danger." Thanking Reinsch for recommending him as his replacement in China, Long replied: "It is the confidence you have inspired, and which you continue to inspire which makes me realize that you are the psychological person."[7]

In fact, Reinsch realized that he was not bringing anything concrete back to China. It was the critical moment of the war and all other interests "shrivelled" before the task of concentrating every effort— manpower and financial—on the Western Front. "I appreciated all this," Reinsch wrote in his memoirs, "but I deeply regretted that a tiny rivulet out of the vast streams of financial strength directed to Europe could not pass to China. Even one thousandth part of the funds given to Europe, invested in building up China, would have prevented many disheartening and disastrous developments." Except for the company of Charles Crane, who would be his guest at the legation for several months, the return voyage was lonely and gloomy for Reinsch.[8]

And yet, Reinsch could not surrender. Peking was not China, and there was strong sentiment for peace and unity throughout the nation. The Second Chinese Consortium was being organized and American business might turn its attention to the Orient. The European war was drawing to a close and the peace conference might establish a just peace and a new international order.

Above all, he pinned his hopes on Woodrow Wilson. For years, Reinsch had applauded Wilson's Christian statesmanship and he had identified himself with the President's goal of not only fortifying America's "just position in the world, but also to help the world recover peace and health, and then to found methods and institutions for their permanent maintenance." In the fall of 1918, Reinsch, like many of his contemporaries, looked upon Wilson as a savior. "Perhaps in all the world, President Wilson is the only man who will raise a strong voice in pleading for international justice and individual rights," he declared in an interview with a Chinese newspaper. "For myself," he told a Japanese reporter on his way back to China, "I am proud that I work in China chiefly because of the propagating of the gospel which I rightly call 'Wilsonism.'"[9] Therefore, when Wilson betrayed him, Reinsch had no choice but to resign as minister and to seek other ways of realizing his dreams.

*   *   *

On the seventh anniversary of the Chinese Republic—October 10, 1918—Hsu Shih-ch'ang was inaugurated president of China in Peking. He was a weak figure and a man without any great abilities. Because he had been governor of Manchuria and a lieutenant of both Yuan and Tuan, Hsu was suspected of holding Japanese affiliations and militarist loyalties. And yet he responded to the yearning for peace, and now doffed the mantle of reconciliation and reunion. On October 24, 1918, President

Hsu issued a peace mandate and called for a general disbandment of troops. He forced the northern *tuchuns* to acquiesce in his policies and eventually arranged for an armistice and peace talks with the south at Shanghai.

Reinsch was elated by these developments, which demonstrated Hsu's independence of the military. He called upon Washington to give the peace movement moral support as well as definite assistance in the form of carefully controlled short-term loans. "This appeal vital matter," he cabled on October 30, 1918, "for as long as no such foundation is provided, the military clique, with the aid of proceeds of Japanese loans, will continue their debauching action to the end of defeating constructive policies of the President." Then, quickly following up on a similar Japanese proposal, Reinsch recommended that the United States lead a joint démarche endorsing Hsu's program and urging its prompt execution. Finally, when the south dragged its feet on sending a delegation to the peace conference, Reinsch advised that the surplus customs revenues be released to the Peking government for diplomatic expenses and the demobilization of troops. The State Department concurred and the threat was sufficient to bring the southern delegation to Shanghai.[10]

Meanwhile, Japan subverted the efforts of the foreign powers to encourage the peace movement. On December 3, 1918, one day after the delivery of the Allied representations to the Peking government, Tokyo issued a public statement that "left the door open for the old system of double dealing." It reasserted Japan's claim to a special position in China and declared its inability to discourage financial and economic enterprises of private Japanese subjects or to interfere with loans and arms contracts which had already been concluded. Under instructions from Washington, Reinsch made repeated protests. Only after the Allied ministers approved a ban on further loans and arms shipments did Japan agree to curtail military shipments after April 1919.[11]

The Shanghai Peace Conference finally convened on February 20, 1919, but it collapsed within two weeks. Southern leaders were furious that the northern militarists had continued to receive Japanese arms and money and suspected that the Allies were backing the Peking government. Acting through Consul-General Sammons and his personal representative, Major Arthur Bassett, Reinsch labored to get both sides to reopen the negotiations. He also tried to reassure the south that the United States and the Allied Powers sincerely wished to curtail militarism in China. He instructed Sammons to add, however, that while the Chinese might look to the foreign powers for support, the basic effort "cannot be performed by outsiders. When such a policy has been declared by national leaders willing to stand by it, the opposition cannot remain formidable."[12]

Reinsch also wanted to leave Peking for a visit to central China. He believed that anything that emphasized the Shanghai Peace Conference would have a beneficial effect on the peace movement. Aside from the president, Reinsch maintained in February 1919, the Peking government could no longer be recognized as the real seat of national authority. The State Department refused to grant Reinsch permission because it feared that his trip would be viewed as an interference in China's internal affairs and would conflict with Washington's policy of cooperation with the other powers. In reply, Reinsch denied that he had any political motives and claimed that he merely intended to visit American consulates at Hankow, Nanking, and Changsha. "The propriety of such visits as I have suggested cannot be justly attacked from any source," he maintained. "The political implications which will be formed are entirely inferential but they would also be decidedly salutary."

Reinsch's political purposes, however, were obvious. He later admitted that "national unity feeling is strong" in the cities he proposed to visit. Nevertheless, he believed that the risk was warranted. "America still has a treasure of moral authority with the Chinese people inherited from the past," he explained. "If we should too plainly identify our political influence with Japanese intrigue, Americans in China— supporting a clique that under Japanese control does everything in its power to oppose and belittle American influence—would certainly be chargeable with a failure to gauge the situation and all the damage consequent thereon."[13]

Meanwhile, Reinsch urged that the United States join with the other powers in offering Hsu strong moral and financial support for his program of reform and demobilization. "This does not mean intervention," he opined, "but simply [a] straightforward statement on the basis on which financial support can be given." Demobilization, he pointed out, was the basis of all reform and the only way to rid China of the military menace and Japanese influence. "The freeing of four hundred million from this curse . . . is the most important object to be achieved in order to make the world safe," he declared. "It is in the hands of the American Government co-operating with Great Britain, France and Japan to bring about this achievement for justice and peace."[14]

The Shanghai Peace Conference reconvened in April, but broke up on May 13, 1919, over the question of the status of Parliament. China remained divided and the warlords dominated the north and the south. Reinsch had worked like a "trojan" to ensure the success of the peace movement. But it was a futile task. The Wilson administration had focused its attention on Paris and wanted nothing to interfere with the delicate Consortium negotiations. It therefore directed Reinsch and Sammons to discontinue their secret contacts with Chinese leaders and forbade Reinsch from visiting central China. The Far Eastern experts in the State Department thought that Reinsch's motives were well intended, but felt that his actions might be misused or misinterpreted by others. "He [Reinsch] cannot carry it through because he is weak and Japan is strong," Nelson T. Johnson observed. In any event, subsequent developments indicated that the Chinese had to work out their own differences and that any form of foreign intervention probably would have failed.[15]

*   *   *

Meanwhile, Reinsch had labored to implement his plan for international control of Chinese finances, which he had discussed with policy makers in Washington during the summer of 1918. Upon his return to Peking, he refined them in consultation with his advisers and Chinese and foreign officials and businessmen. From these deliberations, Reinsch, in a major reversal of his former position, formulated a comprehensive plan for Chinese financial and economic development.

At the top of Reinsch's system stood the new Consortium, composed of the leading powers acting as trustees for China. Each national group would be so inclusive that no financial institution desiring to participate would be excluded. The Consortium would support the credit of the Chinese government and stimulate economic development by making all administrative loans and some industrial loans. But to retain flexibility and to avoid monopoly, China would be free to conclude industrial loans elsewhere as long as the Consortium was informed of the terms. Complete equality of opportunity would govern bidding for construction and supply contracts under uniform standards established by expert commissions. In all cases, there would be a "complete disassociation of banking from construction and from furnishing of materials and equipment." The developmental needs of Chinese national life would be the sole criteria for all projects. "Finance ought to be placed on a business basis and divorced from all connection with extraneous political influence," he maintained.

Furthermore, efficient national administration would be provided by various expert commissions composed of Chinese and foreign representatives, in finance, communications, internal improvements, and police. But since the ultimate objective was the creation of an honest Chinese civil service, foreigners would not dominate these commissions. Finally, Reinsch's plan called for the creation of an expert financial board consisting of the heads of the various services—customs, salt, tobacco, wine, revenue—and one or two Chinese members, which would supervise and police the entire structure. The powers of the board would be technical, but extensive; they would include complete control over government accounting and auditing, preparation of data for the annual budget, and the right to demand the dismissal of Chinese officials. While this board would be in close contact with the Consortium, as the chief financial agency of the government, it would represent China—not the powers who were its creditors.[16]

Reinsch's scheme made special provision for a revived plan to neutralize China's railways. The entrenchment of foreign national interests in railway spheres of influence was the fundamental cause of China's troubles and the violation of the Open Door. "If reform can be introduced here," Reinsch pointed out, "all other difficulties will be more easily handled." Under railway neutralization (commercialization or unification, as it was dubbed by its advocates), all railway concessions would be renounced and pooled into a Chinese National Railway System. The existing foreign-owned lines would be redeemed and new ones would be constructed by floating loans through an international group, probably the Consortium. All equipment would be "standardized on the basis of efficiency and equal opportunity to all industrial nations" and all construction and equipment contracts would be "let by public bidding under the standards established." Reinsch hoped that this plan could be implemented at the Paris Peace Conference and thus enshrined in the "public law." But he felt that the same results could be achieved if the Consortium followed the principles that he outlined.[17]

Reinsch's program was a culmination of his progressive-expansionist *weltanschauung*. It sought to achieve flexibility and efficiency, to disassociate banking from construction, to destoy the spheres of influence and secure the Open Door, to apply Western technical know-how and to create an honest, effective Chinese administrative system. China would obtain stability, prosperity, and eventual political and economic independence. The United States would obtain a huge foreign market and a position of world leadership, for Reinsch was confident that American standards would prevail and American experts would predominate. And mankind would benefit from the exploitation of China's resources and market and the resulting peace in the Far East. However, it also underscored Reinsch's temporary loss of faith in China's ability to organize itself, as well as his determination to block further Japanese expansion.

Reinsch worked hard to win support for his proposals in China, Washington, and Paris. He was assisted by Arnold, Charles Denby, Jr., a State Department trade adviser, and especially Paul P. Whitham, the new assistant commercial attaché, all of whom submitted similar proposals to their superiors in Washington. Nevertheless, Reinsch's plans encountered opposition and obstruction from a variety of sources.[18]

Chinese moderates and liberals, as well as the reactionaries and the pro-Japanese clique, denounced all forms of foreign control of China's finances and administration. Convinced of the crucial importance of his program and confident that there were sufficient safeguards, Reinsch failed to appreciate the extent of Chinese resentment against foreign control. Subsequently, Reinsch modified his plan so that the Consortium would have an option only on industrial loans at rates offered by others and he discussed the possibility of giving the Chinese greater authority in the direction of the national railway system. With the assistance of William H. Donald and the encouragement of the State Department, Reinsch launched a publicity campaign to educate the Chinese to the true nature of the Consortium proposal. Reinsch declared:

> The arrangement for these reforms will be made by the Chinese Government as a sovereign act necessary to give the Chinese Government the efficiency required in modern times. Without this efficiency the Chinese Government cannot be sovereign in any true sense. The foreign creditors are entitled to the guarantee that these reforms will be carried out. Their representatives are therefore entitled to full information as to every part of public finance, which in fact the Chinese public is entitled to, as is the public of any free state. . . . It will be seen that the essential securities are in the interest of the Chinese people even more than in the interest of the foreign creditors.[19]

The British and the French supported the new Consortium with reservations, but they had problems in organizing their groups. Japan, however, tried to subvert it. The Japanese tried to induce the Chinese to request a loan from the old Consortium, which would place Tokyo in a position to control the new international syndicate. Japan also stymied the Consortium negotiations, which were being conducted in Paris simultaneously with the Peace Conference, by insisting on the exclusion from the scope of the Consortium of industrial loans and enterprises in Manchuria and Mongolia. Reinsch pleaded with the State Department not to be blackmailed into accepting the Japanese conditions, which he warned would wreck the Open Door and cause endless complications. On these matters, Reinsch had little to worry about. The State Department was anxious to organize the Consortium as quickly as possible and wanted to give it control over all Chinese loans.[20]

But major differences appeared on other aspects of Reinsch's program. The State Department rejected Reinsch's neutralization scheme and would not allow it to be brought up at Paris for fear that it might embarrass the Paris Peace Conference and imperil the formation of the Second Consortium.[21] Reinsch's repeated demand that the American Group send a representative to Peking also created tension between himself and Washington. Reinsch insisted upon American participation in all negotiations from the start, especially in the matters of currency reform, demobilization of troops, and the reorganization of Chinese finances. Reinsch recognized that the actual transfer of funds must await "reconciliation." But he wisely pointed out that now was the time to work out policies based on first-hand knowledge of the situation.[22] The American Group finally sent Abbott to China in 1919 for the vague purpose of investigating the financial situation. The American Group clearly did not give Abbott a mandate to engage in substantial negotiations. There is also evidence that the pro-Chinese Chicago banker was sent to Peking to keep him out of trouble in the United States and to give Thomas Lamont, the chief spokesman for J. P. Morgan & Co., a free hand in the crucial Consortium negotiations in Paris.[23]

Reinsch was not satisfied with this sop and he was determined to make the most of Abbott's visit. He was particularly worried that the Japanese might convince the Chinese that they would be wasting their time if they dealt with him. Reinsch deliberately routed the banker's trip to Peking through Shanghai, rather than through Japan and Korea. Once Abbott arrived in China, Reinsch persuaded him to consult with the Chinese on the details of a loan proposal, for a five-year plan of orderly financing and constructive enterprise. Reinsch pleaded with Washington to permit Abbott to indicate which of the Chinese proposals were sound and could expect a favorable hearing. However, the American Group, supported by the State Department, objected. It vetoed Abbott's tour of Canton and Hankow to meet with Chinese business leaders and it ordered him to return home in May 1919, to advise on personnel.[24]

This incident underscored a basic difference between Reinsch, on the one hand, and the State Department and the American Group on the other. Reinsch still believed that independent American action should be pursued both as a safeguard for American interests and as a weapon to gain the powers' adherence to American principles governing the Consortium and the Open Door. "I must strongly emphasize," Reinsch declared before leaving Peking in 1919, "the present situation can be met only by immediate action leaving consortium proposal in force, but not allowing it to be made the means of eliminating American [and] British enterprise and influence."

After all, Britain and France still refused to give unqualified recognition to the principle of equal opportunity in railway construction and they might try to consolidate their spheres of influence after the war. Japan sought additional concessions and forced the Chinese to cancel an American electric works contract in Foochow. "Our allies are not all as altruistic as the United States," Reinsch observed as he argued for the export of railway equipment for China. Independent action would also force Japan to drop its conditions for entering the Consortium. It is not "probable," Reinsch advised, "that the Japanese at present will come into the consortium unless they should understand that the train will start without them."[25]

Finally, the United States had to restore Chinese faith in America and lay the basis for strong economic, political, and cultural ties between the two great Pacific nations. The Chinese resented the fact that Washington made everything contingent on the formation of the Consortium. "As America has not forfeited her right to deal directly with China," he opined,

> we could at any time make an independent loan which would immediately solve the present troubles of China by putting into the hands of the President the means necessary for disbandment of troops and reorganization upon approval by a new national parliament. . . . The cost of such a policy would be negligible compared to the loss which will be involved in blood and treasure if we continue to be inattentive to the Chinese situation and fail to realize that far from being a Sino-Japanese affair it is one upon which our future national life and security are essentially dependent.

Similarly, Reinsch pointed to the lingering impression that Americans sought valuable options "with no intention of carrying them through." Reinsch therefore urged that some concrete work be started on the Grand Canal or the Siems-Carey railways. "The Chinese must be shown what

Americans can do when they get started," he once more insisted to William Carey and his colleagues at AIC.[26]

*　　*　　*

The Paris Peace Conference became Reinsch's last great hope. Recognizing that the conference would be primarily concerned with settling issues arising out of the war, Reinsch counseled the Chinese not to present their demands for the annulment of all foreign concessions and leased territories, the abolition of the Protocol of 1901, and the restoration of tariff autonomy. Although he expressed sympathy for China's aspirations, Reinsch pointed out that China could not reasonably ask for tariff autonomy and the abolition of extraterritoriality until it could guarantee foreigners legal protection and freedom from abuses in taxation. Instead, he advised the Chinese to rely upon the gradual strengthening of China's independence and integrity through the abolition of localized preferences and foreign financial assistance under American leadership. Reinsch's step by step program sounded logical in view of the Japanese threat and China's internal anarchy. But it also indicated that Reinsch was unwilling to forgo all of the advantages of the treaty system and that he misjudged the strength of China's rising nationalism.[27]

On Shantung, however, Reinsch would not compromise. China's case was weakened by the treaties of 1915 and especially by the secret agreement which Ts'ao Ju-lin negotiated in September 1918, without consulting the Foreign Ministry. In exchange for Japanese withdrawal of its civil administration along the railway, China recognized Tokyo's right to inherit Germany's privileges and also granted Japan a half interest in the Shantung Railway. This meant that Japanese promises to set aside an international concession and to return the German leased area to China were worthless: Japan would still retain absolute economic control of Shantung. "It would not be easy to imagine a deal which illustrates the worst features of secret diplomacy," Reinsch observed. "The civil administration offices which were set up without a shadow of a right are treated as a valuable asset to be used in obtaining further advantages. The public determinations of the peace conference are sterilized before the event. . . ." Reinsch painstakingly demonstrated the vital importance of the railway and other economic interests as the basis of Japanese power. He therefore insisted that the complete return of Shantung to China offered the only just solution.[28]

But Reinsch also saw the work of the peace conference in larger terms. Because it would attempt to write rules to assure future peace,

Reinsch proposed that the conference ratify three general principles "to be given full connotation in action and institutions." First, the powers must surrender their spheres of influence and abolish all local preferences. Second, the powers must pledge themselves to replace the old system of international politics with a trusteeship that would benefit China. Finally, the conference must condemn secret diplomacy and lay on the table all of the agreements extracted from China since August 1, 1914, in order to determine those that conflicted with China's integrity and the Open Door. The agreements that were not submitted would be *ipso facto* invalid and all the concessions granted by the corrupt Chinese politicians would lapse unless they were ratified by the Chinese Parliament.[29]

Reinsch maintained that the acceptance of these principles would enable China, with the assistance of foreign experts and capital, to control its own development; it would also reduce international friction, free the world from "the curse of militarism," and produce material benefits for the entire world. Without such a settlement, Reinsch warned, competition for spheres of influence and special privileges would poison the atmosphere and increase the likelihood of war. Or still worse, if Japan—the new Prussian menace—were given a free hand or a so-called Monroe Doctrine, "forces will be set in motion which will make a huge armed conflict absolutely inevitable within one generation," Reinsch predicted.

At the same time, the Chinese masses must be given hope and encouragement so that they could free themselves from the "corrupt gang which, now by our sufferance, holds authority in Peking." In an impassioned plea to American policy makers, Reinsch declared:

> Never before has an opportunity for leadership toward the welfare of humanity presented itself equal to that which invites America in China at the present time. The Chinese people ask for no better fate than to be allowed the freedom to follow in the footsteps of America; every device of intrigue and corruption as well as coercion is being employed to force them in a different direction. . . . If it were only known that an exchange [sic] in concert with the Liberal powers would not tolerate the enslavement of China either by foreign or native militarists, the natural propensity of the Chinese to follow liberal inclinations would guide this vast country toward free government and propitious developments of peaceful industrial activities, even through unavoidable difficulties in the transition of so vast and ancient a

society to new methods of action. . . . If China should be disappointed in her confidence at the present time the consequences of such disillusionment on her moral and political development would be disastrous, and we, instead of looking across the Pacific towards a Chinese nation, sympathetic with our ideals, would be confronted with a vast materialistic military organization under ruthless control.[30]

Reinsch bent every effort to educate American policy makers to the large issues at stake at the peace conference. He counted upon the American delegation, especially Wilson, to exert strong leadership at Paris. Besides, there was little else that he could do in Peking. Worried about the predisposition of the State Department to concentrate on European affairs, Reinsch told Lansing before the opening of the conference that "there is no single problem in Europe which equals in its importance to the future peace of the world, the need of a just settlement of Chinese affairs." Reinsch also pointed out that the principles applied to the Chinese situation could be used wherever similar conditions prevailed. A victory for the Open Door in China, Reinsch noted, would also strengthen the principle of equal opportunity in Turkey, Persia, and Morocco. Dissenting from Acting Secretary of State Frank Polk's statement that the "Peace Conference has more important work than strengthening up relations between China and Japan," Reinsch retorted:

The Far Eastern Question is not merely one of relations between China and Japan; in fact whether China is to be left free to develop as a peaceful industrial state, or is to be made the material for supporting and strengthening the most reactionary militaristic society now existing in the world, that is a question the solution of which will affect the future of our country fully as much as anything the Peace Conference can do.[31]

It was all in vain. On April 30, 1919, Wilson yielded to Japanese and Allied pressures and agreed to give Japan all of Germany's former economic privileges in Shantung and the right to establish an exclusive settlement in Tsingtao.[32]. Reinsch was stunned when he received confirmation of the Shantung decision from the State Department on May 2. He demanded an explanation of the American action so that he could respond to inquiries from the Chinese government and the press. He also endorsed the Chinese refusal to sign the peace treaty unless they could make reservations, and urged support for China's request that

Japan make a definite commitment to return Shantung to China and to withdraw its military forces from the railway.[33]

Throughout the summer of 1919, Reinsch vigorously criticized the Shantung decision and demolished Wilson's defense of the arrangement. Reinsch felt that the Shantung decision "destroyed all confidence in a league of nations which had such an ugly fact as its cornerstone." He predicted that there will be "a great deal of talk of friendship for China, of restoration of Shantung, of loyalty to the League of Nations, but it will be dangerous to accept this and to stop questioning what are the methods actually applied; . . . We cannot rest secure on treaties nor even on the League of Nations without this questioning of the facts," he declared in his letter of resignation. "Otherwise these instruments will only make the game a little more complicated but not change its essential character." Nor did Reinsch believe that Japan would have walked out of the conference if it had not gotten its way on Shantung. Colonel House had panicked, Reinsch stated in his memoirs; with "friendly firmness" the president could have obtained a different solution.

Above all, Reinsch castigated Wilson for failing to undestand that the economic rights granted to Japan subverted the entire Shantung settlement. Japan retained political influence and the means to discriminate against other nations. Reinsch thus defined the Shantung decision as a threat to American security and an abandonment of the Open Door. Furthermore, it caused the Chinese to lose confidence in the "power, justice, principles and actions of western nations," and might force China, as a last resort, to adopt a policy of "Asia for Asiatics," and an alliance with Japan "against the Occident."[34]

*   *   *

The Shantung decision had two important consequences for Reinsch. It touched off the May Fourth Movement and occasioned his resignation.

Chinese nationalism had gained momentum since the Revolution of 1911. At the beginning of 1919, students denounced the validity of the Twenty-One Demands and demonstrated for internal peace. On May 2, 1919, Reinsch informed the State Department that there existed disquieting signs of a massive national uprising with anti-foreign overtones.[35] Reinsch sympathized with the growth of Chinese nationalism, and he may have played a small part in encouraging it. He worked with the Young China party to bring China into the war in 1917 and he encouraged the students to take a more active role in national affairs after the Peking government fell into the hands of the militarists and pro-

Japanese politicians. He had strong ties with the young progressive editors of Chinese newspapers and the students who returned from abroad. And he was a frequent guest at the National University, which became the center of nationalist ferment.[36]

On May 4, 1919, after deomonstrating in the streets of Peking, students from the National University called at the American legation and asked to see the minister. Reinsch was visiting the temple above Men Tou-kou, outside Peking, and was spared the ordeal of explaining what had occurred at Paris. The students thereupon vented their anger on the pro-Japanese clique which they held responsible for China's humiliation; Ts'ao Ju-lin barely escaped with his life. The demonstrations quickly spread to other cities and the May Fourth Movement soon attracted broad popular support. Chinese nationalists successfully organized an anti-Japanese boycott and secured the dismissal of the pro-Japanese officials.[37]

Reinsch hailed the nationalist movement and believed that a new era had dawned in China. For the first time in the history of that ancient people, popular opinion had been mobilized and was actually influencing government action. The movement also renewed Reinsch's hope for representative and responsive government, the reunification of the country, and rapid modernization. In addition, Reinsch endorsed the anti-Japanese boycotts, which he thought would stimulate Chinese industry and might also expand American exports.[38]

To be sure, this American progressive remained distrustful of violent revolution. He deprecated the students who advocated extreme measures and worried that the movement, if it were carried too far, might assume general anti-foreign overtones. Reinsch also realized that continued unrest might provoke Japan into encouraging the northern militarists to "establish order." But he vigorously insisted that nothing be done to interfere with the student movement. In conversations with Tuan and other officials, Reinsch defended the demonstrators and criticized the Peking government for jailing the students. Concerned about a general anti-foreign backlash, Reinsch opposed the attempt of the British Municipal Council to arrest and expel from the international settlement Chinese who wore boycott badges. The State Department instructed Reinsch to oppose any outside interference as long as there was no violence. But Reinsch also wanted to indicate positive support for Chinese aspirations. Behind the scenes, therefore, Reinsch and Arnold organized the Anglo-American community in a demonstration of sympathy.[39]

Reinsch took a broad view of the unrest in China. He felt that a rupture with the past was bound to be unsettling. Besides, if democracy were to succeed in China, the masses had to be aroused in a political sense. The student demonstrations had achieved that result. In the end, Reinsch hoped that the students would return to their books and that more moderate elements would assume leadership of the nationalist movement. Before leaving China, Reinsch told Chinese businessmen that they had to "make sacrifices for their own Commonwealth," both in terms of political involvement and financial assistance. In this work, he told a farewell audience, Americans as friends could help. But there were certain things which could be done only by the Chinese themselves. "You want friends not guardians," he reminded them. "A friend will use his influence so as to create a favorable situation for your activities."[40]

The Shantung decision also forced Reinsch to submit his resignation and, more significantly, caused his break with Wilson. Reinsch had been thinking for almost a year of returning to the United States and had actually decided to resign two weeks before the announcement of the Shantung award to Japan. Family considerations, especially the education of his children, were a factor. He was also piqued with the State Department for rebuking him for his lengthy telegrams (one cost ($597.96), questioning his motives in connection with his trip to central China, denying him the personnel he requested, and expressing irritation with his insistence that his messages be shown to the president. Above all, after six exhausting years of tireless effort, Reinsch was discouraged by his failure to awaken Americans to the importance of China. He believed that, as a private citizen in the United States, he might have greater success in reaching the men who controlled America's economic life.[41]

The Shantung decision, however, hastened Reinsch's departure. By nature and experience, he was probably unprepared for the president's betrayal of China and his personal disavowal. The Chinese did not upbraid him for what happened at Paris. But Reinsch knew that his position was no longer tenable. He had lost face with the Chinese by assuring them of American support. "Rightly or wrongly," he explained to Polk, "the Chinese had felt that China had entered the war under America's wing and that America would stand sponsor for her at the Conference."[42]

In a letter dated June 7, 1919, Reinsch submitted his resignation to President Wilson. Reinsch complained that he had not been given the staff he needed and criticized the administration for failing to devote sufficient attention to the critical situation in the Far East. "Unless this was corrected and the government feels strong enough to take adequate action, the fruits of one hundred and forty years of American work will be lost," he warned. "Our people will be permitted to exist there only on the sufferance of others, and the great opportunity which has been held out to us by the Chinese people to assist in the development of education and free institutions will be gone beyond recall." Reinsch singled out the failure of the United States to aid China after Peking broke relations with Germany and the insult of the Lansing-Ishii Agreement. The general tone of the letter, however, was moderate and expressed appreciation of Wilson's confidence in him. Publicly, Reinsch continued to maintain that his resignation was prompted by his state of health and his desire to reenter affairs at home.[43]

However, after Reinsch acquired additional information about the Shantung decision, he composed, but probably did not send, two angry, damning letters: one was addressed to Lansing, the other to Wilson. He was rankled by the knowledge that the president had relied upon the "vague promises of Japan" instead of the "carefully considered expressions" of the American minister and the Far Eastern experts at Paris.[44]

The administration appreciated Reinsch's feelings. Long wrote an analysis of Reinsch's letter of resignation that was both sympathetic and critical. Long thought that Reinsch's anti-Japanese tone was understandable since the minister had been in the midst of the Japapnese intrigues and he had been "the most active of the foreigners who have fought it." On the other hand, Reinsch was unjustified in faulting the State Department for not providing him with sufficient personnel; he had failed to delegate authority and had often bypassed the legation staff. Disregarding the failure of American business and the administration to support the Open Door effectively, Long put his finger on part of Reinsch's problem: "He, himself, is much overworked, and has been for several years; has carried on by an enormous nervous energy and is consequently now in a highly nervous condition; and is tired out and discouraged at the physical impossibility of achieving what was too much for any one man to do." Long therefore agreed with Wilson and Lansing that Reinsch could not be of "much further use in his present state of mind." However, the administration delayed accepting his resignation until August 18, and kept him in China until the middle of September in order to keep him out of the United States while the Senate was conducting hearings on Shantung and the peace treaty.[45]

*   *   *

In China, the news of Reinsch's resignation was received with genuine regret. Tributes poured in from consular officials, private citizens, organizations, and newspapers. "What you have accomplished almost seems miraculous especially when one considers the inadequate support our Washington Government has afforded," E. Carlton Baker, the anti-Japanese consul-general in Mukden declared. Baker also joined other consular officers in expressing their deep personal loss since "no former Minister ever took such a deep and sympathetic interest in the welfare of the Students." The vice president of the Shanghai Commercial Federation aptly expressed the feelings of the Chinese: "Your services to China can never be forgotten by those who love their country and who have seen in you a warm friend and teacher. During your incumbency here as American Minister you have done everything humanly possible to help save our country from its enemies internal and external." From the United States, the vice president of General Electric, M. A. Oudin, wrote: "All those who have knowledge of Far Eastern conditions are aware of the very great services you have rendered this country during your six years in Peking. None of our previous Ministers has done more for American interests in China than you have done." During his final weeks in China, Reinsch was feted by one group after another. And when he left Peking on September 13, he was given an enthusiastic send-off attended by high dignitaries.[46]

Reinsch worked to the very end. In conversations with President Hsu, Tuan, and other Chinese officials, Reinsch appealed for political unity and reform and urged them to cooperate with the Consortium. In reply, they complained that the United States had failed China and they opposed even limited foreign financial control. Meanwhile, throughout the summer of 1919, Reinsch tried desperately to obtain some financial assistance for China and to break the impasse in the Consortium negotiations at Paris. He proposed both Japanese-American short-term loans to preempt independent action by Tokyo and the formation of a three-power consortium, without Japan. Washington agreed with American bankers that short-term loans would not serve any useful purpose. But at the end of August, Lansing, frustrated by Japanese maneuvers and aware of China's financial plight, was ready to prod Japan by sounding out Britain and France on a three-power consortium. By the time Reinsch left Peking, however, he had failed to utilize America's vast economic power, either independently or cooperatively, to make the Open Door a reality and he made no progress in establishing the foundation for a great Sino-American partnership.[47]

On September 11, 1919, Reinsch conducted a long and thorough-going review of Chinese affairs with the legation staff and urged it to carry on the fight for American enterprise. His final message to the State

Department, before boarding his ship in Shanghai, expressed the same theme. "All influential men and parties are desirous of American lead," Reinsch cabled. "The opposition is greatly weakened. The matter is in your hands."[48]

NOTES TO
CHAPTER XII

1. Dreher to Vanderlip, 14 August 1917, Vanderlip Papers; Reinsch to Long, 7 December 1918, Reinsch Papers.

2. Reinsch to Lansing, 20 July 1917, 123.R271/56, 9 April 1918, 123.R271/73, DSNA; Williams to Reinsch, 1 February 1918, Reinsch Papers.

3. Reinsch to Lansing, 2 January 1917, 123.R271/50, 1 September 1917, 763.72/6693, DSNA; Reinsch to Long, 17 May 1918, Reinsch Papers; Lansing to Reinsch, 5 September 1917, 763.72/6693, 21 June 1918, 123.R271/74a, DSNA; Reinsch to Vanderlip, 14 May 1918, RG 84, Peking Post file, 851.6, NA; Reinsch to Straight, 21 May 1918, Reinsch Papers.

4. Reinsch to Long, 26 July 1918, Long Papers; Long Diary, 7, 8, 12, 14 and 15 August 1918, *ibid*.; Lansing Desk Diary, 14 August 1918, Lansing Papers; Polk Confidential Diary, 8 August 1918, Polk Papers; Reinsch to Tumulty, 7 August 1918, Wilson Papers; Ray S. Baker, *Woodrow Wilson: Life and Letters, Armistice: March 1 – November 11, 1918* (New York, 1939), 333, 363; memo of conversation, Reinsch and Wilson, 14 August 1918, submitted to Lansing, 893.51/1960, DSNA; Reinsch to Wilson, 31 August 1918, RG 84, Peking Post file, 851, NA; Reinsch, "Memorandum on Chinese Finance," 14 August 1918, Reinsch Papers; Reinsch to Alma, 24 August 1918, *ibid*.; Reinsch, *An American Diplomat*, 354–56.

5. Memo of offices and firms consulted with Minister to China, August 1918, Reinsch Papers; Reinsch to Lansing, 1 November 1918, 893.77/1694, DSNA; Williams to Trade Advisers, 25 July 1918, 893.77/1690, DSNA; Reinsch, *An American Diplomat*, 354.

6. Memo of offices and firms consulted with Minister to China, August 1918, Reinsch Papers; Reinsch, *An American Diplomat*, 354.

7. Wilson to Lansing, 22 August 1918, 893.51/1979, DSNA; Reinsch to Alma, 24 August 1918, Reinsch Papers; Reinsch to Long, 7 December 1918, 28 January, 22 April 1919, *ibid*.; Long to Reinsch, 14 March, 23 May 1919, *ibid*.; Long Diary, entries for August 1918, Long Papers.

8. Reinsch, *An American Diplomat*, 321, 356–57.

9. Reinsch to Wilson, 11 November 1916, Wilson Papers; Reinsch interview with *Osaka Manichi*, 5 October 1918, Reinsch Papers; translation of Reinsch interview in *Shih Shih Hsin Pao*, 12 October 1918, *ibid*.

10. Reinsch to Lansing, 19 October 1918, 893.00/2893, 26 October 1918, 893.00/2896 and 763.72/11913, 30 October 1918, 893.00/2898, 14 November 1918, 893.00/2976 and 763.72/12250, 23 November 1918, 893.00/2981, DSNA; Reinsch to Polk, 10 January 1919, 893.00/2954, 11 January 1919, 893.00/2931, DSNA; Reinsch to Pontius, 14 November 1918, 893.00/2976, DSNA; *FR 1918*, 110–21, 135; *FR 1919*, I, 290, 294–95; Reinsch, *An American Diplomat*, 319–22.

11. Reinsch to Polk, 10 December 1918, 893.51/2079, 24 February 1919, 893.51/2142, 6 June 1919, 893.00/3180, DSNA; memo of conversation, Reinsch and Hayashi, 5 December 1918, Reinsch Papers; Reinsch to Obata, 3 April 1919, *ibid*.; *FR 1919*, I, 289–93, 298–303, 310–27; Reinsch, *An American Diplomat*, 326–27.

12. Sammons to Polk, 22 March 1919, 893.00/3075, DSNA; Reinsch to Sammons, 28 March 1919, 893.00/3087, DSNA; *FR 1919*, 316–27.

13. Reinsch to Polk, 15 February 1919, 793.94/759, 19 April 1919, 123.R271/96, 23 June 1919, 123.R271/102, DSNA; Polk to Reinsch, 10 April 1919, 123.R271/60, 15 April 1919, 123.R271/94, DSNA, 3 May 1919, Reinsch Papers.

14. Reinsch to Lansing, 30 October 1918, 893.00/2898, 8 November 1918, 893.51/ 2078, DSNA; Reinsch to Polk, 10 December 1918, 893.51/2079, 11 January 1919, 893.00/2929, 15 February 1919, 793.94/759, 26 April 1919, 893.51/2192, DSNA; *FR 1919,* 293–94, 316, 323–24.

15. Reinsch to Polk, 26 April 1919, 893.51/2192, 17 May 1919, 893.00/3131, 6 June 1919, 893.00/3180, DSNA; Polk to Reinsch, 15 April 1919, 123.R271/94, DSNA, 3 May 1919, Reinsch Papers; Johnson to Miller, 5 April 1919, 793.94/785, 22 April 1919, 893.00/3062, DSNA; *FR 1919,* I, 344–64.

16. Reinsch, "Memorandum on Chinese Finance," a summary of a conversation between Reinsch and Wilson, 14 August 1918, 893.51/1960, DSNA; Long Diary, 12 August 1918, Long Papers; Miller to Lansing, 24 October 1918, *ibid.*; Reinsch to Lansing, 19 October 1918, 893.00/2893, 23 November 1918, 763.72119/3173, DSNA; Reinsch to Polk, 10 December 1918, 893.51/2079, 20 December 1918, 893.77/1723, 17 January 1919, 893.77/1706, 15 February 1919, 793.94/759, 6 March 1919, 893.51/2166, DSNA; *FR: Paris Peace Conference,* II, 491–98; Reinsch, "Memorandum on the Consortium," Reinsch Papers; Reinsch, *An American Diplomat,* 355–56.

17. Reinsch to Polk, 20 December 1918, 893.77/1723, 17 January 1919, 893.77/ 1706, 10 March 1919, 893.00/3040, DSNA; *FR: Paris Peace Conference,* II, 491–98.

18. Arnold to Cutler, 18 July 1918, RG 151 (Records of the Department of Commerce, Bureau of Foreign and Domestic Trade), file, 524, NA; Whitham to Cutler, 22 November 1918, 27 January 1919, RG 151, file 492.1, NA; Whitham to Herring, 27 January 1919, *ibid.*; Denby memo, 31 January 1919, 893.77/1711, DSNA; Reinsch to Polk, 12 February 1919, 893.77/1715, DSNA.

19. Reinsch to Polk, 3 June 1919, 893.77/1782, 11 July 1919, 893.51/2310, DSNA; "Memorandum on the New Consortium," 5 July 1919, in Reinsch to Phillips, 7 July 1919, 893.51/2348, DSNA; American Mission to Phillips, 4 July 1919, 893.51/2301, DSNA; Lansing to Reinsch, 24 July 1919, 893.51/2338a, DSNA; Donald to Reinsch, 16 July 1919, Reinsch Papers; interview, Reinsch and Tuan, 29 August 1919, *ibid.; New York Times*, 4 July 1919; Frederick V. Field, *American Participation in the China Consortiums* (Chicago, 1931), 169.

20. *FR 1918,* 169–99; *FR 1919,* I, 420–504; Reinsch to Polk, 12 February 1919, 893.77/1715, 26 June 1919, 893.51/2284, 7 July 1919, 893.51/2302, 11 July 1919, 893.51/2310, DSNA; Polk to Reinsch, 18 December 1919, 893.51/2079, 4 February 1919, 893.77/1710, 11 April 1919, 893.51/2173, 11 July 1919, 893.51/2302, DSNA; Polk to MacMurray, 10 August 1918, 893.51/1951, DSNA; Miller to Lansing, 24 October 1918, Long Papers; State Department Aide Memoire, 21 February 1919, 893.51/ 2122, DSNA; memos of conversation, Long and Japanese ambassador, 31 January 1919, 893.51/2132, 21 February 1919, 893.51/2130, DSNA; Marshall to Long, 21 June 1919, Long Papers, 1 July 1919, 893.51/2518, DSNA; Field, *American Participation in the Chinese Consortiums,* 147–54, 176.

21. Polk to Lansing, 15 February 1919, RG 151, file 492.1, NA; Redfield to Polk, 19 February 1919, *ibid.*; Polk to Redfield, 11 March 1919, *ibid.*; Polk to American Mission, 12 March 1919, 893.77/1724, DSNA.

22. Reinsch to Lansing, 8 November 1918, 893.51/2078, DSNA; *FR 1918,* 161, 197–98.

23. Polk to Reinsch, 18 December 1918, 893.51/2079, DSNA; Reinsch to Polk, 29 March 1919, 893.51/2156, DSNA; memo of conversation, Long with J. P. Morgan, John J. Abbott, H. D. Marshall, 20 December 1918, Long Papers; Long Diary, 29 June 1919, *ibid.*; Abbott to Lamont, 10 March 1919, in 893.51/2193, DSNA; Polk to Wallace, 14 May 1919, 893.51/2192, DSNA.

24. Abbott to Lamont, 20 February 1919, 893.51/2177, 10 March 1919, 893.51/ 2193, DSNA; Reinsch to Polk, 29 March 1919, 893.51/2156, 26 April 1919, 893.51/ 2192, 12 May 1919, 893.51/2220, DSNA; Polk to Reinsch, 12 May 1919, 893.51/2220, DSNA; Polk to Wallace, 14 May 1919, 893.51/2192, DSNA.

25. Reinsch to Polk, 28 January 1919, 893.51/2145, 12 February 1919, 893.51/1715, 29 March 1919, 893.51/2156, 14 May 1919, 893.51/2192, 25 July 1919, 793.94/939, DSNA, 26 July 1919, Reinsch Papers; Reinsch to Phillips, 7 July 1919, 893.51/2302, DSNA; Reinsch to Lansing, 18 August 1919, 893.51/2372, DSNA.

26. Reinsch to Polk, 31 December 1918, 893.811/313, 11 July 1919, 893.51/2310, DSNA; Reinsch to Phillips, 2 July 1919, 893.51/2293, DSNA; Reinsch to Lansing, 10 September 1919, 893.00/3235, DSNA; Reinsch to Carey, 24 December 1918, Reinsch Papers.

27. Hawkins Tapes, 2; *FR: Paris Peace Conference,* II, 491–509.

28. Reinsch to Lansing, 3 December 1919, Reinsch Papers; Reinsch to Polk, 12 December 1918, 893.77/1696, DSNA.

29. Reinsch to Lansing, 19 October 1918, 893.00/2893, DSNA; Reinsch to Polk, 8 February 1919, 793.94/746, 12 February 1919, 793.94/759, DSNA; *FR: Paris Peace Conference,* II, 491–98; memo, "Major Desiderata for Peace Treaty, 1919," Reinsch Papers.

30. *FR: Paris Peace Conference,* II, 493–94, 520–25; Reinsch to Polk, 23 June 1919, 123.R271/102, DSNA; Reinsch, *An American Diplomat,* 328–38.

31. *FR: Paris Peace Conference*, II, 491–98, 509; Polk to Reinsch, 2 February 1919, Reinsch Papers; Reinsch to Polk, 11 April 1919, *ibid*.

32. Memo, Wilson to Ray Stannard Baker, for Communication to the Chinese Delegation, 30 April 1919, 793.94/820½, DSNA; Williams to Long, 27 April and 5 May 1919, Long Papers; Robert Lansing, *The Peace Negotiations: A Personal Narrative* (Boston, 1921), 257–63; Fifield, *Wilson and the Far East,* 218–93.

33. Polk to Reinsch, 5 May 1919, 763.72119/4824, DSNA; Reinsch to Polk, 28 April 1919, 763.72119/4764, 1 May 1919, 763.72119/4833, 14 May 1919, 763.72119/ 5003, 30 May 1919, 793.94/824, 31 May 1919, 763.72119/5173, 23 June 1919, 763.72119/5412, 3 July 1919, 763.72119/5317, DSNA; author's interview with Hornbeck, 5 January 1965; Reinsch, *An American Diplomat*, 361–62; Fifield, *Wilson and the Far East,* 315–33.

34. Reinsch to Wilson, 7 June 1919, 123.R271/101, DSNA; Reinsch to Polk, 2 May 1919, 763.72119/4837, 21 July 1919, 862.01/25, DSNA; Reinsch to Lansing, 28 July 1919, 763.72119/5350, 23 August 1919, 763.72119/6347, 10 October 1919, 793.94/ 1027, DSNA; Reinsch, "Six Years of American Action in China," Reinsch Papers; Reinsch, *An American Diplomat,* 359–63.

35. Reinsch to Polk, 22 January 1919, 793.94/773, 2 May 1919, 763.72119/4839, DSNA; Sammons to Reinsch, 26 March 1919, 893.00/3066, DSNA; Bose, *American Attitude and Policy to the Nationalist Movement in China, passim;* Warren Cohen, "America and the May Fourth Movement," *Pacific Historical Review,* XXXV (February 1966), 83–100; John K. Fairbank, *The United States and China* (Cambridge, 1958), 169–70.

36. Reinsch, *An American Diplomat,* 358; Tong, "Dr. Reinsch: A Popular American Minister"; John B. Powell, *My Twenty-Five Years in China* (New York, 1945), 46.

37. Reinsch to Polk, 4 May 1919, 893.00/3089, 8 May 1919, 793.94/828, 16 May 1919, 693.1112/25, 11 June 1919, 793.94/838, DSNA; Sammons to Polk, 6 May 1919, 893.00/3118, DSNA; Reinsch, *An American Diplomat,* 318–19.

38. Reinsch to Polk, 9 May 1919, 793.94/828, 17 May 1919, 893.00/3130, 19 May 1919, 693.1112/25, 11 June 1919, 793.94/838, 4 July 1919, 893.00/3151½, DSNA;

Reinsch, "Six Years of American Action in China," Reinsch Papers; Reinsch, "The Far East as a Factor in International Developments," 224.

39. Reinsch to Polk, 12 May 1919, 793.94/829, 7 June 1919, 793.94/830, 9 June 1919, 793.94/836, 11 June 1919, 793.94/838, DSNA; Lansing to Polk, 22 June 1919, 793.94/848, DSNA; Arnold to Reinsch, 16 May 1919, RG 151, file 492.1, NA; Reinsch, *An American Diplomat,* 370–71.

40. Reinsch to Lansing, 29 August 1919, Reinsch Papers; Reinsch remarks at a farewell reception, September 1919, *ibid.* Warren Cohen points out that American officials preferred to work with Chinese businessmen rather than with students. Cohen, "America and the May Fourth Movement."

41. Reinsch to Wilson, 7 June 1919, 123.R271/101, DSNA; Reinsch to Polk, 28 January 1919, 763.72119/3528, DSNA; Polk to Reinsch, 28 January 1919, 763.72119/3528, 10 April 1919, 123.R271/60, DSNA; Alma to Daisy, November 1918, Reinsch Papers; Reinsch to Long, 7 December 1918, 28 January and 22 April 1919, *ibid.*; Long to Reinsch, 14 March 1919, *ibid.*; Reinsch Statement to the Associated Press, 8 October 1919, *ibid.*; Reinsch, "Six Years of American Action in China," *ibid.*; Hawkins Tapes, 12; Reinsch, *An American Diplomat,* 363.

42. Hawkins Tapes, 2; author's interview with Hornbeck, 5 January 1965; Reinsch, *An American Diplomat,* 361–62; Reinsch to Polk, 6 June 1919, 893.00/3180, DSNA.

43. Reinsch to Wilson, 7 June 1919, 123.R271/101, DSNA; Reinsch, *An American Diplomat,* 363–67; Reinsch Statement to the Associated Press, 8 October 1919, Reinsch Papers.

44. Reinsch to Lansing, 24 July 1919, Reinsch Papers; Reinsch to Wilson, 5 September 1919, *ibid.*

45. Long to Reinsch, 23 May 1919, Reinsch Papers; Long to Lansing, 5 August 1919, 123.R271/105, DSNA; Wilson to Lansing, 4 August 1919, Long Papers; copy of extract from letter of the President, n.d. August 1919, *ibid.*; Long to Wilson, 12 August 1919, *ibid.*; Long Diary, 1 September 1919, *ibid.*

46. Huston to Reinsch, 20 August 1919, Reinsch Papers; Baker to Reinsch, 4 September 1919, *ibid.*; F. C. Tong to Reinsch, 19 September 1919, *ibid.*; Oudin to Reinsch, 19 September 1919, *ibid.*; clippings, *Peking & Tientsin Times,* 19 August 1919, *China Press,* 21 August 1919, *ibid.*

47. Interview, Reinsch and Hsu, 21 August 1919, 893.00/3237, DSNA; interview, Reinsch and Tuan, 29 August 1919, Reinsch Papers; Reinsch to Lansing, 31 July 1919, 893.51/2343, 16 August 1919, 893.51/2369, 6 September 1919, 893.51/2407, 10 September 1919, 893.51/2415, DSNA; Wallace to Lansing, 7 August 1919, 893.51/2360, DSNA; Lansing to Davis, Wallace, and Marshall, 27 August 1919, 893.51/2386b, DSNA; Lloyd G. Fulton, "Japanese-American Relations, 1918–1922: Attempts to Nail Down the Swinging Open Door" (Ph.D. dissertation, Michigan State University, 1975), 183–90.

48. "Notes Taken at the Meeting of the Staff of the American Legation," 11 September 1919, RG 84, Peking Post file, 800, NA; Reinsch to Lansing, 15 September 1919, 893.51/2433, DSNA.

Chapter XIII

CHINA'S
ADVOCATE

Reinsch's time was running out, but he had no intention of relying upon others to realize his dreams. "When I return to the United States," Reinsch informed Long before his resignation, "I expect to devote the rest of my life to developing the relations between China and our country." Reinsch's problem was to find a position which would enable him to carry on his life's work and, at the same time, would give him sufficient income to support his family and provide for it after his death. Before leaving Peking, therefore, Reinsch obtained a three-year appointment as adviser to the Chinese government at an annual salary of $20,000. He also accepted Davies's offer to join his law firm and, in October 1919, Reinsch moved his family to Washington, D.C. Reinsch's exact relationship with the firm of Davies & Jones in unclear. Davies probably arranged the association as a convenience for his friend. It placed Reinsch in a strategic location so that he could reach America's political and business leaders. It gave him an office, an address, from which he could pursue his own literary, speaking, lobbying, and business activities. Reinsch offered legal and consulting services to businessmen interested in China, he handled appeal cases from the United States Court for China, and he represented Pacific Coast shipping interests and later the Far Eastern Republic. But his primary client, officially and unofficially, was China.[1]

Reinsch assumed the title of counselor to the Chinese government in preferance to the broader title of general adviser. In fact, Reinsch advised Peking on a whole range of matters—legal, political, and economic. An editorial in the *Washington Herald* aptly captured Reinsch's role:

China was far-sighted when she made Dr. Paul S. Reinsch her special adviser. . . . You see him going about his new work here in Washington with an air of serious ardor that bodes ill for the Japanese or any other enemies of the fundamental rights of a people that he has come to admire and believe in. His touch is here today, there tomorrow; first it is the Shipping Board that succumbs to his plea for increased facilities in transportation between the Pacific ports of the two republics; then it is a conference with the expert propagandists for China's cause. Next it may be a call on the State Department to let in light on a new phase of the conflict in the Far East, from his new employer's standpoint. Always it is the man-on-the-job, earning his large salary, to be sure, but more than that. It is a republican at work for a republic to save it from the "penetration" and exploitation of an ambitious monarchy.[2]

Reinsch soon discovered, however, that the appointment gave him neither the rewards nor the satisfaction that it promised. Publicly and privately, Reinsch was severely criticized because he had used his position as United States minister to get the job. Reinsch waged a frustrating and often fruitless battle to collect his salary from the bankrupt government in Peking and embarrassingly had to call upon the help of his Chinese and American friends. "I never thought that I should have to worry about this thing," he complained to Roy Anderson. He was also upset because he was treated like all the other foreign advisers; he was a "mere ornament" whose advice was generally ignored. Finally, no matter how hard he labored to generate public support for China's cause and business interest in Chinese investments, his efforts were vitiated by China's ongoing political turmoil. First Chang Tso-lin and the Chihli faction drove Tuan and the Anfu clique from power in the summer of 1920; the next year, Tuan Ch'i-jui and Chang joined forces and installed Liang Shih-yi as premier; in 1922, however, Wu P'ei-fu and a coalition of warlords seized power in Peking. This game of political musical chairs, which was played in Canton as well as Peking, subjected China to continuous instability as well as foreign ridicule and danger. Meanwhile, the Peking government teetered on the brink of financial bankruptcy and, failing to obtain money from the Consortium, it defaulted on several foreign loans.[3]

In the hope of influencing the direction of political affairs, Reinsch submitted a "Memorandum on the Chinese Political Situation," during his visit to China in the summer of 1920. Reinsch argued that the

Chinese people would no longer be satisfied with grand promises of reconstruction and reform. The leaders of China could restore national unity and gain the moral and financial support of the Chinese masses only when they instituted regular, honest constitutional government. "No force can stop the development of popular government in the present age," he warned.

Reinsch then proposed the convocation of a great constitutional convention and the prompt election of a Parliament, with representation based on the commerical, industrial, and educational organizations as well as the provincial assemblies. He also called for a federal system. Reinsch assigned to the central government responsibility for foreign affairs, defense, coinage, communications, and justice. But the provinces would retain considerable autonomy and would be free to adapt their administrative systems to local needs and traditions.

Recalling the evils produced by Yuan and Tuan, Reinsch also took issue with those foreigners who continued to prescribe a strong man to cure China's political malaise. Instead he emphasized the need for disinterested expert administrators and financial reform; careful supervision of expenditures, a just and productive tax system, and added cooperation between the government and the bankers would advance Chinese independence and development. Reinsch also stressed the importance of protecting China's credit through the prompt payment of all foreign loans.[4]

Now that he no longer represented the United States government, Reinsch offered forthright advice which reflected his progressive background and his view of China's experience. But his suggestions were ignored or forgotten by the men who controlled the seat of government. Increasingly, Reinsch looked for encouragement from educational and business leaders and the provinces. "If only the good people could unite," he lamented to Alfred Sze, the Chinse minister to Washington, "China would be very strong indeed."[5] Left to his own devices, Reinsch bent most of his energies toward creating a favorable image of China. This is probably what the Peking officials expected of the well-known and respected former minister and Far Eastern expert. He was their high priced publicist, or propagandist.

Reinsch's writings and lectures, now largely polemical, emphasized three themes. First, Reinsch scored Japan's imperialism in China. He maintained that Japan could obtain needed raw materials and markets without seeking political power or special preferences. An Open Door, combined with its geographical proximity, would give Japan an advantage over other powers in East Asia. Indeed, if Japan would terrace its hillsides instead of burdening its people with war fleets, and would industrialize its economy like England and Holland, it could feed its population and become the prosperous workshop of Asia. Furthermore, by playing its "trump card"—making a liberal settlement on Shantung —Japan could influence China and also remove from mankind the terrible threat of war. Reinsch, however, was not optimistic that the Japanese would adopt such an enlightened policy by themselves. He believed that the Japanese military controlled the government and sought imperial dominion under the guise of the "peace of the Far East" or an Asian Monroe Doctrine. "I cannot escape the conclusion," he told the *New York Times*, "that the activities of Japan on the continent aim at a political control of the resources and population of the continent as far as it is possible, and that there is nothing that can turn that aside except the stone wall of resistance."[6]

Second, Reinsch attempted to present a positive picture of developments in China. He argued that the Chinese economy was sound and that Chinese society was bursting with energy. "Wherever one goes in China," Reinsch wrote in 1922, "one finds a spirit of planning and curiosity for the new. Wherever three or four men meet together they discuss plans and proposals for enterpises—industrial and educational. . . . Everything is in germination." The Chinese people wanted peace and reunion and were struggling to rid themselves of the incubus of the warlords. Nor did the political charade in Peking and Canton really make a difference. "In any other country it would seem that under such conditions, everything was going to pieces. But in China," he observed to San Franscisco businessman Hanford E. Finney, "the industrial and commercial life of the people goes on independently of politics." Reinsch had much more difficulty explaining the Chinese government's default on the loans of the Chicago bank and the Pacific Development Corporation. Nonetheless, he wrote in his syndicated column in November 1921: "China will meet her obligations. They are a light burden, infinitely light, compared with those of other nations. What the Chinese people desire is that these should not be made the starting point for involving them in commitments that will stand in the way of a free development of their new national life."

Reinsch stressed the importance of taking the long-range view. He predicted that China would become the predominant factor in the Far East. Consequently, the United States could not be indifferent to China's political, economic, and ideological development. "We are indeed blind if we do not realize that the fate and future of China, that great continental nation, are inextricably bound with our own," he declared in Hon-

olulu on his return to the United States in 1919. Moreover, Reinsch still
envisioned a great partnership between the two great Pacific powers of
the future. "China will soon be called the Asiatic United States," he told
a gathering honoring the Chinese delegation to the Washington Conference (1921–1922). "She has the same continental outlook. She is new in
resources, though old in civilization; young in politics, though matured
in social experience. She comes from a different stock but she seeks the
same aims as we have."[7]

Finally, Reinsch dwelt on the role of the United States in Far Eastern affairs. He asked Americans to be patient and indulgent as China
worked out its internal problems. He invariably appealed for large loans
to disband Chinese armies and major investments for railway construction and other public works. Then he called upon the United States to
use its influence to bring about a just settlement of the Shantung question. That issue, he argued, threatened the revival of spheres of influence
in China and might thrust the world into a major war. In addition, the
United States had to prevent any outside interference in China's internal
affairs in order to protect the Open Door and permit China to develop
along peaceful and democratic lines. "We have no better friends in the
world than the Russians and the Chinese," Reinsch stated in a lecture at
the Army War College, "and if the democracies of those two countries
can develop along sound lines, we do not have to worry about the future
ourselves. But if there is injected a foreign political control to organize
the resources and populations of this region in accordance with the policy
of military imperialism, then we shall be, in the future, confronted with
a very different situation, and by adhering to and advancing and supporting the policy of integrity and of equal opportunity in China we are
instinctively working for the protection of our country from a very great
danger."[8]

Reinsch's impact is difficult to measure. The Shantung question
kept the Far Eastern situation before the American public, which remained overwhelmingly sympathetic to China. But the scores of speaking invitations and requests for articles and interviews attest to the fact
that Reinsch was regarded as America's leading Far Eastern expert as well
as China's true friend and able spokesman. Charles McCarthy admitted
to a Japanese friend that Vanderlip had done the Japanese cause "a great
deal of good." But it was too bad, he added, "that you do not have a
representative in this country of the same stuff as Dr. Reinsch." When
the Council on Foreign Relations tendered a luncheon for the Vanderlip
party after its return from the Orient, Reinsch was invited to present the
Chinese side. It was unfortunate that Reinsch could not attend, Fred

Rogers lamented to MacMurray, for "he could not have well let go by unanswered the remarks of Mr. Schurman and Mr. Taft, and certainly would have been able to have shown a more hopeful side for China."[9]

Meanwhile, Reinsch tried to sell China to American business interests. "I believe we are on the right track," he wrote Edward Bruce, the head of the Pacific Development Corporation. "If people can be set to work in specific things in which they are interested—like commerce, education, art—something can be accomplished." Working closely with Hsu Un-yuen, the former president of the Bank of China, Reinsch managed to preserve the valuable security of the tobacco and wine taxes in "the hands of investors friendly to China." At the last minute, the Pacific Development Corporation took over the Chicago bank's option and loaned China $5 million.[10]

Reinsch also had limited success in obtaining ships for the Pacific trade. Upon his return to the United States in 1919, Reinsch promised reporters and businessmen in Honolulu and San Francisco that he intended to do something to relieve the shortage of shipping on the Pacific. The United States had to build up its merchant fleet if it was to "meet trade competition from Europe in the Orient on an equal footing." The immediate assignment of fast cargo vessels with large carrying capacity to the Pacific, he argued, was the "most outstanding need of our national commerce." Reinsch was therefore retained by Pacific Coast interests to represent them before the Shipping Board.[11]

Reinsch appeared before Judge Barton Payne of the Shipping Board on December 3, 1919, and called for fortnightly passenger service from Pacific Coast ports to the Orient and the assignment of fast passenger-freight vessels covering three routes. Reinsch and Pacific Coast shippers seemed to suffer a setback when Judge Payne declared that the Shipping Board's first task lay in the extension of trade to South America. But Reinsch persisted. After conferring with Judge Payne on December 19, Reinsch won an agreement to assign to Pacific routes several 535-foot, 17-knot vessels then under construction. Pacific Coast businessmen were delighted with Reinsch's work and continued to seek his advice.[12]

Reinsch's repeated efforts to organize a Sino-American bank also bore fruit. During the winter and spring of 1919, Reinsch worked with a broad group of Chinese capitalists, headed by Hsu Un-yuen. Reinsch tried to interest IBC, National City, the Asia Banking Corporation, and several other major institutions, but they declined to participate in the joint venture. In the end, Reinsch and Edward Bruce succeeded in forming an American group composed of the Pacific Development Corporation, Chase National Bank, and Hayden, Stone. However, many problems attended the final arrangements for the Chinese-American bank. A Japanese-controlled newspaper tried to frighten away American investors by declaring that the bank was "full of officialdom." After a long struggle, during which Reinsch hurt the feelings of the Chinese partners, it was agreed that the Americans would retain managing control of the bank.[13]

The bank opened its doors in Peking on February 6, 1920, under the name of the Commercial and Industrial Bank. It was pronounced an immediate success. The bank attracted large amounts of deposits and soon opened branches in other major cities. But the Chinese were slow in adopting American methods and often ignored the American manager. "Today we have dual management," T. W. Overlach complained to Reinsch, "and dual management means ultimate disaster."[14]

During the following years, Reinsch maintained close interest in the bank. But he felt there was a need for another Sino-American bank, especially since the Commercial and Industrial Bank confined itself largely to commercial and exchange business. In the summer of 1920, therefore, Reinsch signed an agreement with a Chinese syndicate led by Chou Tzu-ch'i and Li Sum-ling to organize the Pacific Commercial Bank, which was to devote itself to commercial and industrial business in central and southern China. Reinsch's senatorial campaign and the depression of 1920–1922 interfered with the attempt to find American partners. Once the Chinese share was subscribed Chou became impatient and asked Reinsch not to fail "our friends' confidence." Reinsch and Li tried to avoid Wall Street and concentrated their efforts on Midwestern banks. Then, at the end of February 1921, a Boston capitalist, John Fahey, signed the articles of incorporation and a preliminary agreement, with the understanding that the American syndicate would not be required to raise its share of the capital until financial conditions had improved. The Americans, however, never raised their share and apparently lost interest in the project.[15]

Overall, the results of Reinsch's labors were meager. Peking's default on the Pacific Development Corporation loan did not make things easier for him. Undeterred, Reinsch knocked at the doors of American bankers and industrialists. In addition, he continued to endorse the Consortium for the financing of political loans and for some industrial matters. But he still insisted that Americans proceed independently in order to secure the prosperous development of American enterprise in China and avoid a monopolistic situation. "Unless this freedom of action is preserved," he warned Thomas Lamont, "the Consortium would meet with a storm of disapproval."[16]

*   *   *

Reinsch's inability to influence Peking politicians and American businessmen exemplified the failures of his last years of life. Everything seemed to conspire against him. Reinsch's health deteriorated rapidly and the winter of 1921 was particularly hard on him. "I have not been well; in fact, as near a nervous breakdown as I have ever been in my life," he confided to Stanley Hornbeck. "Therefore the continued difficulties in China weigh on me particularly. We can only work and hope."[17] Reinsch was overworked, burdened with responsibilities, and plagued with financial worries. Several bad investments and Peking's failure to pay his salary added to his distress. That, in turn, forced him to work harder through lecturing and writing. Faced with high living expenses in Washington and the need to provide for Alma and the children, Reinsch reluctantly sold some of the art objects he had collected in China and his stock of fine wines which he had left behind in Peking.[18]

Even the writing of his memoirs became a chore. Reinsch apparently never intended to write a memoir or autobiography. But the hoped-for royalties and the desire to propagate his message forced him to undertake the task. Because of his many responsibilities, Reinsch dictated his account of his China experiences in spare moments, drawing heavily on copies of his diplomatic correspondence which he brought back to the United States. But the task took much longer than expected and he was forced to ask his publisher, Doubleday, to extend the deadlines. In order to broaden its appeal, his editors at Doubleday insisted that he personalize his experiences as much as possible and remove lengthy discussions and analyses of the great issues that he enountered in China. Doubleday also forced him to change the title to *An American Diplomat in China* from "Six Years of American Action in China," which he felt aptly expressed the theme of his diplomatic career. Overwhelmed by work and exhaustion, Reinsch finally allowed Doubleday to edit the manuscript, which resulted in several factual errors and the elimination of perhaps half of Reinsch's account.[19]

Reinsch suffered his greatest public embarrassment when he ran unsuccessfully for the Senate in 1920. Opposed to another bid by Joe Davies (who lost to Irvine Lenroot in the 1918 special election) and hoping to avoid a bruising battle at the Wisconsin State Democratic Convention, Charles McCarthy launched a boomlet for Reinsch in the spring of 1920. Reinsch did not encourage McCarthy's effort and it seemed to have fizzled by the time Reinsch left to accompany a congressional summer junket to the Orient. But at the Wisconsin State Democratic Convention, Davies withdrew from the race and in a thrilling speech asked the delegates to endorse Reinsch unanimously.[20]

Reinsch was guiding the congressional party in Manila when Davies's congratulatory cable reached him. Reinsch coolly thanked Davies and made arrangements to return to the United States. But the nomination greatly upset him. Throughout his career, Reinsch had scrupulously avoided partisan politics. He had no desire to enter Wisconsin politics at this difficult time, particularly when Wilson's foreign policy would certainly be a major issue in the campaign. He also realized that the nomination was the work of his friends who were primarily interested in preserving party unity. Friendship and gratitude dictated that he accept the nomination. But he was not an enthusiastic candidate.[21]

Reinsch arrived in Madison on September 23, declaring that he was seeking the Senate seat "in order that I may carry into our national political life the safe and sane progressive legislation for which our state is noted." After taking care of personal matters, Reinsch moved on to Milwaukee for two days, during which he addressed the State Democratic Committee and started to organize his compaign. Reinsch then left for Washington and New York, where he spent the next two weeks conducting Consortium negotiations for the Chinese government. Davies had already rebuked Reinsch for his cavalier attitude toward the Senate race. "I am a great deal concerned by your suggestion that you 'may' go to Wisconsin for the campaign," Davies told his friend. "I certainly hope that you will go and will leave no stone unturned."[22]

By the time Reinsch returned to Wisconsin on October 10, James Thompson had entered the race as an independent candidate, which threatened to deprive Reinsch of the La Follette progressive vote. Nevertheless, Reinsch launched an energetic campaign which took him to almost every corner of the state. As expected, he ran an honest and decent campaign and spoke directly on the issues. He strongly endorsed the League of Nations and denied that Article X would entangle the United States abroad. But he broke with the national Democratic platform when he suggested that League decisions be subject to congressional recall. He also condemned the Shantung decision, but softened his attack on Wilson by pointing out that the peace treaty did not hand over the province to Japan as had been alleged. Obviously uncomfortable with the issue, Reinsch groped for a middle position that would enable him to criticize Wilson without wrecking Democratic party unity.[23]

Claiming that they were more important than the League, Reinsch generally focused on domestic issues. He denounced the Esch-

Cummings Act for its special favors to the railroads and maintained that the higher rates would hurt manufacturers, merchants, and farmers. He opposed the use of the injunction against labor unions and defended the right of collective bargaining. He called for greater decentralization of the banking system and expanded credit to farmers and businessmen. Urging prompt development of the depressed northern portion of the state, Reinsch also stressed the need to conserve Wisconsin's forests and natural beauty.[24]

While Reinsch evidently tried to woo the labor, farm, and internationalist vote in Wisconsin, he remained true to his convictions. Reinsch's platform was permeated with idealism and Wisconsin progressivism. In the midst of a campaign speech he expressed the hope that "Wisconsin will always maintain this standard of commonwealth." Reinsch's progressive inclinations, his feeling for justice and human decency, had in fact been intensified by the World War and his experience in China. The achievement of economic democracy was the great problem of "your age," he told the commencement class at the University of Cincinnati before his nomination. "Our whole life must be permeated with that social justice, that regard for men as human beings, which is indeed present in political democracy but which needs to permeate all our economic, industrial, and commerical development before American humanity can reach its fullest growth."[25]

Despite the high level of his campaign, the support of his friends, and the endorsement of the *Milwaukee Journal,* Reinsch suffered a disastrous defeat at the polls. He finished a poor third behind Irvine Lenroot, the regular Republican candidate, and James Thompson. Reinsch had to contend with a national Republican sweep and a weak and demoralized Democratic party in Wisconsin. Still, Reinsch's pride was wounded. More important, his energies were wasted by this unwanted foray into Wisconsin politics.[26]

*   *   *

Discouraged and ill, Reinsch returned to Washington to carry on his work for China, to organize an American syndicate for the Pacific Commercial Bank, and to complete his memoirs. However, President Warren Harding's announcement, on July 11, 1921, that a conference on the limitation of armaments would convene in Washington later that year, gave new purpose to Reinsch's efforts. Reinsch believed that the inclusion of Far Eastern matters on the agenda of the Washington Conference of 1921–1922 would enable statesmen to get at a source of world tension. In addition, China was presented with a unique opportunity to enlist the support of public opinion, to obtain a favorable settlement of the Shantung issue, and to remove some of the unjust restraints on its sovereignty and independence. What the Japanese had obtained through their "sharp practices during the war, the position they had so carefully built up, is swept away, and there is now some chance for equal opportunities and for the rights of China," Reinsch declared to Roy Anderson.[27]

The calling of the conference also raised Reinsch's hopes that he might exert a constructive influence on Chinese policy and play an important role in the deliberations. There is no evidence that his advice was solicited by Peking. Nevertheless, Reinsch sent numerous recommendations to President Hsu and Foreign Minister W. W. Yen. He immediately urged the Chinese government to appoint an able, distinguished, and well-prepared delegation. He also counseled the Chinese to concentrate on those matters which were essential to China's welfare and safety and from which "all other desirable results will then naturally flow." Moreover, the Chinese were justified in suggesting the means by which conflict might be lessened or eliminated in the Far East. In that sense, Reinsch declared, "the case of China is the case of the whole world. Unless the difficulties in China are removed the entire world will suffer."[28]

Then in the first of many memoranda he submitted in the course of the next six months, Reinsch outlined the demands which China could place before the conference. The first category went to the heart of international relations in China. In it, Reinsch called for the safeguarding of China's territorial and administrative integrity, the strengthening of equal opportunity, the elimination of all localized political and economic preferences, the "unification" and "nationalization" of all foreign railroads in return for proper compensation arranged through a Consortium loan, and provision for the eventual return of all foreign concessions and settlements. In other words, Reinsch proposed that the Washington Conference reaffirm the Hay Open Door notes, but without any reference to the "so-called spheres of influence." Twenty years earlier, because of China's weakness and the immaturity of America's overseas economic system, American policy makers had recognized the reality of the spheres of influence. During his six years as minister to China, Reinsch had attempted to neutralize the spheres of influence through the extension of American economic power. Now the Washington Conference offered the opportunity to abolish altogether the spheres of influence and to achieve the objectives of the Open Door policy. "As long as claims for special preferences are actually given diplomatic sanction the principle of the open door is to that extent rendered an empty formula," he told the Chinese delegation to the Washington Conference.[29]

In a second category, Reinsch proposed ways in which China might strengthen itself and vindicate its sovereign rights. The powers must grant China financial independence by increasing the import duty to 10 percent, as a first step toward complete tariff autonomy, and by subjecting foreign residents to certain national and local taxes. "The Chinese government," he insisted, "must have the means of supporting itself and fulfilling the functions of modern government in education and internal improvements. The lack of resources keeps it weak and is a source of loss and danger for all." In addition, the conference must remove foreign post offices in China and suppress the opium traffic. In essence, the powers must accept China's right to work out its own destiny even if it made mistakes. On the other hand, Reinsch advised the Chinese not to press for the abolition of extraterritoriality until the government could guarantee the protection of foreign life and property. When China soundly established "the basis of sovereignty itself," he argued, "the abolition of extraterritoriality will only be a question of time."[30]

For Reinsch, a just settlement of the Shantung question became the touchstone of the conference's ability to bring peace and stability to the Far East. If the powers allowed Japan to retain control of the Tsingtao—Tsinan railway, they would undermine Chinese sovereignty and development. They would also strengthen the spheres of influence and imperil equal opportunity. "Every American merchant in China appreciates that if a trunk line in the interior of China is held by a foreign government, American commerce there, hitherto enjoying an entire equality, will be in the same position as American commerce has been in Manchuria. . . ," Reinsch responded in an interview for the *Philadelphia Public Ledger*. Afraid that China would succumb to Japanese pressure for direct negotiations on Shantung, Reinsch insisted that Peking stand firm. "American opinion is that advantage can now be gained for China by utilizing Shantung proposal of Japan, being careful not to make a comitment [*sic*] but making the world understand that no essential concessions have been offered by Japan and that the railway matter is fundamental," he wrote in a cable, dated September 20, 1921, intended for the Chinese president, premier, and foreign minister.[31]

For a while, Reinsch was his old self. He enthusiastically and energetically carried his case to the Peking government, United States officials, and the American public. His analysis of the situation and his proposals showed flashes of brilliance. But it was all in vain. The Peking government was in disarray and the Foreign Ministry probably never bothered to read his memoranda. Reinsch had no formal connection or any influence with the Chinese delegation to the Washington Conference, which often ignored instructions from Peking and which had its own team of American advisers. In fact, when Sze learned of Reinsch's intended cable of September 20, he asked the State Department to urge him to be more conciliatory. The State Department was already irritated by the inflammatory propaganda issued by the unofficial foreign advisers and friends of China, of which Reinsch was but one. MacMurray therefore called in Reinsch for a long talk and persuaded him to modify his advice to Peking.

Subsequently, the Nine Power Treaty renounced the spheres of influence and exclusive preferences and the separate Sino-Japanese treaty on Shantung produced a settlement that was quite favorable to China. However, in his last major performance, Reinsch was confined to the wings, and he had virtually no effect on the drama that was played in Washington.[32]

*   *   *

With the Washington Conference behind him, Reinsch made plans to go to China during the summer of 1922. Alma wanted to visit family and friends in Germany, and Paul arranged to meet her in Europe. Accompanied by S. Gale Lowrie, a former student at Wisconsin and professor of political science at the University of Cincinnati, and Dr. Henry J. Furber, a retired Chicago attorney, Reinsch sailed from Vancouver in July 1922. Reinsch's primary aim was to collect his unpaid salary and to renegotiate his contract with the Chinese government. Privately, Reinsch hoped to rescue China from its financial distress. He therefore stated publicly that he would assist the Koo Commission, which had recently been established to recommend ways of rehabilitating Chinese finance. However, Chinese officials denied to Jacob Gould Schurman, the United States minister, that Reinsch had been invited to help the Koo Commission or that he had any connection with the Ministry of Finance. Consortium representatives in Peking suspected that Reinsch was really trying to arrange an unsecured loan for the bankrupt Chinese government.[33]

Shortly after arriving in Peking, Reinsch was forced to enter a hospital for treatment of his left eye. Two weeks later he was released and he delved into a round of activity. Reinsch addressed several audiences, conferred with government officials and Chinese friends, and investigated investment opportunities for American businessmen.[34]

Above all, Reinsch attempted to raise what he called a constitution interim loan. He declared that foreign bankers would lend the Chinese government $2 million a month, for at least ten months, without any security, to assist China during the transition to constitutional government. Such a loan, he argued, would bring down the warlord system and set China on its feet. In repeated conversations with representatives of the Consortium and with Schurman, Reinsch tried to convince them of the soundness of his proposal and to obtain their backing. But his approaches were strongly rejected. The Consortium representatives worried that Reinsch would create the impression that his proposal had merit and support, misleading Peking officials into expecting an immediate loan. The Peking manager of IBC thought that Reinsch was acting irresponsibly, especially since he had criticized Peking's reckless borrowing, and he doubted if the former minister believed the absurd "piffle" which he was disseminating. Schurman refused Reinsch's numerous requests to communicate directly with Secretary of State Charles Hughes in the legation's code. Claiming that Hughes had asked his views on the subject, Reinsch reportedly threatened Schurman with an official reprimand. But Schurman held firm and did not cable Reinsch's message. For Reinsch, it was a final, desperate, and futile effort to help China. Reinsch was at the end of his rope and he was clearly losing touch with reality.[35]

After collecting part of his salary, Reinsch renewed his contract with the Chinese government on September 28, 1922, for another three years on the same terms. Although he was quite sick, Reinsch then left Peking for a tour of the south. On October 10, 1922, as he boarded a train bound for Hankow, Reinsch suffered a mental breakdown: he had hallucinations that the Japanese had marked him for assassination and he became violent. A physician aboard the train diagnosed his case as "delusional dementia," and declared him unfit to travel. Reinsch was taken to the Hankow International Hospital and, after his condition stabilized, he was moved to Shanghai. There his doctors discovered a brain tumor. On January 22, 1923, they reported that Reinsch had contracted encephalitis and pneumonia. The end came quickly. On January 26, 1923, Paul Samuel Reinsch died at the age of fifty-three.[36]

*   *   *

America had given Paul S. Reinsch a mandate to make the Open Door work. Reinsch eagerly accepted it. Since the late nineteenth century, the United States had looked to the markets of China to solve its economic, political, and social problems. Reinsch matured intellectually during the 1890s, the crucial decade of modern American expansion. While he differed slightly on matters of detail, emphasis, and tactics, Reinsch shared the basic assumptions of Open Door expansion and the policies of America's leaders. Indeed, much of his writing and teaching during the years of his successful and productive academic career was devoted to explaining, publicizing, developing, and systematizing the ideas of American policy makers, notably John Hay and Elihu Root.

However, from the time he began his studies in the 1890s to his appointment as minister to China in 1913, Reinsch's views concerning the Open Door policy underwent two major changes which reflected the transformation of international politics in the Far East. First of all, he rejected the old notion that the foreign spheres of influence were compatible with the Open Door; now he insisted that they must be destroyed, or at least replaced by one big American-dominated sphere encompassing virtually all of China, in order to sustain equal opportunity and China's independence. Second, he eliminated Japan as the protector of the Open Door and as the model for Chinese modernization; instead, he argued that the United States (perhaps in combination with Great Britain) must serve as the guarantor of China's integrity and peace in East Asia, and he looked to America to foster and shape China's development.

Having secured the diplomatic position which he had pursued for over ten years, Reinsch prepared and launched a hard-headed program to realize the objectives of and concrete benefits from the Open Door policy. He cultivated the Chinese and won valuable concessions from them; he defended American rights and Chinese integrity against the foreign powers as well as against the corrupt and conniving Chinese politicians and *tuchuns*; he tried to neutralize the spheres of influence, and when that failed he fought to eliminate them completely through a revised declaration or understanding on the Open Door; and he showed Americans what was needed to rationalize overseas enterprise and mobilize American economic power and good will. Initially, Reinsch relied on independent American action to make the Open Door effective; however, circumstances forced him to accept a combination of international cooperation, expressed in the Second Chinese Consortium, and independent American activity. But Japanese-American cooperation, he argued, would be self-defeating.

As befitted a United States diplomat, Reinsch always thought first in terms of advancing American interests. Nevertheless, he often operated on the premise that American interests coincided with those of China and he believed in the viability of a great Sino-American partnership. And yet Reinsch did not live in an ivory tower—no more than did the politicians and business leaders who governed the United States and who frequently equated American interests with the good of the world.

As minister, Reinsch was a man of action; he was one of the most dynamic representatives the United States ever sent to China. He was pragmatic, flexible, bold, and resourceful. Reinsch learned very quickly how things operated in China and he acted accordingly, within certain limits set by his ethical system. He accepted the role of self-interest and the need to harness it for higher goals. He was willing to compromise— to give Japan predominance in Manchuria and to furnish loans and capital to Britain and France—but he wanted a *quid pro quo* in return. America had bargaining power and leverage, and he expected Americans to use it in order to protect America's long-range interests. Finally, he predicted correctly that if the United States confined itself to the rhetoric of the Open Door, without giving it economic, political, diplomatic, and even military substance, America would lose China's good will and would be forced to fight another and more terrible world war.

Reinsch needed help to attain his objectives. He placed his faith in corporate titans as well as in shady promoters, Chinese officials and the Cantonese clique mandarins, British diplomats, businessmen anxious to protect their stake in East Asia, and American leaders, particularly President Woodrow Wilson. All of them disappointed him. That was a great shock to Reinsch, for he believed that men generally kept their word and acted in the national interest. But since Reinsch was so committed to the American system and his personal image of China, he could not cast most of the blame for his failures on either American businessmen or the Chinese themselves. Instead, he made a small corrupt gang of Peking politicians and warlords and, especially, Japan the source of all his problems. Japan became the incarnation of all that was evil in the world. During the last, sad years of his life, Reinsch became so obsessed with the Japanese menace that he believed that his enemies sought to assassinate him. Reinsch's early death spared him from witnessing further Chinese disintegration and Japanese aggression. It also prevented him from seeing the vast overseas empire developed by the United States, though it would be in Canada, South America, Europe, and the Mediterranean— not China.

To some extent, Reinsch had unrealistic expectations; sometimes, he was also naive and ignorant of Chinese affairs. The United States had other priorities and commitments, and its resources were not unlimited. Although they were indeed timid, narrow-minded, and inexperienced in Asian affairs, American business leaders had sufficient objective grounds for refusing to invest in China. The Anglo-Japanese Alliance was certainly abused by Tokyo, but Britain needed it as long as it faced a life and death struggle in Europe. The Chinese were entering a period of real revolution and they did not share Reinsch's vision of China's future or his dream of a Sino-American partnership. For the most part, the Chinese officials with whom Reinsch dealt sought to advance their own interests and to destroy the entire imperialistic structure imposed on China. Although Japan's policies were expansionist, opportunistic, and self-serving, its power in East Asia was a fact; Japan—not America—was geographically and culturally close to China. Therefore, even had Reinsch succeeded in diverting that small rivulet of American capital to China, it is highly doubtful if it would have made any difference. Above all, Reinsch mistakenly believed that his conception of the Open Door, which would solve America's problems, would also serve the interests of the other nations of the world.

Still, it would be misleading to emphasize these personal weaknesses. Reinsch was very much a product of his age and he was limited by his experiences and assumptions. He also shared the idealism that was common among his American contemporaries. He believed in the importance and influence of ideas in transforming mankind and his world; he assumed that truth, justice, morality, and beauty were the foundations of the universe; he taught that man had to strive unceasingly toward higher goals and ideals. Reinsch had a vision of a better world in which prosperity, progress, and peace overcame poverty, backwardness, and conflict. Moreover, as a progressive, Reinsch's optimism about the modern age led him to underestimate the cost and time necessary to transform China and to exaggerate the benevolence and power of American capital, technology, and expertise.

Moreover, developments during his years in China placed Reinsch in an impossible situation. Reinsch's program contained elements that were sound and reasonable. But everything seemed to conspire against it: Yuan's monarchical ambitions and the interminable internal strife; the European war and the shattering of the balance of power in East Asia; the competition among American bankers and their distrust of the Wilson administration; the Lansing-Ishii Agreement and Wilsonian diplomacy at the Paris Peace Conference.

The Open Door was not a total failure until the late 1930s. But had America determined its Chinese policy earlier—how much of that fabled market it could really expect to obtain and how much effort it was willing to make—it might have saved Reinsch some of the anguish and exhaustion which affected his mind and eventually shortened his life. Reinsch himself often wondered if American leaders were merely paying lip service to the Hay doctrine in China. Frustrated and angered by the lack of concrete American assistance, Reinsch repeatedly questioned the intent of Washington policy makers and New York financiers. More than once, American leaders had the option of withdrawing from China and abandoning the Open Door in the Far East. But they never seriously considered that possibility, nor did they undertake a serious reexamination of the assumptions which had underlaid American policy since the late nineteenth century. Some suggested adopting alternate tactics—Japanese-American cooperation, for example—while they continued to maintain their desire for friendship with the Chinese and for economic, political, and moral influence in China.

It was a bitter twist for a tragic career—that of a man who had hoped to be an envoy of peace, understanding, and progress. On the day of Reinsch's death, John V. A. MacMurray paid a personal tribute to his former chief. "He was a great minister," he wrote to Alma Reinsch, "who gave brilliant and inspiring service to our country under circumstances that might have discouraged and daunted a less devoted and resolute man."[37] It was a sincere and fitting appraisal of a man who had dreamed noble dreams and who had fought throughout his life to realize them.

NOTES TO
CHAPTER XIII

1. Reinsch to Long, 22 April 1919, Reinsch Papers; Reinsch to Tumulty, 14 July 1921, *ibid.*; Lansing Desk Diary, 27 October 1919, Lansing Papers; Hawkins Tapes, 9; Hawkins to author, 27 January 1967. Reinsch's contract with the Chinese government was dated 13 September 1919. See 893.018/561½, DSNA.

2. Clipping, *Washington Herald,* 24 December 1919, Reinsch Papers.

3. Williams Diary, 12 October 1921, Williams Papers; Ruddock to Long, 21 May 1921, Long Papers; clipping, Bureau of Public Information, 25 March 1920, Reinsch Papers; Reinsch to Hsu Un-yuen, 7 September 1921, *ibid.*; Reinsch to Y. C. Tsur, 21 October 1921, *ibid.*; Reinsch to Anderson, 29 December 1921; *ibid.*; Reinsch, "The Consortium and Chinese Finance," address before the Chinese Political and Social Science Association, 2 October 1922, *ibid.*; Clubb, *20th Century China,* 100–7.

4. "Dr. Reinsch's Memorandum," *Peking & Tientsin Times,* 28 August 1920, Reinsch Papers; Reinsch, "Financial Independence of China," 15 September 1922, *ibid.*; Reinsch, "The Consortium and Chinese Finance," *ibid.*; Reinsch to Chou Tzu-ch'i, 12 February 1920, *ibid.*

5. Reinsch to Sze, 21 December 1920, *ibid.*; Reinsch to Hornbeck, 4 February 1921, *ibid.*

6. *San Francisco Chronicle,* 10 and 12 October 1919; *Seattle Post-Intelligencer,* 17 October 1921; *New York Times,* 14 October 1921; Reinsch, "America and the Far East," lecture delivered at the Army War College, 30 September 1921, Hornbeck Papers; Reinsch, "Japanese War-Fleets or Terraced Gardens—Which?" Reinsch Papers; Reinsch, "Manchuria, Mongolia and Siberia," *Nation,* CXIV (3 May 1922), 523–25.

7. Reinsch, "The Far East as a Factor in International Developments," 221–23; Reinsch, "The Attitude of the Chinese towards Americans," 7–13; Reinsch, "Vital Forces in China Today," *Current History,* XVI (September 1921), 934–36; Reinsch, "Chinese Humanism and Ethics," address delivered before the New York Society of Ethical Culture, January 1922, Reinsch Papers; Reinsch to Hanford Finney, 18 April 1921, *ibid.*; extract from Reinsch address at a dinner for the Chinese Delegation to the Washington Conference, 14 December 1921, *ibid.*; interview with Reinsch, *Christian Science Monitor,* 31 May 1920, *ibid.*; clipping, *Pacific Commercial Advertiser,* 2 October 1919, *ibid.; New York Times,* 10 May 1920, 21 November 1921; *San Francisco Chronicle,* 11 and 18 October 1919; *Seattle Post-Intelligencer,* 14 November 1921.

8. Interview with Reinsch, *New York World,* 14 March 1920, Reinsch Papers; interview with Reinsch, *Christian Science Monitor,* 14 December 1921, *ibid.*; Reinsch, "America and the Far East," Hornbeck Papers.

9. See correspondence and clippings in Reinsch Papers for Reinsch's speaking and writing activities. McCarthy to Shibata, 6 July 1920, McCarthy Papers; Report on luncheon given by the Council on Foreign Relations, 14 July 1920, in Rogers to MacMurray, 10 August 1920, MacMurray Papers; Wilbur Morse to Reinsch, 25 July 1920, Reinsch Papers.

10. Notes taken at the meeting of the staff of the American Legation, 11 September 1919, RG 84, Peking Post file, 800, NA; Reinsch to Bruce, 3 January 1921, Reinsch Papers; Hsu Un-yuen to Reinsch, 9 February 1920, *ibid.*

11. Clippings, *Honolulu Star Bulletin,* 1 October 1919, *Seattle Times,* 3 December 1919, Reinsch Papers; Reinsch, "Pacific Trade and the Merchant Marine," *San Francisco Bulletin,* 1920, *ibid.*; Robert Davies to Reinsch, 25 November 1919, *ibid.*; Lynch to Reinsch, 14 April 1920, *ibid.*

12. Reinsch to Lynch, 27 December 1919, Reinsch Papers; Payne to Reinsch, 10 December 1919, *ibid.*; Lynch to Reinsch, 14 April 1920, *ibid.*; Reinsch, "Pacific Trade and the Merchant Marine," *ibid.*; clipping, *San Francisco Chronicle,* 16 January 1920, *ibid.*

13. Reinsch to Lansing, 1 November 1918, 893.516/61, DSNA; Reinsch to Polk, 22 April 1919, 893.516/66, DSNA; Polk to Reinsch, 20 May 1919, 893.516/65a, DSNA; Hsu Un-yuen to C. L. L. Williams, 1 May 1919, RG 84, Peking Post file, 851.6, NA; memo of interview on Chino-American Bank, 19 December 1918, Reinsch Papers; Reinsch to Long, 22 April 1919, *ibid.*; Arnold to Reinsch, 3 May 1919, *ibid.*; Reinsch to Wiggin, 9 May 1919, *ibid.*; Reinsch to Bruce, 9 July 1919, *ibid.*; Hsu Un-yuen to Reinsch, 9 February 1920, *ibid.*

14. Hsu Un-yuen to Reinsch, 9 February and 7 June 1920, Reinsch Papers; Thomas to Reinsch, 9 February 1920, *ibid.*; Overlach to Reinsch, 27 April 1921, *ibid.*

15. Memo of Agreement between Chinese Subscribers and Paul S. Reinsch, 29 August 1920, Reinsch Papers; Reinsch to Chou Tzu-ch'i, 9 November 1920, *ibid.*; Chou to Reinsch, 3 November 1920, 4 January 1921, *ibid.*; Reinsch to Harry Merrick, 5 and 29 January 1920, *ibid.*; Merrick to Reinsch, 29 January 1921, *ibid.*; Reinsch to Roger Williams, 9 November 1920, 12 January 1921, *ibid.*; Li Sum-ling to John Fahey, 17 February 1921, *ibid.*; Li Sum-ling to Reinsch, 26 April and 1 May 1921, *ibid.*

16. Reinsch to Stevens, 13 November 1920, 8 March 1921, *ibid.*; Reinsch to Lamont, 8 October 1920, *ibid.*; Reinsch, "The Far East as a Factor in International Developments," 226.

17. Reinsch to Hornbeck, 4 February 1921, Reinsch Papers; Li Sum-ling to Fahey, 17 February 1921, *ibid.*

18. Hawkins Tapes, 6, 9; Hawkins to author, 8 December 1964; Willing Spencer to Reinsch, 26 January 1920, Reinsch Papers; Reinsch to Thomas Brady, 10 February 1921, *ibid.*; Reinsch to William B. Feakins, 24 March 1922, *ibid.*

19. Reinsch to Hornbeck, 17 May 1921, Reinsch Papers; Reinsch to Stone, 4 October 1920, n.d. [October 1920], 14 February 1921, *ibid.*; Hawkins Tapes, 3; Reinsch, "Six Years of American Action in China," Reinsch Papers.

20. McCarthy to Reinsch, 13 March 1920, Reinsch Papers, 20 April 1920, McCarthy Papers; McCarthy to Louis Wehle, 6 May 1920, *ibid.*; clipping, *Milwaukee Sentinel*, 28 February 1920, Reinsch Papers; *Milwaukee Journal,* 31 March and 22 July 1920.

21. Crane to Reinsch, 25 July 1920, Reinsch Papers; Reinsch to Davies, 4 August 1920, *ibid.*; Hawkins Tapes, 7.

22. *Milwaukee Journal*, 24 September and 12 October 1920; Davies to Reinsch, 11 and 24 September 1920, Reinsch Papers.

23. *Milwaukee Journal,* 26 September and 20, 23 and 29 October 1920.

24. *Ibid.*; 26 September, 15, 20, and 24 October and 2 November 1920.

25. *Ibid.*, 18 September and 20 October 1920; "Regeneration," Reinsch Commencement Address to the Class of 1920, University of Cincinnati, Reinsch Papers.

26. *Milwaukee Journal,* 3, 4, and 5 November 1920; Herbert Margulies, *The Decline of the Progressive Movement in Wisconsin, 1890–1920* (Madison, 1968), 275–80.

27. Reinsch to Hsu Shih-ch'ang, 13 July 1921, Reinsch Papers; Reinsch to Anderson, 14 July 1921, *ibid.*; interview with Reinsch, *New York Times,* 2 October 1921.

28. Reinsch to Hsu, 13 July 1921, Reinsch Papers; Reinsch to W. W. Yen, 12 July 1921, *ibid.*; cable, Reinsch to Yeh Kung-chow, August 1921, *ibid.*; Reinsch memoranda, #1, "General Considerations," #2, "Foreign Finance in China," #3, "Spheres of Influence," *ibid.*

29. *Ibid.*; Reinsch memo, #4, "Commentary on the Ten Points Presented by the Chinese Delegation," Reinsch Papers.

30. Reinsch to Yen, 12 July 1921, Reinsch Papers; Reinsch to Hsu, 13 July 1921, *ibid.*; Reinsch memo, #1, "General Considerations," *ibid.*

31. Reinsch to Frederick W. Wile, for the *Philadelphia Public Ledger,* 23 May 1921, Reinsch Papers; interview with Reinsch, *New York World,* 14 May 1920, clipping, *ibid.*; Reinsch memo, "Shantung," December 1921, *ibid.*; telegram, Reinsch to president, premier, and minister for foreign affairs, 20 September 1921, *ibid.*; Reinsch, "Japan Is Pressing China To Sign Shantung Pact," *Seattle Post-Intelligencer,* 10 October 1921.

32. "Memorandum on the Attitude of China in the Washington Conference," Lansing Papers; Lamont to Hughes, 9 November 1921, 893.51/3527, DSNA; Williams, "Memorandum for Mr. MacMurray" [September 1921], Williams Papers; MacMurray memo on a conversation with Dr. Paul S. Reinsch, 20 September 1921, 793.94/1289, DSNA; Lamont to Hughes, 9 November 1921, 893.51/3537, DSNA; Koo to author, 21 January 1966; Noel H. Pugach, "American Friendship for China and the Shantung Question of the Washington Conference," *Journal of American History,* LXIV (June 1977), 67–86.

33. Reinsch to Lowrie, 2 January 1922, Reinsch Papers; author's interview with Hawkins, 10 August 1971; Hawkins Tapes, 6, 10; "News and Notes," *American Political Science Review*, XVII (May 1923), 272–73; Schurman to Hughes, 4 August 1922, 893.01A/48, DSNA.

34. Reinsch to Lewis, 2 September 1922, Reinsch Papers; Reinsch to Hornbeck, 8 September 1922, Hornbeck Papers.

35. Reinsch to Wu Pe'i-fu, 2 September 1922, Reinsch Papers; Reinsch, "Financial Independence of China," 15 September 1922, *ibid.*; Reinsch, "The Consortium and Chinese Finance," 2 October 1922, *ibid.*; Schurman to Hughes, 29 September 1922, 893.01A/49½, DSNA; J. P. Morgan & Co. to Hughes, 9 November 1922, and enclosures, 893.51/4040, DSNA.

36. Schurman to Hughes, 11 October 1922, 123.R271/117, DSNA; Cunningham to Hughes, 26 January 1923, 123.R271/123, DSNA; Harold Quigley to Frederick Ogg, 17 November 1922, Frederick Ogg Papers, University of Wisconsin Archives; Hawkins Tapes, 6–7.

37. MacMurray to Alma Reinsch, 26 January 1923, Reinsch Papers

A NOTE
ON SOURCES

The importance of the Paul S. Reinsch Papers (The State Historical Society of Wisconsin, Madison, Wisconsin) for the writing of this study is self-evident. For many years the Reinsch Papers were in the possession of Stanley K. Hornbeck. Hornbeck subsequently gave the papers to Professor Fred Harvey Harrington who, until his appointment as president of the University of Wisconsin, was planning to write a biography of Reinsch. President Harrington then turned over the papers to The State Historical Society of Wisconsin, as desired by the Reinsch family.

The collection reveals Reinsch's manifold activities, his personal ambitions and goals, his role in securing concessions in China, and his method of operation. Although some materials were lost, probably in shipment from China to the United States, the papers are rich in official and private correspondence, memoranda, speeches, and unpublished manuscripts. They also include documents from the files of the American legation in Peking and several volumes of scrapbooks which record Reinsch's activities and major developments in the Far East as well as his academic career.

In the autumn of 1963, Mr. and Mrs. Horatio Bates Hawkins (Reinsch's brother-in-law and sister-in-law) annotated the Reinsch Papers and made sixteen tape recordings. These now form a part of the Reinsch collection. In addition some of Reinsch's papers were mixed in with Hornbeck's papers, which are now deposited at the Hoover Institution of War, Revolution and Peace (Stanford, California). I also obtained information and insights into Reinsch's personality through interviews and correspondence with Hawkins, Hornbeck, V. K. Wellington Koo, and Reinsch's daughter, Claire Reinsch Cadura. See the notes for specific references to correspondence and interviews.

Nevertheless, significant material on the life and career of Paul S. Reinsch may be found elsewhere. And the student of United States Far Eastern policy during the Reinsch period must use other government and private collections.

The Reinsch Papers and Hawkins Tapes are the starting point for a study of Reinsch's early life and career as an academic, scholar, and Wisconsin figure. They should be supplemented by documents in the University of Wisconsin Archives (Memorial Library), including the Records of the University of Wisconsin Regents, the Papers of the University Presidents (Charles Van Hise) and the files of College of Letters and Science

(Dean Edward A. Birge). In addition, there are several relevant collections at The Wisconsin State Historical Society: the Edward A. Birge Papers, the Richard T. Ely Papers, the Robert M. La Follette Papers, and the Charles McCarthy Papers. The Thomas A. Flint Papers (The State Historical Society of Wisconsin) contain the lecture notes of Reinsch taken by one of his students. The John Burgess Papers (Columbia University Library, New York) have Reinsch's report on his tenure as Roosevelt Professor in Germany. The papers of The Carnegie Endowment for International Peace (Columbia University Library) document Reinsch's contributions to the peace movement. On the other hand, the Joseph Davies Papers (Library of Congress, Washington D.C.) disappointingly did not contain any Reinsch material. The Stanley K. Hornbeck Papers provide evidence of Hornbeck's evolving role as Reinsch's student, associate, family friend, and personal confidant, as well as some of Reinsch's classroom material. Reinsch's intellectual and scholarly interests may be traced by reading his extensive works, many of which are cited in the notes of this book. A comprehensive list of Reinsch's publications may be found in the bibliography of my Ph.D. dissertation, "Progress, Prosperity and the Open Door: The Ideas and Career of Paul S. Reinsch (University of Wisconsin, 1967).

Reinsch's ambition for a diplomatic position are clearly indicated in the Reinsch Papers and are discussed by the Hawkinses on their tape recordings. The details of his efforts are documented in other collections, notably the John C. Spooner Papers (Library of Congress), the Robert M. La Follette Papers (at both The State Historical Society of Wisconsin and the Library of Congress), the Charles R. Crane Papers (Institute of Current World Affairs, New York), the Ely Papers, and the University of Wisconsin Archives, especially the Van Hise Papers. In addition, the State Department kept a file on Reinsch from the time he applied for the position as minister to Japan in 1902. See the Paul S. Reinsch file maintained by the Bureau of Appointments (National Archives, Washington, D.C.). The story of Wilson's search for a minister to China may be traced in the papers of Woodrow Wilson, William Jennings Bryan, and Ray Stannard Baker (all at the Library of Congress), Charles Crane and Colonel Edward House, especially the latter's diary (Yale University Library, New Haven, Connecticut).

While the Reinsch Papers are indispensable for an understanding of Reinsch's motives, objectives, and methods, the records of the Department of State are the most important single source of information on Reinsch's diplomatic career in China and the development of United States Far Eastern policy. Reinsch wrote voluminous and lengthy dispatches and telegrams to the State Department on almost every aspect of United States-Chinese relations, Chinese internal developments, and the international situation in the Far East. Many of Reinsch's dispatches and comprehensive reports were never read or were ignored by officials in the State Department. Yet, on the more important topics and incidents, the replies to Reinsch, the internal memoranda and discussions in the State Department, and the exchanges between the White House and secretaries of state Bryan and Lansing supply an important and extensive source of information.

An excellent sample of this material may be found in the valuable and highly regarded printed collection of State Department documents, entitled *Foreign Relations of the United States, 1912–1919*, with supplements (Washington: Government Printing Office, 1919–1934) and the special volumes on *Russia, 1918* (3 vols., Washington: Government Printing Office, 1932), the *Paris Peace Conference* (13 vols., Washington: Government Printing Office, 1942–1947) and the *Lansing Papers 1914–1920* (2 vols., Washington: Government Printing Office, 1939–1940). The *Foreign Relations* series, however, contains only a selection of the diplomatic correspondence and, for the Reinsch period, often omitted the interesting intra- and inter-departmental correspondence. In addition, the editors often printed extracts of very long dispatches and deleted documents marked confidential. The *Foreign Relations* volumes contain many of the contracts negotiated when Reinsch was minister to China. But the magnificent and more comprehensive collection edited by John V. A. MacMurray, *Treaties and Agreements With and Concerning China, 1894–1919* (2 vols., New York: Oxford University Press, 1921) should be used as a supplement.

The serious student of Reinsch's diplomatic career and Wilsonian Far Eastern policy must therefore examine the original State Department decimal files in Record Group 59 (General Records of the Department of State). The most important groups for this work are files 893 (internal affairs of China), 793.94 (relations between China and other states), and 763.72 and 763.72119 (World War I). These files are avilable on microfilm. Still, a visit to the National Archives is necessary to investigate those State Department files in RG 59 which have not and probably never will be filmed. Among the more significant are Reinsch's personnel file (123R.) and those dealing with economic relations between the United States and East Asia (693.).

In addition, there are other files which I found extremely useful and important to this study, many of which are ignored by diplomatic historians. The Peking Post file, in Record Group 84 (Foreign Service Post Records), contains a considerable amount of correspondence between Reinsch and American businessmen and between Reinsch and American, British, and Chinese figures in China. In some cases, copies of this correspondence were sent to Washington and included in RG 59; but a good deal of it remained in the legation's files in Peking until they were eventually transferred to Washington. The activity of representatives of the Department of Commerce became important during Reinsch's tenure. The correspondence between the Commerce Department's agents in the Far East as well as the department's involvement in foreign policy making may be followed in RG 40 (General Records of the Department of Commerce) and, especially, RG 151 (Records of the Bureau of Foreign and Domestic Commerce). Significant information on the Consortium negotiations and loans to China during World War I may be found in RG 39 (Records of the Department of the Treasury, Bureau of Accounts). Finally, there is a collection of Wilson–Bryan correspondence, particularly useful for the Twenty-One Demands, in the National Archives, which has also been microfilmed (microcopy, T-841).

Besides the records of the United States government in the National Archives, a number of private collections of government officials proved to be essential to the writing of this study. Among the more important were the John V. A. MacMurray Papers (Princeton University Library, Princeton, New Jersey). MacMurray's correspondence provides another, often critical, view of Reinsch's conduct and personality as well as information on events in China when Reinsch was absent from Peking. However, MacMurray generally agreed with Reinsch on the principles of American diplomacy in the Far East. The Edward T. Williams Papers (Library at the University of California, Berkeley, California) were helpful for a few incidents in Sino-American relations, but they do not shed much light on Reinsch's diplomacy. The State Department files are a more fruitful source for Williams's ideas and positions on China policy. The papers of Breckinridge Long (Library of Congress) have long been recognized as a major source of information on United States Far Eastern policy, 1917–1919, especially for the China loans and the Consortium negotiations. They include numerous memoranda of conversations with the Chinese and Japanese ministers to the United States as well as his interesting diary which contains candid comments on leading personalities and diplomatic decision-making.

Reinsch's relationship with Wilson and insights into the president's China policy may be derived from the Wilson, Baker, and House papers. Bryan's influence on Far Eastern policy was erratic, but his involvement was at times significant. Nevertheless, the Bryan Letterbooks in the William Jennings Bryan Papers (Library of Congress) proved useful in understanding his role in the Twenty-One Demands. Lansing's role and ideas are best followed in the State Department records, but the Robert Lansing Papers, specifically his desk diary (Library of Congress) should also be consulted. The papers of Colonel Edward House and Frank Polk (Yale University Library) were occasionally useful for this study. Several important items, including some Reinsch letters and corre-spondence dealing with Pacific shipping and the Sino-American steamship company, were found in the William G. McAdoo Papers (Library of Congress). The John Bassett Moore Papers (Library of Congress) contain some material on the Huai River Conservancy project. The Elihu Root Papers (Library of Congress) did not yield anything substantial on Reinsch or on United States Far Eastern policy during the Wilson era.

There are also several relevant collections of papers of private individuals and groups involved in American diplomacy in China. Because they figured so prominently in Reinsch's plans, the papers of Frank A. Vanderlip (Columbia University Library) and Willard Straight (Cornell University Library) are especially important. The Warren Austin Papers (University of Vermont Library, Burlington, Vermont) and the Otto Kahn Papers (Princeton University Library) supply additional background information on AIC's activities, but they were not cited in the notes. The papers of the American Na-tional Red Cross (Archives of the American National Red Cross, Washington, D.C.) are essential for a full understanding of the evolution of the Huai River Conservancy project. The Frank J. Goodnow Papers (The Johns Hopkins Library, Baltimore, Maryland) provide information on political and constitutional developments in China and Yuan's monarchical scheme.

The massive records of the British Foreign Office (Public Record Office, London, England) are a storehouse of information on Far Eastern international politics. I made use of a few selected files for this study of Reinsch, but much more could be gleaned from them. They should be supplemented by the Sir John Jordan Papers (Public Record Office), which contain some references to Reinsch and United States policy. The general impression that one receives from these British records is that the United States occupied a relatively minor role in Chinese affairs and that American leaders were clumsy and ignorant in the game of Far Eastern international politics. British officials often viewed American initiatives with suspicion and disdain and America's potential strength with envy and concern.

For the last years of Reinsch's life, the Reinsch Papers and the Hawkins Tapes again became the primary source of information. The Hornbeck Papers also contain a few revealing items of correspondence. The McCarthy Papers should be consulted for Reinsch's nomination for the Senate in 1920. A letter in the Frederic Ogg Papers (Uni-versity of Wisconsin Archives) describes the state of Reinsch's health shortly before his death.

I found newspaper accounts and editorials frequently helpful in the preparation of this study and I read a number of them for selected topics and time periods. Milwaukee and Madison newspapers, as well as the *Daily Cardinal* (the University of Wisconsin's student newspaper) covered Reinsch's activities during his pre-1913 career. I generally consulted the *New York Times* for major developments in Far Eastern diplomacy during Reinsch's years in China. In some instances, I read *The Times* (London) to compare how the British covered these events. I used the *San Francisco Chronicle* and the *Seattle Post-*

Intelligencer to sample West Coast opionion as well as its interest in Pacific shipping and the China trade. The *Journal of the American Asiatic Association* reported Straight's public statements and the shifts in official American policy in the Far East. Its editorials offered an indication of the thinking of Wall Street–East Coast bankers and businessmen. I followed Reinsch's senatorial campaign in 1920 through the pages of the *Milwaukee Journal* and the *Wisconsin State Journal*.

Just about every historian of Wilsonian Far Eastern policy has referred to Reinsch's published memoir, *An American Diplomat in China* (Garden City: Doubleday Page & Co., 1922). Based largely on copies of the diplomatic correspondence which Reinsch kept in his personal files, it is generally a reliable source of information on Reinsch's objectives and major activities. Because of errors and omissions made by his editor, however, it should be compared to the original and much longer typed manuscript, which may be found in the Reinsch Papers. Nevertheless, the reader of both accounts should be aware that Reinsch sought to justify his actions, some of which were questionable, to exhort Americans to stand firm against Japanese expansion, to paint a reasonably positive picture of China, and to emphasize the future economic and political importance of China to American needs and interests. Several other published memoirs, autobiographies, and diaries have been cited in the notes.

Besides my own study, "Progress, Prosperity and the Open Door: the Ideas and Career of Paul S. Reinsch" (Ph.D. dissertation, University of Wisconsin, 1967), Reinsch has been the subject of two other dissertations. The earliest effort was made by Daniel J. Gage, "Paul S. Reinsch and Sino-American Relations" (Ph.D. dissertation, Stanford University, 1939). It is based almost exclusively on published sources, especially the *Foreign Relations* series, and is marred by a strong pro-Japanese bias. It essentially denigrates Reinsch's program and shows little understanding of his objectives or of American Far Eastern policy.

More recently, Patrick John Scanlan wrote "No Longer a Treaty Port: Paul S. Reinsch and China, 1913–1919" (Ph.D. dissertation, University of Wisconsin, 1973). Scanlan has used the Reinsch Papers and the more important parts of the State Department decimal files, but he has neglected other primary sources on the American side. He has, however, used some Chinese language materials, which I have not been able to utilize. Scanlan is highly critical of Reinsch, whom he argues was generally ignorant of Chinese affairs and never really learned much about China during his rather long tenure as United States minister. On the other hand, Scanlan depicts Chinese policy as being wise, realistic, and consistently well formulated. While Scanlan provides some sound criticisms of Reinsch and some new information on the Chinese side, his interpretations are frequently simple-minded and exaggerated. In addition, his understanding of American policy making is at times weak. While the focus of her study is more restricted, Madeline Chi, *China Diplomacy, 1914–1918* (Cambridge, Massachusetts: Harvard East Asian Center, 1970) offers a more balanced account based on Chinese, American and British sources.

Finally, I have benefited greatly from the contributions of other historians in the areas of American progressivism, United States foreign policy, Sino-American relations, and East Asian history. Most of the books, articles, and dissertations which I have used may be found in the bibliography of my dissertation. In the notes of this study, I have cited the more important works as well as those which came to my attention after the completion of my dissertation.

INDEX